To Prevent & Cure Cancer

1976
2006
30 years

ARIZONA®
CANCER CENTER

All proceeds from your purchase
of the Commemorative
Book Plate
personally signed by
Coach Lute Olson

will go to the
Bobbi Olson Fund
at the *Arizona Cancer Center*
to find a cure for
Women's Cancers

Order at:
1-800-327-CURE
or
www.arizonacancercenter.org

Lute!

Lute!

The Seasons of My Life

Lute Olson and David Fisher

Foreword by John Wooden

Thomas Dunne Books
St. Martin's Press ✿ New York

THOMAS DUNNE BOOKS.
An imprint of St. Martin's Press.

www.thomasdunnebooks.com
www.stmartins.com

Book design by Michael Collica

Library of Congress Cataloging-in-Publication Data

Olson, Lute.
   Lute! : the seasons of my life / Lute Olson and David Fischer ;
foreword by John Wooden.
      p. cm.
   Includes index.

   ISBN-13: 978-0-312-35433-6
   ISBN-10: 0-312-35433-9
   1. Olson, Lute.   2. Basketball   coaches—United   States—
Biography.   I. Title.

GV884.O45 A3 2006
796.323092 B—dc22

                                                    2006048378

First Edition: October 2006

10 9 8 7 6 5 4 3 2 1

To the women in my life

Acknowledgments

The adage that there is no "I" in "TEAM" is certainly true. This book would never have had excelled to this degree without the assistance and support of some very special "teammates." I want to thank my family: Vicki Olson Price, Jody Brase, Greg Olson, Christi Snyder, Steve Olson, Matt Brase, Julie Brase Hairgrove, and Yvonne Gragson for taking the time to share stories on their papa and brother-in-law. To my dear friends Betty and Paul Weitman, Bobbi Stehbens, Bernie Comfort, George Kahlil, Ginny Murphy, and Judge Stanley Feldman, thank you for enhancing and supporting me in this endeavor. To the great players and families of my professional career, Scott Thompson, Jim Rosborough, Josh Pastner, Miles Simon, Joe Turner, Jason Gardner, Joseph Blair, Khalid Reeves, Bruce Wheatley, Bruce "Q" Fraser, Dylan Rigdon, Harvey Mason, Reggie Geary, Pete Williams, Tom Tolbert, Jack Murphy, Sherilyn Byrdsong, Al LaRocque, Andy Thurn, Ronnie Lester, and Steve Kerr, you have made each day of my life a real joy. Bob Avery had the vision for this book and brought together the team of David Fisher, Peter Wolverton, and Jay Acton. To you, a sincere thanks. A very special thanks to Dr. David Alberts and his wife, Heather, who work so hard to combat the insidious disease called cancer.

This book, *Lute: The Seasons of My Life*, is a love story of the greatest magnitude. To my high school sweetheart and wife of forty-seven years, Bobbi, wherever your spirit resides, know that you are remembered with love every single day. To my wife and life partner, Christine, you did come to my rescue. You are the sunshine of my life. You kept this project alive. I love you.

Lute Olson
June 30, 2006

David Fisher would like to acknowledge the assistance of the following people: Laura Stevens for her incredible support, Mickey Freiberg for his fortitude, and Jack Styczynski for his professional knowledge and personal good humor.

Foreword

Lute Olson, one of the coaches enshrined in the Naismith Basketball Hall of Fame, is one of the finest teachers and strategists that the sport of basketball has produced. This is well documented by the success of his teams at every level—be it interscholastic, junior college, or college. His college teams at Long Beach State, the University of Iowa, and more than twenty years at the University of Arizona have all been outstanding and superior to those of his predecessors.

Coach Olson's teams are always fundamentally sound, but equally impressive is his ability to get outstanding individuals to work into the team concept. Regardless of the individual ability of his players, they all seem to be able to maintain the physical, mental, and emotional balance so necessary to be able to execute near their own particular level of competing. Furthermore, his teams are very adept at maintaining the floor balance so necessary for productive rebounding, getting good percentage shots when on offense, and limiting those of the opponent when on defense.

However, more importantly, Coach Olson is an outstanding family man and one who truly and deeply cares about others. He has both the love and respect of all who know him well and the respect of all those who understand the great sport of basketball.

John Wooden
UCLA (Ret.)

Lute!

1

We lived so many unforgettable days and nights together. On March 27, 1988, at the Kingdome in Seattle, we defeated Dean Smith's North Carolina Tar Heels in the Elite Eight. For the first time, the University of Arizona Wildcats were going to the Final Four. When the buzzer sounded, the kids started celebrating at midcourt. But I stood in front of our bench, looking up into the stands, waiting for Bobbi to make her way down to the floor. This was our victory. I didn't know it at the time, but the network had focused its cameras on us. She finally made it through the cheering crowd and, for an instant, we just looked at each other. We knew what it had taken to get to this moment. I took her in my arms, lifted her off her feet, and kissed her. As millions of people watched, we danced round and round.

It would be almost another decade before we would finally win the national championship. This time we beat Rick Pitino's Kentucky squad in Indianapolis. The press conference after the game seemed to go on forever. As I answered question after question after question, Bobbi stood patiently on the side, occasionally leaning against the wall. If I close my eyes, I can still see her standing there. It was after one A.M. when I finally started to stand up, but a reporter asked one last question. I looked at Bobbi and asked her, "Will you wait one more second, dear?"

She smiled. "I've waited forty-five years for you," she said. "I'm surely not going to stop now."

We were blessed. I really believed we would be together forever.

It was love at first sight.

Or maybe love at first touch. I don't know how old I was the first time I touched a basketball. Certainly too young to remember, but once I picked it up, I never put it down again. I knew right away what I was supposed to do with it. Nobody had to tell me. That was obvious: throw it up in the air, try to throw it through that hoop. That's it, that's the essence of the game. Shoot the ball through the hoop. I don't know why it captured me so completely, but it was fun, it was a challenge, and it was something I could play by myself or with one friend or with many friends.

It's an irresistable game. It's fun to practice and even more fun to play games. Hand a basketball to a five-year-old or a sixty-five-year-old and if there's a basket nearby, they'll do exactly the same thing. They'll take a shot. And then they'll take another shot. It's a simple game. In fact, it's so simple I've spent my entire life trying to figure it out.

I don't really know how to explain my passion for basketball. But when I'm out recruiting, walking through the halls of a high school looking for the gym, and all of a sudden from somewhere in the distance I hear that rhythmic spat-spat-spat-spat, it's like a shot of adrenaline for me. I know this is where I should be. This is what I'm looking for. I'm home.

I've been a basketball player and a high school and college coach. I've been coaching for half a century. My teams have won more than a thousand games. We've won league championships, a national championship, even a world championship. I've been named Division I College Coach of the Year twice, and many of the players I've coached have had wonderful professional careers. I'm extremely proud to have been elected to the Basketball Hall of Fame. Basketball has been the Olson family business as well as its passion; my five kids grew up with my players, and my late wife, Bobbi, was so very much an equal part of my success that after her death in 2001 the University of Arizona named the home court after both of us: the Lute and Bobbi Olson Court. My grandson played for me at Arizona, and my granddaughter was a great player and is currently a WNBA coach. I've spent more hours of my life than it's possible to calculate, many tens of thousands of hours, teaching and coaching in gyms throughout the world, and after all that, after a lifetime of basketball, I've never lost my passion for the simple act of shooting the ball through the hoop. It is an amazing thing. One day I picked up a basketball and it never let me go.

The game of basketball has taken me around the world, several times. It's provided me with an unbelievable range of experiences, from coaches in gorilla costumes to psychics, from real tragedy to great triumphs. It's enabled me to form countless wonderful friendships, and do the one thing I wanted to do more than anything else, be a coach.

I learned how to play the game in the small town of Mayville, North Dakota. I also played football and baseball and even threw the discus and the shot put. I enjoyed them all, they were all fun, but mostly what those sports did was keep me occupied until basketball season started. I played basketball every chance I got. When two feet of snow covered the court, I'd sweep it off and start shooting. We'd play outside with gloves on when it was twenty below zero. Playing with gloves got to be easy. Mittens were tough, though.

At night my brother Marv and I would play in our bedroom. We made a round basket out of coat hangers and hung it over the door. Our room was on the second floor and we'd close the door, roll up a couple of pairs of socks, and play H-O-R-S-E. We usually got away with it as long as we only took set shots. That was the basic shot of the time; you keep your feet planted on the ground. But as soon as one of us took a jump shot—boom! The whole house shook, and next thing we heard was Mom coming upstairs pretty fast and pretty angry, warning us we'd better stop playing and get to bed.

Mayville was a fine place to grow up. The entire population seemed like it was on a first-name basis. My high school class had only forty-three students. But it was the kind of small town where people cared about their neighbors and willingly helped out without needing to be asked. The values I learned in Mayville haven't changed much throughout my life, no matter how far away I've gone.

My grandparents were Norwegian. When they immigrated to America they looked for a climate similar to the one they had come from: basically, cold weather and warmhearted people. They found it on the farms near Mayville. We once traced the genealogy of my family on my mother's side all the way back to the year 872. Appropriately, as I'm well known among basketball fans for my seemingly immovable, perfectly groomed full head of gray-white hair, we can trace our lineage to King Harald the Fair-Haired.

Norwegians are strong, stoic, hardworking people. We accept life as it comes to us, even when it gets hard, and usually we do it without complaint or great displays of emotion. That's probably an accurate description of my personality. Bobbi and I celebrated our four hundredth win at Arizona by warming up some leftover pizza in the oven. I'm also a product of the American Midwest. I believe the simple things of life are the most important: family, honor, integrity, teamwork, the open man gets the ball, and you win by defending well.

If I have a public image, it's that I'm taciturn. It's true that generally I don't show much emotion in public. I don't often yell at my players or officials—I've never once thrown a chair, the best I ever did was a clipboard—and I never curse. People like to joke that I once went on vacation to the Hoover Dang. But believe me, that emotion is there. I get just as excited and angry and tangled up inside as everyone else; the difference is that generally I show it through my facial expression. My wife for forty-seven years, Bobbi, used to say that I really did have a terrible temper; she'd call me a "very stubborn Norwegian." But as anyone who has ever played for me will confirm, I have a way of letting people know when I'm upset. I have a withering stare. Mike Gatens, who played for me at Iowa, once said, "I've never seen anyone get so upset and not curse. But he can say more with a stare than anyone else can with words." I admit it. There are times I just stand there glaring at officials. They feel it, too. I've had officials come over to the sidelines and ask, "Is there something you want to say to me?"

Usually I try to respond with a joke, "No, you've made all the right calls, so I was just looking at you so that you'd know I agree with every one of them."

Technically, the person who literally has put his body in front of mine numerous times to protect the team from being charged with a technical foul is my longtime assistant coach Jim Rosborough. In major college basketball the assistant's job is to know when the coach is truly upset and get between him and the official.

With my players I'm not one of those touchy-feely Jimmy Valvano–type coaches. I liked Jimmy Valvano a lot; he was a good coach and a good person. The difference between the two of us is the difference between Italians and Scandinavians. I don't believe in being a buddy to my players until after they graduate. Then often we become close. I don't know if that is the right way or the wrong way to coach a team, but I really didn't have a choice. I am who I am.

I remember that after we'd beaten Missouri in the Elite Eight in 1994 to get into the Final Four, we returned to our arena, the McKale Center, for a celebration. The place was completely packed. Our fans were elated. I asked each of our players to say a few words, then I made some comments. Bobbi told me later that, as I began speaking, one of our players, Joseph Blair, came to her and asked, "Do you think it would be okay if we messed up the coach's hair?" That was a big deal for the kids. My hair has always been a sort of symbol of my demeanor. It's always under control.

"Oh, of course it would be," she told him. When Joseph hesitated, she wondered, "What's the matter?"

He asked her sort of sheepishly, "Think you could come with us?"

I learned at a very young age how quickly life can change completely and forever. My family lived on a small farm outside Mayville. One Sunday morning just before my sixth birthday we were in the yard getting ready to go to church. My father, Albert Olson, had just finished trimming my hair. He brushed the hairs off the back of my neck and began walking toward the house. As he started going down the cellar steps he collapsed and died instantly of a massive stroke. He was forty-seven years old. He was a good, hardworking man. And in an instant he was dead.

My older brother, Amos, came home from college to run the farm. One afternoon eight months later, he was out plowing. It was a cold North Dakota day. Once you get a tractor moving in a furrow it'll pretty much stay on course, so my brother hopped out and was walking alongside, probably trying to stay warm. Nobody knows what happened, but somehow he tripped, and the plow blade cut open his leg. He died from gangrene. I never really got the chance to know him. I know he was a talented musician; he played the piano and sang in a quartet that was planning to go to Europe. I remember just staring at his picture in his high school yearbook. Within a year my father and my brother were dead. I have no doubt that if my father or my brother had lived I would have spent my life as a farmer.

I had terrible, terrible nightmares for a long time. Funerals have always been very hard for me.

I never heard my mother complain. Never. She just accepted tragedy and went on with her life. She did what was necessary. Alinda Olson was her name, and she was a beautiful woman. We sold the farm and moved into town. She worked as a short-order cook in the morning and cleaned rooms at the hotel in the afternoon. My first job was filling the salt and pepper shakers and stocking the soda cases for her at the restaurant. It was a good job for a second-grader.

It seems like I was always working somewhere. Hard work was also part of that Midwestern ethic. I've done some strange jobs in my life. By the summer of seventh grade I was flagging for crop dusters. My partner and I would get up at 3:30 in the morning so we could be at the field at sunrise. We'd stand at the corner of a field waving a white flag. That plane would fly right over our head and hit us with the DDT and everything else it was carrying. We didn't think anything about it. We never even wore masks. When the plane completed its first run, we'd pace off a certain number of feet and he'd make another pass. We'd probably do six fields a day.

In eighth grade I had a paper route. I know a lot of young people have paper routes, but it's a little tougher in North Dakota, where, at 5:30 in the morning, zero degrees would be considered a heat wave.

I spent several summers working on a farm. Cleaning out the barn was bad, but the worst job I ever had was banking grain inside the bins. The grain had been harvested before it was ripe, so it would "heat" inside these bins. I'd go in there first thing in the morning and move the grain so it would air out. The dust and the smell and the heat were just horrible. That was more than sixty years ago and I can still taste it. I was also a corn shocker. After corn had been cut it was wrapped in twine. Those bundles were about six feet tall and weighed as much as fifty pounds. My job was to stand up two of them at the same time and balance them up against each other, then start piling on additional bundles. Trying to hold up one of those suckers while lifting up a second bundle and balancing them was not for the weak or the poorly coordinated.

I was an egg checker for a little while. I was actually the overnight guy in a gas station, but it was the place farmers brought their fresh eggs. My job was to look at each egg under a light to make sure there wasn't a little chicken in it. If it didn't have a chicken, it went in the egg container.

The most embarrassing job I ever had was dressing dummies. I had a part-time job at a ladies' store called Buttery's in Grand Forks. My primary job was vacuuming the carpet, but I'd also have to change the clothing on the anatomically correct female dummies in the window. That may not sound tough, but just imagine being sixteen years old and standing in the window of a ladies' store on the main street trying to put the clothes on a naked female dummy. Sometimes it made me wish I was shocking corn.

So as a coach I never worried much about keeping my job. I did what I thought was right and was willing to live with the consequences. I knew if things got bad, I could always earn a living dressing dummies. Feel free to make your own joke right here.

No matter what job I was doing, as soon as I got some free time I would go to a court and shoot baskets. Whatever I was doing, there was never any question in my mind what I intended to do. When I was thirteen years old, my high school social studies class had a unit on occupations. We studied occupations that we thought would be of interest. Even then there was only one thing I wanted to do: I wanted to be a teacher and a basketball coach. And, truthfully, I didn't really want to be a teacher if I couldn't be a coach.

That decision became the driving force of my life. I continued my education pretty much so I could earn my teaching degree so I would be able to coach.

I was a pretty good player, too. I was about 6'3" in high school and I was a good athlete. I played basketball, baseball, and football for Mayville High. But in 1950, at the beginning of my junior year, my mother decided to move to Grand Forks to be closer to my sister, Kathleen, who was working there as a nurse. She moved in October and allowed me to stay in Mayville for the basketball season. I wanted to stay there. These were my friends, the people I'd grown up with, my teammates. So I lived with their families, a week with one of them, two weeks with another one. That way no single family would be responsible for feeding me the whole time. It seemed to work out very well: The basketball team went to the state Class B tournament that season. We'd played together most of our lives; we were confident we could win the state championship our senior year.

My mother wouldn't let me stay in Mayville alone. At the end of the basketball season she told me she wanted me with her in Grand Forks. That was almost fifty miles away, much too far to commute, so I had to go. I accepted the move without too much complaint and just went on with my life. I played American Legion baseball that summer for a man named Fritz Engle, who had just become the basketball coach at Grand Forks Central High School. Fritz Engle was a big Cleveland Indians fan. At that time the Indians had a fine player named Luke Easter. Mr. Engle told me I reminded him of Easter. Luke always had a wad of chewing tobacco in his cheek and I had a wad of licorice or sunflower seeds in my cheeks, so, for the only time in my life, I was known as Luke Olson. I remember that one of the kids I played against that summer was Roger Maris, who was a senior at Fargo Shanley High School. Roger Maris was a North Dakota high school legend; he was all-state in football and basketball as well as baseball.

I pitched against him one time. My recollection is that he was one for three against me. He was a left-handed hitter so I threw him curveballs that broke in on him. He hit one of them foul a long way. A long, long way. There was the ball field, there was a grassy area behind the field, and beyond that there was a road. I think that ball landed on the road. Fortunately, foul.

The story we all heard was that Roger Maris had turned down several offers from major-league teams to play football for Bud Wilkinson at Oklahoma. I don't know whether this story is true, but supposedly he took a bus all the way down to Oklahoma. When he got off the bus, there was no one at the terminal to meet him. So he turned around and came back to North Dakota and signed a baseball contract.

The year before we moved to Grand Forks, the high school basketball team had been favored to win the state Class A tournament but had been upset by Bismarck. The entire starting lineup had graduated and in my senior year I was the tallest player we had, so I became the starting center. In Mayville, we had played a run-and-gun game, get up and down the court as quickly as possible. We didn't spend a lot of time setting up plays. We got the ball, we shot the ball. We played the way kids wanted to play. But Coach Engle played a ball-control offense. We played slow and deliberate. The slowest, most deliberate, torpid offense in the entire world, pass after pass after pass. Coach Engle would have made Princeton's coach Pete Carril, who was famous for his slowdown offense, seem like a wild and crazy guy. Coach Engle didn't believe in things like the fast break. He stressed fundamentals; he was extremely methodical and detailed. He understood the game of basketball. Take advantage of every possession. We defended very well. But our offense was just pass, pass, pass, pass, then pass, and if you didn't see an opening, pass it back out and start again.

Nobody complained about it. We did just as we were taught. And we won. We won games by scores like 28–24, a big offensive game would have been 32 points, but we won. I played center. We had a forward named Duke Evenson, so our team became known as "the Luke and Duke Show." I was "Leaping Luke." It was a very smart group of players: Every single one of the fifteen people on that team graduated from college, which was pretty amazing at that time.

The 1952 state championship was held in the new field house at the University of North Dakota in Grand Forks. In the semifinals we upset favored Bismarck, which had been the number-one team in the state all season, by cutting off their outlet passes and slowing down their up-tempo offense. We played Williston High in the finals. They had a 6'8" big-bodied center named Jon Vohes whom I had to guard. He probably outweighed me by sixty pounds. I don't remember being nervous about it; confidence was an important part of Coach Engle's strategy. It was a very close game. With about a minute left I got the ball on the right side of the lane and hit a short hook shot to put us ahead. We won the state championship. I've been part of at least two thousand games. I've had some thrilling victories and some truly excruciating defeats. But that game, that's a game I never will forget. North Dakota State Class A Champions.

A question I've often been asked is, What did I pick up from the coaches I played for? I've always responded that you can learn from every coach; you pick up some good points as well as negative points. They end up shaping your own philosophy of the game. From Coach Engel I learned the importance of even the smallest details, but I also knew that this was not the way I would want my teams to play the game. Coach Engel had great success playing a slowdown offense. He had an outstanding high school coaching career, proving to me that it wasn't necessarily the type of offense you use, but rather how well you execute it. But I knew that just wasn't my style of play.

I hadn't wanted to move to Grand Forks—I wanted to stay with my friends in a place I knew and loved—but the move turned out to be the most important of my life. In Mayville I'd played in the band and sung in the choir at the Lutheran church. The first Sunday morning I went to the Lutheran church in Grand Forks the pastor said, "I understand you sing?"

My mother had been talking to him. I nodded, "Yeah."

"Why don't you come to choir practice?"

It was at my first choir practice that I met a young woman named Bobbi Russell. Roberta Rae Russell officially, but I never knew anyone who called her anything but Bobbi. She had dark hair, brown eyes, and olive skin, and she was beautiful. Growing up in Mayville, I'd thought every Norwegian had blond hair and blue eyes, so for me she was very exotic. Her mother was Norwegian, her father was a mixture of European cultures. Whatever it was, I was immediately attracted to her. It really was love at first sight.

At least it was on my part. Bobbi always told me that she didn't like me at first. Actually, what she said was she couldn't stand me. She thought I was arrogant. The second time we met was at a dance. Supposedly one of her friends pointed me out to her. "Look at that new boy over there. He just moved in from Mayville. Isn't he cute?"

Supposedly she replied, "I don't think he's cute at all." Maybe that's all true, maybe she wasn't attracted to me right away, but within a couple of weeks she was letting me walk her home.

She lived in East Grand Forks, about three miles away. She'd grown up in Grand Forks, but her father had built some apartments across the Red River in Minnesota and they'd moved into one of them. Her father owned the local Dairy Queen and a small restaurant in which a lot of the kids hung out. It turned out her aunt was the choir director and all her friends still went to this church. Bobbi was a year behind me in high school, and she was a cheerleader at East, our biggest rival. We got to know each other on those walks home. I was really lucky we'd met in the spring. In the spring, summer, and fall the weather was beautiful and the walks home were enjoyable, but in the winter the temperature went way below zero, so that walk became a true test of my love for her.

I never missed one of them. I hadn't ever taken the time to wonder about the meaning of love. It wasn't very complicated for me. I was happy when I was with her; I missed her when I wasn't with her. I wanted to be with her all the time. And I just couldn't imagine not being with her. I guess that's as good a definition of love as I've ever known.

After we met I only went out with one other girl. I was going to Augsburg College, a small Lutheran school in Minneapolis. It was a very conservative school. No dancing at parties; the girls weren't even allowed to wear makeup. I went to a school party with another girl; maybe we went out three times. We were friends. But for the next half century, it was Bobbi. Only Bobbi. We got married in 1953, less than two years after we'd met, right after she graduated from high school. I was nineteen years old, she was eighteen.

She'd moved to Minneapolis to be near me and was living at a woman's boardinghouse on Lake of the Isles. She even had a curfew. Getting married seemed like the right thing to do. We got married during Thanksgiving vacation because it was between football and basketball season. We were married in the Lutheran church in Grand Forks, North Dakota, but then we had to go to her mom and dad's house in East Grand Forks, Minnesota, with our pastor, who married us a second time because we'd taken out our marriage license in Minnesota. I couldn't afford an engagement ring, so we had simple but lovely wedding bands. Bobbi always had great style. We were planning to go to Minneapolis for our honeymoon, but we got caught in a snowstorm and spent the night in the Westward Ho Motel on the outskirts of Grand Forks. That was our honeymoon, one night in the Westward Ho. I had $40 in my pocket when we got married. That was our entire savings. So we know for sure she didn't marry me for my money.

There were about 1,800 students at Augsburg College. Augsburg didn't give athletic scholarships. But what it did offer was a fine education and an atmosphere that made me comfortable. I was a small-town kid, this was a small college. Perfect. During my senior year at Central High my sister Kathleen and I visited the campus. One of the first people I met there was the basketball coach, Ernie Anderson, although when we met he was dressed in full custodial gear, mopping the gym floor. He put down his mop to shake hands, which was about his entire recruiting technique.

Recruiting definitely has changed a lot since those days.

I played three sports—basketball, football, and baseball—at Augsburg. In football I played both offense and defense, I was an offensive tackle and a defensive end. Just like any other athlete, there were plays I will never forget. I remember one game we punted and I raced downfield. I had a clear shot at the receiver, but he put a great move on me and faked me out completely. I lost my footing, but as I was going down I stuck out my long arm and clotheslined him. Caught him right in the neck. I can still see his feet flying out from under him as his body went down quick and hard. That's the way I remember it. That might not have been the way it happened, exactly, but no athlete likes to remember the tackles or the baskets he missed.

In basketball we played an up-tempo game. Of necessity. The necessity was that Coach Anderson and football coach Edor Nelson were the entire athletic department, so they had to do everything. Coach Anderson just gave us three or four plays; the rest of the time we just went all out.

It was at Augsburg that I got to know an African American for the first time in my life. This was 1952. While in other places in the country many restaurants, public school systems, facilities, movie theaters, and sports arenas, as well as colleges and universities, were still segregated—whites only, blacks only—that wasn't true in the Midwest. Iowa's football team had the first black captain in the Big Ten in 1937. In 1944 the Hawkeyes' Dick Culbertson became the first black basketball player in the Big Ten. But to live in Mayville you pretty much had to be Norwegian, so I just didn't know any black kids growing up. Grand Forks had a little bit of a Hispanic community, but that was a different part of the town. Augsburg was integrated. Nobody made a big deal about it, I can't even recall anyone talking about it. That's just the way it was. It wasn't a matter of us accepting it; truthfully we barely even noticed it. One of my roommates on the road was a black kid from Minneapolis named Richard Green. Richard was a very bright kid who came from a stable and loving Minneapolis family. I don't really remember too much about the time we spent together, which I guess is a mild statement itself. I do know that Richard continued his career in education, becoming a principal, as well as a basketball and football coach. Eventually he became the chancellor of the New York City school system.

I had a tuition grant of $200 a semester, but I had to work for it. I cleaned the men's and women's locker rooms and swept the classrooms in the phys ed building. What I didn't know at the time was that when I became a high school teacher those skills would become just as necessary as my participation on the field. To pay my expenses, particularly after Bobbi and I got married, I always had several different jobs. Coach Anderson was well aware of my financial problems, so he'd usually set the practice schedule around my work schedule. I worked at the post office during holidays, I drove a beer and soda truck, I painted houses. For a time I even worked at the legendary Dave's Popcorn Stand in Minneapolis. Dave had started with a little cart, but eventually owned a corner. His popcorn was famous. Dave didn't have much of a formal education, but he had wisdom. I remember one of the things he told me, mostly because I use it myself. It proved to be important advice. "The definition of a failure," Dave told me, "is someone who leaves for tomorrow what could be done today."

Dave was telling me to just do it, don't put things off, a long time before Nike used it. Unlike that clothesline tackle, this is a pretty accurate memory.

Whatever I did, Bobbi was supportive. We were partners in everything we did. She worked at a local car dealership to help support us. Our first child, our little girl, Vicki, was born a year after we were married. Bobbi took a little time off, but within a couple of weeks she was right back to work. We bought our first car so we could commute, a 1942 Pontiac for which we paid $225. And we had to finance it.

When I wasn't in school or working or watching the baby, I was probably playing basketball. I don't remember putting down the ball

for any great length of time. Bobbi never objected. Even when sometimes it was tough on her with first one baby, then two, then three . . .
She liked sports, but she loved me. And she knew what made me
happy. Bobbi never felt competitive or threatened by my love for basketball. Instead, she understood it and accepted it. She wasn't a participant. I have to be honest: Bobbi couldn't shoot at all, and she couldn't
play any defense, but she embraced the game. She carved out her own
way of participating, whether it was driving our own five kids back and
forth to practice and activities, entertaining players and recruits at
home with her famous apple pancakes with homemade cinnamon
syrup, or later going on recruiting visits with me. Basketball was at the
center of our family life.

I did take my turns with our baby, which convinced me that one of
the greatest inventions of the twentieth century was the disposable di-
aper. We didn't have that in 1953. What we did have was the constant
smell of ammonia. There were three other young couples with babies in
our building, but only one washer-dryer, which was pretty much kept
busy twenty-four hours a day.

I had a double major at Augsburg in history and physical education.
When I graduated, I had several high school teaching offers, but I was
only interested in offers that included the chance to be head coach of
the basketball team. Actually, I had a couple of better offers that included the head football job, but there was no way I was not going
to be a basketball coach. One of the offers came from Mahnomen High
School, a small school about eighty miles north of Minneapolis. They
offered me $3,200 a year to teach six classes and coach three sports.
I took the contract home with me to talk it over with Bobbi. It just
felt right, it felt like a good situation. I signed the contract and sent it
back.

What I didn't know was how much Mahnomen wanted me. To convince me to accept the job, they'd sent me a second contract, this one
for $3,600. $400 was a lot of money for us. The two contracts crossed in
the mail. I went to see the superintendent and told him I'd just sign the
second contract. No, he said, you've already signed your contract.

He was right. I'd signed the contract and I certainly would honor it.
But I still haven't forgotten that $400.

I taught American history, world history, phys ed, and an Introduction to Business course. Introduction to Business? My personal introduction to business was losing a $400 raise. The first thing I taught my
students was take your time before signing your contract. I was the

head basketball coach, the head baseball coach, and the assistant football coach.

The athletic department consisted of myself and Ron Raveling, who had hired me. Ron was a former college football star at the University of Minnesota as well as an NCAA boxing champion. He was big, probably 6'5", at least 260 pounds, and strong. He was the head football coach and believed in the hands-on teaching. The first week we scrimmaged he decided that he and I should play against the first-string defense. I'd heard of hands-on teaching, but this did seem a little excessive. We put on helmets, but no pads, and ran plays against the defense. At first the kids couldn't believe they were allowed to hit their coaches, but once they accepted the premise, they seemed to thoroughly enjoy it. They certainly enjoyed it a lot more than I did.

One advantage of teaching in a classroom, I learned quickly, was that there was no tackling in world history.

There was one clause in my contract that I will never forget. At least, never forget again. On the morning of our first football game I told Ron I was going to rush home and have a quick bite to eat, then I'd come right back to tape ankles. Ron smiled knowingly. "Well, don't forget the other part of your job."

Other part? "What's that?"

"Gee, Lute, you know you should have read your contract."

That didn't sound promising. "What are you talking about?"

He pointed to the chalk spreader. "You have to line the field on game days."

Until that day I don't think I ever really appreciated how many long, straight white chalk lines there are on a hundred-yard field. There were other surprises to come. The whole athletic staff consisted of Ron and me. So he was my assistant baseball coach. When we were getting ready for baseball tryouts I told Ron, "You know, I haven't seen the baseball field?" In small towns the high school often played on the town field. But I hadn't seen any town field either.

There was a good reason for that. "That's because we don't have a baseball field."

Okay. "Then where do we play our games?"

"We're the visitors. Every game. All our games are on the road."

I enjoyed teaching. It was pretty straightforward stuff. I couldn't change history. I just had to make sure I stayed a few chapters ahead of the kids. Most of my classes were required courses, so I had some kids who loved the subject, others who accepted it, and a few who absolutely hated it. One thing I learned that year: If you're going to be a high school teacher, the best subjects to teach are math and advanced science. Courses like physics and chemistry. Because the kids who take those courses do it for a reason, not because they are required courses. It makes for a much more enjoyable classroom atmosphere.

But it was the basketball coaching job that really mattered to me. I can't tell you why I'd decided years earlier that I wanted to be a coach, only that I did. And I didn't go into it with any kind of long-range plan to someday coach a major college basketball team. This job wasn't intended to be a stepping-stone to bigger and better jobs. The only future I was looking forward to was the next game. Bobbi and I were realists. We would do the best job we could and see what happened.

This was my first basketball team. My team. I certainly hadn't developed a philosophy of coaching, I didn't have any coaching experience, and, in retrospect, I had very little knowledge. My preparation consisted of reading every book about basketball instruction and strategy I could find and attending the annual coaching clinic held in Minneapolis. But I also brought my enthusiasm, my experience as a player, and a great love of the game of basketball to the job.

As any successful coach will tell you, there really is only one way to learn how to coach. You have to coach. You can read every book, go to every clinic, watch numerous games on television, and talk to other coaches, but there is no substitute for doing it. There's a lot of trial and error involved. Coaching isn't only understanding the Xs and Os. That's a significant but small part of coaching. In addition to dictating strategy, coaching is working with other people, being able to communicate, applying discipline when it's necessary, and going through a thousand scenarios. To improve as a coach, whether you win or lose, you try to learn something valuable every game, even every practice.

Among the several important lessons I learned my first season was that you play with the players you have. You have to let your personnel dictate your strategy. There is an old saying in basketball: You can't teach height. As a high school coach, the only recruiting you can do is walk through the halls the first few days of the school year and try to convince the tallest kids to come out for the team. I was very fortunate to have inherited a team that had played together for quite a while, including a 6'4" center. Two years earlier they'd won twenty games, so I had the nucleus of a very good team. Luckily for me, Mahnomen had played in the same conference for more than thirty years and had never won a league title, so there wasn't a lot of pressure on me.

Perhaps the most important lesson I learned that season came from necessity. Keep it simple. I didn't know enough to make it complicated. I taught what I knew. I drew on my experiences as a player to decide what I wanted to run offensively and defensively and how I wanted to conduct my practices. We played good, hard, basic basketball. Our offense was wide open—run the court, look for the open man, try to take high percentage shots—although way back then nobody was using terms like "high percentage." We used a lot of pick-and-rolls. On defense we played primarily man-to-man, we had a pretty good press, and occasionally we'd go into a zone.

Just as in football, I wasn't afraid to mix it up with my players. Truthfully, I loved it. There's no tackling in basketball, either. Usually I'd emulate the key player from our next opponent. I figured if my player could guard me, he would be ready to guard an opponent closer to his own height and ability.

It was also a new experience for Bobbi. There were no instructional books for coaches' wives. We never sat down and talked about it, but both of us wanted my team to be a sort of extended family. Early that first season she invited all the players to our small home for a casual dinner. The only thing we could afford to serve was spaghetti, so we had spaghetti salad followed by spaghetti for dinner; if there had been a spaghetti dessert she would have served that, too. But it didn't matter what she cooked; that wasn't the point. What we were doing was creating the kind of atmosphere that would endure for the rest of our lives together. Bobbi was the team mother for every team I ever coached. "Mom O," a lot of the kids called her, and many of them considered her their mother away from home. Each season at the University of Arizona we celebrated Senior Day. At our last home game our graduating seniors escorted their mothers onto the court. On several occasions our players asked Bobbi to be their mother for that ceremony. That all began back in Mahnomen.

At Mahnomen we played under some difficult conditions. Probably the best thing that could be said about our gymnasium was that it was better than our baseball diamond, but just barely. It was very old and very small. At most there was room for two hundred fans. On game nights the doors opened promptly at 6:30 and usually closed by 6:40. The court was so narrow the end lines were about a foot away from the walls. And it was so short that the foul line at either end served as the ten-second line going in the opposite direction. The school stage was at one end of the court. The pole holding up the backboard was bolted into the the wall below the stage, so if you drove too hard for the basket you were going to end up squashed against the wall.

Our opponents' courts weren't much better. At one school a basket was right next to a stairway that went down and outside. The doors were covered with a mat, but there were a couple of times that season when players slammed into the mat, went right through it, down the steps and out the doors.

That wasn't even the worst court we played on. In Borup they had a second-floor running track circling the court. It probably was similar to the gym in which James Naismith hung up two peach baskets and invented the game of basketball. These baskets were attached to the wood pillars supporting the track. So when a player drove for the basket it was actually possible for him to go under the track and use a pillar as a blocker.

We also had to deal with the weather. There were days that winter when the temperature got down to forty-five below zero. Nobody knew what the wind chill was; it was too cold for anybody to go outside and calculate it. Bobbi and I had bought our first new car, a Ford Fairlane. When I'd signed my new contract we felt like we were rolling in bucks. It was a neat car, with white sidewalls, the optional radio, and a headbolt heater. It cost $2,800. At night we'd have to plug a little heating element into the Ford's engine block to keep the oil warm enough for the car to start in the morning. When it got really cold we'd also bring the battery in at night to keep it from freezing. We'd drive to games in snowstorms.

Yet it was a wonderful year. We finished the season 22–3. In the district finals we played Ada, a team that had finished third in the state a couple of years earlier playing against much bigger schools. We'd split two games with them during the regular season. At halftime we were leading by fifteen points. They came all the way back to tie the game. With seconds left on the clock one of their players hit a foul shot to put them ahead by a point. We had the last shot, but we didn't make it. I always felt that if I'd been coaching a little longer we would have won that game. I would've hoped out something.

It was a heartbreaker. Up by fifteen at the half and losing in the last few seconds. I hoped I'd never have to go through that particular situation again.

I learned one other very important lesson that first season. I began to understand the tremendous impact a coach could have on the lives of his players. I'd experienced it from the other end, the players' end, because I'd been fortunate enough to play for coaches who had influenced my life. So I knew that coaches can be powerful figures in young lives. High school coaches in particular can make a big difference because they're getting people at a very vulnerable period of their lives. I knew that, but until I was actually a coach I didn't completely appreciate it. That title, coach, carried a lot of respect and gave me the opportunity to affect these kids even though I was only four years older than some of my seniors. I took it seriously. I tried to be a positive role model. For example, some of these kids had never even considered going to college. In many cases no one in their family had ever gone to college. When I would talk to them about their future, I'd never use the word "if," I'd always say "when you're in college." I couldn't reach all of them. About 30 percent of the school population was Native American, and it was very difficult for those kids to break through those cultural barriers. If the weather was bad, we knew these kids in particular would be in school, because many of them were being raised in huts without electricity. Conversely, on a nice day they often skipped school to go hunting or work with their parents. There were so many scholarships available to these kids because so few took advantage of the opportunity. I remember one young man in particular who was a really good football player. A linebacker. He had the ability to go to college and be successful. He was being recruited by two or three small schools. Coach Raveling and I tried so hard to convince him to take a scholarship, and he just didn't want to do it. He just wanted to get back to the reservation.

At least for a few of them I made a difference. One of my players, Al Santwire, intended to go into the military. I don't remember this, but he tells me I pulled him aside and said, "You can go play basketball for these guys and get an education at the same time." So he attended Moorhead State on a scholarship and became a teacher—and a high school basketball coach. We've remained friends through our lifetimes.

In my career I've earned a considerable amount of money. Much more than Bobbi or I ever dreamt possible. Every time I sign a new contract the media want to know the total value of my package. I always tell them the same thing: You weren't there when I was making $3,200 a year and lining the football field on game days, and plugging in my car with an extension cord so it would start in the mornings, so I'm not willing to discuss it now.

To my surprise, at the end of the season Two Harbors High School, a small town on Lake Superior north of Duluth, offered me the head coaching job and a $4,000 salary. I'd enjoyed coaching at Mahnomen, but with three kids it was impossible for Bobbi and me to turn down a 20 percent raise. Two Harbors was a relatively substantial community. They had iron ore money in the district and a beautiful facility. They had two gyms, both of them better than Mahnomen, but their basketball program was in poor shape. I think they'd won about four games the previous three years.

On the high school level you have to figure out how to utilize the talents of the players who show up at the beginning of the year. Baseball is often referred to as "a game of inches," but, believe me, a few more inches in basketball often can make all the difference. One year at Two Harbors my center was 5'11" LeRoger Lind. The first few years I was at Arizona we developed a reputation as a good school for big men. We had good height, and our guards supported our front line. But then we started recruiting great guards. In 1994 we had three great guards, so we went to an innovative three-guard offense. When people asked me how I could make such a drastic change, I pointed that that I'd coached high school basketball for thirteen years, and every year I'd had to change my offense to fit my players.

I'd seen LeRoger Lind playing football, so I knew he was a good athlete. He was playing junior varsity basketball, and he couldn't shoot much. But I knew he was coachable, smart and tough, and had a great work ethic. So I put him in the post, told him to focus on defending and rebounding, and built the offense around our guards. Most of the time we played an up-tempo offense, run and gun, which the kids loved. We went 10–11 that season and improved to 14–8 the following year. When we finally did get the big guy in the middle, Frank Lebo, he ended up blowing out his knee during the season.

For me, this was all part of the learning process. What I learned most at Two Harbors was how much I hated losing. I'd always known that; I just hadn't had a lot of experience dealing with it as a coach. I understood that high school sports was supposed to be about building character and that certainly was part of the program. But dang it, losing on any level is still losing. I'm a perfectionist, that's my nature, but it means I'm setting myself up for disappointment. I never forget losses. I probably remember the losses more than the wins. Even with all the success I've enjoyed on the national level, I can still remember that game we lost to Ada in the district finals in 1957. The reality of coaching is that emotionally you're either at the top or the bottom. There is no in-between. At Two Harbors I had to learn how to lose without it affecting my life and the lives of the people around me. How to keep it in perspective. Fortunately for me, Bobbi was always there to help me. After some of the tough losses she would tell me, "Okay, you've got twenty minutes to get over it. Then we're moving on. You just can't be so serious all the time." And she meant it.

At Two Harbors all I had to do was teach six classes and coach the basketball team and the junior varsity football team. I was at Two Harbors when the Russians put the first Sputnik in space, beginning the space race. The federal government instituted the National Defense Education Act, which offered substantial support for science and math courses, but also established a training program for counselors. I applied for the counselor program and was accepted. I was paid to go to school at the University of Minnesota Duluth. As a high school teacher, your salary rises with the number of postgraduate credits you compile on the way to your masters. I earned ninety units above the bachelor's degree.

Eventually Bobbi and I would have five children, so we needed every penny that I could earn in addition to my salary. In the summers I'd do custodial and maintenance work at the school. The school building was, I believe, three stories. It definitely was high. We'd clean the building, sand and reseal the floors, do whatever had to be done. One summer we had to reshingle the roof. I may not remember how tall the building was, but I can't forget having to climb up long ladders carrying shingles on my back.

Our apartment was on the second floor of a building directly behind the school. One afternoon, I remember, I was cleaning the windows. For safety, you'd have to hook a belt on to the building and lean backward. I was doing this one afternoon when Bobbi came out onto our porch and said to me, "Lute, I'm scared."

Well, I was pretty uncomfortable myself. There I was, suspended in midair, having a casual conversation with my wife. "There's nothing to be scared about," I told her, but definitely without a lot of conviction.

During spring break in 1962 we drove out to Denver to visit my brother, who was living there working for Sears. We were driving through the magnificent mountains and came down into Boulder and just were enchanted. Bobbi suggested, "Why don't you see if you can get a job here?"

When I'd graduated from Augsburg, Bobbi's uncle and her aunt who'd led the choir had moved to Southern California and tried to convince us to come out there. We weren't ready at that time, but things had changed. Both Bobbi and I were getting a little tired of the cold weather. In Two Harbors people used to joke, "Don't go out of town this weekend; summer's coming and you might miss it." And with all our young children Bobbi seemed to be spending an inordinate amount of time dressing and undressing them for the weather.

We were ready to move. Boulder was beautiful and we'd be close to my brother. Three days later I had an offer to work as a counselor at Baseline Junior High School. It was an administrative job, and it didn't involve coaching. We discussed it with the kids; we discussed every move we made with our kids. I didn't want to give up coaching, but this seemed like a better situation for the whole family. I didn't know how I would adjust to working in administration, but I was willing to try it.

By that time we had a little Comet station wagon with approximately no power. We rented a trailer, packed all our belongings—we even had furniture strapped to the top of the car—and drove west. We probably looked like a family moving out of the dust bowl during the Depression.

Two Harbors is on a lake, but we had to drive through Duluth. There's a very steep hill going out of Duluth. Our trip nearly ended going up that hill. I put the car in first gear and told all our kids to lose weight as fast as they could. The only reason I was in first gear is that we didn't have any lower gears. People from Minnesota say it's tough to leave Duluth. It is, mostly because of that hill. During that trip there were many times when Bobbi and I wondered if we'd make it. But we were young and excited, we were really leaving the area we both knew so well, and very optimistic. Truthfully, we were most optimistic when we were going downhill.

Basketball? Well, I figured I'd learn to live without coaching. We had a nice year but a tough year. We loved being in Colorado, but I missed coaching even more than I had anticipated. I played in a city league and I watched a lot of games; I probably saw more basketball games on different levels that year than ever before in my life.

Being a counselor was not fulfilling enough for me. The students I worked with generally were having some type of problem, so often I would end up between their teachers and their parents. The parents didn't have confidence in me because I represented the system, the teachers considered me part of administration and didn't feel comfortable with me, either. I did the best job I could, but I went through the entire year with an empty feeling. I felt out of place. If coaching is your passion, I learned, then you need to coach. And if it isn't your passion, then you shouldn't be coaching.

I've spoken with many coaches who've retired and almost univer-

sally they told me the thing they miss more than anything else is the relationships they established with their players. There are very few
things a person can do that foster closer relationships with other people than those that grow out of coaching. A bond develops over the
seasons made stronger by shared experiences. As a counselor I just
didn't have the opportunity to really get to know the kids. Often, the
only time I'd meet them was when there was a problem we had to re-
solve, and even then I'd only speak to them a few times. So it became
obvious to me—and Bobbi, too—that the only way I was going to get
rid of that feeling in my gut was to get back into coaching.

The money mattered, too. During the year Bobbi and I lived in Colorado we went out for dinner exactly one night. We drove to a town
about fifteen miles outside Boulder where you could get a spaghetti dinner for seventy-five cents. This was it, that was the entire social life we
could afford. It's not that we felt we were missing anything; we were
very happy together and loved being with the kids, but jeez, I should
have been able to afford to take my wife out to a nice dinner more than
once a year.

Southern California was growing like somebody had tipped the
country on end and anyone not tied down somewhere else ended up
there. Entire communities just popped up out of the desert. It seemed
like a new high school was opening every day. Bobbi's uncle was teaching in the Anaheim Union High School District, and he helped me get a
job as the assistant basketball coach at Western High School, home of
the Pioneers. I accepted that job with the understanding that I would
be the leading candidate the following year for the head coaching job at
the brand new Loara High School.

That first season at Loara we had only sophomores and juniors, but
"the Olsonmen," as the team was known, went 12–4 to win the Orange
League Championship.

In California, people are very serious about high school basketball.
It's like high school football in Texas. Another new high school, Huntington Beach Marina, was opening the following year. It was only about
a mile from our house. I got a call from the new principal, who was recruiting me to coach the basketball team. At first I turned him down,
telling him, "I can't leave these kids after one year." But he persisted. He
wanted me. I knew that Huntington Beach had a great basketball tradition. In Anaheim the focus was more on baseball and football. Loara had
one gym, which seated about 800 people, and several outdoor courts.
The new Marina High School gym, when divided, had three full courts

and seated probably 3,000. The city had an extensive youth basketball program. The foundation was there to build a substantial program, and they were also offering me a substantial salary increase.

Bobbi and I had the "Olsonmen" over for a barbecue. We'd won the league championship our very first season, so everyone was already anticipating the following season. Telling them I was taking another job was very tough, very tough. Well, immediately some of those kids wanted to transfer to Marina, but that was impossible.

I spent the next six years coaching at Marina High School. We made the state championship playoffs the last five seasons. There were some very talented teams in our area. We lost to Compton in the semifinals one season—and they had eight players who went on to play top-level Division I basketball. Compton was so good that Reynaldo Brown, a two-time Olympic high jumper with a personal best of seven feet four inches, was only a reserve on that team. Over those six years at Marina we were 158–23, and that's where I really became a basketball coach.

For the first time in my career I had a stable situation in a high school that had quality facilities. I had some good athletes to work with and relatively easy access to some of the finest college basketball coaches in America. Jerry Tarkanian was at Long Beach State, Bob Boyd was at USC, and John Wooden was winning championships at UCLA. These were great coaches; their teams played tough, fundamental basketball. They were innovative and they were tremendous teachers. Fortunately for me, they opened their practices to local high schools, and I'd take my team to watch them. I wanted to expose my kids to that level of play. I wanted them to see the intensity with which those players practiced. I wanted them to see what it took to be a winner. And I wanted to see it myself.

I had a tremendous desire to learn as much as possible about the simple game of basketball. I attended every possible clinic, I studied the instructional tapes, and I reread all the books. That way I was able to learn from the experts, Coach Wooden, Dean Smith at North Carolina, Pete Newell at California. As my assistants one season I had John Kasser, who'd learned Hall of Fame coach Henry Iba's motion offense while playing for Duck Dowell at Pepperdine, and Wally Torkell, who'd been a reserve on Pete Newell's 1959 championship team and could teach Pete's unbelievably tough defense. I spent hours asking questions, learning from my assistants the drills their great coaches had used to teach offense and defense, and how it was applied in games. I took a little bit from every possible source and put them all together to make my own mix. It was sort of like Bobbi creating her own recipe for apple pancakes. Coach Wooden, for example, stressed organization. He didn't waste a minute of practice time. Well, that was a perfect fit with my personality. I subscribed to the belief that games are won or lost in practice sessions. Like Coach Wooden I had my practices scheduled to the minute. Literally to the minute. And there wasn't any time in there to fool around. We lived in a democracy before practice and after practice, but practice was a dictatorship. And I was the dictator. Sometimes after practice I'd go into the locker room and joke around with the players, but on the court it really was my way or go play volleyball.

It was my pledge to my players that the coaching staff would work as hard as they—or even harder. We wouldn't waste their time. We would be just as focused on our jobs as we expected them to be on their work. And we would never ask them to do anything that we wouldn't do. We used drills that I'd learned from other coaches as well as some I created on my own. It was in high school that I devised what I called a Total Performance Chart. During games I had managers keep track of an array of individual statistics. I didn't like the fact that the player scoring the most points almost always seemed to get the most credit. So I created a system that would give me a much more complete picture of player performance. That including rebounding, playing defense, forcing the other team to make mistakes, taking high percentage shots. By this point I was using phrases like "high percentage shots." The box score lists steals, for example, but it's just as important when you force an opponent to travel or double-dribble or throw the ball out of bounds.

The TPC is a plus or minus point system. A field goal is +2, a missed field goal is −2. Taking a poor shot is a −2, being charged with a foul is a −1. Losing the ball is a −2. Blocking a shot is +1, but drawing a charging foul is a +3, because the player gave up his body to make a defensive stop. It's a system that tells me instantly what kind of all-around game each player is having. It's been copied in various forms by a lot of people, and I've continued to use it throughout my career.

We built an entire program at Marina High School. During the daily fifteen-minute nutrition breaks at the school, for example, I always went out to the patio with my assistant coach. The varsity players would gather around us, and if the varsity was there the JVs and the freshman gathered around them. Then I had the middle-school coaches over to the house for clinic-type sessions so I got to know them well and made sure they were teaching the same system we were using in the high school. I even coached junior varsity baseball—with the understanding that every day after baseball practice I could open the gym for basketball games. We had a freshman team, but in addition we also set up a freshman intramural program on the outdoor courts; we had more than 150 kids playing. On Saturday mornings the grade school kids would play at Marina—coached by our varsity players. During the summer we participated in two leagues, which meant our kids were playing basketball four nights a week. So we established a feeder program going directly from sixth grade through high school.

My job meant a lot more work for Bobbi. By now we had five children—three girls, Vicki, Jodi, and Christi, and two boys, Greg and Steve. The one thing that hadn't changed is that we were still just getting by financially, so I continued working at a variety of different jobs. I mention this not to impress people that I worked hard, but rather to remind them how hard coaches work—particularly high school and volunteer coaches—and often without sufficient financial support. With the exception of parents, coaches have more influence on young people than anyone else, even teachers, and they rarely get the recognition they've earned and deserve. I know that to be true because that was my life for a long time.

To supplement my income I got my driver's training certificate. In addition to teaching driver's ed in the school—I got to take my students on a freeway for the first time—on weekends throughout the year and during the summer I worked for the Wright Driving School. Teaching in the school was easy; my students were young, well coordinated, and excited about learning how to drive, but teaching at the Wright Driving School was more challenging. Most of those people had already tried to learn from relatives and friends. They'd had people screaming at them; they were already nervous and uptight.

It was right around that time that Bob Newhart did a comedy routine entitled "The Driving Instructor." "[N]ow what's the first thing we're going to do before we pull into traffic? What did [your previous instructor] Mr. Adams do before he let you pull out into traffic? Well, I mean besides praying . . ." Well, it was almost like that sometimes.

Most of my students were older women who had either lost their husbands or gotten divorced and were going to have to drive for the first time. Often when they started they were already depressed or nervous about their lives. I've always described this job as . . . challenging. Very, very challenging.

I bought a 1964 Nash Rambler through the driver training school. It had a special foot brake installed on the passenger side. One woman, I remember, probably took ten hours of instruction before she was able to make a turn and then straighten out the car. Most of the time, students would make the turn and head directly for the curb, which is when I got to use my foot brake.

One Saturday afternoon I was teaching a woman from Newport Beach. We were driving about fifty-five miles an hour on the Pacific Coast Highway. All of a sudden, with absolutely no warning and for no apparent reason, she slammed on the brakes. We came to a twisting, squealing, screeching stop. I took a deep breath. Actually, many deep breaths. About the only thing a driving instructor can't control from the passenger side is somebody slamming on the brakes. Fortunately, nobody hit us. As calmly as possible, which under the circumstances was probably not that calm, I directed her to the side of the road. When I caught my breath I asked her as gently as I could, "Please, Mrs. Stevens, why in the world did you stop like that?"

It turned out she had a reason. In fact, she looked at me like there was something wrong with me for not understanding. "Didn't you see that stop sign?" she asked.

"Uh, no," I said. We were near the San Diego Freeway. There are no stop signs on the San Diego Freeway. I knew this to be an absolute fact. But I looked behind us. There was a stop sign at the end of an entrance ramp we'd just passed. I took a deep breath. "Let me explain something," I said. "See, in California if there's a stop sign, there's going to be a warning about a stop sign coming up. And, Mrs. Stevens, I promise you, there will never be a stop sign in the middle of a freeway."

Call me Bob Newhart. For two summers I also drove a gasoline transport truck for Texaco. Ten hours a day, four days a week. I liked sitting way up high in that truck. Once, I remember, I was on the Golden State Freeway, which must be seven or eight lanes wide. At one place the Ventura Freeway branches off. As I'm watching I see this lady in the left lane suddenly realize she wanted to get on the Ventura, so she cut right across all seven lanes as if she were the only person on the road. People were slamming on their brakes, cars were squealing to a halt. I was far enough behind to see it all happening, so I had time to slow down somewhat gradually. You see something like that, it makes you wonder who taught that person to drive.

Without doubt, the question I am asked most often by young people who want to coach college basketball is how to get started. I tell them flatly, first look at what I did—and then don't do it. Because it's exactly the wrong way to get started. Don't start in high school. It's even hard to move up from high school to the junior college level. If you want to become a college coach, you have to take any job you can get in a college program. Even if you have to volunteer, do it. It's almost impossible to move up from a lower level because college athletic directors—the people who do the hiring—can't afford to take the chance. Their job is on the line. The rule of thumb is that no athletic director is going to hire more than two head basketball coaches—because if he has to hire more than two coaches, he isn't going to be the athletic director anymore.

I was very fortunate. When I got my opportunity to move up to junior college there wasn't quite so much pressure on ADs to win consistently as there is now. The finances were different, and the media coverage was substantially less. I didn't set out to be a college coach, just a coach. I can remember the day everything changed for me. It had been a long day at the school. In the middle of the afternoon I found myself standing in the boys' room making sure nobody was smoking. And I realized I didn't want to do that anymore. I went home that night and told Bobbi, "I don't want to be an old high school coach. I mean, this is crazy. I've got all this education and all this experience and I'm spending my time being a lunchroom monitor and being a cop. It's really degrading."

I hadn't been thinking about it for a long time. I wondered, How did I go to school to become an educator and end up spending my time trying to keep the peace? I had earned my master's in educational psychology. I had enough credits to consider getting a doctorate. And I was standing in the boys' room.

Bobbi was supportive. Bobbi was always supportive. "Well," she asked, "what do you want to do?"

I didn't know. The only thing I knew for sure was that I didn't want to be a boys' room cop cum lunchroom monitor anymore. I started looking at various opportunities, particularly a junior college coaching job, because if a coach stayed in one place on that level eventually they paid him pretty well.

I began speaking to junior college coaches. The former coach at Western High, Roy Stevens, was by then the head coach at Saddleback College in Mission Viejo, and I spoke with him about an assistant's job. The coach at Moorpark College interviewed me about coming in and taking control of his defense. In 1969, the head coaching job at Long Beach City College opened up. LBCC, the largest community college in the country, has almost 30,000 students. I didn't know anybody over there, so I just sent a résumé. If I had known about the politics involved in getting that job, I wouldn't have bothered.

The athletic director, Del Walker, invited me in for an interview. We just hit it off. We liked each other instantly; it was the beginning of a friendship that has continued four decades. Del wanted to hire me, but a former coach who had done extremely well there had been pushing his own candidate. Del put his own job on the line for me, telling the college president he would quit if he didn't hire Lute Olson. That was a pretty amazing thing for a man to do for somebody he'd met only two times. But Del was so highly respected in the community that the president didn't have much of a choice. They offered me the job.

I had to go home and tell Bobbi that I'd been offered the job—and it paid $4,500 less than I was making at Marina High School.

Bobbi knew how much I wanted to take it. "Well," she said, "we've gotten by on a lot less than that."

Maybe not a lot less. Finally, I had my dream job—and it had only cost us $4500.

2

I've been a basketball coach for fifty years. Imagine that, fifty years. I started coaching the same year Elvis Presley had his first hit single. A year before the first satellite was launched into orbit. I've coached high school, junior college, and college. So a question I'm often asked is, How have kids changed since I started coaching?

People are generally surprised when I respond that I don't think kids have really changed very much. The world has changed. Their environment has changed. The pressures on them have changed. There is less discipline in the home, and much less discipline in school. But I really believe kids today are seeking the same thing kids wanted a half century ago: leadership and direction. They want to feel they are part of something bigger than themselves, part of a team. I emphasize to young coaches that what they do with a young man—or now a young woman—is probably going to stay with them for the rest of their lives, because they've got the attention of these kids at a crucial point in their development.

I haven't changed my approach to coaching very much, either. Certainly I've adapted to the changes in society; there was a time when I had strict rules about hair length and all my players had to live in the same dorm and none of them had tattoos. There was even a time I didn't want my players making behind-the-back passes. Times change, the game of basketball has changed, and so those rules have changed. I've never believed in having rules for the sake of having rules, but my approach to my players is substantially the same as it was when I walked into the locker room at Long Beach City College for the first time.

I think if you look at coaches who have been successful over a long period of time you'll find they're demanding, that there is good team discipline, and that everyone involved with the program knows that the coach is in charge and things are going to be done the way he wants them done.

I treat my players with respect, and I expect to be respected in return. I don't worry about hurting my players' feelings. Long after Luke Walton graduated from Arizona, for example, he told me, "Every time I look at the phone caller ID and see it's you calling, my first thought is, Now what did I do wrong?"

My job is to be prepared enough to make each of my players the best player he can be. That's not always pleasant. Sometimes I have to push my players hard. Tom Tolbert, who played for me at Arizona, used to say that for years he thought his real name was God Dang It Tolbert. But the easiest thing for me would be to have a good time and have the attitude that whatever happens happens. Sometimes kids need a kick in the butt, and sometimes they need a hand around their shoulder. I have to admit, most of the time it was my foot and Bobbi's hand.

The kids who went to Long Beach City College were very different than the players I'd coached in an affluent community like Huntington Beach. Long Beach was a multiethnic campus; a lot of our kids came from the lower end of the economic scale. The first year I was there we had a lot of black kids coming in, particularly from Long Beach Poly High, one of the great high school sports programs in America. That changed my second year: The Watts riots took place. It was a troubled time, and black kids were discouraged from participating. That year we recruited only one black kid. Then that changed once again.

We didn't offer scholarships because the school was free for California residents. So what we offered in our program was a chance to be scouted by four-year schools and get a scholarship. A lot of our kids were street-smart kids who'd been exposed to some of the more difficult parts of life at an early age.

But they responded to exactly the same coaching techniques as the kids from Marina High School. Kids are kids—and basketball players are basketball players. They want discipline, direction, and leadership. And if you give it to them, they'll follow you, whether they're listening to Elvis Presley on their transistor radios or Coldplay on their iPods.

We ran the same type of motion offense at Long Beach that I'd run in high school. Some of the schools we played had twenty or more presets, set plays. I think we had four, and we didn't even use those four very often. We were always looking to fast-break, to run the floor. We didn't put a player in the post, in the middle. It was called a five-man motion, so everyone had to be able to catch a pass and put the ball on the floor, pass to the open man, or drive to the basket if the opportunity was there. It wasn't playground ball. Our kids had grown up on the playground. So they had to learn how to play team basketball, which can be very difficult to do. Every player had offensive responsibilities and restrictions, as well as a defensive assignment. The goal was to put each player in a situation in which he could be the most effective. That was a big advantage to the players on our team, kids like Chuck Terry, who had played center in high school because he was the tallest and best player on his team, but wasn't big enough to play the post at a Division I school. Our offensive allowed them to learn the positions they would play at a four-year college. And all of our kids did go on to a four-year college.

This was the first time in my career that I had to recruit players. That was a whole new world for me. In high school you play with the kids who walk through the door. In college you have to go out and find players and then convince them to walk through your door. Obviously it's the key to the success of the entire program. At that time, it was much less structured or competitive than it has become. There were no professional scouting services, no national magazines. The only tool we had was a telephone. People would call me and tell me there was a kid I should look at, or I would call players I'd seen in high school games to introduce myself.

When I was being interviewed for the job, there was some concern about my ability to recruit. I wasn't worried about it. If you can communicate, and you work at it, you're going to be able to recruit successfully. I wasn't the slightest bit nervous about it. Recruiting is primarily a test of your people skills. I like meeting people, so that has never been a problem for me. One decision I made then was that I would always be completely honest with the kids I was recruiting and their parents. I've never promised a single person that he would get a position or playing time. I've laid out the facts: These are the players we have coming back, this is what we think is possible, but there are no guarantees. And I've certainly never offered an incentive prohibited by the rules.

The coach I replaced at City, Rex Hughes, had put together a talented squad before leaving to become an assistant at Nebraska. He had recruited the top kids in the area as well as outside the state. The year I was hired, the administration changed the recruiting policy. I wasn't permitted to recruit outside Long Beach. There were five public schools and one parochial school in the area, and that was it. That was the extent of my recruiting territory. That was fine with me; in fact, it ended up being beneficial because the players we brought in had great camaraderie. Many of them had grown up playing with each other or against each other. They came from a common experience. A lot of coaches complain they have to recruit on a shoestring budget; we didn't even have the shoestring. We didn't get reimbursed for gas or food, for any kind of expenses. I did have one advantage, my family. They immediately became part of the program. We had a little pool at our house, and on occasion the team would come over for a pool party. From the very beginning Bobbi would cook for them, and my kids would be right in the middle of whatever was happening. We didn't try to create a family atmosphere; it was there, and we shared it with our players.

We recruited against four-year schools and during the time I was there we didn't lose one kid we wanted to a college or university. But in fairness, under the NCAA rules at that time, freshmen were not eligible to play at those schools, so we could sell them on the fact that they could come to City and play right away. I told them they would be playing against better competition than on a freshman team and they would learn a lot more. Once they came, they stayed two years. Only one player left after his first year. Dave Frost, who ended up pitching in the big leagues for the Chicago White Sox. When he'd graduated from high school he'd had something like eighty scholarship offers to four-year schools, but we got him at Long Beach City. Even he wouldn't have left, but we didn't have a baseball team, and his father wanted him to accept a full ride to play baseball and basketball at Stanford.

I believe we ran the best junior college program in California. We'd recruit five kids and take one walk-on, a player we hadn't recruited who had the ability to play at this level. But working with the team was only part of building our program. During the season I was in the gym five nights a week after practice, from six to eleven. On Monday and Wednesday nights we ran a six-team league for kids in other junior colleges in the area. On Tuesdays and Thursdays we had an eight-team high school league. Friday nights the best high school players from the area played with our current and former players. I spent Saturdays doing the stat sheets for all the leagues while one of our players wrote brief game summaries. We didn't just build a program in Long Beach, we built a whole basketball culture. Our gym became the place for basketball players to hang out. If you wanted to play basketball, this was the place you had to be.

When I met with my team at Long Beach City College for the first time, I didn't make much of a motivational speech. I told them who I was, I told them what I expected from them and what they should expect from me. Then we started practicing. And we continued practicing. They learned almost immediately how much emphasis I put on practice. If you don't play in practice, you aren't going to play in the game.

One day very early in my first season we were running a repeat drill in which the passer calls out the name of the player he's giving the ball to and that player has to call out the passer's name. As soon as the pass is made, the first player had to run and touch the sideline. You go until the player receiving the pass can make a layup without walking. One kid just couldn't keep up. He had some talent, but he wasn't tough enough. In practice that day he just kept dogging it; he couldn't get to the basket in time to make the layup without walking. It wasn't just an inability to keep up—that's conditioning and with work that can be remedied—it was a lack of hustle and a poor attitude.

The penalty for not making the layup has always been that the group runs the drill again. Finally, my assistant, Wally Torkell, told him, "You know what, Pete, when we finish this drill, you just keep running right out the door." I don't know what happened in the locker room after practice that day, I don't know what teammates said to him, but the next morning he turned in his uniform. He decided it just wasn't worth the effort. That was the last time we had someone not hustling in practice.

I was extremely fortunate to have been given a talented group of players. The team was led by a sophomore, Chuck Terry, who was 6'6", athletic, quick, an unbelievable competitor, and a really nice person. My first season coaching on the junior college level we went 25–6. In the finals of the California Junior College Championship we played undefeated Compton Junior College. They had three future pro players on that team. But we were well disciplined and handled the ball really well. The game was played on our home court, and neither team ever got more than five points ahead. We were tied with seconds left in the game. Chuck Terry came off three screens, just as we had practiced over and over and over, and back-cut in for a layup. But they came right back to tie the score at the end of regulation.

In the first overtime we got the ball and held it for almost the entire five-minute period. There was no limit then on how long a team could retain possession. With seconds to go Gary Anderson made a great cut, caught a bounce pass, and went up for an easy, potentially game-winning, junior college championship–winning layup. It was perfect. The execution was exactly the way we'd been practicing it, and Gary got the shot we wanted. But after the ball hit the backboard, it was between the glass and the basket, on its way down, a Compton player scooped it up and out of there. It was clearly goaltending; the ball had hit off the glass and was on its way down into the basket, but neither official was going to make that call. No official wants his call to determine the outcome of a game. The buzzer went off. Second overtime.

We played even through the second overtime. Again we had the ball at the end. Chuck Terry went up for the winning shot and just got clobbered. This time the officials had to make the call. Hacking. Chuck Terry had two foul shots, two chances to win the game in double overtime. Chuck was the community college player of the year. He missed them both. Both attempts went in and out.

In the third overtime we got beat.

Coaches will tell you every loss hurts, but some losses hurt a lot more than others. This was an opportunity to win a championship my first season, and we had come so close. As I walked into the locker room after the game, I really didn't know what I was going to tell my team. The room was absolutely silent. The guys were just destroyed. They knew they were the better team, that they should have won. There was a green chalkboard on wheels in the front of the room. The words I wrote didn't come from my head, they came directly from my heart. I wrote, "I have never been more proud of a group of guys in my life."

When the kids saw that, several of them busted out crying. Some of the players in that room that night have claimed that I had tears in my eyes, too. I'll deny it, but I'll admit that that was a tough locker room to be in. Nights like that I don't go to sleep very easily, and if I do manage to fall asleep, I know I'll wake up with a start. We didn't have the ability to tape our games then, but if we had, I know I would have sat up all night watching that game over and over, trying to figure out what we could have done differently to change the outcome. I have watched many thousands of game tapes and one thing I know for sure: No matter how many times I look at a tape, the outcome isn't going to change.

Something else happened that night. All the freshmen, the kids who would be coming back the next season, got together in a huddle and vowed that they would win the state title the following year. They vowed to each other that starting in the off-season they would do whatever it required to win.

I had great kids in that program. Gary Anderson, whose layup should have won the game for us, eventually became the coach at Long Beach City College, and his son Ricky played for me at Arizona. The following year we had another great season, 27–5. This was a very close team, and we didn't make a lot of mistakes. Because our program didn't have any budget, we drove to all our games. My assistant, Wally Torkell, and I had to drive our own station wagons, each of us with six players. The kids called Wally the "anti–Coach Olson" because he was as loose as I was tough. So they all wanted to drive to and from the games with him. During the trip Wally might be telling them jokes from *Playboy* while I would be reviewing our offensive plan or defensive scheme or talking about an NBA playoff game. I didn't know why they didn't want to ride with me.

The biggest game that postseason was the regional finals. We were ranked second and we were playing the number-one team, Santa Monica. Winner goes to the state championship. Loser goes home. It was another close game. Once again we played into the third overtime. By that point we were running out of players. I think five of our players had fouled out; we had only two substitutes on the bench. One was a freshman, the other one a sophomore named Al LaRocque. Neither one of them had played very much for us during the season. With twenty-five seconds left in the overtime and the score tied, another starter fouled out. I don't remember this, but Al LaRocque tells me I walked down to the end of the bench and told him, "Al, we need sophomore leadership right now. Go on in and get it done."

That does sound like me. That's what I would have said. I remember what happened, though. With about ten seconds left in the game Santa Monica scored to take a one-point lead. We had a set play we'd practiced specifically for that situation. We used screens to free up a player who received a length-of-the-court baseball pass at the foul line. It worked exactly as we'd practiced it; Al LaRocque caught the pass, took two or three—or maybe even four—long steps and laid it in at the buzzer for the win. Al was mobbed at midcourt. When he finally got up he looked into the stands. Several of our players from the previous season were at the game and Al was going to give them a thumbs-up—this one's for you. Instead, each one of them was standing up—and giving him the traveling signal.

He probably did walk, but in that situation no official was going to make that call, either.

That was the first basket Al LaRocque had scored in more than a month. As we jogged into the locker room he remembers me leaning over to him and telling him, "Big bucket." That does sound like me, too. By that point the game had been over at least five minutes. I'm sure I was already thinking about how we were going to defend against our next opponent.

We played Cerritos Junior College for the championship. Cerritos was coached by Jim Killingsworth, who went on to a great career at Idaho State and Texas Christian. They'd won the title two years earlier and played a controlled half-court style. The game was close through-out, but we hit some free throws down the stretch to pull ahead, then held on to win. We were the California Junior College champions. It was a big deal back then, and in my memory it has always remained a big deal. It was the first one, and it was a great group of kids. There is some-thing so special about winning a state title or a national title. It's an un-believable feeling on any level. You've played every team there is to play and you're the team still standing. You're the top gun. You've beaten everybody there is to beat. Everybody else ends their season with a loss. You go home with a winner. It makes for a very happy off-season.

One day during that summer the phone rang. It was Coach Wooden, inviting me to speak at his annual coaches clinic. I'm certain I re-sponded calmly that I would be delighted. That's the way I respond, calmly, but I'm just as certain I felt anything but calm. I was thrilled. There was no basketball coach—and few men—I admired more than John Wooden. Two years earlier I'd been coaching at Marina High School, and now the most successful coach in the history of college basketball was asking me to lecture other coaches. Coach Wooden treated me with great respect that day, discussing basketball with me as an equal, even occasionally asking my opinion. I'm practiced at keeping my emotions contained, but, dang it! this was very special event for me. Afterward Coach Wooden and his wife, Nell, asked Bobbi and me to join several other coaches and their wives at dinner. We were all sitting at a round table and a waitress came over and asked, "Would you like some wine or a cocktail?"

As we all looked at the wine list, ready for a nice, relaxing glass of wine, or two, Coach Wooden said simply, "No. No, we don't care for any cocktails or wine." You could hear the wine lists snapping closed. As far as any of us sitting at that table were concerned, not only didn't we want any wine that night, we'd never wanted any wine in the past and never would want any wine in the future.

After that I would occasionally get a call from Coach Wooden. It seemed like just about every time a four-year college job opened, the athletic director would call him to see if he could suggest a replacement. He called me several times to ask if I wanted to apply for one of these jobs.

I hadn't spent a lot of time thinking about the next step. I love basketball; I love coaching basketball, but I don't necessarily love everything else that goes on around it. I found the more successful I became—even on that level—the more time I was spending doing things that had little to do with coaching players. I liked what I was doing at City; Bobbi and the kids were very happy living in southern California, so I was happy. We didn't have a lot of money, but we'd never had a lot of money, so that wasn't an issue. We couldn't miss what we'd never had. These jobs were down south or back in the Midwest, and I just wasn't willing to move to those places.

In my four seasons at Long Beach City we won three league titles. You had to win your league title to get into the state tournament. Naturally, I remember in detail the game we lost that cost us that fourth title. We had lost to Santa Monica during the season. It was a game we should have won. With five seconds left we were up a point and had to inbound the ball under our basket. All we had to do was get the ball inbounds and dribble away the last few seconds and the game was over. Instead, our inbounds pass was intercepted, and they laid it in at the buzzer for the win.

Later in the season we played Santa Monica again at our place, and this time killed them. But we lost one more game that year, a tough loss in double overtime. Santa Monica didn't lose again, so they won the league championship. We were easily the best team in the league, we won twenty-seven games, but we had to watch as Santa Monica won the state championship by about 25 points. That was more than thirty seasons ago, and when I think about it, it still bothers me. One inbounds pass from the championship.

I was very happy at Long Beach City College. Several years later, I took the University of Iowa to the Final Four for the first time. We were in Indianapolis. On the Thursday night before the weekend games NBC hosted a cocktail party for the participants. Bobbi and I found ourselves riding up to the party in an elevator with Al McGuire. McGuire had been to the Final Four as a coach; he'd won a national championship at

Marquette. He had this great big smile on his face as he said to us, "Just make sure you take time to smell the roses."

I laughed politely at that. "Al," I said, "when did you get a chance to smell the roses?"

"I didn't," he admitted, then brightened. "But you should." And then he said something that really surprised me. "Where are you going to be coaching next year?"

"What do you mean?"

"Well, you're not going back to Iowa, are you?"

"Well, yeah," I told him. That was my sixth season at Iowa. "We feel like we finally have everything going in the right direction."

"Right," he nodded. "That's why you should go somewhere else." Then he explained, "If I were coaching now, I'd go into a down program, build it up, and as soon as I got it built up, I'd go to another down program and build that one up. Because every year you win, they're going to expect you to win more games. This year you're in the Final Four and they're ecstatic about it. Next year they're going to expect you to be in it and win the whole thing. It's like the car salesman. If he sells sixteen cars one month, the sales manager doesn't say next month I hope you'll sell fifteen! Every year you're at Iowa you're going to make a few more enemies; there'll be a few more people who won't feel they were treated right. Believe me, if I were coaching right now, there's no way I'd stay somewhere more than five or six years. Build it up and go. Build it up and go."

At first I wasn't sure he was serious, but he was. "I don't know, Al. How do you feel about the kids you've recruited? It's like, okay, guys, you did a heck of a job, see you later?"

"Kids get over coaching changes quickly. As soon as the new coach is named, they get all excited about a new coach and a new system. Kids adjust."

The elevator doors opened before Bobbi or I could respond. I don't know what I would have asked him, maybe why he had stayed at Marquette for thirteen seasons. I never looked at any job as a means to get another job. When I was at Long Beach City College I hadn't spent any time at all thinking about moving to a Division I head coaching job. That just wasn't my goal. I didn't need a major college job to feel fulfilled. The program was in excellent shape, and if I had stayed there, I'm confident we would have continued winning. There were very few jobs I would have even considered leaving for, and most of those jobs were major programs that would never have hired a junior college coach.

One of those programs was Long Beach State, only a few minutes away. Apparently Jerry Tarkanian would have agreed with McGuire. In five years at Long Beach Tark had won 122 games. He'd built a national power by recruiting junior college players. In his five years the 49ers had won four Big West Conference championships, had made four trips to the NCAA tournament, and at one point was ranked number three in the country. Then he'd decided to leave and take the job at the University of Nevada, Las Vegas.

The day after Tark resigned, the athletic director called and to ask me to come over and talk to them about the job. I wasn't surprised; the local papers did a good job covering our program. I was expecting to be considered: I was about five minutes away and had been very successful at City College. During that meeting he offered me the job. I knew that several other coaches were being interviewed for this job, coaches who would have considered this a dream come true. Tarkanian had made Long Beach State one of the most desirable coaching jobs in the country. This was a nationally ranked program. But I hesitated. There were rumors floating around that the real reason Tark had left was because the NCAA was investigating Long Beach State for recruiting violations. Supposedly there was the possibility that tough sanctions would be imposed on the program. If that was true, I was definitely the wrong coach. I told the athletic director, "Look, I'm not going to be interested in taking this job if there are going to be problems with the NCAA."

He held up his hand. "No way." He looked right at me and said, "We've been assured there're no problems." He gave me ten days to make my decision.

It was tempting. It was really tempting. By that point I'd gotten my salary up to $18,000 and Long Beach was offering $28,000. The family sat down and discussed the offer. It certainly wasn't the kind of struggling program Al McGuire had recommended, but it had the big advantage of being practically in the neighborhood. Since it didn't involve moving, none of the kids had strong feelings about it. Whatever Bobbi and I decided to do, that would be fine with them.

I didn't know what to do. I was almost forty years old. I'd gone as a spectator to several Final Fours and I'd seen a lot of very good coaches scrambling around like crazy trying to land another job. Some of them were really scared they weren't going to find work. That type of insecurity didn't appeal to me at all. Also, I was comfortable recruiting kids from the Long Beach area. I'd get in my station wagon and drive over to their high schools or I'd get to know them when they came into our gym to play. Recruiting at the four-year college level was very different. That meant recruiting nationally, getting kids from all walks of life. I wasn't sure how comfortable I would be with all that traveling.

While at Long Beach City I'd gotten to know quite a few top college coaches when they'd tried to recruit my players. I spoke with several of them about this job, and so I got several different opinions. Take it. Don't take it. Wait for a better job.

The decision would have been a lot easier if I wasn't feeling so good about the job I had. At City College I was working with kids I really liked; I got home every night, and it wasn't one of those high-pressure win-or-else programs. Bobbi and I talked about it a lot. Sometimes, when we had an important decision to make, Bobbi would get out two legal-size yellow pads. We'd sit down together and each make our own list: why I should and why I shouldn't. We would compare what we had against what we might be gaining. We talked about money, satisfaction, working hours, the additional pressure that would be on Bobbi because I'd be busier. We talked about how it would affect the kids. The one question we just couldn't answer was, Is it worth it?

Finally, I ran out of time. I had to make a decision. The fact that I still had so many reservations about this job convinced me I shouldn't take it. That's what I told Bobbi, "You know, I just don't think it's worth it. It's something I might enjoy, but I know what we've got here."

"You're sure?"

I nodded. I wasn't, but it was the decision that made the most sense. Later that morning Coach Tex Winter called to see what I was thinking. Tex had become a legend at Kansas State. I told him, "You know, Coach, I don't think I'm going to take it. I feel so comfortable where I am."

"Let me tell you just one thing, Lute," he said. "I guarantee you this, if you don't take it, you're gonna spend a lot of time wondering if you could've done it."

Well, that just added to my confusion. Tex Winter was somebody I really respected. I thought about what he'd said. Finally I decided that he was probably right. If I didn't take the job, I would always wonder how I would have done. If it didn't work out, I still had my ninety education credits and a fine record on the junior college level. I called Bobbi and told her we were taking the job. Then I called Long Beach State and accepted it.

Not everybody was happy I took the job. An individual who had applied for the job and might have gotten it if I'd stayed at City College was pretty angry. He went behind my back and told the African-American players at Long Beach that, basically, I was a racist. He told them I didn't want to coach black players. As proof he pointed to the fact that I'd recruited mostly white players the first year I'd been at City.

I was furious when I found out about it. Furious. That was about as vile a lie as I could imagine. I did recruit mostly white kids, but that was because after the Watts riots black kids didn't want to go to Long Beach City. I spoke directly with the players on my new team, I told them the truth. I also asked Chuck Terry and a couple of the other kids I'd had at City who were then playing at State to talk to their teammates. We buried that story pretty quick.

Other people had pushed Long Beach to hire a coach with more Division I experience than I had. I'd spent thirteen years on the high school level and four years in junior college. So I already had been coaching seventeen years before I took this job. I had plenty of experience. I also had a lot of confidence: Basketball is basketball. In Division I the players may be quicker, they may be able to jump higher, shoot better, defend better, but the game is the same. Adjusting to a Division I program wasn't difficult for me at all. I just kept doing the same things I had been doing the same way I had been doing them. Except more.

I started recruiting right away. Tark had left the nucleus of a fine team, but I brought in four very talented players. I discovered that I enjoyed recruiting more than I thought I would. Not necessarily the traveling part of it, but meeting new people, telling them what we could offer, talking basketball. This was the first full-time basketball job I'd ever had; even at City I had to work as a counselor during the week. At State I was the basketball coach. Period.

Also for the first time there was a lot of pressure on me to win. Tark the Shark had given the school a very big taste of success. The students and alumni expected it to continue. But Tarkanian ran his program very differently than I did. Tark had recruited a few of our kids from City. I remember talking with one of my former players after his first team meeting. "It's really different, Coach," he told me. "They got everything set up to make sure we stay eligible. It's all planned for us, the courses we're supposed to take, the professors, our schedule; it's all about playing basketball."

I knew for sure that was going to change right away. At my first meeting with the team I made it clear that they were at the university to earn a degree—and play basketball. They weren't going to get any grades they didn't earn, and they weren't going to be playing basketball if they didn't earn their grades. "Nothing is set up for you," I told them. "You either get your grades or you don't play. We'll give you as much help as we can, we'll get you tutoring if you need it, but it's up to you to stay eligible." I tried to change the way these players looked at school.

Basketball is a means to an end, I told them, it's not an end in itself.

Don't let basketball use you, I told them, use basketball.

I think a few of those players were pretty shocked by my attitude. Several of them believed they were at Long Beach State to hone their skills for pro basketball, not necessarily to go to school. They looked at basketball as their full-time job. A few of them were really upset by *my* attitude. They didn't believe they should have to take the full schedule of courses needed to earn a degree.

I remember in particular one of Tark's players looking at me like I was crazy. This was a talented player who eventually had a solid pro career. And a stubborn kid, too. If you pushed him too hard he was going to fight back. We butted heads pretty good, and I told him straight-up, "There's the door. Either you do it the way we want it done, or just go on out the door and don't come back." We had a rocky year together, but to my surprise, many years later, I found myself recruiting his son, and he wanted his son to come play for me.

That was the beginning of the most stressful season of my career. Taking that job was a mistake. It's always difficult for a new coach to come in and replace a winning coach, but this was an unusually tough situation. Tark was more than a winning coach; he'd given the campus an attitude. Most people just wanted more of the same. I came in with a new system, a new way of doing things, a new attitude. With respect to Tark, I did things differently.

But the talent was there. He was a great recruiter. I've coached a lot of very good teams, but I think this was probably the best team I've ever coached. Certainly this group had the most ability. Maybe it wasn't quite as good at point guard as some of my other teams, but overall they could play with anybody. Five members of that team eventually played pro ball, four of them in the NBA. We finished 24–2. We lost to Marquette and Colorado, both of them in overtime, and in both games we got hammered by the officials. We played Marquette at their arena in Milwaukee, Wisconsin—in the middle of winter, in the middle of a very cold winter, which was just the way their coach, Al McGuire, planned it. Al once told me that he always scheduled the teams from warm-weather climates in December or January. That way, when they came to Milwaukee, their players would be as uncomfortable as possible, and when his kids went to the warm weather they would be happy as could be.

Al was always very tough to beat at home. He played every angle. He invented angles. With Al, even the circles had angles. He used to bring in the same two officials from Chicago to work all his big games: He found them in Chicago's Catholic League. Marquette, a Catholic Jesuit university, was very good. According to Al, this was "BLT—Butch Lee Time." This was the core of the team that won the 1977 national championship. They had Butch Lee and Bo Ellis. They didn't need any help from these officials, but they got it anyway. We had a very good ball-handling team. We probably averaged ten or eleven turnovers a game. Against Al—and you were always playing against Al, not just Marquette— we committed thirty-six turnovers. We didn't just get beat, we got beaten up. These officials just weren't going to call a foul against Marquette unless it involved a power tool. The game was like the battle of Gettysburg, only with more injuries. I think we ran out of bandages with eight minutes left in the game. Still, a few minutes into the second half we were actually leading by as many as 18 points; that's when Al went ballistic. He exploded. It didn't matter why; whatever it was, it wasn't a big deal, but he turned it into an event and didn't quit until he got a technical foul. That got the crowd into it. If I had been a little more experienced I would have immediately gone out and gotten a technical of my own. I would have argued until the crowd quieted down. I would have done something to change the momentum. After that we didn't have a chance. They caught us in regulation and beat us in overtime.

We played a very difficult road schedule because Tark would make these contracts with quality teams where they would play at Long Beach first and then we'd work out the rest of the contract later. Which was similar to never. I thought it was important to set everything straight with these people, so we visited Colorado when they had Scott Wedman, we played San Francisco when they had a good program, and we went to New York City to play Long Island University in Madison Square Garden.

That was my very first trip to New York, my first game at Madison Square Garden. I was thrilled to be there, but maybe just a little apprehensive. I remembered the story Abe Lemons, the legendary coach, told about his first trip to New York. Abe was a wonderful character. In a statement every coach understood, he once announced that the alumni wanted to buy out his contract, "But I couldn't make change for a $20 bill so they had to let me stay." He brought his Oklahoma City team to New York sometime in the early 1960s. His first morning in the city he had an egg for breakfast, and when the check came he was stunned. It was $7.50. Seven fifty for an egg that cost probably thirty cents back in Oklahoma City? He signaled for the waitress to come over, and when she did, he asked her very politely if she would please bring him the chicken that had laid that egg—because his whole life he had wanted to see a chicken that could lay an egg worth $7.50.

I was being introduced to a whole new world of college basketball, and some of that world wasn't particularly appealing. It was during this trip to New York with Long Beach State that I first met the street agents. Streets agents are the hustlers of college basketball; they live off the kids. I was walking into the Garden when one of my assistant coaches introduced me to "the Rat." That was what everybody called him, the Rat. He seemed to be very proud of that, too, like he had earned that name. I didn't feel comfortable calling anybody the Rat, but Mr. Rat didn't sound much better, so I avoided calling him anything. In fact, I tried to avoid him completely. These street agents made their living by putting coaches in contact with the better city players; they got paid a certain amount for arranging a meeting between a school and a player; they got paid more if the coach got to make a home visit, and even more if the player visited the campus. Not only did these people have shady names, they looked shady and they acted shady. I just never dealt with them.

We came into New York with a reputation as an aggressive, running team. In those days West Coast games were rarely on TV on the East Coast, so this was an opportunity for a lot of pro scouts to see our players for the first time. The Garden was packed with scouts. We intended to run LIU off the court, so they held the ball. And held it. And held it. And held it. It turned out that everything in New York was fast—except LIU. In the first half they made Princeton look as if it were playing a hurry-up offense. I don't remember exactly, but at halftime I believe the score was something like 6–2. The crowd was booing. We were a top-ranked team, and they wanted to see us play our up-tempo basketball. In the second half LIU did play, and they played well, so the score ended up in the fifties and we beat them.

We easily could have been undefeated. We finished the season ranked ninth in the polls. We were ranked second nationally in field goal percentage, third in average margin of victory, and seventh in offense. I didn't think there was a team in the country that was better than us. But we never got to find out how good we really were; we didn't get an opportunity to play in the NCAA tournament.

Just after New Year we were getting ready to go on the road to play

San Jose and Pacific. That was a tough trip; even with all the talent Tark had recruited, he had never been able to sweep that trip. The night before we were going to leave, the president of the university called me. He said, "Coach, I'm sorry to tell you this, but the NCAA has placed us on three years' probation." I sat down. I was stunned. Claiming Tarkanian had committed numerous recruiting violations, the NCAA had prohibited us from going to postseason tournaments, limited the number of games that could be televised, and took away two scholarships. In addition, two of our starters were declared academically ineligible because they'd done so well on standardized tests that the NCAA suspected someone else had taken the tests for them.

Jerry Tarkanian's problems with the NCAA throughout his career have been well documented. I never knew what was true. Tark was personable, Tark was a character, Tark was a great recruiter; his record proves he was a great coach. I do know that several years after leaving Long Beach he sued the NCAA, basically for continued harassment, and eventually won a large cash settlement. Whatever the facts were, probation was devastating to my program at Long Beach. While you want to win every game during the season, everything you do is in preparation for the postseason tournament. That's where teams earn their reputations, and we'd lost that opportunity.

We were preparing to leave on the longest, most difficult road trip of the year when two of my players were declared ineligible and I had to tell the team we couldn't go to the NCAA tournament. The kids were devastated. I was afraid that with postseason prospects gone the kids were going to start playing for their own futures, rather than worrying about the team.

We won both games on the trip. When we played at the College of the Pacific, one of the kids I'd recruited, Bobby Gross, started in place of one of our ineligible players and had a triple double. Among the people watching that game with a rooting interest was Pacific's athletic director, a guy named Cedric Dempsey. That was the first time our paths had crossed. We continued winning for the remainder of the season. We knew how good we were, even if we weren't going to get the opportunity to prove it.

Of course I was upset about being penalized for the actions of another coach, but I wasn't sure what I was going to do about it. At least not for another month. We were playing at home one night and Bobbi just happened to be sitting behind the wives of two officials in the athletic department. She couldn't believe what she heard. They were talking about the probation, she told me, and they said something about it being worse than they expected. "They knew it was going to happen," she said.

Apparently the administration had known from the very beginning that the NCAA investigation was going to result in penalties. They had lied to me. I was furious. Coincidentally, we found this out at the same time the university was pressuring me to sign a contract extension. I told them I wanted to wait till the end of the season before deciding if I was going to stay, but there was no way I was coming back. I had a migraine headache that had lasted about three months. Bobbi felt the same way, "I don't care where you coach," she told me. "Alaska, anywhere, as long as you're going to be happy."

I didn't have any plans, I didn't care if I had to go back to junior college or take a high school job. It didn't matter to me. The one thing I knew for sure was that I wasn't going back to Long Beach.

We didn't tell anyone. I didn't want to ruin what was left of the season for the players. I didn't want them to believe I was jumping ship. But after we'd beaten Santa Barbara I was being interviewed by Tommy Hawkins, the former NBA player who'd become a broadcaster. He asked what seemed like an innocuous question, "So, Coach, are you gonna be back at Long Beach State next year?"

"I don't know, Tom," I said. "I need some time to think about that."

He was surprised. "Well, with a team as good as you've got, and with the guys coming back, it seems like it would be a natural that you'd come back."

"Well, it's been a long season," I said. "I just need some time to think about it."

Until that interview I don't think anyone even suspected I wouldn't return to Long Beach State. An attorney in Los Angeles named Al Schallau happened to be watching. Schallau was a graduate of the University of Iowa—and Iowa was looking for a new basketball coach.

I was home a week or so later just getting ready to go out the door to speak at the All-City High School Banquet when the phone rang. This is how it always starts. The phone rings and your life changes. Bobbi put her hand over the receiver and told me, "It's someone from Iowa who wants to talk to you."

It was Al Schallau. "I'm an Iowa grad," he introduced himself. "I watched your team play several times, then I saw you in that interview with Tommy Hawkins, where you said you weren't sure you wanted to come back to Long Beach. Let me ask you, any chance you'd be interested in the Iowa job?"

"It's nice of you to ask, Al," I replied, "but I don't think so. I don't think we want to go back to that climate." I didn't know where I'd be coaching the following season, but I was pretty certain it would be in the west. My family, all of us, had really grown to love Southern California. We loved the climate, we loved going to the beach in Coronado. We definitely didn't miss bundling up every time we walked out the door or plugging in the car at night. If I had taken the time to think about it, I might have wondered why Schallau, who was trying to recruit me for Iowa, was living in California.

"Well, I've called Bump Elliott"—Bump Elliot was the athletic director at Iowa—"and if you have any interest in the job Bump'll call Long Beach and get permission to talk to you."

"I don't know. Look, right now we haven't made any decisions. I've got to run to this banquet and . . ."

Al Schallau then did a very smart thing. He called back a couple of nights later and spent almost three hours on the phone—with Bobbi. He did a great job of selling her on Iowa. If she wasn't completely convinced, at least she was open to the possibility. "You know, Lute," she told me. "It wouldn't hurt to talk to them."

I told Schallau I'd be willing to speak to Bump Elliott. Whatever the regulations were at the time, Elliott followed them and got permission from Long Beach to speak with me about the job. Only a year earlier I'd been going through a similar situation about the Long Beach job. Even though I had very serious reservations, I'd taken it and regretted it. This was not a mistake I intended to make a second time. Elliott and I spoke for a long time. All he asked was that I come to Iowa City to take a look around and meet with the athletic committee. Well, I was already scheduled to fly to Denver to take a look at a prospect playing in the Colorado state high school tournament, so I told him I'd be there if he arranged a ticket from Denver to Iowa City.

The night I arrived on the University of Iowa campus I met with the hiring committee. Bump Elliott's primary concern was that he and the coach like each other, because they were going to be spending a lot of time working together. There are a lot of people in sports who use the word "communicate," but many of them seem to think that means you tell them what they want to hear. That wasn't what Elliott was looking for. Bump Elliott was open and frank about the job, and I told him about my interest in it as well as my concerns. We seemed to get along very well. They offered me the job that night.

I didn't know much about the situation at Iowa except that it wasn't good. This wouldn't be like Long Beach, where I'd taken over a successful program. Iowa basketball had reached rock bottom. Years earlier Coach Ralph Miller had turned the Hawkeyes into a national power. In 1970 they'd gone 14-0 in the Big Ten, and then Miller had left to take a job at Oregon State. For Iowa, it'd been downhill after that. This last season they'd finished tenth in the Big Ten, and they were losing their four leading scorers and four leading rebounders. It was a program in desperate shape.

I called Bobbi later that night to discuss it, and we spent several hours on the phone. We didn't have Bobbi's yellow pads to make notes. It was a big move for us, but it was a good time to make it. Our daughter Vicki was in college, and Jodi was a high school senior and would be in college in September. Both of them could go to school at the university. Greg was a sophomore at Fountain Valley High School, which had 4,500 students; He wanted to play football and it was doubtful he'd be able to make the team at Fountain Valley. Christi and Steve were in middle school, so the move wouldn't affect them quite as much. Money wasn't a major issue. Iowa was offering only a few thousand dollars more than I was making at Long Beach. I would have the opportunity to host a weekly local TV show and a radio show, as well as run summer camps, but those deals were completely up to me. They weren't part of the package. We thought it would be enjoyable to live in a university town. And the weather . . . well, not everything could be perfect. Only a couple of days earlier I'd had very little interest in the job, but by the end of our conversation Bobbi and I were excited about moving to Iowa.

Bump Elliott surprised an awful lot of people when he introduced me as his new basketball coach. In Iowa the news was greeted by a great chorus of "What's a Lute?" Very few people had ever even heard my name. This was a brave thing for him to do. I had only one year's experience at Division I, so nobody knew very much about me.

Some people in California were maybe even more surprised. Maybe they accepted the fact that a coach would leave a program being penalized for the actions of a previous coach—but what really puzzled them was how I was going to adjust to that cold Iowa weather. I told them, "Are you kidding? People from North Dakota used to go to Iowa to spend their winters."

During spring break Bobbi and I flew into Cedar Rapids. From there we would drive to Iowa City so she could find a home for us. As the plane was landing, it really hit us what we'd done. We'd committed to moving our lives to a place she'd never seen. Feeling confident that I'd made the right decision didn't stop me from being apprehensive. I wanted Bobbi to love it there; with a little luck and a lot of hard work, this was going to be our home for a long time. It was a cold, overcast steel-gray day. There were no leaves on the trees; it felt about as far from California as it was possible to travel. Bobbi took one look around and said, "Write to me, please."

Our real estate agent, Steve Richardson, met us at the airport. I wanted Bobbi to have the best possible first impression of our new home, but from Cedar Rapids to Iowa City there is no scenic route. Steve and I had decided it was best to stay off the interstate. Instead we took a side road that went through a nice area north of Iowa City. We drove into Iowa City along the river. Iowa City actually is a really nice college town, and I think after looking around for a few minutes Bobbi felt a little better about the move.

That's what I thought. The next day she looked at houses while I got settled in my new office. When we met for lunch I asked, "Well, how's it going?"

She had this weak smile on her face. "We saw all three of the houses," she said. The tone of her voice said it clearly, What have we done?

Bobbi did pick out a house, and when the California school year ended, we packed the whole family into the station wagon and took off for Iowa. When finally got there we drove right into a massive storm. It was night by the time we got into our house. Our furniture had already been set up by the movers, so we all went to bed. Just after we lay down, there was an incredibly loud crack of thunder right over our house. The sky exploded with lightning. Later we found out that a tornado had touched down just north of Iowa City. Well, we'd never experienced anything like that in California. All we had was earthquakes. And maybe the occasional landslide. But tornadoes? The next thing we knew, Bobbi and I had all five kids and the dog in bed with us. That's the way we spent our first night in Iowa.

So we knew it had to get better.

3

Several hours after it was announced that I'd taken the Iowa job two of the players I'd recruited at Long Beach City College, center Dan Frost and guard Cal Wulfsberg, got hold of me in my hotel room. Both of these kids had played one season for me before I'd left for Long Beach State. I don't know how they found me. "So, Coach"—I believe it was Dan Frost who said it—"when do you want us there?"

I'd been the coach for about four hours. Recruiting had officially begun. It never ended. Frost and Wulfsberg were playing in a junior college tournament in New Orleans with Fred Haberecht, who was probably the best junior college center in California. After I'd told Frost I'd love to have them play for me at Iowa, Haberecht took the phone and said, "I'd like to play there, too, if there's an opening."

It was like hitting a trifecta. I called Bobbi. "Guess what? I just got a call from Cal and Danny and the center at Rio Hondo, Fred Haberecht. They all want to come here." We were both elated. Like so many of the people who played for me, Cal and Danny had become part of our extended family. Our kids had been to just about every game and seen them play, and both of them had spent time at our house. Cal Wulfsberg, in fact, later married my daughter, although eventually they divorced. But it was a great way to begin my career at Iowa; I had the nucleus of my team, and Bobbi and the kids would have some players they knew.

There are no instructional tapes that teach recruiting. No coaches clinics. No books. The only way you learn how to recruit is to go out and recruit. The most important thing about recruiting is keeping it in perspective. Or, as I once explained the process to a good friend, "How would you like to have your life depending on the whims of an eighteen-year-old?"

Maybe it's not quite life and death, but it is the difference between success and failure. My first day at Iowa was the easiest day of recruiting I ever had. Every day after that was the hardest. I had to learn how to recruit on a national level. It wasn't easy. I remember that my assistant coach, Jim Rosborough, once spent a long time recruiting Glenn "Doc" Rivers, who lived in Chicago. We thought we had a pretty good shot at him until we read an interview in a Chicago newspaper. "I'd never go to Iowa," he'd told a reporter. "There's too many cornfields there."

I couldn't argue with that. There were a lot of cornfields there, and long, cold winters. So I knew we didn't really have much of a shot at kids who loved the comfortable weather in the South and the West. We had a lot of difficulties to overcome. For example, at that time Iowa City's airport didn't have a jetway. You just walked down the stairs onto the tarmac and into the terminal. On the tarmac it seemed like the wind was always blowing and it was bitterly cold. Unfortunately, as you opened the door to the terminal the very first thing you saw, hanging on the wall directly facing the door, looking right at you, was a huge, a gigantic, color picture of a pig. It wasn't even an attractive pig—for those people who like pigs—but it was a big, ugly pig. And beneath it was written, in large black letters, "IOWA: NUMBER 1 IN CORN AND NUMBER 1 IN HOGS."

We learned very quickly that when we walked through the door with a recruit I had to be standing on his far side, the side away from that wall. I just kept asking him questions so he would be looking at me rather than the hog.

Bobbi had it pegged. The first time she walked through that door and saw that pig, she looked at me, she looked at the pig, nodded and laughed, and said, "Right." That was all she said, "Right." It was a giant pig looking at you. What else was there to say.

Obviously we weren't the only program to have to overcome problems like this. For example, Washington State University is in Pullman, Washington, about an hour and a half from Spokane. The drive from Spokane to Pullman is mostly hills and farmlands, not exactly what kids from cities want to see. Coach George Raveling told me once that he solved that problem by making sure his recruits arrived at night, then he had them driven to Pullman in a van without any windows.

What we learned to do was go after kids from our part of the country and emphasize the many positive things about the university and our program. We also tried to schedule campus visits on Big Ten football Saturdays in the fall, when the whole day is one long party, or in May, when Iowa City was particularly beautiful.

I was naïve. I knew that some schools recruited by a different set of rules. I'd learned that much at Long Beach. But I hadn't really dealt with it until I began recruiting at Iowa. I remember going to the home of a very poor kid on the Gulf Coast of Louisiana. We were sitting in his living room and the television was on though the sound was off. I asked his father a couple of times to turn off the TV, and he politely explained to me that it was on because it was the only light source in the room. We had a nice visit, until this young man's father asked me, "So, what's your final offer?"

As soon as he said that, I knew we had no chance at this kid. When it became obvious that a player or his family was looking for something beyond what the rule book permitted, I dealt with the situation directly. I told potential recruits and their parents that maybe some of the NCAA rules seemed silly and out of place, but that we intended to follow every rule in that book. "So if it's a case of where you're looking for something beyond what's a legal offer, we won't be part of that. You don't have to tell us that's the reason you're not interested. Just eliminate us, and that's fine."

Recruiting was an art. It took a great deal of time and effort to develop a relationship with a young player—and even then you never knew what might influence his final decision. I remember being at a high school game in Minnesota to watch a kid we really wanted and had been recruiting heavily. I thought we had a very good shot at him. I was talking to him after the game when a coach from the University of Minnesota interrupted us to say hello. It was only then that I found out that this kid was dating the coach's daughter. That was another kid we weren't going to get.

There are some recruiting battles you just aren't going to win. One year we were recruiting a very good prospect from Texas. He finally narrowed his choices to us and a major church-sponsored university. I went to visit his parents and gave them my best pitch, but the coach of the church school convinced the university president, a famous evangelist, to visit the player and his parents. The evangelist told his mother, "I had a vision. I saw your son playing for us." No way I could compete with a vision.

Many years later, when I was at Arizona, I was on the other side of a similar recruiting war. A McDonald's All-American from California was being recruited by just about every major program. We were high on his list, but he was having a difficult time making his decision. Finally, his mother went to see a psychic she trusted. Apparently this psychic knew absolutely nothing about college basketball, but she told this player's mother, "I see your son playing for a wise man with white hair." There may be a lot of wise men coaching, but very few of them have hair whiter than mine. We got that kid.

Every player was an entirely different experience. Early in my career in Tucson there was a player from the Pacific Northwest who was interested in our program. I couldn't imagine that Washington or Washington State wouldn't get him. But we recruited him anyway. It seemed like every time I spoke with him on the phone he ended up in an argument with his mother. I finally mentioned that to his high school coach, who sighed and told me, "Yeah, it's true. They fight like they're married."

When this player decided he really did want to come to Arizona, I was surprised. I asked him if he was certain he'd be comfortable going to school so far away from home. And he said, "Comfortable? The reason I want to come to Arizona is because it is so far away from home."

Recruiting on this level was new to me, but I learned very quickly how to do it. The most important thing I could do, I found, was to be completely honest. Just be myself and try to forge a relationship with a kid where we felt comfortable with each other. I decided right away that we would recruit in-state first—the one advantage we had is that kids love to play in front of their family and friends—then look east, to Chicago. Pretty much until that point Chicago had been used as a connecting point to fly to other places, whereas I thought we should be focusing our efforts there. Our goal each year was to get the best high school player in Iowa and then go to Illinois and anyplace else. I hired Jim Rosborough primarily because he had very good contacts in the Chicago area. Roz was an Iowa graduate who was teaching middle school on the west side of the city. The kids from his school went to Farragut High School. There was a kid playing at Farragut who hadn't been scouted and Roz believed he could play. Shortly after I was hired, he called the office to make us aware of this player. That's how we met.

Among the countless things I had to do as soon as I took the job was hire two assistant coaches and a graduate assistant. I didn't know any-body in that area. I retained Dick Kuchen, who later became head coach at California. When Rosborough heard I needed a graduate assistant, he applied for that job. What he lacked in experience—which was everything—he made up for with his personality, his willingness to work, his passion for the game, and his knowledge of Chicago. I hired him and told him Chicago was his territory. All I wanted from him was the best players in the city every year.

Isiah Thomas was recently voted the best player ever to come out of Chicago. We worked especially hard to recruit him. Pretty much every university in America recruited Isiah Thomas. He lived in a terrible neighborhood on the west side of Chicago, but I don't think I ever saw him without a smile on his face. He was that kind of kid. At that time there wasn't any limit on the number of times you could watch a high school kid play or practice. It was obvious Isiah was going to be an impact player on whichever program he picked. I think I saw every game he played his entire senior year. It was a four-and-a-half-hour drive to Chicago, and I made it twice a week. Bobbi was usually with me. If you really want to get to know your wife, try driving nine hours with her twice a week in the snow and ice, in all types of midwestern winter weather, to say a few words to a high school basketball player.

I remember one evening we were standing outside the locker room with Coach Lou Henson from Illinois, Bobby Knight, Ray Meyer of De-Paul, a representative from North Carolina, another one from Kentucky, maybe thirty people. Illinois had brought an entire busload of boosters to the game to cheer for Isiah. Finally, he came out of the locker room. One thing that hasn't changed about kids, they are meticulous about their hair. His hair was exactly the way he wanted it. Every single strand was in exactly the right place. But as he approached us, an Illinois booster slapped an Illini hat on his head and their group started cheering, "We want Isiah! We want Isiah!"

I was thrilled. I knew that was it for Illinois. Isiah was a quiet kid, and the last thing he would have appreciated was all that noise and attention—and someone messing up his hair. Believe me, when it came to hair, I knew exactly how Isiah felt.

I knew we were close to getting him. What I didn't know was that Isiah's high school coach was a big Indiana and Bobby Knight fan, and that one of his former players, Tom Miller, was an assistant at Indiana. And I didn't know the coach allowed Tom Miller to run through drills with the team.

Indiana had an assistant coach practicing with him; we had a pig on a wall.

Still, we almost got him. Eventually it came down to us, DePaul, and Indiana. DePaul really thought they were going to get him, but kids generally keep the in-state school in the running until the very end; otherwise they won't have a very good chance of being selected the state's Player of the Year. I knew that Isiah's mom, Mary, loved our program, and I think she really wanted him to come to Iowa. Mary Thomas was an amazing woman. Supposedly a gang came to her house one night to recruit Isiah. She met them on the porch with a sawed-off shotgun and told them, "There's only one gang around here—and I run it. Now get off my porch."

Mary Thomas and Bobbi became good friends. Mary also greatly respected my assistant coach, Jim Rosborough, probably because he was a white man who'd had the guts to teach in an inner city school on the West Side, and Roz was heavily recruiting Isiah. Finally, though, Isiah picked Indiana. Even now, decades later, it still bothers me that we lost him. But after he'd announced his decision, Mary called us and said, "I really would have liked him to go to Iowa, so if there are any mothers in Chicago of kids you're recruiting, you let me know and I'll call those mothers for you." And that's exactly what she did for us for a number of years. She was one of our best recruiting weapons in Chicago.

Even then we almost did get Isiah. He wasn't happy at Indiana after his freshman year and had decided not to return to school. We couldn't talk with him because he had not gotten permission from Indiana to talk to other schools. But we knew. Mary did not want him to transfer, telling him, "You stay one more year at Indiana and then I'll let you go hardship," meaning she would allow him to make himself eligible for the NBA draft. That's what happened.

Mothers loved Bobbi. I was a good recuiter of players; Bobbi turned out to be a terrific recruiter of families. Once I told reporters, "We've signed more All-American mothers than you can shake a stick at." Unfortunately, it was their children we wanted.

I can't even begin to calculate how many miles I've traveled recruiting players. Whatever the number in front, there is a line of zeros behind it. We covered the entire Midwest, from the rural farms to the cities. A player we wanted named Charlie Sutton, for example, who eventually played at Oregon State and then went on to the pros, lived on a farm. When Roz and I got out there Charlie and his father were working outside. Charlie came up to greet us carrying a couple of pails of feed. His father joined us and we stood there talking for a few minutes, and I think Charlie felt he was done with his chores. "Why don't you come on in, Coach?" his father said, and then looked at his son and told him, "Charlie, you come on in, too—soon as you get done cleaning the barn."

Standing in that front yard I don't think we could see another house. In contrast, Ronnie Lester, who became one of the greatest players in university history before going on to the NBA, lived in Chicago's Robert Taylor Homes, at one time the largest housing project in the world, but basically an island of poverty, violence, and drugs on the South Side. When my assistant coach Floyd Theard and I made our home visit, Ronnie asked us to make sure we called before we got there so he could meet us in the parking lot and escort us upstairs. This building was basically a vertical ghetto. When we got upstairs to his apartment, we had to wait outside as his mother, Nadine, pulled open three or four deadbolts before she could open the door. And this was four o'clock in the afternoon.

Bobbi played an important role in the recruiting process. We didn't plan it, but we had always done so much together that her participation just evolved. When recruits made their one campus visit, they would always, always come to our house for breakfast. Bobbi's homemade apple pancakes with cinnamon syrup became legendary throughout college basketball. One year, for example, we were at the Final Four in Minneapolis, walking through a crowded concourse, when I heard someone shouting my name. It was Phil Hubbard, whom we had tried to recruit several years earlier, but eventually lost to Michigan because Cazzie Russell was his hero. Bobbi hadn't spoken to him since his visit to Iowa City. Phil Hubbard walked all the way across the concourse and the first thing he said was, "Mrs. O, are you still making those great pancakes?"

She never lost her touch, or her secret recipe. Many years later, when we were recruiting Jason Gardner at Arizona, he had one condition. "Mrs. O," he asked her seriously, "if I come to Arizona, will you keep fixing my pancakes?"

When I made my almost-nightly phone calls to potential recruits, Bobbi often would speak to them and their parents. She wasn't just trying to persuade them to come to Iowa—well, not directly at least—she wanted to get to know them as people. She'd talk to them about their schoolwork and their girlfriends and things in their life other than basketball, and then she'd get to know their parents.

When it was permitted under NCAA rules, she also made recruiting trips with me. I'd be in the living room with the recruit and his father; she'd be in the kitchen with his mother. Bobbi wanted parents to feel that she would be watching out for their sons, just as she would like it if one of our sons was going away to school. She wanted their parents to know that we tried to create a family atmosphere, and if their son needed someone to lean on a little bit, she would be there for him. There were very few mothers of kids we recruited that Bobbi didn't know well. Ronnie Lester, who came to Iowa from the Chicago projects, remembered that throughout his career there Bobbi and his mother spoke regularly on the phone, and when his mother came to Iowa City, Bobbi and his mother would go shopping. All day.

Mostly, successful recruiting required putting in long hours. Long, long hours. For a time Bobbi wrote a column for the *Cedar Rapids Gazette*. Once, someone wrote in and asked her, How do a basketball coach and his wife spend New Year's Eve? Her answer was a good summation of our life. "Well, Lute informed me we were going to see some games. So we started at 10:30 that morning and went to four different high school games in three different tournaments in Illinois.

"We had to fly because first we went to Bloomington, Ill. . . . then we flew to Kankakee, Illinois. . . . Then he took me out to dinner. He had promised me a good meal. We went to Pontiac, Illinois, and saw the final two games of a tournament there . . . We were landing at midnight. Our pilot asked us about a minute before twelve o'clock, 'Do you want to be up in the air for midnight or on the ground?' I said I always love being on the ground . . .

". . . What really tickled me was that, though I didn't want to spend New Year's Eve that way, it turned out to be a very nice New Year's Eve."

It was at Iowa that we really learned how to recruit. In addition to the three junior college players, I also was able to bring in three true freshmen recruits. At our first team meeting I showed them a movie. Actually, it was a game film taken at Long Beach City College. "This is the offense we're going to be running this year," I told them. Running, I emphasized, was the key word. We were going to run a motion offense. Five men constantly moving, setting screens for each other, working for an open shot. Frost and Wulfsberg had learned it at City College, but for everybody else it was a new concept. The only other Big Ten coach running a similar offense was Bobby Knight at Indiana.

I also told them that we would be stressing defense probably more than they were used to. "Defense allows you to be consistent," I said. "Even on those nights when you're not hitting your shot, you can keep your opponent from scoring. Your offense determines how many points you're going to win by; defense always keeps you in the game." They may have thought I was exaggerating—until practice started. Defense means team defense. On offense, an individual can dominate his opponent. But on defense a team has to work in unison. Each move by one player dictates the moves of his teammates. The only way to learn that is to do it. To practice it hour after hour. Day after day. Practice may not make perfect, but it does make better. To quote Abe Lemons again, "One day of practice is like clean living. It doesn't do you any good."

I made several changes to promote our program. An executive at a local NBC station in Waterloo, Iowa, named Bill Bolster—who eventually became president of CNBC—wanted to broadcast a few of our games. The previous coaches had turned down the opportunity to televise our games because they felt that it would hurt attendance. They figured if people could watch the game at home for free they wouldn't come to the arena. I felt exactly the opposite. We needed a stage so that people could see we were playing exciting basketball and get to know our players. That exposure would bring them to the field house. It would also help with recruiting; kids liked to play on television. Bump agreed with me. We started with an abbreviated, minimum six-game package.

One thing I didn't change was our uniforms. Iowa is a very tradition-conscious state. Bump Elliott once tried unsuccessfully to update the mascot, Herkey the Hawk. Herkey is large-headed hawk wearing a football jersey. Bump got Disney to design a more cartoonish costume. That hawk didn't fly. They showed the new hawk at one football game. People were really upset, wondering, What are you doing to our hawk? He just got blitzed. After one game the old Herky was back.

That first season in Iowa was rough. We had the talent to have a really good season, but mostly we had bad luck. Cal Wulfsberg, our point guard, injured a knee in our first game and was lost for the season. We didn't have another pure point guard. Just before Christmas our shooting guard, Scott Thompson, contracted mononucleosis and never regained his strength. One of our top freshman recruits was declared academically ineligible and transferred. Then Dan Frost, our best player, broke his hand and missed six games. We finished 10–16.

Believe me, I suffered through every loss. Maybe I didn't show it—that's the stoic Norwegian in me—but losing just tore me up inside. I remember walking to the postgame press conferences going over and over the game in my mind, trying to figure out what I could have done differently, what I should have done that might have made a difference. If you start out as I do believing that every game is winnable, when you lose you have to figure out what went wrong so it can be corrected.

One thing we did get from the very beginning was tremendous fan support. Even though most people in the state had no idea what a Lute was when I was hired, they gave me the opportunity and the time to succeed. There was unbelievable interest in the program. I began going to functions in small towns throughout the state to promote our program. Wherever people would listen, I would talk to them. These dinners or cocktail parties were always packed. I think they realized we were building a program and that it would take some time.

By the end of that first season we had the foundation of the program in place. My players knew what I expected from them both on and off the court, and I knew what the players expected from the coaching staff. As the program began growing, I found I had to spend many more hours off the court preparing for practice, games, and recruiting than I got to spend at practice, games, or recruiting. I would never refer to coaching as a full-time job; it was much more than that. If we had only worked full-time, we never could have gotten done everything that needed to be done. Games took the least amount of time. Preparation was the key to success. I didn't care how much time it took; for me, this was the fulfillment of a lifelong passion. Everything had changed since I'd started playing in Mayville—except the ball and the basket. It was the same ball I'd played with on the dirt lots of Mayville and the object was still the same: Put that ball in the basket.

We were both better and luckier about injuries in the 1975–76 season, finishing 19–10, fifth in the Big Ten. It was a substantial improvement. But there was at least one game that season that I will never forget. We were playing at Indiana. Bobby Knight's squad would go undefeated that season, 32–0, and win the national championship. They were so much better than we were that it wasn't much of a game, but they still got every close call. Maybe that's just the way the officials saw the game, maybe they were intimidated by Knight; whatever the reason, eventually it got ridiculous. In the second half Cal Wulfsberg was bringing up the ball into the offensive court when Quinn Buckner literally knocked him down and took the ball away from him. It was a flagrant foul, but the officials wouldn't call it. I was outraged. When Buckner got across half-court I was the only defender he had to beat. I don't know what got into me, but all of a sudden I found myself standing right out there in the middle of the court. I couldn't help myself; it was such an outrageous foul and such a frustrating game because they were killing us that I couldn't take it anymore. I had to do something. Obviously, I was charged with a technical foul, and Buckner beat me anyway.

That reminded me of another coach who found himself in a similar situation. He had run out onto the court and the official gave him a T, then warned him he was going to get another T for every step it took him to get back to the bench. The coach thought about it for a second—then called out his assistants and had them carry him back to the bench.

The thing that surprised me most about that game was the reaction of the Indiana fans. In the last three minutes of the game the Hoosiers were winning by almost fifty points and their fans were still going crazy every time they scored. When we scored they would all boo. Everybody on our bench was wondering what was going on. Eventually they beat us 102-49—and we found out that we were in the middle of a fast food promotion. If they scored a hundred points or more, fans got a free hamburger at McDonald's, but if they held their opponent to under fifty points they got the whole meal. So we fed the entire arena that night, in what became known in Iowa lore as "the Hamburger Game."

I didn't blame Bobby Knight for that score. As I remember it, he didn't leave his starters in or intentionally run up the score. They were just that much better than us. Actually, my relationship with Bobby Knight was pretty good my first few years at Iowa. The first time we played Indiana in Iowa City I asked him to come to our game-day luncheon and say a few words. He did it, and he was fine, but then he never let me forget it. He really can be charming. Bobbi met him for the first time the night we went to St. Joseph's in Chicago to see Isiah Thomas. Knight was there, and he came over and introduced himself politely to her. Afterward Bobbi was almost gushing, "Oh, he's just so nice, so charming."

I've always felt his reputation worked to his advantage when he was recruiting a player. He'd go into their home and the parents would be uptight, wondering if he was going to get angry and throw a lamp, and the kid would be nervous, wondering if he was going to grab him by the shirt and start shaking him. Then he ends up being this really nice guy.

He is a nice guy, at least until you beat him. Then he's not so good.

I think it was four years after the Hamburger Game when the Hoosiers—led by Isiah Thomas—came to our place and we beat them 93-60. If it wasn't the worst defeat of his career at Indiana, it was right up there with the worst of them. Toward the end of the game our field house got very quiet. Then, from the upper level, a fan yelled, "Hey, Bobby, how about a hamburger?" The place exploded in cheers.

I think my real problems with Bobby Knight began during another game at Indiana. It was a very close game at halftime. Normally at halftime the officials leave the court and the teams go to their locker rooms. But as I started walking toward our locker room I noticed that Knight had an official named Earl Fouty corralled on the sidelines at midcourt and was ripping into him. Earl was a wonderful guy, but he was from Indiana. At the beginning of each season he'd appear on Bobby Knight's TV show. He was completely honest, but you definitely didn't want him working the game when you were playing Indiana or Purdue. At the end of the game he had to go home. I wanted to know why Knight was screaming at him. I knew it wasn't about the TV show. I stood a few feet away, just listening. I heard a lot of loud F-this and F-that. It was classic Bobby Knight. Finally Fouty looked over Knight's shoulder and saw me standing there. "Hey," he said, "get to your locker room. This is none of your business."

"None of my business?" I said. "You're officiating the game and you're being degraded like this, and it has nothing to do with me?" Actually, I thought the opposing coach arguing with the official had everything to do with me.

"Get off the court," Fouty told me. When I refused he warned, "Get off the court or you start the second half with a T."

I left, but I wrote a letter to Wayne Duke, head of the Big Ten, explaining the situation. It did not have the effect I had hoped. Bobby Knight was screaming at Earl Fouty—and I ended up getting reprimanded by the conference. Knight was not reprimanded, and nothing happened to Fouty. After that night my relationship with Bobby got worse and worse, although at every opportunity he reminded me, "Hey, how can you be this way? I even came and spoke at your lunch." At every single opportunity.

Eventually our relationship got so bad that basically we stopped talking to each other. We'd shake hands before the game and after the game, but for three or four years that was the extent of our relationship. I didn't miss our confrontations and I suspect he didn't, either.

Bobby Knight has always been a great basketball coach. He's honest and he gets the maximum performance out of his teams. He's always run a very clean program, but he has a horrible temper, and when it blows he gets into difficulty. If you're on the receiving end of that, it is not a pleasant place to be. I've always believed that he just didn't feel people understood him. I also believed I understood him.

Bobbi rarely said anything negative about anybody. But when Gene Keady became Purdue's head coach in 1980 Knight sent a dozen roses to his wife, Pat. I remember Pat telling Bobbi about it. "That Bobby Knight is so nice," she said.

Bobbi said simply, "Wait."

A couple of years later, we were in Indiana, having an early shootaround to loosen up for the game, when Knight came up to me and asked if we could talk for a few minutes. "Look," he said, "it shouldn't be this way between us. Both of us follow the rules, we go after the same kind of kids, we have great programs."

It was much more a clearing of the air than any kind of apology, but it was still a nice gesture. "I have no problem with that," I told him. "But I want you to know that I'm not going to let you intimidate me. We can be cordial with each other when we see each other. That'd be a lot less tension for both of us."

We didn't become close friends, but after that we got along well. When I took the job at Arizona he called the athletic director, Cedric Dempsey, and told him he had hired "an H of a coach." That was really nice of him, I thought, but then I started wondering if he might just be happy I was leaving the Big Ten.

You can only be "an H of a coach" if you have the players. Our decision to focus our recruiting efforts in Chicago began to pay off when 6'2" point guard Ronnie Lester committed to Iowa. Ronnie had been heavily recruited by schools as diverse as Princeton, Arizona, and Louisville. He was an inner-city kid. He told me that after visiting the University of Arizona he had decided not to go there because "they had some real funny-looking trees." He picked Iowa because we had been there to recruit him first and often—we went to his games and his practices—and because we recruited his whole family, his mother as well as his three sisters. And it also helped that he visited the campus on a beautiful weekend in May.

What made Ronnie so good was his tremendous self-pride and determination. He just demanded perfection from himself. This was the first player I ever had who literally would iron his socks and his shorts. You'd go into his room and everything would be in its place. He was very hard on himself, much harder than I would have been. He had more trouble adjusting to Iowa City than to college basketball. He was used to the hustle of a big city; Iowa City is very laid back, very friendly place. His freshman year, every chance he got he was at the Greyhound station taking a bus back home. But after that year he got used to it, and loved it, and even began spending summers there.

On the court he was as good as any point guard I've ever had. He fit our offense perfectly because he was so quick. We finished 20–7 in 1977, and we were competitive in every game. We won twelve games at home, tying a decade-old record. When I look back on that season, one game really does stick out. It was one of the most memorable games of my own career, against Purdue, that February: I got thrown out of the game with three technical fouls. Just imagine what might have happened if I weren't Norwegian.

Actually, one of them, the second one, was a mistake. The official, once again, was Earl Fouty. We were playing at home. I have a habit of keeping a plastic water bottle next to me on the bench. Several times during a game I'll grab it by the long thin nozzle—a plastic straw—and have a quick drink. The fact that I'd already been tagged with one technical means I wasn't especially happy with the officiating. I don't remember the specific call that set me off, but as I got up I grabbed my water bottle by the nozzle. Apparently one of our managers had refilled it and hadn't quite tightened the lid. As I raised my arm holding the bottle I could feel the bottle just go flying straight up in the air. I was still holding the nozzle, but the bottle was making a slowly spinning arc directly onto the court. It may have gone as high as fifty feet into the air. I sat down before it landed and tried to look as innocent as possible. The water bottle landed at least three feet from Earl Fouty. I'm not sure if he knew where it had come from, but if he hadn't, the fact that the entire Purdue bench was pointing at me was a pretty big hint.

I got the third technical when I angrily kicked a rolled-up towel and was invited to leave the court. My players had never seen me that angry. After the game I apologized to the team, but I told them, "I'll be danged if I'm going to just sit there and take what this officiating crew has done to us this season."

With twenty wins we had a real chance of getting invited to the National Invitational Tournament at Madison Square Garden in New York. At that time the NIT was considerably more prestigious than it is now. The NCAA invited only forty teams to the Big Dance, and you had to win your conference to get a bid, so a lot of very talented teams ended up playing in the Garden. I thought going to a postseason tournament would give national exposure to our program—a postseason tournament is a good recruiting tool—and a trip to New York would be a lot of fun for our team. Iowa hadn't been to a postseason tournament since 1970. So after our season ended we kept practicing—right up until the NIT selections were announced and we hadn't been invited. Then we put the balls away . . . for about an hour.

Our success that season had generated tremendous enthusiasm. It seemed like the whole state had embraced the team. Iowa fans loved their Hawks. During the winter we'd visit I-clubs all over the state, and in some towns we'd have more people there than there were people in the town. After a couple of years, on Saturday morning before a home football game, we started letting the team play skins and shirts; they would choose up sides for pickup games. We opened the doors to the field house and let people in for free, and at times as many as 10,000 people showed up to watch the kids play. Tickets to our games suddenly became hard to get. Bobbi and I had never been treated as celebrities before, so we weren't ready for the loss of privacy that came with our success. Certainly it was flattering, but it also became a problem. We couldn't go out to the store without somebody stopping us to talk Hawkeye basketball. It was impossible to have dinner in a restaurant without several people interrupting to ask for an autograph. One time we were in a restaurant when a very nice woman came up and asked for an autograph for her son. I was always polite. "Of course," I said. "How old is your son?"

She said matter-of-factly, "He's thirty-one."

Based on our success in 1977 and the fact our key players were returning, I was confident we were going to be very good in 1978. I told the reporters, "We could be strong enough to challenge for the conference title next season." Some coaches like to minimize expectations; I try to be realistic and honest. At the beginning of the season most coaches look at their schedule and try to figure out how the season is going to progress. This game we should be able to win, this one is going to difficult to win. This one is probably a toss-up. Most of the time I'm fairly close. I know my personnel and I know the league. The nonconference games are a little tougher to predict. But as I've learned through experience, as much as I know, it's impossible to know. Once the ball goes up, there are so many variables that have an impact on the season.

Nobody I know has yet been able to devise a defense against injuries. You can't outcoach an injury. No matter how good your conditioning program is, no matter how good your trainers are, basketball is a high-speed, all-out contact sport, and players are going to get hurt. In pro basketball if a player gets hurt you can go outside your organization to find a replacement player. In college you have to find that player on your bench. Every team suffers injuries every year. The only thing you can hope for is that your best players don't go down for a prolonged period of time. This [1978] was one of the most disappointing seasons of my career. We finished 12–15, including 5–13 in the league. We just never got healthy. At one point during the season three of our four top forwards were out with injuries.

I'm not at all superstitious. I don't believe in charms, but just in case I'm wrong, I'm very selective about the tie I wear for a game, and if we don't do well, that tie will definitely go into the do-not-use-again pile. I would always go home after the pregame shootaround and sit, relax, and read through the scouting report again. Bobbi and I would always ride together to a game, and we'd always have a bottle of fizzy water in the car. We'd always take the same route. We'd always listen to relaxing music—but we weren't superstitious.

No matter what I tried that season, it made no difference. I went through a whole pile of neckties. I would like to believe that at home and during practice I was the same person and coach that I was during the winning seasons. But if that were true, then I probably shouldn't have been coaching. When the passion for winning disappears, it's time to find something else to do. And I was as passionate as ever. So it hurt, it hurt a lot. As always, Bobbi and our children were right there, reminding me to keep things in perspective. While the outcome affected Bobbi nearly as much as it did me, after a win or a loss she was always smiling, always sociable, always able to create a protective wall around me.

I try not to make excuses. Every college coach has to deal with similar problems. Certainly injuries were not our whole problem. All season long I sort of felt like I was driving on a sheet of ice; we could never get enough traction to get things going in the right direction. Some nights we would play very well, other nights the same players would look like an entirely different team. Shots just wouldn't go in. There's a name for that: basketball. In a situation like this, I responded as I had my entire life: I worked harder. If I had been flagging for crop dusters, I would have covered more fields in a day; if I'd been driving an oil truck, I would have made more stops; in this case I put in more hours, tried to adjust strategy to fit the situation as player after player went down with an injury, and never lost my optimism that we would win the next game. One thing I never did was doubt the validity of our system. There was a reason we did things our way. I didn't wake up in the morning and figure out what we were going to do that day. I didn't change the entire system or replace my assistant coaches because we were losing. Everything we did every day was based on past success—from recruiting to practicing to game strategy.

I also continued to believe that the lessons we were learning during this season would prove valuable in the future. We never stopped teaching. And the following year all that hard work paid off. It paid off in the most successful season we'd had. We had four kids we'd recruited from Chicago on the team. In addition to Ronnie Lester, we had 6'9" center Steve Krafcisin, 6'6" forward Kevin Boyle, and 6'2" guard Kenny Arnold. Krafcisin was particularly hard to get. He played at St. Lawrence High School, and for a long time I was convinced he was going to come to Iowa. He'd made a verbal commitment. Two nights before he was scheduled to sign his commitment letter I called him, as I did practically every night, and as soon as we started talking I knew something had changed. "What's going on?" I asked.

"Well," he said, "Dean Smith is coming to visit me tonight." Dean Smith? Out of nowhere Dean Smith had suddenly appeared. I knew what that meant: North Carolina had just lost a big recruit and they wanted Steve. Dean never had backups for any players, and generally he didn't need them. Dean Smith had been the coach of the Olympic team, so he brought in tapes of the Olympics, tapes of North Carolina winning championships, he brought one of the great traditions in sports with him.

When I spoke to Steve the next day he admitted he was officially undecided. To me, that meant he was going to North Carolina and just didn't want to tell me. We needed him at Iowa. "Can I come see you tonight?" I asked. "You at least owe me the opportunity to come in and talk to you after Coach Smith has been there." He was very reluctant, but I talked my way into a meeting. I caught a commercial flight right after practice and went to his house. Normally I'm in a recruit's home for about two hours. I was in the Krafcisin house for four hours and I didn't want to leave. I was going to filibuster. I tried everything to get him turned around. When I left, I don't think he knew what he wanted to do.

I missed my flight back to Cedar Rapids, so I had to stay in Chicago overnight. The next morning I was at the airport early in the morning and I looked like a mess. I was wearing the same clothes, I hadn't shaved, nothing. At 7:00 A.M. I was slipping through O'Hare, hoping no-body would recognize me, when all of a sudden I hear a familiar voice, "Lute! Hey, Lute!"

It was Al McGuire, looking McGuire dapper. We had breakfast. Al was going to Peoria to see a kid. Al loved the city kids; he always said he wasn't interested in recruiting any kid who had grass in front of his house. "I'm going to sign this kid today."

I asked him where his assistants were. He shrugged, "I don't know. Rick Majerus [his assistant] is out there somewhere. He thinks he's re-cruiting, but the only kid we're going to take is this kid. But I like to make my assistants feel like they're doing something."

When he asked me what I was doing, I told him the whole Krafcisin story. When he asked me what other school he was thinking about, I told him, "North Carolina."

Al smiled, "Is he black or white?"

I said, "He's white."

"Forget it." Just that simple. He was right. Steve Krafcisin went to North Carolina, but after one season he wasn't happy there and trans-ferred to Iowa. It had taken an additional year, but finally we'd gotten him to play the middle for us.

In 1979 Ronnie Lester emerged as a star on the national level, be-coming an All-American while leading the team to a 20–8 record. For the first time in my career at Iowa we won the Big Ten championship with a 13–5 record. Well, actually, we tied with with Michigan State and Purdue for the championship, but there is no doubt in my mind we re-ally should have won it outright.

We were leading the league by a game near the end of the season when we played Michigan State in East Lansing. The Spartans were led by sophomore "Magic" Johnson. With time running out Ronnie Lester hit a bucket to put us up by two, and Michigan State came down with only a few seconds left to go for the tie. We knew they were going to try to get the ball to Magic, so we really defended him well. I can close my eyes and see it. Eventually they called a time-out. During time-outs I never try to do too much. I just review what we've already practiced. I never introduce anything new. If the team isn't prepared for whatever the situation then the coaching staff hasn't done its job. In this case we knew they were going to try to get the ball to Magic. That was obvious. If you have Magic Johnson you get him the ball. We talked about how we were going to keep the ball away from him. We talked about the screens they might run to get him free for a shot. Everybody knew his assignment.

If we could hold them for less than ten seconds we would win the Big Ten championship. People have often asked if I get nervous in situations when a game—or even a championship—is on the line. The answer is the same when an NCAA championship is on the line as it was in Marina High School. During a basketball game there is so much to do and everything happens so quickly that there isn't time to get nervous. I get more nervous when I have to make a speech in public or when I'm sitting in the stands watching someone I care about playing or coaching than I ever do on the sidelines. I don't want my players nervous, either, I want them to do what we practiced.

Michigan State inbounded. Kevin Boyle was on Magic. He was a great defender, he just wouldn't let Magic get his hands on the ball. The clock was ticking down. With one second left on the clock, less time than it takes to read this sentence, a kid named Mike Brkovich out of Canada had the ball at the top of the key. When he realized he couldn't get the ball to Magic, he launched a desperation shot. Ronnie Lester was guarding him perfectly. He stood his ground, his arms straight up in the air. He didn't move. The shot went wide—and Brkovich jumped right into Ronnie. The game should have been over, but the official called Ronnie for a shooting foul. Two shots.

This isn't an excuse, this is a fact: It was a terrible call. It will always be a terrible call, and I'll never forget it. Brkovich was one of the leading free throw shooters in Michigan State history. He hit both shots. Then they beat us in overtime. That loss dropped us to a tie with Michigan State and Purdue.

At that time only conference winners went to the Big Dance, so all three teams were invited. That foul call turned out to affect basketball history as Magic Johnson's Spartans beat Larry Bird's Indiana State for the national championship, a game they would not have been in without that call.

We always had a difficult time winning at State's Jennison Field House. Well, I guess everybody did. But after this game one of our writers began referring to the "ghost of Jennison," who kept us from winning there. So each year we played there the specter of the "ghost of Jennison" who kept us from winning would rise in the newspapers. One year we were practicing in the morning in the empty field house when suddenly somebody with their head covered with a towel comes down the aisle shouting, "WWWOOOOOooooo, I am the ghost of Jennison here to keep you from winning. Woooooo. Woooo."

The guys looked at whoever this was and wondered, who the heck is this fool?

"Woooooo." When the towel came off, Michigan State coach Jud Heathcote was standing there smiling. That was exactly the kind of personality he had, so if we weren't going to win, I was pleased for him.

We played the cochampion of the Mid-America Conference, the University of Toledo, in the first round. I'd been to the NCAA before, but only as a spectator. I think every coach or player dreams of being involved in the Final Four. The problem is that there's absolutely no time to enjoy it, contrary to Al McGuire's suggestion. From the moment we found out we were playing Toledo, we got busy trying to learn as much as possible about them. In those days few games were broadcast, so we had to hustle to get tapes of their games to break down. We watched those tapes over and over; we spoke to people who had played them and we got some idea of their tendencies. In the early rounds there just isn't enough time to learn a lot about your opponent. We knew it was going to be a tough game; we were a number four-seed, Toledo was a five. And the game was played in Indiana's Assembly Hall—an arena in which Iowa had never won a game.

The moment we got our invitation, the telephone started ringing and just kept ringing. Our games at Iowa Field House had been sold out but if somebody seriously wanted a ticket they usually could get one. But the NCAAs were different. We had a limited number of tickets and a maximum number of people who wanted them. It's strange, in a situation like that many of the people you want to be there to share the excitement with you don't call you because they understand what you're going through and don't want to bother you. But many other people you haven't seen or spoken to in a long time—or don't even know— call and ask for them. Bobbi and the kids manned the phones during this time. They didn't even tell me about our newfound distant relatives.

In the game we had a fourteen-point lead at halftime, but Toledo came all the way back and scored in the last few seconds to beat us 74–72. Many people tried to console us after the game, reminding us that we'd won the Big Ten, that it was the first time since 1970 that Iowa had even gone to the NCAA, but there is no consolation in losing, even in the NCAA tournament.

This was the end of our fifth year in Iowa City. We'd become very comfortable there, although at times the fans' enthusiasm for the program became almost overwhelming. Finally we had to make some changes in our lifestyle. From the day we'd moved to Iowa City our phone number had been listed—an unlisted phone number was a big deal back then; that was something movie stars had—but eventually we had to get an unlisted number. We had to stop going out to dinner as often as we once did. And eventually we even had to move a little farther out of town, to Lake MacBride. It was about fifteen miles outside Iowa City. With the help of our close friend, Bobbie Stehbens, we'd built our dream house on the lake. Before we built it I'd worried that in a major snowstorm I might not be able to get to a game. The highway patrol alleviated that fear, telling me that if I had a problem they would land a helicopter on the lake and fly me to town. But even way out there we didn't have privacy. We left all the trees and reeds on the lakeshore so people wouldn't be able to see the house, but they knew where it was. We'd be sitting in the house and all of a sudden we'd hear a horn blaring and some people would be on the lake in a pontoon boat shouting, "Lute! Lute!" The only way we could get rid of them was for me to walk out to the end of our dock and wave to them. We'd moved out of town to get a little more privacy and ended up out of town with a lot less privacy.

Part of the problem was that we were a very big story in the state. I attended so many dinners and I was on TV so often that people felt that they knew me. We were friends. There was absolutely nothing malicious about it; these are the nicest people in the world, and they just wanted to say hello and wish us luck. In fact, sometimes it seemed like every single person in the state of Iowa wanted to say hello and wish us luck.

Bobbi's role in the program actually began expanding as our kids got older and there were fewer sports events, after-school activities, and lessons she had to attend to and less need to arrange transportation. That left a little more time for her role as the team mother. She became well known for that, and most people looked at us as a team; it was always Lute and Bobbi. She took her role very seriously. For the first time she had started traveling with us to more away games. She'd be on the plane and the bus before and after each game, and win or lose she'd have something encouraging to say to just about every player. Her presence just softened the whole atmosphere. The players loved her; the incredible thing was that just about every one of them believed completely that he was her favorite. She'd come on the bus and one of the kids would tell her, "You really look nice. That's a nice dress."

She would just beam and respond, "Thank you. You'll start tonight." The problem was that she would tell every one of our kids that they were starting. Admittedly, there are times after a loss when I'm not a very pleasant person to be around. Then the players liked to stay far away from me, but not from her. No matter how bad the game had been, she would always find something positive to say. Often on the flights home she'd sit in the back with the players rather than up in front with me. They would discuss things with her they wouldn't tell me—or their own parents. They trusted her. If I was having a problem with a player, she'd be certain to seek him out and try to make the situation a little easier. For me, these were young men with responsibilities. I treated them that way and expected them to live up to the standards we'd set for the team. For Bobbi, they were kids with the ability to play basketball—but still growing and learning. Sometimes they were going to be silly; they were going to make the mistakes that kids make. And when they needed someone to talk with about a problem at home or with a girlfriend, or if they didn't think I was treating them fairly, that was her place.

Harvey Mason, who played for me at Arizona, had been a big star in high school, but his freshman season he wasn't getting a lot of minutes. Like a lot of the players we get, this was the first time in his life he'd sat on the bench. He didn't like it at all. I was riding him pretty hard, he recalls, trying to mold him into our system. He wasn't angry, he was just very sad. On a plane coming back from a road game Bobbi sat down next to him. "How's it going?" she asked him. "How are you feeling?" As Harvey remembers, "She worked her way around to her point, 'Don't let Lute get to you. Don't let Coach get you down.' She sat with me for almost three hours. Basically, she read my mind. She knew I was having a tough time. We didn't talk too much about basketball, but more about life and personalities and dealing with people. She told me she had seen hundreds of athletes come and go and [discussed] how best to deal with Coach.

"After that Bobbi was a special person for me. We talked all the time."

That wasn't an act with her. It was absolutely real. That was Bobbi. She was always concerned about their feelings. Once she was sitting in the stands at a football game with Bobbie Stehbens when Dan Frost approached her and asked her to do something. Whatever it was has long been forgotten. For some reason Bobbi kind of snapped at him. She said something like "Oh, go away. Not now." That was completely out of character. She was always kind, I never remember her being rude to anyone. Whatever happened with Danny Frost, it bothered her for a long time. She knew she'd hurt his feelings and she felt terrible about it. But from that point on, whenever the two Bobbies were together and the situation might have called for a less than kind response, one of them would tell the other, "Oh, look, there goes Danny Frost."

By that point we had been married more than twenty-five years. We'd struggled financially at times. We'd raised five children. We'd gone through thirteen years of high school, four years of junior college, and six years of major college basketball. Then, in 1980, our daughter Jodi gave birth to our first grandchild, Julie Brase.

We were grandparents. Still, sometimes it was like we'd met only a couple of weeks earlier. We never stopped loving each other. I don't think I ever left the house without kissing her good-bye. She had a routine, Monday through Friday: About a half hour before she knew I'd be home from practice she'd stop whatever she was doing and go freshen up. She'd redo her hair, put on a little makeup, a touch of lipstick, and a change of clothes. She just didn't want me to walk in and find her in cleaning or cooking clothes. It wouldn't have made the slightest difference to me, but it was important to her.

One of the reasons our marriage worked so well was that the things that mattered to us didn't require money. It seemed like we were always in tune with each other. It was never a case of me having men's toys or Bobbi caring about the name on a label. It was at Iowa that we became financially comfortable. We weren't rich, but for the first time we had some security. When we married, the only rings we could afford were those simple, basic wedding bands. For our anniversary one year I bought her a beautiful ring with a yellow diamond. It might have been the first diamond she'd ever had. She was thrilled, but the first thing she asked was "Are you sure we can afford this?"

"We'll be fine," I said.

Whatever attention the program had gotten the first five years was barely noticeable compared to what happened in 1980, when we won twenty-three games—and went to the Final Four. The season had not started very well. We were playing in Dayton, Ohio, in the finals of a Christmas tournament. Ronnie Lester, who was without question the best point guard in America that year, stole a pass and got free on a breakaway. One of the Dayton kids chased him, and as Ronnie went up to lay it in, the kid grabbed his left arm and yanked it. Ronnie went flying and landed on his knee. It was diagnosed as a severe sprain, but it was terribly damaging. Ronnie's game was quickness, and the injury just took it away.

We lost four of our first six Big Ten games. Ronnie tried to come back a couple of times during the season, but just never regained complete mobility. Without Ronnie that season we were 8–7; with him playing we were 15–1, and we hadn't really lost that one. We were playing UNLV. With slightly more than four seconds left we hit a basket to go ahead by a point. They inbounded, dribbled upcourt, made a pass, shot and missed, and rebounded and scored. Supposedly that had taken a little more than four seconds, which is absolutely impossible. But that was our only regular season loss with Ronnie Lester playing.

That wasn't our only injury. At different times four other starters suffered serious injuries. And my top assistant, Tony McAndrews, was very lucky to have survived when the plane he was on returning from a scouting assignment went down. He broke several bones and had head and chest injuries, and was lost for the season.

We struggled through the Big Ten, finishing only 10–8. But we were very fortunate that the NCAA changed its rules that year, expanding the tournament field to forty-eight teams. That included twenty-four conference champions and twenty-four at large teams. Ronnie Lester returned for the final two games of the Big Ten season. He wasn't 100 percent, but I let him play with the understanding that he wouldn't take the ball to the hoop. Period. If he had a lane, he'd pull up and take a jump shot. If the player he was defending drove to the basket, he had to let him go; he had to depend on a teammate to cover up for him. I think that was hard for him. He had to stop and think rather than reacting, but we won both games and got our invitation to the tournament.

We knew we'd been on the bubble. We had enough wins to earn an invitation but we'd finished fourth in our conference. Considering all the injuries we'd suffered, getting invited was tremendously satisfying. That feeling of satisfaction lasted a few minutes, then we went to work.

It takes two equally important factors to win the tournament. First, you have to be a really good team or you have no chance. And second, you need to be lucky. Everything has to break right for you. The committee sent us to Greensboro, North Carolina, to open against Virginia Commonwealth. We were a number-five seed, they were a twelve. Going into the tournament you never know what to expect; you just hope that your team is ready to play. With all the injuries we'd suffered that year, with Ronnie Lester at less than full strength, I don't think anybody picked us to get out of the Eastern Regional. We beat Virginia Commonwealth 86-72 and then had to play North Carolina State. N.C. State was in Raleigh, so this was practically a home game for them. They were a strong favorite, but we beat them, too, 77-64. We were in the Sweet Sixteen.

Momentum is simply confidence magnified. You score a couple of baskets, make some defensive stops, and suddenly you're on a roll. Your confidence builds, so you play better, and the better you play, the more your confidence builds. For a brief time your team is able to play the game at a higher level, and you just try to sustain it as long as possible. You can't create momentum, you can't predict it, but you can feel it, and when you're in the middle of a run, you ride it as long as you can.

The crowd feels it, too. And feeds it. During a game the only time I ever hear the cheering is when we get a momentum swing and the arena gets louder and louder. Announcers talk about getting the crowd into the game, and they are absolutely correct. It makes a difference. It has a big effect on the confidence level of the players. The teams I've coached have been known for years for making great runs. That's generally caused by the defense creating quick scoring opportunities. The crowd gets louder, the other team gets a little rattled or gets out of its offensive scheme, and we score again.

I've been on the other side of it, too. When it happens, you try to switch defenses, slow down your own offense to regain control of the tempo, and use your time-outs. Sometimes it works.

After we won those two games in Greensboro, I could feel the momentum moving in our direction. Suddenly everything we'd been trying to do all season, admittedly with mixed success, fell into place. There was a good reason for that: Having Ronnie back just raised the confidence level of the whole team. We knew we were good; we didn't know how good we were at full strength. We went to the Spectrum in Philadelphia for the Eastern Regionals. It turned out to be us against the Big East. A large number of loyal Iowa fans drove to the game, some of them getting caught in a dangerous ice storm. In our first game we played Jim Boeheim's Syracuse Orangemen, the top seed in the region. It was a close game all the way, but we broke away in the final five minutes and won 88-77. That set up a meeting with Georgetown. John Thompson's Hoyas. The number-three seed was led by Sleepy Floyd, and they were favored. Some people had picked them to win the national championship.

It was a typical John Thompson team, big, fast, and physically intimidating. They played you every minute, for every point. Anything you got against Georgetown you earned.

We were the Cinderella team. Nobody had picked us to be there, so this was supposed to be midnight. Time for us to go home. It was one of those great games in which the momentum kept shifting, though most of the time it was shifting toward the Hoyas' end of the court. Georgetown was up by a dozen with 12:45 left in the game. But for the last twelve minutes and forty-five seconds of the game that night we played as close to perfect basketball as possible. It was the kind of stretch every coach fantasizes about: Every rebound goes in your direction, every bounce finds one of your players. In those rare situations the best thing a coach can do is stay out of the way. You do nothing to change fate or luck or whatever winds of fortune have suddenly started blowing in your direction.

During that span we hit fifteen consecutive free throws, we shot almost 78 percent from the field, and we had one turnover the entire second half. One turnover the entire half. Georgetown didn't quit; they shot 50 percent. It was two great teams going at each other with all their ability. We just clawed our way back into the game. We were tied at seventy-eight with about twelve seconds to play. Our ball. This is where composure and experience make the difference. Kevin Boyle, one of our primary go-to guys in that situation, got the ball. He tried to make a couple of moves, but the defense wouldn't give him a thing, so he passed to Steve Waite, who was free in the corner. Steve was not a shooting option. He wasn't an outside threat. But the defense came up to guard him. With the clock ticking down he drove to the basket. He hit a layup and was fouled with five seconds on the clock. This was before basketball added the three-point shot. So this foul shot was for the game. Winner goes to the Final Four; loser goes home. How much pressure is that on a twenty-one-year-old? He was ice. He hit the free throw to put us up three. They scored a meaningless basket as the buzzer sounded. Cinderella was going to the Final Four.

At the press conference after the game Waite admitted, "My first thought when Kevin Boyle passed me the ball was to pass it back so one of our shooters could shoot. But nobody was open. I saw a hole to the basket and decided to take it in myself." That was the play of his lifetime. Momentum? Luck? Fate? More likely it was the countless hours of hard work that had prepared him for those five seconds. When he caught the pass, he knew exactly how to react.

It was not only the most extraordinary game I had ever coached, it was probably the most amazing game I'd ever seen. Coach Roz was a little more exuberant, calling it "the greatest game in the history of basketball of all time."

We got back to Iowa just after midnight. Iowa was going to the Final Four for the first time in twenty-four years. A large crowd was there to meet our bus, and they escorted us to the field house. For more than seven hours 13,000 people had been sitting there waiting for us—and the wrestling team, which had just won the NCAA championship. The doors had been closed at five. It was like walking into a single huge roar. The sound was deafening. Signs were hanging from rafters: THE MORER WE HURT, THE GOODER WE GET. LUTE'S BRUTES EXECUTE, THE FABULOUS FEW. Kids were wearing LUTE FOR PRES T-shirts. When you walk into an arena overflowing with support and love, it's overwhelming. And Bobbi and I were at the center of it. I don't remember saying anything to her—it was probably too noisy to be heard—but I do remember that incredibly warm feeling we shared with every person in that building. Few people are lucky enough to experience such emotion. Had it come earlier in our life together it still would have been exciting, but it would not have meant so much. This was a moment we'd reached together, and we savored it.

The next morning I was back in the office, preparing for our game the coming weekend against the Louisville Cardinals in Market Square Arena in Indianapolis. At the end of the season Denny Crum's Cardinals had been ranked second in the country; we weren't in the top twenty.

The game was a duel of All-Americans, Ronnie Lester versus Louisville's Darrell Griffith. It was a game every bit as good as the buildup. For most of the first half, Ronnie and Darrell matched each other basket for basket. Ronnie scored our first ten points without missing a shot. The score was tied. Then one of our people intercepted a pass and threw it to Ronnie. Ronnie was ahead of everybody and went in for an uncontested layup. A kid from Louisville was chasing him, but he didn't interfere at all as Ronnie went up and came down— awkwardly. That was it. He was done.

Our kids were in shock. There goes our chance, they figured. Believe me, I felt as awful as they did, but I couldn't show it. We called a timeout and I reminded them that we'd played a lot of the year without Ronnie. "We can do it," I told them. "We can win this thing."

It was very difficult playing without our leader. Ronnie was sitting in a large janitor's closet watching the game with his knee in an ice bucket. We were only down 34-29 at the half, but we ended up being down double figures with about ten minutes to go—and then we began making our run. The kids found their confidence. We fought back hard. The momentum had shifted in our direction. With forty-some seconds to go, the Cardinals were up three. Kevin Boyle, who was probably the best defender in the country, was doing a good job guarding Griffith. Kevin was 6'6", lean and quick, and he always guarded our opponents' best player. At Michigan State, remember, he'd guarded Magic Johnson and hadn't allowed him to get the ball with the game on the line. When we played Magic in Iowa City, Kevin held him to a single field goal— although Magic hit a lot of free throws. Kevin had done a great job on Griffith. Now he forced him to the baseline. Griffith had to take a fade-away jumper, practically over the edge of the backboard—and he hit it. Griffith was a phenomenal player, and he made an incredible play. I think that was one of the most amazing shots I've ever seen. There isn't anything you can do about that but admire the player. Kevin had defended him very well, but Griffith was great enough to hit the basket. The lead was five. We didn't score, so we had to foul. Game. The final score was 80–72. Louisville went on to win the national championship and Griffith was the Most Valuable Player of the tournament.

If Ronnie Lester hadn't gotten hurt, we would have won the national championship. I believe that in my heart. Anyone in Iowa will tell you that was the best team we ever had there. But after what we had accomplished in just getting to the Final Four, it was difficult to feel that we had failed. At the end of every season only one Division I team goes home happy. So maybe we weren't happy, but we were very, very proud.

4

It turned out that Al McGuire had been absolutely correct. Our success had created extraordinary expectations. This is how bad the situation became: The following season we'd lost a game on a Thursday night. On Friday Bobbi was doing a little shopping in our local grocery store and the manager came over to her and said, "I can't believe you're out of the house today!"

"What do you mean?"

It seemed obvious to him. "Well, you lost last night."

Bobbi was stunned. "Yes," she said, "we did. But the family still needs to eat."

That kind of thing happened every day. The greatest thing about coaching at Iowa was the tremendous interest in the team and the support for the program. Of course, the worst thing about coaching at Iowa was the tremendous interest and the support for the program. It was as if the entire state had become cheerleaders for our program. I remember a farmer outside Iowa City spent eighty hours filling fifteen hundred trash bags with leaves and arranging all fifteen hundred to spell out GO LUTE!—a tribute which could be seen only from the air. My full head of white hair made me instantly recognizable, so even when we were in the car people would be honking and waving. It truly was too much of a good and well-meant thing.

As often as possible Bobbi and I would take very early morning walks. Just the two of us. It was an opportunity for us to spend time alone and talk about the whirl surrounding us. We'd discuss the kids and the various problems in their lives, we'd talk about the team and anything that was bothering me, we'd review our schedule for the next few days. On one of those walks we were talking about the unbelievable hoopla that was going on around us. Bobbi looked at me and shook her head, then she said, "Can you just imagine what it would be like if we were losing!"

It really was an amazing situation. In some ways we were captives of our success. All of our home games were sold out on a season ticket basis before the season began and tickets to the games had become status symbols. Our players were celebrities, and some of them had to schedule autograph signing sessions. At first only a limited number of our games were televised, but demand became so great that eventually all of our games were broadcast on every NBC station throughout the entire state. Our games were so popular that NBC's top-rated program, *Hill Street Blues,* had to be moved from Thursday night to Sunday night. When NBC executives objected, we invited them to a game. When they saw the enthusiasm—and the ratings we were getting—they understood why their top show was better on another night. In addition to the games, I also had a coach's show on Sunday nights to discuss the games of the previous week, and on Saturday mornings, there was an hour-long Iowa sports program—which covered all sports but featured basketball.

If on occasion my ego did get a little inflated, I always had Bobbi to anchor me. My birthday is September 22, which makes me a Virgo. Virgos are perfectionists; they need everything to be in order. She never let me forget that. One night the whole family was sitting around the dining room table. A local sportswriter had described me as rigid, and I was very loudly disputing that. I denied that I was a perfectionist, that everything had to be in its specific place—until Bobbi pointed out that as I sat there I was carefully arranging the silverware in perfect order around the plate.

On another occasion Bobbi and I were going to Chicago on a recruiting trip. We were planning to visit several prospects, so we were going to be doing a lot of driving. Our neighbor across the street was the top salesman at the Lincoln-Mercury dealership in Iowa City. He asked me "When you go to Chicago what kind of car do you rent?"

An inexpensive one, I explained. We didn't spend a lot of our recruiting budget on fancy cars.

"Let me fix you up with a Lincoln Town Car," he said. Well, naturally I wasn't going to resist too strongly. I explained to Bobbi that it would be impolite to turn him down, that this was his way of contributing to the program. Truthfully, I was feeling pretty good about it. Perhaps even a little cocky. We'd never been able to afford a luxury car and this was a nice gesture. "You know," I said contentedly to Bobbi, "we've really come a long way."

Unfortunately, when I picked up the car at the dealership in Chicago the only car they had for us was a small Mercury Comet. The same make we'd had years earlier when leaving Minnesota. For three days every time we squeezed into the car she'd start laughing and ask me, "Oh, Lute, please tell me again how far we've come."

After we'd been in Iowa for a couple of years a well-respected sportswriter from the *Cedar Rapids Gazette,* Gus Schrader, asked Bobbi to collaborate with him on a weekly column. I think it was called "Ask Bobbi." She didn't write it; she just answered his questions. Basically, it was Iowa basketball from the woman's point of view. What did the players eat before a game? Isn't weaving wall decorations one of your hobbies? When she was asked, How do you react when someone criticizes your husband's coaching? She responded, "I never like to hear criticism, but I never turn around and hit them over the head with my purse or say anything because I feel they paid their way into the game and have the right to second-guess the coach . . . I try not to have rabbit ears . . ."

It was meant to be completely noncontroversial, warm and friendly. My own relations with the sportswriters who covered our program were sometimes strained. We had very different objectives. Mine was to win basketball games and protect the image of my players and our program; theirs was to write a story almost every day and try to attract readers to their newspapers. Finding a new and interesting story every day was difficult. I understood that, but sometimes I thought they were less than fair. A lot less than fair. Conversely, they thought that I was cold, distant, and uncooperative.

Bobbi always tried to cooperate with the media. She liked most of the people who covered our program, and I think they all appreciated her. Once, though, Ron Maly, a *Des Moines Register* columnist, asked her to reflect on the success of our program. She responded that the reaction had been overwhelming, and then, unfortunately, she added, "Lute has created a monster here."

She meant it to be positive. But it didn't come out that way in the papers. It was written as if she was criticizing our fans. It was a statement that never died. Some people thought it was intended to be an insult, which was the absolute last thing that Bobbi was capable of doing. But the writers continually revived that statement. Every time something negative happened they dug up that quote to support their opinions. It was a simple aside, but it just never went away.

The attention we were receiving wasn't limited to Iowa. Just a few years after I had been "Lute who?" I had become known nationally as "What's-his-name, that guy with all the white hair coaching at Iowa?" *Sports Illustrated* regularly covered our program. Instead of attending clinics, I was invited to speak at them. And I was being paid to speak at them. People began asking me about my philosophy of coaching: It was pretty much the same as it had always been, practice hard, get the ball in the hands of the open man, put your players in a position to do those things they do best, and play as a team.

One night our phone rang at 5:30 in the morning. A reporter from *The New York Times* informed me, "A press release came over the wire that you were joining the Nike consulting staff and you're getting paid for your players to wear Nikes. Is that true?"

Did I mention this was 5:30 in the morning? Even if I had been wide awake I wouldn't have known what he was talking about. "I'm on the what?"

He read a few lines from a Nike release supposedly reporting that I had joined the consulting staff. "That's not true," I said. "I don't know what you're talking about."

After a brief pause he asked, "If you had the chance, would you be on their consulting staff?"

At this time Nike was not the power in collegiate sports that it was to become. It was still pretty much a shoe and uniform company. I knew a little about the company. While I was at Long Beach City I'd met a Nike salesman. He was a graduate of Long Beach State and offered to provide a free pair of Nikes to any of our players who would wear them. That was the whole deal. There were no negotiations, no compensation, no contracts: He would provide a free pair of shoes to any player who would wear them. One pair. Several of our players took advantage of that offer.

When I took over for Jerry Tarkanian at Long Beach State *Coach and Athlete* magazine decided to do a cover story about the program. They photographed me kneeling with Leonard Gray, a senior on that team. Both of us were given a pair of gold suede Nikes to wear, and we got to keep the shoes. Years later I discovered that was the very first time Nikes had appeared on the cover of a national magazine. That photograph now hangs in an honored spot at Nike's headquarters.

These are Lute's parents, Albert Olson and Alinda Halvorson, on their wedding day, October 9, 1919. *(Courtesy of the Olson Family Archives)*

Lute at eleven years old with his brother, Marv, and sister, Kathy. *(Courtesy of the Olson Family Archives)*

Olson is out on a typical winter day in North Dakota. *(Courtesy of the Olson Family Archives)*

These are the 1968 Marina High School seniors who lead the Vikings to the Southern California Final Four. Left to right: Mark Miller, Mark Soderberg, Mike Shelley, and Larry Baker. *(Courtesy of the Olson Family Archives)*

Here is Olson (#24) with his Augsburg College teammates in his junior year. The "Flying Midget Cage Circus" was one of the highest scoring teams in the history of the college. Notable on the team was Dr. Richard Green (#12), who went on to serve as chancellor of the New York City Public School System. *(Courtesy of the Olson Family Archives)*

Olson is at home with his granddaughter and future Wildcat, Julie Brase-Hairgrove. Currently, Julie is an assistant coach with the Phoenix Mercury of the WNBA. *(Courtesy of the Olson Family Archives)*

This is the 1980 Iowa Final Four team, including future NBA players, #24 Bob Hansen and #12 Ronnie Lester (current assistant general manager of the Los Angeles Lakers). *(Courtesy of the Olson Family Archives)*

Lute is coaching in Iowa City. Left to right: Scott Thompson, Jim Rosborough, and Lute Olson. *(Courtesy of the University of Iowa Photo Services)*

This is the reunion of the 1988 Final Four Wildcats. Included are former NBA players: Steve Kerr, Jud Buechler, Anthony Cook, Sean Elliott, and Tom Tolbert. Multiple Grammy Award–winner Harvey Mason is eighth from the left. *(Courtesy of the Olson Family Archives)*

Guard Steve Kerr takes a moment to confer with Olson during a stoppage in play. The Pacific Palisades, California, native played for Olson from 1983 to '88. *(Courtesy of the University of Arizona Athletic Media Relations Archives)*

Forward Pete Williams, the Walnut, California, native who played for Olson from 1983 to '85. *(Courtesy of the University of Arizona Athletic Media Relations Archives)*

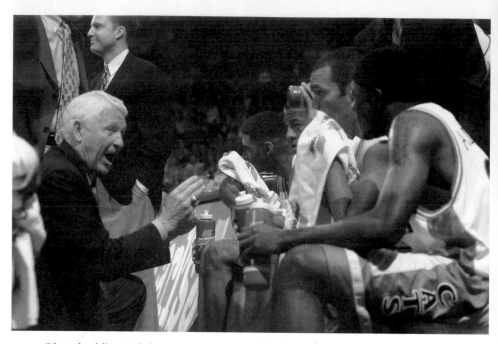

Olson huddles with his team during the 2002–3 season. *(Courtesy of Wily Low/University of Arizona Athletic Media Relations Archives)*

Olson is all smiles after defeating Northern Arizona University on November 24, 2003. The victory was number 500 for Olson as the Arizona head coach. *(Courtesy of Jacob Chinn/University of Arizona Athletic Media Relations Archives)*

This action photo of forward Michael Dickerson was taken during the 1996-97 season. The native of Seattle played for Olson from 1994 to '98. *(Courtesy of Robert Walker/University of Arizona Athletic Media Relations Archives)*

Center A. J. Bramlett during the 1996–97 season. The native of Albuquerque, New Mexico, played for Olson from 1995 to '99. *(Courtesy of Robert Walker/University of Arizona Athletic Media Relations Archives)*

This action photo is from the 1997 national championship game featuring four of Arizona's five starters. Arizona defeated Kentucky, 84–79, in overtime. *(Courtesy of Brian Spurlock)*

Olson waves to supporters following the win over Kentucky to claim the 1997 national championship. *(Courtesy of Brian Spurlock)*

Olson claims the Sears Trophy following the 1997 national championship game.
(Courtesy of Brian Spurlock)

Olson holds the national championship trophy at the welcome-home celebration in Arizona Stadium on April 1, 1997. *(Courtesy of Robert Walker/University of Arizona Athletic Media Relations Archives)*

Olson presents President Bill Clinton with a jersey at a White House ceremony honoring the 1997 national championship squad. Also pictured (from left) is Vice President Al Gore, University of Tennessee women's head coach Pat Summit, Miles Simon, and Michael Dickerson. *(Courtesy of Kathleen "Rocky" LaRose/University of Arizona Athletic Media Relations Archives)*

Olson is on the sidelines during the 2005–6 season. *(Courtesy of Ben Rider/University of Arizona Athletic Media Relations Archives)*

Olson and the other members of the Naismith Memorial Basketball Hall of Fame class of 2002. *(Courtesy of the Associated Press)*

Olson with former players prior to a San Antonio Spurs vs. Portland Trailblazers game. Left to right; Steve Kerr, Damon Stoudamire, and Sean Elliott. *(Courtesy of the Olson Family Archives)*

Olson certainly looks the part at his annual Celebrity Chefs charity event.
(Courtesy of University of Arizona Athletic Media Relations Archives)

Two families unite at the wedding of Christine and Lute in Las Vegas on April 12, 2003. Absent: Steve Olson who resides in Italy. *(Courtesy of the Bellaggio Hotel)*

Lute and Christine surrounded by her University of Arizona Chi Omega sisters at the Annual Greek CATwalk, October 9, 2005. *(Courtesy of the Chi Omega Archive)*

Olson with wife Bobbi at the ceremony dedicating the playing surface in the University of Arizona's McKale Memorial Center "Lute Olson Court" on March 11, 2000. *(Courtesy of Robert Walker/University of Arizona Athletic Media Relations Archives)*

But when the *Times* reporter called—at 5:30 in the morning—that was all I knew about Nike. I was not involved with them in any way. As we later discovered, the reporter had misread the press release, which can happen at 5:30 in the morning. It wasn't Iowa's coach who was joining Nike's staff, it was the coach at Iona College in New York, Jimmy Valvano.

It turned out that Sonny Vacarro, a Nike employee, had started a program to encourage collegiate teams to wear Nike equipment. A few days after this morning call Vacarro called me. "I know you got called about this," he said. "Here's the situation. We're forming an advisory staff and we'd like to have you to join us."

Nike was inviting several respected college basketball coaches to join this staff. Among them were several coaches I'd long admired. People who did it the right way. I took some time to think about it, almost a year, but eventually I became one of the original members of the Nike advisory board. It is an association I've continued throughout my career.

As Al McGuire had warned me, our success led to even greater expectations. With the exception of Ronnie Lester, who had missed much of the season anyway, we had the whole team returning, and we'd added three promising freshmen. We'd lost in the semifinals. Anything less than getting back to the Final Four would be a big disappointment. We were talented and experienced, and, logically, we should have done better the following season. In basketball, logic sometimes becomes your best foul shooter missing two free throws with the score tied and no time on the clock. Or one of your worst shooters from the field hitting a driving layup to win a big game. Or in the 2006 NCAA tournament, Villanova forward Will Sheridan, who averaged slightly more than two field goals a game for the entire season, hitting seven of eight shots from the field against us to lead his team to an 82-78 victory in the second round of the NCAA tournament. Logic often is that thing you just didn't expect to determine the outcome of the game.

And we were good. We were ranked in the top ten. At the beginning of the season it looked like we were going to fulfill a lot of those expectations. We opened 8-1. Johnny Orr, who ran up a 16-5 record against us when he was coaching Michigan and had just taken over at Iowa State, told their fans, "It used to be a picnic to play in Iowa City." So when Iowa State came to town, someone politely set out a complete picnic in front of their bench for him. We beat them by twenty-six points. We finished 21-7, but lost the Big Ten title to Indiana.

The NCAA made us a third seed and sent us to the Midwest Regional to play the Wichita State Wheatshockers—in their arena. So it was a home game for them. Wichita was led by the original "Big Dog," Antoine Carr. As a third seed we had a first-round bye, while they played a first-round game. I've never liked that kind of matchup. They were talented and already had a win in the tournament. Whatever nervousness their kids might have had was gone. This was our opening game and there was a great deal of pressure on us to repeat last season's magic.

We played well, opening up a fifteen-point lead. But Wichita roared back to tie the score with seventeen seconds left. It was our ball. We called a time-out to talk it over. We set up a play that would get Kevin Boyle free in the lane. The play developed well and Kevin got a good look, but his shot bounced off the front of the rim. Carr rebounded and we got called for a foul. He was shooting one-and-one for the win. I signaled one of our players to call a time-out so we could review our strategy for the last few seconds. I just didn't realize that we didn't have any time-outs left. That's a technical foul, the penalty was two shots and possession of the ball.

Carr shot the one-and-one before shooting the technical. And he missed his first shot. If he hadn't had to shoot the technical, the ball would have been in play, and maybe we would have gotten into overtime. Nobody knows what might have happened. But I know what did happen. Randy Smithson, the son of Shockers' coach Randy Smithson, shot the technical foul. He hit both shots. They took the ball out of bounds and we were forced to foul again. The final score was 60–56. No one play ever determines the outcome of a game, but when a mistake in the last few seconds changes the final score, it sure seems like it does. And when you've made that mistake, there's not a lot you can do except stand up, admit it, explain it, and take responsibility. "I wouldn't have taken a time-out, obviously, if I had known we had already taken our five," I told reporters. "We had a communications problem. Apparently I was the only one on the bench who didn't know we were out of time-outs, and the unfortunate thing is our staff thought I was aware of it."

I think that's probably the year that critics began to whisper—sometimes pretty loudly—that my teams couldn't win the big games. We'd lost our first game twice. Dealing with criticism is part of a coach's job—possibly the most unpleasant part, particularly when you think that criticism is unfair. I wasn't the first coach subject to that criticism; among others who heard the same complaints were Syracuse's

Jimmy Boeheim and Kansas and North Carolina coach Roy Williams. They reacted the same way I did: They didn't bother to respond. They just went out and kept winning basketball games.

Those critics forget that in order to lose the big game you first have to get into it. And usually getting there requires winning some big games. That year, for example, we beat Indiana the two times we played them, and they eventually won the national championship. And when you get to the NCAA, every game you play is against one of the best teams in the country. The team that beat us, Wichita State, made it to the Elite Eight. There isn't too much a coach can do about that kind of criticism except try to ignore it, which is what I did. It was criticism I would hear again in my career, but it's a subject that Bobbi and I never spoke about. We accepted the reality of the situation.

I know how disappointed our fans were. But nobody felt worse about losing that game than I did. A game like that practically rips your heart out. Even when we win a game I play it over and over in my mind, so imagine how many times I reran this game. I don't think there's any game you lose in the tournament that doesn't sit with you all summer, whether it's in the first round or the championship game. But this loss was especially frustrating.

Winning doesn't make me forget the losses. But winning does make it easier to get over them. After a while our supporters got over the loss to Wichita State, too; instead of focusing on it, they began looking forward to the next season; they began talking about our new recruits. Anticipation replaced disappointment. The first few years we were there, people wondered if the team would be any good; now they debated how good we would be.

I don't remember exactly when Bobbi and I began to consider leaving Iowa. It wasn't part of any plan. In my entire career only once had I actively gone after a new job, and that was when I left Marina High for Long Beach City. I've been fortunate to be in the right places at the right time. Other programs had always approached me to see if I had any interest in their head coaching job. After we began having some success at Iowa, athletic directors began contacting me to see if I had any desire to make a move. The first job that we actually considered was the University of Southern California, and that had come after our fifth year at Iowa, in 1979.

USC was an extremely appealing situation. We had raised our family out west. And we knew that kids who grow up in the West and enjoy that lifestyle are going to end up living in the West. While our kids liked

Iowa, they loved California, so Bobbi and I knew eventually they'd go back there. We still had many friends there, too. Also, I was pragmatic. At Iowa, it was very difficult to recruit beyond the Midwest. I knew that wasn't going to change. So, in 1979, I knew it was going to be very difficult—if not impossible—to ever get to the Final Four at Iowa.

I'd always believed that USC had the potential to become one of the great basketball powers in America. Recruiting would be a lot easier. I'd have the whole west from which to draw players.

It wasn't that we actively wanted to leave Iowa City. But the lack of privacy continued to be a concern. People saw me on TV all the time, so they often acted as if they knew me. At times it was particularly hard on Bobbi because people would practically knock her over to get to me for an autograph. Then there was the weather. In everything we did the weather was always a factor. Long road trips during the season could be very . . . challenging. We would split the team into two groups and fly on small planes, eight-to-ten seaters. During the winter, when the wind was blowing, things could get scary. Sometimes those small planes seemed like they were flying sideways. Planes did crash. In December, 1977 the entire Evansville basketball team had been killed when the plane crashed on takeoff. My assistant coach, Tony McAndrews, had been badly hurt in a crash.

There wasn't much we could do about it, though. One time, I remember, we had to wait quite a long time while repairs were made on our plane. When they finally let us board, one of the players asked me, "You think it's fixed, Coach?"

I responded truthfully, "Well, I guess we'll know pretty soon."

At times I'd leave my car at the airport for two days, and when I got back it would be buried, completely buried, under a snow pile, or literally encased in ice. When we started considering the USC job those were the things we knew we wouldn't miss. What we would miss were the friends we'd made, the support we received, the magical fall afternoons, and the warmth of a college town.

Bobbi and I flew to Los Angeles over a three-day weekend and met with the president of the university and the athletic director. We discussed salary and other opportunities. They had a small dinner party with about twenty administration officials and top boosters. As part of the inducement they told me they were going to build a brand-new arena on campus. "You're going to have a great place to play," I was told. They did build that beautiful new arena—twenty-six years later. While we were there, Bobbi and I looked around at homes.

We were ambivalent. When we got back to Iowa City Bobbi told me, "I like it here. I can very easily live here. But if you decide we need to be out there, that'd be fine, too."

The determining factor turned out to be location. I turned down the job at USC because there really wasn't anyplace affordable nearby where we could live comfortably. If I took the job, I'd have to spend a lot of time stuck in freeway traffic, which I truly disliked. Also, university officials told me they intended to hire their new coach at the end of the season, so they were not in a hurry to negotiate a contract with me. I didn't like the prospect of being left hanging for several months. Ironically, one of the reasons I even considered the USC job was that I didn't believe Iowa, with all of our recruiting difficulties, could get to the Final Four—and we got there the very next season.

Our two youngest kids, who were still in high school, desperately wanted me to take the job. They were huge USC fans and were devastated when I turned it down. So in a moment of weakness Bobbi and I told them that they could apply to USC, and if they were accepted, we'd let them go. That's exactly what happened, which is how a trip to explore a job offer ended up costing me a considerable amount of money.

With the exception of our children, Bobbi and I didn't tell anyone we were making this trip. We were hoping to keep it a secret. I didn't intend to put Iowa in a bidding situation. If I was going to take the job, I would take it. Money wasn't the issue, it was all about lifestyle—and what I believed to be the opportunity to build the kind of program John Wooden had built at UCLA. But even before we got back to Iowa, university officials knew all about the trip. It wasn't hard to figure out: USC had made all the travel arrangements. When Bobbi and I got on the airplane in Cedar Rapids we were seated in first class. Lute and Bobbi sitting in first class to LA? That had to mean we were going out there to look at a new job, because at Iowa, and at Arizona, we were not allowed to fly first class. When we returned, Bump Elliott told me, basically, that I had a lifetime contract at Iowa. "We're glad you're staying here," he told me. "And you'll be here as long as you want to be here." Officially, though, my contract was extended nine years. In fact, while I appreciated that gesture, the circumstances bothered me. I didn't talk with USC to put pressure on Iowa, it wasn't a threat, and I was sorry that Iowa had to be reminded of our success before taking steps to keep me there. The reaction of our fans was even more gratifying. We had a game the day it was announced I'd turned down the job offer. I didn't really know how the fans would respond. I would not have been surprised if there was a lot of anger, so I was a little nervous when I walked onto the court that night. The place erupted in cheers: 13,300 fans started chanting, "Lute! Lute! Lute!" I was embarrassed, but absolutely thrilled. My Norwegian ancestors residing in my DNA still resisted that kind of adulation, but the rest of me enjoyed it. It is nice to be appreciated for doing something you love to do. I made sure I got my hands high in the air and waved to all parts of the field house.

Finally, Iowa began moving forward with plans to build a new arena. It was something everybody had been talking about for a long time, but just had never gotten started.

We certainly needed it. The old field house had been built in 1927. It was a great place to play, but not such a great place to watch a game. Pillars obstructed the view from a lot of seats; it only held 13,300 fans, and the permanent seats were a long way from the court. Initially we wanted the new building to have 18,000 seats, which would have made it the largest arena in the Big Ten. But it was going to be paid for by a combination of bonds and private donations, and university president Sandy Boyd didn't believe we could raise sufficient money, so instead we settled for 14,500 unobstructed seats. He was also concerned that people who donated money for a sports facility wouldn't donate additional funds to academic building plans. Experience has proven that's not what happens; once people begin donating money to a university, for whatever reason, they generally continue.

The cost of the new facility was $17.2 million. We figured it would take us two years to raise that money. Three thousand volunteers worked on the fund-raising campaign in twenty Iowa cities. More than 10,000 people contributed to the effort, a huge number for a state like Iowa. I traveled around the state with the cochairman of the campaign. Among the fund-raising techniques we used was selling a license to buy season tickets. The total cost for the seat was $2,500. The problem was that in only eight months we ran out of seats to sell. We added another five hundred seats. And they were sold immediately. Even before the arena was built, it was sold out for the entire season. Obviously if we had put in 19,000 seats we still would have sold them all. We broke ground for the new arena, the Carver-Hawkeye Arena, named after Roy Carver, the largest individual contributor, in July 1980. I thought there was a pretty good chance I'd spend the rest of my career in that building.

It wasn't quite that long. It seemed like I had become a hot property. I had done nothing, absolutely nothing, to let people know that I was interested in another job, but it seemed like every time a coach was fired, the athletic director would want to speak with me. In addition to USC; Stanford, Washington, the University of California, and several other schools called to see if I had any interest in their head coaching job. I said no to every inquiry. We were happy in Iowa, cold but happy. After turning down USC, it would take a very desirable situation to make us seriously consider leaving. Truthfully, though, after all the years I'd spent coaching high school, it really felt very nice to be wanted by major college basketball programs. I'd spent a lot of years reading articles about these teams, watching them practice and play, admiring their coaches, and feeling that I was an outsider. Now I was right in the middle of it. Those same programs were offering me their head coaching job. Of course it was flattering.

In early 1982 the University of Arizona had called Bump Elliott and asked permission to speak with me about taking over their program. Their coach, Fred Snowden, the first African American ever to coach a Division I team, was being eased out. "What do you want me to tell them?" Bump asked. "You want to talk with them?"

I'd been to Tucson only a few months earlier watching high school kids playing in the Basketball Congress International senior tournament. It seemed like a nice, small city. "No way," I said. "Our new arena's going to open in December. I've been out there helping them raise the money for it. If I left they'd hang me at the border."

I don't know who else Arizona approached, but eventually they signed Ben Lindsey, who'd coached Grand Canyon College to the Division II national championship. When I read about it I thought, well, that's the end of that one. But then he had an absolutely terrible year. Arizona finished 4–24 and 1–17 in the Pacific Ten Conference, the most losses ever in the Pac-10.

Cedric Dempsey, whom I'd met years earlier when he was the athletic director at College of the Pacific and I was coaching Long Beach State, had become Arizona's athletic director earlier that year. The basketball program was in shambles. Apparently there were problems both on and off the court. Dempsey realized almost immediately that the situation was beyond repair, and the longer he let it continue the worse it would get. Arizona was already behind in recruiting. Under state law at that time, coaches were limited to one-year contracts, so Lindsey's contract had expired. Dempsey made a gutsy move: He fired his coach after a single season.

I didn't know any of this was going on. We were playing our way through the NCAA tournament. We made it to the regional semifinals, the Sweet Sixteen, at Kemper Arena in Kansas City, where we met Rollie Massimino's Villanova team. It was a very close game. Down the stretch they were up 55-54 when our 6'7" forward Bobby Hansen, a great free throw shooter who later played nine seasons in the NBA, got fouled. Two shots for the game. With Bobby on the line I felt confident this was our game. Unbelievably, he missed both of them. We lost the game and were eliminated.

After spending some time with my team I was walking toward the pressroom to meet reporters when Dempsey introduced himself to me as the athletic director at the University of Arizona. Apparently, he had already received permission from Bump Elliott to talk to me. Both Elliott and Dempsey were on the NCAA tournament committee. He came right to the point. "We'd like to have a chance to talk to you about our job. Would you have an interest?"

I had just lost a very tough game in the Sweet Sixteen. I was feeling pretty far down, trying to figure out where I might have gotten the two points we needed to win the game, playing the inevitable mind games. "Gee, Cedric," I told him, "this isn't such a great time right now. Why don't you give me a call tomorrow."

The next day we met in Dempsey's hotel room. The "we" being Bobbi and me and all our kids who were in town for the game. Dempsey later told people that, rather than interviewing me, he had been interviewed by the entire Olson family. He had a private jet in town, he said, and he suggested that instead of returning to Iowa City, Bobbi and I fly with him back to Tucson. Well, it was cold in Iowa City. It had been snowing the day we took off for Kansas City. A few days in a nice warm city seemed pretty appealing to me.

Moving is part of a coach's job. Very few people get to stay in one place for most of their career. You just get to the point in your career when you think the time is right to make that move. I went to Iowa when the program was down and needed a lot of work. We turned that program around. It seemed like a good time to apply the McGuire Rule.

Bobbi and I were fortunate enough to have a choice. Dempsey called it an interview, but he had made it obvious that Arizona wanted me. Only later did I find out that—once again—Gene Bartow was in another wing of the hotel waiting to be interviewed if I turned down the job. Gene Bartow is a good friend who had been at Illinois when I came to Iowa. From there he accepted the toughest job in college basketball—succeeding John Wooden at UCLA. That was an impossible situation. In 1976 Bartow's Bruins were 26-4, that's twenty-six wins and four losses, and he was still heavily criticized because 26–4 was Coach Wooden's *worst* record in his last nine years in Westwood. In his two years at UCLA Bartow was 52–9, but that wasn't good enough. So finally he took the job at University of Alabama-Birmingham and started what became a very solid program.

As before, Bobbi and I wanted to keep this visit secret. The team had flown home on a charter. I told the reporters covering our game that Bobbi and I were just going to sit in the sun for a few days. The it-has-been-a-long-season statement. I didn't think anybody knew about this trip, but when our jet landed in Tucson at 1:30 in the morning a reporter from Iowa's school paper, *The Daily Wildcat,* was there to greet us. We offered him the we-are-in-Tucson-to-get-some-sun-it's-been-a-long-season, but we couldn't figure out how he'd discovered we were coming.

Cedric took us up to the Westwood Look resort, which was northwest of the city. We figured that staying that far away from downtown would provide at least some privacy. The next morning I was walking around to the front of the hotel to get to the continental breakfast. An older woman was coming out, so I held the door for her. She looked at me, paused, and said, "Lute Olson. What are you doing here?"

I was really surprised that she had recognized me. "Where are you from?" I asked her.

"Oh, I'm from Iowa," she explained. "But we're vacationing up here." The owner of the Westwood Look was an Iowan, I soon learned, so probably half the guests staying there were from Iowa. It got worse. To get to the continental breakfast I had to walk down a hall separated from the dining room by a glass wall. The dining room was filled with Iowans. In fact, at that moment there were probably more Iowans in that hotel than anywhere else in the entire western United States. Some big secret.

I met with the hiring committee in the afternoon. Again, it wasn't an interview; it was an opportunity for them to convince me that I should take the job. One of the members was a local homebuilder; he told me he would arrange for our home to be built and sold to us at his cost. A banker was there; he offered me a mortgage at the lowest possible interest and no points. The owner of the local Buick dealership, Paul Weitman, offered to provide a courtesy car. I was being recruited in the best possible way.

Cedric explained that under state law he could only offer me a one-year contract. We didn't really negotiate. The one thing I told him was that I wouldn't take the job for less than I was making at Iowa. That was the only figure I mentioned—"I won't come here for less." In Iowa, in addition to my salary, I had an annuity that was about to become vested, meaning it would be real money. A banker told me he would put together another annuity to match that deal. They put together what seemed to me to be a fair package.

As much as I know about basketball is pretty much equal to what I don't know about negotiating a contract. If there was one thing I could do over in my career, I would never negotiate my own contracts. No matter how big the jobs got, I was still the coach who'd signed the high school contract paying me the least money. I've had numerous assistants leave my staff to take head coaching jobs and I always advised them, Do the interview and get the job offer, but don't talk contract. Hire someone who negotiates contracts for a living. There was a time when athletic directors refused to negotiate with attorneys or agents— and kept refusing until the coach they wanted started walking away. When I was in the midst of negotiating with Arizona, it didn't even occur to me to hire someone to do it for me. My negotiating stance was pretty firm: I wouldn't accept less than I was already making. Instead of nine years guaranteed, I was offered a one-year deal.

At one point it occurred to me that none of this would have been happening if Bobby Hansen had made those foul shots. I would have stayed in Kansas City through the weekend. If we'd won that game and the next, I would have been so immersed in recruiting and preparing for our next game that I wouldn't have had time to speak to Dempsey. Cedric was under tremendous pressure to hire a coach as quickly as possible so that he could begin recruiting. So if Bobby had made even one of those shots, who knows where Bobbi and I would have ended up, but he didn't, and the life of everyone in my family was changed forever.

After I met with the committee, Bobbi and I spent the afternoon looking around the neighborhoods of Tucson and the evening at the Skyline Country Club for their Sunday evening seafood extravaganza. Cedric Dempsey had asked us to make our decision by the following morning because Bartow was waiting in another wing of the hotel. To complicate our decision, it seemed like the entire state of Iowa had found out what I was doing and where I was staying and wanted to speak to me. At least those Iowans who weren't staying in the hotel. The governor called while I was in Tucson and told me how much I was valued in Iowa. Several of the most successful businessmen in the state called. The banker called to remind me I had only one year left before my annuity vested. Bump called. The president of the university left a message requesting that I not make any commitments, "Come back and let us talk to you." I didn't like that. If Bump knew I'd received several feelers from other schools, the university, felt I was that valuable, the administration should have stepped up before being faced with the possibility I might leave.

Our kids wanted us to accept the offer. Bobbi and I discussed it; I think both of us were ready to move. It was everything, the lack of privacy, being with family, returning to the West, and from a recruiting standpoint I still had strong contacts in California. We called Cedric Dempsey and told him we accepted his offer. Then came the hard part—telling everybody else.

Some people thought I had lost my mind. We had a terrific squad coming back. The preseason polls had us ranked number four in the country, while Arizona was ranked high in the bottom ten. I was certainly one of the most popular people in the state; I had my television show, the university had done a commemorative book, people thought I would stay at Iowa forever.

These were very difficult calls to make. You just hate having to tell people something they don't want to hear. I told Bump Elliott we were flying back to Iowa so I could talk to the team but that I had accepted the Arizona job. That was the fair thing to do. Bump had to find another coach immediately. When Bump asked me to recommend my replacement, I told him that my assistant, Jim Rosborough, would be an excellent selection, though I knew he was under great pressure to hire a high-profile coach with Division I experience. Eventually he hired George Raveling from Washington State. That meant George could finally get a van with windows in the back, although now *he* had to figure out how to hide the pig.

We wanted to tell our friends and the team's incredibly loyal supporters the news in person. We owed them that. I met with the team the night we got back to Iowa City. Tough, very tough. I had known some of these kids since their sophomore year in high school. I'd seen them become men. The younger players had come to Iowa expecting me to be their coach. I'd been through the basketball wars with the upperclassmen, and that is a bond that lasts forever. This was my team and I was leaving. I knew some of them would be terribly disappointed. There were some tears that night, not all of them from the players. I told them that at some point in their lives they would understand why I'd made this decision, but that I thought this was the best decision for my family. "Right now I think the best thing for Bobbi and me is to get out west, 'cause that's where our family is." I assured them that Bump would bring in an outstanding coach. "You guys are going to be really good," I told them. "You're going to have a great season."

The team took it well. A lot of the fans and media did not take it well. They felt abandoned. I didn't see the newspapers, but I heard that one paper ran the headline, "Lute Goes for the Loot." That was completely erroneous; the contract I signed at Arizona was almost identical to my contract at Iowa. In fact, it turned out to be substantially less because I lost that annuity, but the rumors persisted. Supposedly Arizona gave me a Rolls-Royce. Supposedly I had a private jet at my beck and call. Supposedly, supposedly, supposedly.

I listened in astonishment as Bob Brooks, a Cedar Rapids radio sports reporter I'd known almost since the day I arrived, a man I considered a friend, made all these claims that weren't true. Among several other things, he said my family had been given three cars. I got so upset I called him. "I'm really disappointed in you," I told him. "I always thought we were friends. The least I should expect is that you'd be honest in terms of what you're reporting."

He apologized and went on the air to correct the story, but the overall impression was that I was just another sports mercenary, that I'd left for a better deal. Our fans felt I'd betrayed them. Almost a quarter century later some people are still upset. I still get letters asking me to come back. Or I'll run into Iowans at an airport or in a restaurant and they'll say, "I'm from Iowa. When are you coming back home?"

I signed my contract with Arizona on March 29, 1983. From my first day I told the media I didn't want to develop a team, I intended to develop a program. "I have always been a firm believer that you build a program with good people. We never recruit the great players who are questionable people. We would rather have a good player who is a good person. Hopefully, they'll be great players as well.

"We will put a group of kids on the floor who will play hard and with a great deal of intelligence. We never talk about wins when discussing turning a program around. Instead, we say that we will get it done as soon as possible."

That sounded optimistic, but the reality was that there was no program. I had no staff and very poor facilities and it was really very late in the recruiting season. Most of the better high school players had already decided where they were going. I only had six scholarships available, and most of the on-campus visits permitted under NCAA regulations had already been used. I had three terrific kids committed to Iowa, but I was going to be in Arizona. This wasn't like my first year at Iowa, where I could bring in players I had coached in junior college. This time I really was starting from the very bottom.

The moment it was announced that I'd taken the job I was deluged with phone calls and messages from coaches who wanted to join my staff. I brought Scott Thompson and Ken Burmeister with me from Iowa. Both of them were great recruiters. Roz stayed in Iowa City. A member of Coach Ben Lindsey's staff, Ricky Byrdsong, applied for the last job. Ricky was one of those people you like immediately, and then as you get to know him you like him even more. Ricky's wife, Sherialyn, was an assistant coach with the woman's basketball team at Arizona, so if I didn't hire Ricky and he took a job somewhere else, we were going to lose two coaches. I knew Ricky. I'd gotten to know him when he was an assistant at Eastern Illinois. I'd often see him at the games when I was recruiting in Chicago. In those situations I pay attention to what other assistants are doing. Some coaches work hard, they watch the game and make evaluations. Others spent their time socializing, doing everything but what they were supposed to be doing. You watch, and you remember, just in case a situation exactly like this one should arise. Bobbi and I had dinner with Ricky and Sherialyn. I remember he was nervous and he was funny. Bobbi liked him immediately. So he completed the staff.

I held a press conference on April 1, then got in the car and drove to Phoenix to watch a high school tournament. The kid we wanted most was Kevin Johnson, who was from Sacramento. He agreed to come to Tucson for the weekend. I was convinced that once he saw the beautiful campus and understood he would get a lot of playing time as a freshman he'd commit. It was quite a relief knowing I wouldn't have to worry about hiding that pig ever again. But his high school baseball coach wanted him to go to Cal, and when he learned that Kevin was making a campus visit, he called a baseball practice for Saturday, which apparently he had never done before. As a result KJ never had a chance to visit Arizona and ended up going to Cal. So we missed our first choice.

Bobbi had stayed in Iowa to pack up the house. I was living in a hotel in Tucson, but I hardly used it. I was on the road recruiting all week long, and then I'd come in on Friday to meet the people we were bringing in for the weekend. As soon as those kids left on Sunday, I was back on the road. I didn't promise anyone that if he came he would start immediately, but I did explain the situation. The four leading scorers and the four top rebounders from the previous season were gone. The players who were still there hadn't been able to start on a team that went 1–17 in the Pac-10. "Whether you start or not is going to be completely up to you," I said, "but the opportunity is there to make a difference immediately."

Generally, when we get interested in recruiting a player, we try to determine how well he'll fit into our system. We look for three things: Is this person physically able to play at our level? Is this person going to be successful in the classroom and do the things on the court that we expect? Finally, does he have the character to represent us in the community? Every coach in every sport would say this: We look for good people who can play basketball. The one program I can speak for is the University of Arizona's: Character matters. We don't recruit players, no matter how talented, who might prove disruptive to the team. We try to be very thorough in learning everything possible about a potential recruit. We don't just talk to his high school coach; we'll speak to his counselors and we'll talk to other coaches in his league because we may get a very different report from them. We might even talk to the custodian. High school custodians often have a real sense of what's going on in their schools. That's what we usually do. But in this situation we didn't have the time to do any of it. We had to rely on our instincts and the judgment of people we knew.

This was a very unusual situation. We had to do several years' work in a few months. When I visited these players in their homes, I was pretty blunt with them. "We've used up ten of the eighteen official visits to the campus that we're allowed. We need to sign at least six people. So if it's a case where you've made up your mind that you're going somewhere else and just want to come to Tucson, we can't bring you in that way. We just can't afford it. We need a commitment from you that you're really open to the possibility of coming to Arizona and that if you come out there and it's a good match, we can count on you coming to school."

Fortunately, that's pretty much what happened. Among the first group to visit were Michael Tait, an all-Southern California guard, high school All-American Reggie Miller, and Eddie Smith, a power forward graduating from Dodge City, Kansas, Community College. We were able to sign Tait and Smith.

Scott Thompson was our primary recruiter on Reggie Miller. They developed a really good relationship and I thought we had a great shot at him. But when Reggie came to Tucson for his visit, I took him to the home of my friend Paul Weitman. We were sitting out by the pool when Reggie asked Paul's eight-year-old son, Craig, to show him what was behind the house. I found out later that as they were walking in the brush Reggie asked Craig nervously, "Are there any snakes around here?" Apparently Reggie was fearful of snakes.

Craig really wanted to be helpful. "Oh, sure," he said earnestly, "we see lots of snakes around here. We got all kinds of snakes."

Turned out there were no snakes at UCLA.

Although Michael Tait stayed at Arizona only one year, he played a significant role in the program: He convinced his friend Pete Williams that Arizona was the place to go to school.

Pete Williams, a wiry 6'7", 190-pound power forward playing at Mount San Antonio Junior College, was one of the first kids I'd scouted. He was being recruited by Texas Christian, Colorado, and Jerry Tarkanian at UNLV. Tark was a friend of Williams's coach, Gene Victor, so if he had really wanted Pete he probably could've had him. I went to the Williams home with Bobbi and Coach Burmeister. Bobbi spent a lot of time in the kitchen recruiting his mother, assuring her that she would look after him. She also made a point of telling Mrs. Williams, proudly, that during our nine years at Iowa all but one of our players had earned their degrees—and that one kid had transferred after his freshman year—and we expected to achieve those same results at Arizona. Gene Victor set up a special 7:00 A.M. workout so we could watch Pete play. Afterward we were able to convince him to visit the campus.

He arrived in Tucson with several other recruits. We formed a four-car caravan to drive the kids from the airport to the campus. He was with Scott Thompson. This was Pete's first time in the desert, and as we raced to the campus we kicked up quite a dust storm. "Man," he said, looking back at the dust, "it's like we're on a mission to rebuild Arizona basketball."

Scott looked right at him and said, "That's exactly what we're going to do." Pete Williams eventually committed to Arizona and became the cornerstone of our program.

Although I'd had immediate success at Iowa bringing in junior college players, it isn't something I like to do. At Iowa, the kids I was bringing in had played for me. I knew them and they knew my system. I didn't know Pete Williams or Eddie Smith, but I felt like this was the only way we could go. If I had brought in high school kids, we would be setting ourselves up to get our brains beaten in. And after a couple of losing seasons the top recruits wouldn't even look at Arizona. I took the JC kids, knowing that as a result we would be able to bring in much better freshmen and sophomores than we would have otherwise. To win, you have to start by winning.

From the tournament in Phoenix I'd flown to California to see some more kids and speak at the *Los Angeles Times* all-star team banquet. Because of our success at Iowa, the kids knew who I was. Many of their parents and coaches remembered me from my days in Long Beach. What I didn't know was that in the audience that night was an all-city player named Steve Kerr, who was there with his mother. Apparently, his mother was impressed because I spoke at length about academics. Going home that night she told him, "That's the kind of man I'd like you to play for."

After the initial signing period ended, we had one scholarship left, but nobody to give it to who we believed could help us right away.

On July 29, at the very end of the summer signing period, I went to look at some high school sophomores and juniors playing in a summer league at Long Beach State. I was already starting to think about the following season. There was one high school junior in particular I had been scouting since his freshman year. I went to watch him play, but it was a thin 6'2" towheaded guard on the opposing team who caught my attention. That kid's interesting, I thought; he plays very well. He's intelligent, shoots the ball well, and is a real leader on the floor. When the game ended I found his coach. "Tell me about number twenty-five," I said.

"He's a great kid," he said. "His name is Steve Kerr. He graduated from Palisades, but he's got nowhere to go." Apparently he was planning to enroll at Colorado and try to walk on to the basketball team there.

"What kind of player is he?"

"Just what you saw. A heck of a shooter, a leader. He plays really smart."

There was just something about him that intrigued me. He wasn't quick; he wasn't a great athlete. He looked like he would have a difficult time playing at a top college level. But for some reason I was intrigued by him. He played like a winner. I found out when he was playing the next day so I could get there early to watch the warm-ups. You can learn a lot about a young player by watching how he shoots during warm-ups or how he reacts to being taken out of the game or how he relates to his teammates or what he does when sitting on the bench. Once again Steve Kerr played very well. I called him at home that night—the NCAA did not allow face-to-face contact during this period—and introduced myself. He knew who I was, he said, then told me he'd heard me speak at the banquet. I asked him if he would have an interest in taking a look at our program. Yes, he responded, yes he would.

The next day I called his high school coach, Jerry Marvin, whom I knew from my high school coaching days. Jerry told me, "There are two kids who've played for me through the years who didn't get the recognition they deserved. Neither one got recruited much. One was Kiki Vandeweghe, the other one is Steve Kerr. I think Steve can really play." Vandeweghe had led UCLA to a national championship and at that time was in the midst of an all-star pro career.

Jerry told me that the only college Kerr had visited was Gonzaga. When he was there, he'd worked out against their graduating seniors and alumni. Actually, that was illegal at the time, but he didn't know that. In that game a graduating senior had just torn him apart, a senior named John Stockton. Based on that workout, Gonzaga didn't offer him a scholarship. The Gonzaga coach had told him, "We like you, but you're just not quick enough to play at this level."

I asked Jerry Marvin to do me a favor. The next day was July 31, the last day we were allowed to recruit off campus. "Would you set up an open gym with some of your alums, some college guys, so I can come in and watch Steve play again."

Bobbi came with me the next night. We watched him play for about two hours. Again, he just did the right things. What I did not know until many years later was that the setup had been a true setup. And I was the guy getting set up. All of Kerr's friends knew I was going to be there to look at him, so they did everything possible to make him look good. They made sure he got clean looks at the basket, they didn't defend him as intensely as they might have, they made sure he played on the team with the better players. After the game, as Bobbi and I were getting in the car, I asked her what she thought. Bobbi had watched a lot of basketball and I trusted her judgment. She looked at me skeptically, "You've got to be kidding me." Meaning, I had to be kidding her because Steve Kerr couldn't play in our program.

Well, I still liked him. I spoke with his father, Malcolm Kerr, who was president of the American University in Beirut, Lebanon. Both of Steve's parents had been teachers at UCLA, and he had been a ball boy for Coach Wooden. I explained to Mr. Kerr that we were interested in Steve but that we had no campus visits left to offer. If they wanted to see the university, they would have to pay for it themselves.

Some time passed. There was so much to be done before the season started and, admittedly, recruiting Steve Kerr was not a priority. I didn't believe he could come in and play a lot at the beginning, but with a little experience I thought that eventually he could be a useful part of the team.

When Steve didn't hear from me, he thought I'd lost interest. He was ready to enroll at Cal State Fullerton. He talked about it with his father, who asked him, "Well, where do you want to go?"

"Arizona."

"Well, let me call Lute and see if there's a scholarship available."

His father called and asked me that question directly. "Yes," I told him. "If he wants to come, we'll take him." He had never been on our campus, but he had enough confidence in his ability to believe that he could compete successfully on our level. He was the last player we recruited for that first season in Arizona. Even though he was from California, he took the longest route to get to Arizona—until recently, when we began recruiting in Europe and Africa. He had been visiting his father in Beirut before he reported to school. The day he was supposed to leave, they shut down the airport. They had to sneak him out of the Middle East through Damascus, Syria.

I don't think I or any of my assistants got one full night's sleep for the first four or five months we were in Tucson. We practically lived on the road. Sometimes, truthfully, we even forgot where we were. Ken Burmeister was a great recruiter, but he was used to recruiting kids from the Midwest. One of the things we all spoke about was how much easier it would be recruiting players because of the beautiful weather in the desert. So one day, when Ken was talking to a kid we were recruiting from Southern California he asked, "So, how's the weather out there?"

The player was surprised at the question. "It's incredible," he said.

Burmeister continued, "Maybe, but it is sunny? You know, we get 360 days of sunshine in Tucson."

"Coach, it's unbelievable out here as well. This is Southern California . . ."

It was an incredibly hectic time. Not only did we have to put a representative team on the floor that season, we had to start building for the future. There was another player I was really interested in who was entering his senior year at Mater Dei High School in Santa Ana, California. I'd known the head coach there for a long time. In early September Burmeister, Ricky Byrdsong, and I went to the school to watch a workout. When it was done, we met with the coach. He told us, "I'd like to tell you you've got a good chance at him, but I really don't think you do. He's Catholic, his brother is a priest, and he's got a sister who's a nun. Notre Dame wants him, and that's where his mother wants him to go."

We had scheduled a home visit for later that day. "Here's what we're going to have to do," I told my assistants. "We're going to put a premium on what we're going to do for his development as a person. The basketball is going to have to be pretty much pushed aside." That was our plan.

When we walked into the house later that night, it was like walking into a Catholic church. There were pictures of the priest and the nun and religious statues all over the house. They were lovely people. We sat in their screened-in porch. After we'd established a rapport, we started talking about the fact that our kids were required to do some community service; we spoke of how important we felt morals and ethics were in our program and how we tried to build a family atmosphere. Only then did I talk about academics and basketball.

When I finished my presentation, I asked my assistants if they had anything to add. Burmeister talked about the family atmosphere we'd created at Iowa and our intention to do it at Arizona. When he finished I asked Ricky Byrdsong, "Anything you can think of we haven't covered?"

At that time I still didn't know Ricky that well. He was a big African-American man with a welcoming aura about him. As soon as I asked that question I knew it was a mistake. He felt compelled to say something, anything, but he didn't really know me very well, either. Finally, he looked at the parents and said earnestly, "You know, in nine years at Iowa, Coach Olson was never arrested."

For the next few minutes I was afraid Ken Burmeister might die of laughter. That was the end of any serious discussion. When we left I told the player that I knew his mother wanted him to go to Notre Dame, but if that changed "I hope you'll come and look at us." He did go to Notre Dame, but after one season there he decided to transfer. Unfortunately, by that time we'd filled his position and didn't have a scholarship to offer him.

We had finished recruiting for our first season at Arizona even before Bobbi and I had moved into the new house. I didn't speculate about how good the team would be; my goal was to be competitive in every game. And if things didn't proceed as well as we hoped, well, I could always take some satisfaction from the fact that in the nine years we'd spent in Iowa, I had never been arrested.

5

We had to rebuild the program at Arizona from the court up. A complete program consists of the team and staff, the facilities, and community support. We'd addressed the immediate problem, putting a competitive team on the floor, with our nonstop recruiting. And then we focused on all other needs.

Just about every part of the program needed a substantial upgrade, from the sneakers to the arena. Every coach knows that few things can get players as excited as great-looking uniforms, so one of the first things we did was redesign the uniforms. We replaced the nylon with a mesh material and put the players' names on the back.

The way McKale, our arena, was constructed, permanent bleachers bordered our one full court. The court itself was made of a composition material. That had to go, I told Cedric. Although it took a year, we replaced the bleachers with retractable seats and installed a large wooden floor. When the seats were retracted for practice, instead of one court, we had six baskets, six teaching stations. In the middle of the court we put our brand-new logo, a cactus growing out of the "I" in Arizona. The new logo was an easy way of emphasizing that this was a new program.

Our athletic director, Cedric Dempsey, had used originally the logo on some letterhead stationary. When Scott and I were searching for ways to jazz up McKale, we decided that this logo would look great on the court. It's unique. Anybody who sees it knows it represents the University of Arizona. Years later the university created a new logo, and I was asked about changing the logo on the court. Sure, I told them, after

I'm gone you go right ahead and change it, but as long as I'm here that's going to be on the court.

We had no video equipment, the locker room had been divided into small, cramped areas, and there was no official booster club. We created the Rebounders, a basketball support group. The membership dues enabled us to buy the video equipment we needed. One large donor, Albert Cohen, who owned Universal Battery, donated enough for us to rip out the walls of the locker room and make it a bright and pleasant place. Step by step we were creating an entirely new program.

Finally, we had to rebuild our fan base. The average attendance was about 3,000 people. Arizona might have been the only collegiate program in the country where the baseball team outdrew the basketball team. The situation was so poor that when recruits visited the campus they were taken to hockey games at the convention center rather than basketball games because there was a lot of excitement at the hockey games. Now, I like hockey, but that was ridiculous. We couldn't even give away tickets, literally. Our players often had extra tickets, in their pockets, but nobody wanted them.

The previous season they had sold exactly one—that's one—season ticket. Kids love to play in front of large, loud crowds. I knew it was absolutely vital to make it fun for people to come to the games. At Iowa, the moment the team burst onto the floor the entire arena would just erupt. It was like standing in a sea of noise. But that was part of a tradition of excellence. In Iowa, kids had been listening to Hawkeye basketball since they were five years old. At Arizona there was no tradition. I told Cedric we needed to do something to fill up McKale, to make it a difficult ticket to get. Davis-Monthan Air Force Base was just outside the city; I suggested we give tickets to people stationed there. I wanted to bring in Boys Clubs and Girls Clubs and any other clubs who would come. The problem was that in the Pac-10, teams split the gate proceeds, and there were specific rules against giving away too many tickets.

One thing I have to say about Cedric Dempsey: He had guts. In addition to going along with almost every request I made, he announced a new ticket policy. For the first time in history, the university was going to charge a priority seating fee. Instead of simply purchasing season tickets, people would have to pay an additional sum to guarantee the location of their season tickets. He took a tremendous beating in the media, but it certainly emphasized the point we were trying to make: Get your tickets now because good things are going to happen and you won't be able to get them later.

I did everything I could think of to build up our program. I spoke to business groups and social groups. I spoke at every Elks Club and Men's Club and Chamber of Commerce and Rotary Club that would listen to me. I went to every high school banquet and to countless luncheons. At every stop I said the same thing, "You'd better get your tickets now, because soon you're not going to be able to get in. McKale's going to be the place to be."

To drum up interest all over the state during the preseason, we took the team on the road, running intersquad scrimmages in Yuma, Nogales, Casa Grande, as many gyms that would let us in.

I practically pleaded with the students in fraternities and sororities to come to our games. "We're not going to get this done alone. It's not going to be, You have a good team and then you get the fans. If we're going to get this going we need your help. You have to come to the game and be a participant. You can't just be a spectator. You have to come to McKale and put everything into it just like the team is going to put everything into it." I finished with an enthusiastic go-go-go cheer. And then I asked for questions. One night, after listening to my passionate plea, a young man raised his hand. "I got one question," he said. "Can we bring coolers in there?"

We knew we would have at least one fan. Soon after I arrived in Tucson I met George Kalil. George owned a large beverage bottling plant in Tucson but he was better known as the basketball team's greatest fan. He went to every game, win or lose. George had started traveling with the team when Fred Snowden was coaching and asked me if he could continue doing that. I wasn't sure that was something I wanted to continue. At Iowa only members of the team—and Bobbi—were allowed on our bus. Certainly we never let a booster get that deeply involved in the program. I asked him to let me think about it. Meanwhile, George became a tremendous source of information for us. He knew everybody in Tucson. Scott Thompson would have dinner with him several nights a week to ask him numerous questions: Who is this person? Can we trust him? Can we do our laundry with this store? Who are the car dealers we want to work with? He was our shortcut to getting to know Tucson.

Meanwhile, I did some checking on George. Our trainer, Ricky Mendini, told me George Kalil had been a real asset to the program; he was always willing to help out when help was needed, never asked for anything in return, and never interfered or did anything to embarrass the program.

I didn't give him an answer for two months. We invited him to a party at our house with all the players and coaches at the very beginning of practice. George was sitting in our backyard with Bobbi. Just the two of them. Bobbi was knitting and she asked him casually, "So, George, are you going to be traveling with us?"

"I don't know yet," he said. "I asked Lute a couple of months ago and he told me he'd think about it."

"Well, George," Bobbi blurted out, "as of now you're a member of the official traveling party." We had our players, my assistant coaches, some student managers, a wonderful office staff, and now George Kalil. My first Arizona team was complete.

Our first day of practice was October 15, 1983. I set the tone for the season in the first minute of the first day of practice. I don't spend a lot of time giving warm welcoming speeches. I don't tell any jokes or funny stories. I'm serious and I expect the players to be serious. We go to work. What surprised me that first day was how much work needed to be done. I was astonished at the lack of knowledge of the basic fundamentals. There was absolutely no concept of team defense. Some of the kids had decent individual skills but didn't understand a team offense. On the court, basketball isn't a thinking game; things happen too quickly. It's a game of reaction. The keys that allow players to react are repetition and recognition. Being in the right place on the court isn't luck, it's the result of instruction and practice. Many of these players had no basketball concept; they had never been taught how to play team basketball.

It wasn't just the lack of knowledge that surprised me, it was also the lack of physical skills. Our first practice lasted almost four hours. Four hours is a long, long practice; generally we average about two hours. We had four teaching stations, four baskets in use, and everyone was working on fundamentals and controlled drills most of the time. We scrimmaged for only twelve minutes at the very end. Then, when the players were exhausted, we shot foul shots. We had a rule that you have to make ten consecutive free throws before you can get a drink of water. Usually that takes a few minutes. At that practice we sat and watched and waited and waited. It took about a half hour. I remember Scott Thompson and I looked at each other and sort of shook our heads. I don't think either one of us realized until that first practice how much work needed to be done just to be competitive.

I was tough on the team and honest with them. I told them how much work needed to be done. In fact, I probably told them that many times in many different ways in many different decibel levels that first day. And again the second day and the third day . . . I explained that there would be no excuses for a lack of effort. If they wanted to play for the University of Arizona, they were going to have to work—and probably harder than they had ever worked before.

I've always believed the hardest thing to teach is how to play as a team. Play hard, play together, play smart. There isn't a lot of teaching done in some high schools; the coaches roll out the balls and let the kids play. The players who get recruited by Division I schools usually have been the stars of their high school teams. They've had the ball in their hands most of the time and pretty much a green light to shoot it. Defensively, the coach has tried to protect his top offensive player from foul trouble by not assigning him to guard the best player on the other team. The message they've gotten is that defense is not as important as offense. So unless they've come from an exceptional high school program they have no concept of team offense or defense. They don't know where the other players are on the court, or where they are supposed to be. I wanted my players to understand the game. If they were able to grasp the larger concepts of offense and defense, they would understand positioning and team play.

On the first day of practice we began with the fundamentals. To play the game to the best of your ability you have to understand the basics. There is a coaching story told about legendary Notre Dame football coach Knute Rockne, another Norwegian. Supposedly, his team had been beaten the previous Saturday and he was furious. At the beginning of the team meeting Monday afternoon he told the squad, "You guys don't know anything about this game. We're going to start with the fundamentals." With that, he held a football over his head and said loudly, "Now, this is a *football*."

One of the fabled Four Horsemen of Notre Dame, Sleepy Jim Crowley, was sitting way in the back of the room, and as Rockne held up the ball, he shouted, "Please, Coach. Not so fast."

We weren't quite starting from that point. Just pretty close. For the most part these very talented athletes had never learned the fundamentals of basketball. We really were starting from the sneakers up. In a general sense, every step of the game can be taught, or at least how to take that step in the most effective way. Basketball isn't choreography. I don't believe in a highly structured offense in which we run set plays—

in fact, we rarely practiced more than six plays and those were to be used only in specific situations—but there is a correct way of doing things on the court, and that's what we set out to teach.

Everything in the game of basketball is predicated on positioning. That was true in high school in North Dakota and has remained true throughout my career. You have to know where you are on the court every second. Our defensive mantra is ball, man, you. Where is the ball? Where is the man you're guarding? And where are you? Ball, man, you. We started at the bottom, with footwork. Footwork is a fundamental skill, and a lot of players are never taught the correct, the quickest, way to move into position. If you draw a line down the middle of the court, the foot closest to that line—we refer to it as the inside foot—is always up. If you were on the left side of the court, your right foot would be up, cutting off the inside lane; if you're on the right side of the court, your left foot is up. With your inside foot up, you're not as vulnerable to picks and you're in a position to move quickly in a single motion; it's a single straight movement. And there is a proper way to slide. We started with those sliding drills. Footwork, defensive stance, your hand and arm positions, positioning—these are the fundamentals we taught starting that first day.

We emphasized playing defense. There aren't many young players who just can't wait to play defense. Every kid knows that scoring is a lot more fun than preventing other players from scoring. Players who don't know how to defend correctly are just trying to stop specific plays rather than playing basketball. Good defensive play can be learned. So on that October day in 1983 we started by teaching defense. The philosophy that I wanted the team to understand is that every movement of the ball required them to adjust their defensive position. It is amazing how many players never understand that. Basketball is a chess game, the fastest-moving chess game in the world. Good defensive play begins with an understanding that there are scoring positions on the court, places from which an individual player can score when he gets the ball. That position is different for every player. If a player gets the ball outside his scoring position, his team is at a disadvantage, so our objective on defense was to make that happen. We want to push the offense out as far as possible. We taught our players how to deny the pass, how to keep their man from getting the ball out on the wing.

Only after we'd concentrated on defense did we begin working on our offense. On offense our objective is to do exactly what we try to prevent on defense—to get the ball to a player in his scoring position. In everything we did, we taught our players both sides of the ball. Then we broke up for drills.

We had four stations, three players at each station, broken up by position. We did the same drills over and over and over.

The basic drill that we taught was called the seven-in-one. The seven-in-one encompassed seven basic defensive maneuvers, the defender against his man in seven positions. Denying the ball was only the first part of the drill. As practice progressed we added more situations: how to respond when your man has the ball, going into the post and fronting your man. Eventually the drill required the player to incorporate the footwork and defensive stance and arm positions and everything that we taught them.

All of our players could shoot the ball. I knew that. What we intended to do was teach them how to play the game of basketball.

We opened our first season at Arizona with a 72–65 victory at home over Northern Arizona. After all our promotional efforts there were only 3,000 people in the stands. An empty arena makes you feel empty inside. Obviously the way to change that was to win games, but after that first win we lost six in a row. I had never lost six games in a row in my life, not even playing against my brother Marv in our bedroom in Mayville. I knew our kids were trying, but that didn't stop me from being furious. After we lost to Pan American, 65–60, I was livid. I walked into the locker room carrying a clipboard with all the stats on it. "You're one and four," I screamed. "I can see why you were a bunch of losers last year. We have to compete. We can't just go through the motions. We—" I was just lost for words. In anger, I sailed that clipboard across the locker room. It hit the wall and bounced off and just missed Pete Williams's head. Then I turned around and stomped out.

That is the only time in my career I've ever done anything like that. Well, except for that time we lost to UNLV, or that unfortunate incident in Minnesota when I flipped my water bottle over my shoulder and accidentally hit an extremely loud and offensive fan, and that other time . . . Well, nobody in that room had ever seen me so angry. Not the players, not my assistants. They didn't know what to do. After I left they didn't know whether to just sit there or go take a shower or what. Everybody was surreptitiously looking around waiting for someone else to make the first move. I don't know how long they ended up sitting there—and I didn't care.

Game by game, though, we were getting better. Most of our opponents were bigger and more experienced than us. Pete Williams, our rock in the middle, was only 6'7", 190 pounds—and that was provided he had a big pregame meal. Every game he was going against players two or three inches taller and as many as sixty pounds heavier. He had to rely on his quickness, his determination, and his work ethic to compete. When we played Providence he had to guard 6'9" Otis Thorpe, who was basically 225 pounds of muscle. Pete didn't back down, although he said he had never even been close to anybody that big before in his life. I think he was a little awed. At one point in the game somebody got cut and Thorpe—who later played seventeen seasons in the NBA—got blood on his jersey. In the huddle Pete was shaking his head, "That dude is so big and he's got blood on his jersey and he's *still* out there." Pete played well, he hit a few jumpers, he outhustled Thorpe, but we lost the game in overtime.

At the Sun Bowl Tournament in El Paso, we beat Texas Tech 51–49 in overtime, then lost in the finals to the home team, UTEP, also in overtime and by the same score. Even with some very questionable officiating—I did say after the game that "the Most Valuable Player trophy should go to the referee"—we had a last shot to win at the buzzer, but guard Brock Brunkhorst missed a thirty-footer.

We opened the Pac-10 season at USC. We lost, 71–61, but we played well enough to win that game. Our fans were beginning to get interested in the team, and the crowds were getting bigger. You could hear the enthusiasm growing game by game. The louder and bigger the crowds got, the better the team responded.

For the team, for the community, so much changed forever on the night of January 18, 1984. The phone rang in the middle of the night. It was Scott Thompson calling to tell Bobbi and me that Steve Kerr's father, Malcolm Kerr, had been assassinated at the American University in Beirut. We didn't know the details at that time, but apparently Malcolm Kerr had gotten off an elevator and started walking to his office. A terrorist was waiting there and shot him in the back of the head. Mrs. Kerr said once that the terrorist war against America didn't begin on 9/11, it started on January 18, 1984.

George Kalil had heard a report on the radio that Malcolm Kerr had been murdered. He didn't know for sure if it was Steve's father, so he called Scott Thompson. "It sounds like it is," George said. "But I don't want to break the news to him if it isn't true."

Scott had called him. Steve knew. His pastor had called him at three in the morning, afraid that he would hear the news on CNN or a reporter might find him and ask for a comment.

This was a devastating blow. We had all met Malcolm Kerr. He had been in Tucson only two weeks earlier and had spent some time with the team. At moments like that you just take a deep breath and do whatever little you can do to help. If Bobbi and I really were the family we wanted to be, this was a time to show it. Steve was in his dorm room. I believe George and Scott were with him when I reached him. He was in a state of shock, obviously. I asked him to come over to the office where we could talk. There wasn't too much anyone could say. The most important thing is that Steve knew he had people around him who cared about him. I told him, "I just want you to know that you need to do whatever your mom and your brothers need you to do. Basketball is unimportant right now. You just have to let us know when you feel like practicing again and playing. You tell us what you need."

We were scheduled to play Arizona State, our biggest rival, in three days. I didn't expect Steve to play in that game. I knew this would be tough on all the kids. For some of them, it was the first time death had come so close. Particularly such a sudden and brutal death. There was no way of predicting how they would react.

The team practiced the next day. I tried hard to keep things as normal as possible, but it was very hard. Producers from the *Today Show, Good Morning America*, local news stations, reporters were calling the office to arrange an interview with Steve. Our tragedy was their morning news. Steve didn't want anything to do with them.

I watched him move through those days. He was only a freshman then, eighteen years old, but he handled the situation with such maturity. He spent the next night at our house. Bobbi had been close to him, but during this period they became much closer. Steve and our son, also named Steve, went into the hot tub. Very quietly, so quietly I didn't know about it, Bobbi brought them out beers.

The next morning he told me, "Coach, I can't stop thinking about this. The only place I can put it aside for a little bit is if I'm playing."

When he came to practice on Wednesday, Scott Thompson told him, "You don't have to be here, you know."

He replied, "This is my family. I want to be here."

This is the way a legend is born. The largest crowd of the entire season, more than 10,000, showed up for the game. ASU had been beating us regularly and usually pretty easily for a long time. They'd won the last nine games we'd played. We didn't do anything different in the locker room before the game, although I think we probably were a little more tense than usual. I don't remember talking about the situation; I didn't want the kids getting too emotional. We went over our scouting report on ASU and reviewed our strategy. We were fast and I didn't think they could run with us. So we were going to fast-break at every opportunity. Prior to the game we had a moment of silence to honor Malcolm Kerr, but really to show Steve how much the community sympathized with him.

As a player, Steve had progressed much faster than we had anticipated. He was our sixth man, the first player off our bench. The game was relatively even until he entered the game in the middle of the first half. I had no idea what to expect from him. And, truthfully, I was worried for him. The first shot he took was about a twenty-five footer, far outside his shooting range. He drilled it. The crowd just erupted. I mean, it was an explosion of sound. That was the beginning of a night anyone who was there will never forget. Steve hit five of seven attempts from the field and added five free throws. The team came together that night for the first time. I think we all played better than we were capable of at that time. Steve had fifteen points as we routed ASU 71–49.

We celebrated in the locker room after the game. That wasn't disrespectful to Steve, it's just that the team had worked so hard and this was the first time we'd seen results. It wouldn't be accurate to say that we did it for Steve, but certainly that was a big part of it.

A Wildcat tradition began that night. When Steve scored, our public address announcer, Roger Sedlmayr, celebrated by saying, "Basket by Steeeeeeeve Kerrrrrrr." That night, right after he finished, the band repeated, "Steeeeeeeve Kerrrrrrr." And then the crowd picked it up. From that night on, for the rest of Steve Kerr's career at Arizona, every time he scored, Roger would make his call, "Basket by Steeeeeeeve Kerrrrrrr," and the crowd would echo him.

Two weeks later we played ASU at their arena. We were down nine with fifty-three seconds to play—and we came all the way back to win when Eddie Smith's buzzer shot bounced around the rim, and rolled, and finally fell through with no time left on the clock. We lost to Ralph Miller's top-twenty Oregon State team in early February; they hit their first eight shots, but we never quit, losing by five, but after that we knew we could play with any team in the Pac-10. If any single game turned our season around, it was that loss. Two weeks later we beat them at McKale 69–58. We finished 11–17, but that's misleading. We competed in every game for the rest of the season; we just had to learn what it took to win. We ended the season by winning six of our last eight games. It made me wish that we could replay the first half of our season.

That first year in Arizona was a learning experience for all of us. Bobbi and I didn't repeat the mistakes we'd made in Iowa. We lived in a gated community near a golf course, which offered us some privacy, and Bobbi turned down several requests to write a newspaper column. I think the whole family was excited about being back in the West. I remember our close friends from Iowa, the Stehbenses, came out for their first visit, and as soon as they got off the plane we drove them around Tucson. We wanted to share the beauty of the area with them. And after about two hours of this I asked Bobbie Stehbens if there was anything in particular she wanted to do. Oh, yes, she said, "We'd like to go to the house and take these winter clothes off."

It's hard to call an 11–17 record a success, but it was—considering we had started from almost nothing. At least this was a foundation we could build on. That first team gave the program credibility. It was the blueprint for success. Top-rated high school players who would not have considered Arizona a year earlier now at least paid attention when we contacted them. Our recruiting enabled us to build a nationally competitive team.

Joe Turner was one of those kids. He was a mobile 6'9" center from a very bad neighborhood in Bakersfield, California. He used to say it was one of those neighborhoods where it was considered bad luck to step on the chalk body outlines in the street. Just about every Division I program in the country was recruiting him. No one in Joe's immediate family had gone to college, so there was no one with experience to advise him. He once said, "Anywhere I was going to go would be a big step up." Later he told us about some of the offers he'd been receiving, "They told me I could write my own ticket. I could have a car, live wherever I wanted to live—I could even have an apartment my first year. You can have girlfriends. One place told me I could go fishing all day. I wondered, if I'm fishing, when do I practice? All the cold weather places told me the weather was beautiful all year round. I remember visiting one school on the East Coast in the spring. They told me it was always like it was that day. I knew that wasn't true; I'd seen the news, I knew it snowed there. One school gave another player $500 and told him to take me out and have a good time."

Burmeister, Byrdsong, and I went to his house. We told him how we intended to build our program and the type of kids we were recruiting. He had a lot of choices, but he wanted to play on a winner. The results of our first season, particularly the second half of that season, convinced him that we were going in the right direction, and he wanted to be part of it.

Around campus he became known as Smiling Joe Turner. No one ever saw him with a scowl on his face. Joe Turner stories have become legendary at Arizona. Once, for example, I believe we were in South Carolina and he and Craig McMillan were waiting for an elevator on the fifth floor of our hotel. Joe was watching the numbers as the elevator came down to their floor and saw that it had stopped on the eighth floor before reaching them. When the elevator door opened, a couple was inside. To Joe, a stranger was simply a friend he'd never met. He got in the elevator and told the couple, "I'll bet I know what floor you're on."

"What floor?" the man asked.

"Eight," Joe said confidently.

The woman smiled, "How'd you know that?"

"Easy," Joe said, pointing to his brain, "I've got ESPN."

Recruiting is an art as well as a skill. High school statistics don't tell you very much about a player. The leading scorer may simply be the biggest kid or the strongest on the court or the competition he played against may have been weak. What we were looking for in particular were big kids who ran the court well and could handle the ball. A lot of good things start with a post player who has good hands. Big strong players who occupy the blocks but can't pop out for a jump shot didn't fit into our offensive scheme. So up front we looked for quickness. For perimeter players we looked at their ability to handle the ball and shoot it. So far, we were looking for the same things as every other coach.

We also put a lot of emphasis on attitude and disposition. In our evaluation that was as important as playing ability. Does a player have heart? Does he fit in? That's probably what had appealed to me when I looked at Steve Kerr. Even in a pickup game you could feel his passion for winning. Among the things I always look for is how a player responds to his teammates. When someone throws him a bad pass, what does he do? Some kids yell at their teammates. Other kids take the blame when it isn't their fault. That tells me whether or not a player will blame others when the inevitable problems occur. I like to watch young players when they get taken out of the game. Does he come out with a sour look on his face or does he encourage the kid who's replacing him, tell him who he's guarding? When he sits on the bench, does he stay in the game? Does he cheer for his teammates, or is he sulking because he's not playing? I remember watching Jason Terry, from Seattle's Franklin High School, whom we recruited years later, playing at the Basketball Congress International. BCI rules mandated that every kid played a certain number of minutes. I just loved Jason Terry because when he was on the bench, he was right there in the middle of the game, standing up and cheering every good pass, every bucket. For him it was all about the team. We knew he could play the game, but it was that team attitude that made him such a desirable recruit.

The reality is that one great player can make a team, but he can also destroy that team. I gave my teams a somewhat limited right to choose the people they wanted to play with. When recruits came for their campus visit, they were generally escorted through the weekend by two of our players. They met just about everybody on the team. After the weekend the players and coaches involved with that recruit would get together and discuss him. What did you guys think of him? How did he interact? Is he going to fit in? Is he too quiet or too loud? Did he drink a lot? It wasn't so much a secret ballot vote as a general consensus. He's cool. He doesn't fit in.

When I was at Iowa, for example, one weekend we had an outstanding 6'11" kid come in for his visit. Clay Hargrave, our 6'3" forward who led the Big Ten in rebounding, was his host. We took the recruit out for dinner and he was really short with a waitress. Clay took him aside and told him, "That's not the way we operate here. We treat everyone with respect, whoever it is."

The recruit sort of spouted off, telling him, "I know what I'm doing."

Clay told me the next day, "He might as well go home. He's not fitting in here."

I was disappointed. This was a player with tremendous potential, but there really was no choice. As I drove this player to the airport I said, "I'm sorry, but this hasn't been a very good visit for you. I just wanted to tell you that I really appreciate your coming here, but we're not going to continue recruiting you. It's just a case of our team doesn't feel you fit into this small-town environment."

I'll never forget his response. "I know where I've been and I know where I'm going."

One place he wasn't going was Iowa City. He did end up playing in the Big Ten and eventually played in the NBA, but it never would have worked for him at Iowa. Or for us.

That system worked well for several years. And then a very talented player with a very large ego came to Tucson for his campus visit. This was a kid my assistant coach, Kevin O'Neill, and I had been recruiting for several years. Kevin O'Neill had replaced Scott Thompson when Scott took the head coaching job at Rice. Kevin was . . . Kevin was . . . one of a kind. A very unique kind. He was an unbelievable recruiter. When he was recruiting 7'6" Shawn Bradley, a devout Mormon from Salt Lake City, for example, O'Neill would read Mormon scripture with him. One Halloween weekend we had two standout high school players, Sean Rooks and Mark Georgeson, coming for their campus visit. Kevin and Ricky Byrdsong were recruiting them. When they arrived at the airport, Ricky was there at the gate to meet them. He led them out to the curb where Kevin drove up—dressed in a gorilla costume. Ricky didn't even hesitate as he said to the two kids, "I'd like you to meet Coach O'Neill." Kevin wrote a hundred letters a week to prospects—and put a stick of gum in every letter he mailed so the recipient would remember him—his way of telling the kids he recruited, "Whatever happens, I'm gonna stick with you."

This was a player that we all wanted, and Kevin believed we could get him, but it became apparent when the team met on Monday that nobody liked him. The message was clear: They didn't want him on the team. We did not offer him a scholarship. He went on to become an All-American at another school.

Among the players we brought in were Craig McMillan, our first McDonald's All-American, and junior college transfers Bruce Fraser and John Edgar. Fraser, who earned his nickname "Q" by ceaselessly asking questions—supposedly, a teammate once told him not to ask any more questions, to which he responded, "Why?"—was one of our easiest recruits. His father was a high school coach in Long Beach, and he took my place when I left City College. Our families had been good friends for many years, and Bobbi and I had watched Bruce grow into a player good enough to play in our program.

We were in the middle of a building project. The first year we'd dug the foundation. Now the walls were going up and the building was beginning to take shape. We surprised everyone that second season by going 21-10. We tied for third in the Pac-10 with a 12–6 record, but all six of our losses were by four points or less. I knew we deserved to be invited to the NCAA tournament, but I wasn't sure the committee would agree with me. Being on the bubble is an uncomfortable place to be. The day the pairings were announced, I was so nervous that Bobbi and I got in our car and drove twenty-five miles up the Catalina Highway to Mount Lemmon, a beautiful hiking and skiing resort. We got there a lot faster than usual. We were holding hands when it was announced we were a tenth seed. It was only Arizona's fourth invitation to the tournament, and the first since 1976. In those days our fans were thrilled simply to be invited, so even though we lost to Alabama in the first round, most people considered the season a success. When you don't have great expectations, it isn't difficult to meet them. We even sold out several games at McKale that year, and for the second consecutive year we led the Pac-10 in average attendance.

A lot of teaching took place that year, both on and off the court, and it wasn't all positive. One of our six set plays was a desperation play to be used when time was running out. We set screens to release a player to go long and receive a baseball pass. It was called the home-run play. Early in the season we were at New Mexico and blew a lead to let them back in the game. At the end of the first half we tried to run the home-run play, but Joe Turner had no idea where he was supposed to be and the play failed. I was furious. We only ran six set plays, so how could he screw up one of them so badly? At halftime I just lit into him. "Joe, do you know what play we were running there? Do you know what you were supposed to be doing?"

Joe didn't say anything. He just nodded his head.

There was a very large chalkboard in the front of the locker room. It was half the size of the entire wall. "Okay, come up here and show me what we were doing. Come on, come up here."

Joe sort of ambled sheepishly to the front of the room. I handed him the chalk and on this large board he drew the key about the size of a quarter. It was so small it was almost impossible to see. Then he looked for help. He looked first at Pete Williams. Every person in that room knew how hot I was; they weren't about to help him. Pete lowered his head. Joe was getting more and more desperate. "Go ahead," I told him, "where are you?"

He took the chalk and drew an X about the size of a dollar bill over the key. He more than covered the entire key with his X, figuring that if he covered everything he had to be right. I saw the humor in the situation— several years later. But not that day. That day I was boiling mad. "You don't know what the play was," I said, grabbing the chalk out of his hand. Not only didn't he know the play, in the Xs and Os the X is used to represent the defense. I just told him, "We practice this play over and over, and we get a chance to use it, you blow the opportunity for us . . ."

I don't know if we would have scored on that play even if we had executed it perfectly. What I do know is that we lost the game by one point. I'm not sure that any of those players had ever seen me so angry—but I know they got the message. The difference between winning and losing is what happens every day in practice.

The words we've always tried to instill in our players were teamwork, responsibility, integrity. Well, my commitment to those words got tested in Seattle, Washington. In late February of that year we were 11–4 in the Pac-10 and had a legitimate shot at our first conference championship. We went up to Seattle to play Washington. This was the Huskies' Hall of Fame coach Marv Harshman's last home game, and the crowd was big and very loud. Maybe the officials got into the spirit of the day because there were several questionable calls, particularly near the end of the game, and we lost 60–58. It was very frustrating. We'd worked really hard for two years; nobody really expected us to be contending for the championship. After the game that night, several players, among them Pete Williams, Joe Turner, and Morgan Taylor, went out and missed curfew. I don't remember which assistant coach checked their rooms, but when he told me these players were gone I was furious. We left a note on the door of their hotel room: "See coach in the morning."

I was too angry to meet with them. They had let down their teammates. We were flying to LA that morning for a game with UCLA. If we won, we still had a good shot at the championship. I didn't say a word to any of them at the hotel, at the airport, on the plane to Los Angeles, or on the bus from the airport to the hotel. I knew what to do and I knew what the consequences of my decision might be, but I didn't think I had a choice. The day you don't back up your rules is the day they cease to have any meaning. Finally, at pregame practice I told Williams and Taylor, "Turn your jerseys over." That meant they were no longer starting. Williams was our best player, but in practice he and Turner worked with the second team.

After practice I met with the players who had missed curfew. I asked each of them to tell me why they'd done it. I wasn't looking for an apology, I wanted an explanation. What was so important that they had let down their teammates? There was no explanation. What Pete Williams remembers most about that meeting was that, as Turner and Taylor spoke, I looked them right in the eyes, but when he stood up I looked down at the floor. I couldn't even look at him. That's probably accurate. That's how disgusted I was with all of them.

Before the game I explained to the rest of the team why I was benching two starters and an important reserve for the most important game of the year. "Nobody is bigger than the program," I told them. "No individual is more important than the team."

I kept them on the bench for the entire first half. They did play in the second half, but we were out of sync. We lost 58–54. I don't know if we would have beaten UCLA even if the three of them had played the entire game. We lost the conference championship by one game to Washington and USC. It was tough, but after that I don't think anyone doubted that when I said something I meant it. The rules applied to everyone equally.

Our fans didn't like it any more than our players. Numerous people called the office or wrote to complain. How could you do this? We may never have have a chance to win the Pac-10 again! But there was one letter in particular that I remember. We were recruiting a high school junior named Sean Elliott, and his mother, Odie May Elliott, wrote, "I just want you to know that you're the kind of coach I want my son to play for." Months later Sean Elliott committed to Arizona.

I try to keep rules to a minimum, but I do enforce the rules that we make. One of them is being on time. Every member of our traveling party is given a schedule and expected to follow it. That means that if they're late, the bus leaves without them or the plane leaves without them. Believe me, through the years we've left a lot of people behind. I can close my eyes and see George Kalil practically running after the bus, or Bruce Fraser or Luke Walton sprinting through the airport to catch up with us.

I've always been very serious about following the rules in my own life, which is why I demand it of my players. Ethics matter to me, and that almost caused me to leave Arizona after my second season. One afternoon in March 1985 I was getting ready to play a round of golf with my close friend Paul Weitman when a reporter from the *Arizona Daily Star* called. He asked me several questions about our uniforms. Apparently this reporter thought he'd uncovered some sort of shady deal. I had a contract with MacGregor Sporting Goods to run some clinics. We'd bought our uniforms from Sand-Knit, which had been a division of MacGregor, without a competitive bid. The reporter believed I'd made a deal with MacGregor and overpaid for our uniforms.

The reporter was entitled to ask the questions, and I told him the truth. Sand-Knit were better made than other uniforms. We paid more for them because they would last longer. "If a program is going to be first class it has to do things in a first-class manner . . . Over a five-year period," I told him, "dollar for dollar they're the best. Sand-Knit measures every kid . . ." I returned to the golf course and told Paul about it, then forgot all about it.

But the next morning there was a big story on the front page of the *Star*. Not the front of the sports page, the front page of the newspaper. Basically, the reporter was accusing me of giving a kickback to MacGregor by purchasing our uniforms from them in exchange for payment for the clinics. In the story he noted that our uniforms cost more than similar uniforms worn by the Phoenix Suns, but he failed to mention that the Suns uniforms came without anything on them and they then paid to add lettering and numbers, making the price higher than we paid. I was furious about the story. Absolutely furious. I understand that my objectives and the needs of the media are sometimes very different. Sometimes that results in real friction. I may not like some of the things they write, I may get testy about it sometimes, but as long as what they write is true, I can't really object too much. But there was no truth to this story at all. The phone started ringing. Several members of the university's administration called to tell me they knew the story wasn't true, but suggested that the best thing to do was just leave it alone. You can't fight the newspaper, they told me, so don't even bother. It isn't worth it.

"I don't care," I told them. My whole career had been built on following the ethics and morals that I preached to my teams. I didn't feel I had any choice. "No one is going to question my integrity," I said. "They can make up whatever kind of stories they want, but I'm not going to let them question my integrity." I called the local TV and radio stations and told them I wanted to respond to this story. I held a press conference and told them the whole story was a lie. There was nothing true or accurate about it. Their research had been so poor that they hadn't bothered to find out that Sand-Knit was no longer owned by MacGregor.

I found out later that the story had been written by the sports editor, not the reporter whose byline was on it. I never found out why. That night about a hundred people actually picketed the *Star* building, and by the next day the sports editor had been fired. But I was still angry that the university hadn't immediately defended me and had even suggested I shouldn't fight back.

A few weeks earlier I had gotten several calls from University of Kentucky athletic director Cliff Hagan. I knew that Kentucky's coach, Joe B. Hall, was retiring, so I assumed Hagan was calling to see if I was interested in the job. I wasn't. We were happy in Tucson, so I didn't even return Hagan's calls. But this story, and the reaction of the university, got me so angry that on Monday morning I finally returned Hagan's call. It was exactly what I thought: He invited me to Lexington to discuss taking over at Kentucky. The timing was perfect. Bobbi and I were already planning to go to Lexington the next weekend for the Final Four. I agreed to meet with him.

Kentucky is one of the most prestigious jobs in basketball. I wouldn't have to worry about building a program; Kentucky was always competitive. I wouldn't have to be concerned about filling the arena; it was always sold out. Obviously I was flattered. I didn't think of myself as the kind of premier coach they would want for that job. I built the program at Iowa, but we'd only been 11–17 my first year at Arizona. Accepting this job would instantly make me a major figure in college basketball.

Coincidently, I assumed, on the flight to Lexington Bobbi and I were seated next to a couple who lived in Tucson but owned a coal business in Kentucky. I don't think it was a setup, but it was quite a coincidence. The man, Don Johnson, made a point of telling me how great the Kentucky job was—adding that the only way people in Kentucky would get upset about uniforms was if the Wildcats weren't wearing the best available.

In Lexington I met with the hiring committee. During that meeting someone pointed out that the weather in Kentucky was not as nice as in Arizona. "I grew up in North Dakota," I told them. "I went to school in Minnesota and coached in Iowa City." So I knew about cold weather. I visited Rupp Arena and spent some time with Joe B. Hall. Meanwhile, the media had found out that I was meeting with Kentucky. Then things got crazy. It was Iowa all over again. Assistant coaches were trying to get hold of me to ask for a job. Practically everybody we knew in Tucson was calling to urge me to stay in Arizona. We were deluged with telegrams, phone calls, and mailgrams. The other coaches there for the tournament told me, basically, I'd be insane to turn down the job. Finally, it got so hectic Bobbi and I left the hotel and moved out to Don Johnson's horse farm.

It became pretty clear that the job was mine if I wanted it. We didn't talk about money, but I assumed that it wouldn't become an issue. My primary concern was the relationship of the top alumni to the program. They were used to doing things a certain way, and I wanted to make sure there wouldn't be any problems when I made some changes. Cliff Hagan assured me there would be no problems. I had a lot of questions, and Scott Thompson was talking to Joe Hall's assistants for me, trying to get answers. I was also talking to Paul Weitman, who was urging me to forget about Kentucky and come home.

The only person who got the phone number of the place we were staying was George Kalil. He wouldn't tell us where he'd gotten it, no matter how much Bobbi asked. He was being loyal to his source. George had been in the arena for the Final Four and someone told him that Dick Vitale had reported that I was taking the Kentucky job. George knew Vitale from his trips to Tucson for our annual Fiesta Bowl tournament. He shouted up to him, "Dick, are you sure Lute is going to Kentucky?"

"I'm really sure," he said.

George was trying to be optimistic, "Are you positive?"

"Well, I'm pretty sure," he admitted. Then he added, "If you want to keep Lute, you guys better get your money together."

George responded, "If Lute makes the decision to leave, it won't be just about money."

So when George finally got me on the phone he told me, "Don't go."

I told George I wanted him to go the hotel to pick up all the mail and messages.

On Sunday morning I met with C. M. Newton, who was then the athletic director at Vanderbilt, for some advice. I had known C. M. for a few years and trusted him. He had played at Kentucky and had been the commissioner of the Southeast Conference. He knew the Kentucky program inside and out, and answered all my questions.

It was an incredibly difficult decision to make. I really was torn. Cliff Hagan wanted an answer by ten o'clock that night. Bobbi and I sat down with our yellow pads and began discussing our options. It quickly became obvious that Kentucky had made one very large mistake: They hadn't invited Bobbi to these meetings.

We listed all the positives and negatives. The weather in Arizona, the prestige of the Kentucky job. We'd grown very comfortable in Tucson, but Kentucky was the most prestigious job in the sport. We knew the salary would be substantially more; the entire package was probably worth $500,000, but it meant moving the family again. I knew there would be enormous pressure to win, but I already put enormous pressure on myself to win. And it also meant moving back into the fishbowl. Kentucky's basketball coach was probably the best-known person in the state. Finally, after we'd spent most of the day trying to make our decision based on all the variables, it came down to a gut decision. It just didn't feel right. I called Cliff Hagan at ten o'clock that night. He was at an awards banquet. "I'm sorry," I told him. "I really appreciate the opportunity to talk with you about this job, but I think I'm going to with-draw my name from consideration."

I know he was surprised. We flew back to Tucson on Monday. That af-ternoon Don Johnson called and asked Bobbi and me to come back. He explained that Kentucky hadn't hired a new basketball coach since 1930, when Adolph Rupp was hired. When Rupp retired, his well-respected assistant, Joe B. Hall, had simply been elevated to the head coaching job. Kentucky just didn't have any experience in this process and didn't know the proper way to proceed. He told Bobbi, "You should have been part of the whole thing. We blew it. Please come back."

We couldn't, I told him. We'd made our decision.

When we got home, we told the media, "The overriding decision in pulling my name was the fact that we love Tucson." That was ab-solutely true.

On Tuesday Kentucky hired Eddie Sutton. A couple of years after Ed-die Sutton took the job, the program was put on probation. My gut feel-ing had been absolutely right.

As soon as we got back to Arizona I went to work. I wanted to put this behind me as quickly as possible and focus on the job to be done at Arizona. That summer we took our returning players on our first Euro-pean tour. It was a great opportunity for our kids to get some valuable game experience and have some fun. Very few of them had been out of the country, so this was a chance for them to be exposed to different cultures. I wanted them to know that there is a lot more to life than Tuc-son and basketball. I also wanted them to play a lot of basketball. Nike was one of the sponsors of the trip. I think this tour was one of their first attempts to break adidas's domination of the European market. We told our players the trip was going to be so low-key that I was even go-ing to let my assistants coach several of the games.

The tour included Yugoslavia, France, Spain, the Netherlands, and Italy. We ate regional food, which meant trying new foods for the first time. If at times I forgot my players were still teenagers, watching them looking with great curiosity and disdain at a variety of foods they had never seen was a perfect reminder. When we got home I remember ask-ing one of the kids what he had liked best about the trip, and he re-sponded, "That hamburger we had in Holland."

By the time we got to Challans, France, I was pretty disgusted with our accommodations. One of the places they put us was some type of juvenile dormitory. It was slightly better than a prison. The beds were basically thin mattresses laid on top of wooden slats. They were not built for basketball players. They were too short for most of our kids, and when someone rolled over during the night the slats popped out with a loud snap and they fell through the frame. Then they had to carefully fit the slats back into the frame and very slowly lay back down. There were no towels, no soap, very little of anything.

Our host was an American playing ball in France named Tony Parker. Tony had his three-year-old son with him—the son is now starring in the NBA. When we arrived at the arena for the game I told Tony to go inside and tell the organizers of the tour that we weren't going to play unless they fulfilled their promise and put us in a good hotel. "Tell them they can do whatever they want to do, but in about an hour they're going to have to explain to all the people who bought tickets why they don't have the American team."

I'm not sure Tony thought I was serious at first. Not a lot of basketball teams travel all the way to Europe to *not* play basketball. But I was absolutely serious. I told the team to stay on the bus. Bobbi, the whole team, and some boosters who were traveling with us just sat and sat until Tony straightened out the situation. Things didn't become first class overnight, but we were moved to a pretty decent hotel. We played in a tournament in Dieppe against the national teams from the Soviet Union, the Netherlands, France, and several other countries. The tournament gave us the chance to bang heads with much more experienced players, among them the great 7'3" 300-pound Russian Arvydas Sabonis. He was the biggest player I had ever seen. Our players referred to him as "Lurch," after the character in *The Addams Family*. He looked like a mountain, only bigger and stronger. We finished the trip with a very credible eight wins and seven losses, playing under international rules, which gave Steve Kerr and Craig McMillan the opportunity to shoot the newfangled three-point shot, which was about to be made legal by the NCAA and change college basketball.

We'd reached the point where we could compete for blue-chip prospects with the well-known basketball powers. But as it turned out two of our most valuable recruits that year were not highly recruited at all. Kenny Lofton was living in the projects of Gary, Indiana, with his partially blind grandmother. He was 5'11", and he wasn't really a pure point guard. He was more of a scorer than a passer. That meant he had to play the two guard, the shooting guard. Schools like Michigan and Illinois thought he was too small to play that position for them. Syracuse needs tall, rangy guards with long arms because they play that 2–3 zone, so he wasn't right for them. In one way or another, he didn't fit into most top ranked programs, so he was being recruited mostly by lower Division I teams like Kent State.

The first time Ken Burmeister and I saw him play was on an outdoor court. You could see right away what a tough kid he was. There wasn't any question in my mind that he would fit our system. Our philosophy was different: Our feeling was that he could play either guard position for us. We want our point guard to be an offensive threat. If a point guard can score, he has to be defended and opens up other opportunities; if he isn't a scorer, his defender is back helping guard the post. What impressed me most was his competitiveness, his quickness, and his confidence. He was just lightning. And his natural athleticism. We felt he could defend pretty much anyone because of his quick hands and quick feet. And he certainly was confident: He felt he could score on anyone and stop everyone else from scoring.

Kenny's game was speed. I knew the way they played basketball in that area: The kids run up and down the court as fast as they can, and when the horn goes off, they look up at the scoreboard to see who won. He didn't have a natural feel for the game; he played at one speed. Full. I thought that with some coaching we could contain his skills within our offense. So Kenny accepted our scholarship offer.

In Long Beach I was restricted to recruiting within the area, and I still believed in searching the local area for players. But in the first two decades I spent at Arizona I was able to recruit only five players from Arizona. Of course, four of them ended up in the NBA: Mike Bibby, Richard Jefferson, Channing Frye, and the first Arizona native we recruited, 6'7" Sean Elliott.

When I came to Arizona Sean Elliott was a high school sophomore. He attended our summer camp that year; we knew he was big, we weren't sure he was a prospect. By the end of his junior year, he was playing pickup games with our kids at the Tucson Country Club or the university's Bear Down gym and holding his own. Surprisingly, Elliott was not recruited nationally. A lot of the big schools didn't know too much about him. The only school that really came after him hard was the University of Texas at El Paso. So we were confident we were going to get him. One of our boosters owned several McDonald's franchises in Arizona and was a good friend of McDonald's owner Ray Kroc. In those days the selection committee for the McDonald's all-star game was Ray Kroc. There was no committee. If you knew Ray Kroc, you could get your recruits in that game. So Sean became a McDonald's All-American.

After he was invited, he put his arm through a window and came within a fraction of an inch of cutting some ligaments. His arm was in a big cast and he couldn't play in the McDonald's game. That injury prevented other schools from seeing how good he was. So no other big schools showed any interest in him.

From California we recruited 6'8" Anthony Cook, 6'9" Bruce Wheatley, and 6'3" Eric Cooper. Ironically, we also got the best player from Iowa, 6'8" Brian David. I remember posting up Bruce Wheatley in his living room. I actually walked him through a couple of moves to show him how we did things at Arizona. I don't think he was used to being pushed around in his living room by a coach trying to recruit him. I suspect that surprised him a little.

There was a lot of talent in that group, and I was confident we were going to have a successful season. But it was a couple of days before practice when I got the feeling this might be a special team. One of the requirements for all our players is that they complete a two-mile run in a specific time before they are permitted to practice. Guards and perimeter players have to do it in under 12:30 while the big guys have to do it in less than thirteen minutes. Players who can't run the court don't fit in our offense. Wheatly was a big, slow kid. His first attempt took him approximately 45 minutes. I decided to give him a break. "I'll give you thirteen minutes and thirty seconds," I told him.

Everybody else on the squad had done it. On the day he came out to make his next attempt the entire squad showed up to help him. They didn't have to, they had done their job, but they did. Scott Thompson had the stopwatch. It was drizzling a little. Each one of the players ran a lap with him to keep him going. It was almost as if they were carrying him. He made it in something like 13:39. That wasn't good enough, but his teammates kept telling me, "Come on, give it to him. He slipped at the beginning." The fact that they were there to support him was the real reason we gave it to him.

I was about to begin my thirtieth season coaching basketball. I couldn't begin to calculate the number of games I'd watched or coached, the number of players I'd seen, the number of practices I'd run. And yet I was looking forward to the beginning of the season as if it were the first one. It was just as much fun, just as exciting. Maybe even a little more exciting this year because I was confident we were going to be a very good team. This time, when I looked through the schedule, there wasn't a single game in which I thought we would be overmatched.

We started the season slowly, winning five of our first nine, but then found our game and ran off six- and seven-game winning streaks. We finished 23-9 and, more important, won our first Pac-10 title. We started selling out games. I learned a long time later that Steve Kerr and Bruce Fraser used to listen to me telling people at every banquet, "Get your tickets now because you won't be able to get them pretty soon." They'd sort of roll their eyes and think, are you kidding me? What's he talking about? The arena was barely half full. But by the end of the season they actually discussed buying several tickets behind our bench as an investment.

A year earlier our players couldn't even give away their tickets. But as the season progressed, students started stopping them on campus and asking if they had any extras. In the stores on campus clerks began trying to trade pizza and hamburgers or admission to the movie theater for tickets. Years later I found out that Brock Brunkhorst actually attached two tickets to a test paper when he handed it in. The results of that attempt have long been lost to history. That year was the beginning.

It wasn't just winning, it was that we were playing exciting basketball. One play I will never forget had little meaning in the outcome of the game, but I don't know that I'd ever seen a crowd respond quite like that. We were playing Oregon at McKale and had a comfortable lead near the end of the first half. Kenny Lofton intercepted a pass and took off downcourt. He went into the air, did a complete 360-degree turn in midair, then slammed the ball through the basket with both hands. Bam! The arena erupted. The crowd went wild. McKale seemed like it was shaking. Oregon called time-out, mostly just to let our fans quiet down, but after the minute-fifteen time-out ended, the crowd was just as loud. Naturally, everybody wanted to talk about Kenny's slam dunk. Those people who didn't see it knew they'd missed something wonderful, and they didn't want to miss it the next time.

Within a couple of years we were selling out every seat, every game, every season. Season tickets became impossible to get. If a couple got divorced or someone declared bankruptcy in Tucson one of the first things the judge wanted to know was whether they had season tickets. In one bankruptcy action the court ended up with a pair of tickets. The judge held a lottery for the right to buy the tickets and raised $60,000 for charity. To give as many students as possible the opportunity to see a game, we instituted a lottery system in which students can win the right to buy tickets for half the games, which means twice as many students as we have available seats get in during the season. And every game is broadcast on television and radio. But that all got started during the 1985–86 season.

If anyone doubted this was a new era at Arizona we settled that by beating UCLA twice, the first time Arizona had ever beaten the Bruins twice in a season. Early in March we beat them at Pauley Pavilion in Los Angeles, the first time we'd beaten UCLA on their court since 1923. Since 1923. That's a long losing streak. Until the 1985–86 season we pretty much had been patsies for them, the kind of games that they counted as wins when they looked at their schedule at the beginning of the year. But since that year our rivalry with UCLA has become one of the most competitive in college basketball. There are many people who consider it the West Coast version of Duke–North Carolina or Kentucky-Louisville. Reggie Miller was playing for Coach Walt Hazzard at that time, and he didn't like to lose at home. Even before it was called trash talking he was talking trash, and after the game he was still talking. "Maybe you won this one, but I'm going to be in the NBA."

As it turned out, he was absolutely right. But what he did not add was that he was going to be playing in the NBA with five members of our team.

After the game Bobbi approached Coach Wooden, who was sitting in the stands, and asked him to autograph her program. It was not something she normally did, but in this instance it seemed appropriate. I had so much respect for him, I'd grown up as a coach learning from him. To me, it was almost as if this game marked a changing of the guard. Coach Wooden graciously signed the program. I'm not someone who avidly collects souvenirs or mementos, but this one I have hanging on the wall of my home. When visitors wonder why I have a framed UCLA program on display, I tell them, "This was the beginning."

We received our second invitation to the NCAA tournament, this time as a ninth seed. Again we lost in the first round, to Auburn.

Our rebuilding program was doing well, but there was still a lot of construction to be done. The previous season we'd been ranked for the first time—we were number seventeen for a week—but during the 1985–86 season we never made the polls. I've never really cared about polls; the only reason they're important is that high school kids pay attention to them. Being ranked makes recruiting easier. The better teams get the most media attention, they appear on television most often, and as a result they get the better high school kids. If you're not in the top twenty-five, for example, ESPN doesn't even talk about your program. Out of the top twenty-five, out of the mind of the better young players.

I've always believed West Coast teams suffer in the polls because of the three-hour time difference between coasts. Our games start too late to attract a large audience in the East and finish too late for stories to make the morning papers. That means a lot of poll voters don't see West Coast teams often enough to make a fair judgment. Obviously, once our program was established, voters began paying attention to us, but it has always been a problem.

The day this season ended we focused on recruiting for next season. And the season after that. Mostly we needed to get bigger and tougher. We were recruiting a big, strong player from Cerritos Community College named Tom Tolbert. The day after we lost to Auburn we were sitting in his living room. During the visit both Tom and his parents told us he wanted to come to Arizona.

The most difficult thing for a heavily recruited player to do is learn how to say no. Programs can literally spend years recruiting a kid. Coaches know from experience that every year we're going to get a few of the kids we want and lose some of the kids we've been pursuing. It's a way of life for us. It's a lot harder on the kids. They only go through the recruiting process once. And maybe for the first time in their lives they have to tell a coach, thanks, but I've picked someone else. We try to make it easier on kids by telling them we understand that they can't go to five schools. Four of us are going to be very disappointed and only one of us is going to be thrilled. "You have to understand," we say, "that this is a process we're used to going through. The only thing we ask is that you tell us your decision as soon as possible. If it isn't us, we're not going to get upset; we're going to follow your career with interest and we're going to be rooting for you—except when you play against us."

Tom Tolbert told us he was coming to Arizona. The problem was, he had already told Coach Jerry Tarkanian he was going to UNLV. Tom Tolbert, as we were to learn, is a free spirit. Initially, Tolbert had attended University of California Irvine, but the coach there told him he couldn't play on that level—a little below us—and suggested he go to junior college and play football. Tolbert transferred to Cerritos Junior College and became a hard-nosed basketball player. Exactly what we needed. And what Tarkanian wanted.

Both schools recruited him hard. And as Tolbert later explained, his decision came down to the fact that he just didn't trust himself in Vegas. Vegas was only a five-hour drive from his home, meaning his friends could be there every weekend, which had the makings of a disaster. "If I went to Vegas, I could see myself there ten years later being a pit boss."

Finally he told us he was coming to Arizona. For him, that was the easy part. The hard part was telling Tark. Tark can be very persuasive. A UNLV assistant called Tom Tolbert the day before players were permitted to sign an official letter of intent to confirm that he was ready to sign. When Tolbert explained that he had changed his mind and was going to Arizona, the assistant said, "I think you owe it to Coach Tark to tell him you're not coming." The assistant asked if Tolbert was going to be home later that day.

"Yeah, my brother has a Little League game but I should be here for a while." Tolbert waited at home for the call till five o'clock, then left for the Little League game.

When he got home later that night a neighbor told him, "This guy was here to see you. A limo or Town Car pulled up and this bald guy got out and knocked on the door and then left."

Tolbert always said it was a good thing his brother had a ball game that night. Maybe he would have been able to tell Tark on the phone, but chances are pretty good that if he had been home when Tark showed up in person he'd be a pit boss in Vegas today.

Tark was pretty upset. Our paths had first crossed when I was coaching Long Beach City College and he was at Long Beach State. I replaced him at Long Beach State when he left for UNLV—and our program was put on probation because of his recruiting practices. Now it was Tark's turn to be upset, and he was furious. He believed I'd come in at the last minute and stolen Tolbert. That wasn't true, but he believed it. So he gave me the nickname "Midnight Lute." Midnight Lute. Makes me sound like a riverboat hustler; break out the chips and hide the ladies, here comes Midnight Lute! The media picked it up and claimed that there were bad feelings between Tark the Shark and Midnight Lute. That wasn't true. Maybe there were some hard feelings, but we've always respected each other.

Sometimes, when Tom Tolbert and I battled each other the next two seasons, there might have been a time or two when I secretly wished Tolbert had been home that night.

Two players from my very first team at Long Beach City College later played for Tarkanian at Long Beach State. Tark recognized that I could develop players for his program; so he invited me to his gym to watch his workouts and occasionally we'd go to a high school game or dinner together. We had a very good relationship. In addition to being a great coach, Tark is extremely personable. When he speaks to someone, he makes that person feel like he's the most important person in the world. I think the only people who didn't like Tark were the NCAA investigators.

I suspect he didn't like them very much, either.

In addition to Tom Tolbert, we successfully recruited two other kids who would play important roles in our program, Jud Buechler and Harvey Mason. Both of them wanted to come to Arizona. So Midnight Lute never struck again.

6

Maybe the old army recruiting pitch should be changed to "Become a basketball coach and see the world." Because I certainly have. That basic lure of the game, throw the ball in the basket, is universal. I was fortunate enough to become successful at the same time basketball was becoming popular on almost every continent. While some countries were still trying to learn the fundamentals of the game, many other nations had become capable of competing on the international level. At one time the United States and the Soviet Union had dominated international basketball, but by the mid-1980s that was no longer the case.

In 1984 I was asked by the USA Basketball committee to coach the American team in the Jones Cup, an international tournament held in Taipei. Bobby Knight had picked the major college stars for our Olympic team that year, so they gave me the younger players. It was a very competitive field because a lot of countries were using this tournament to prepare for the Olympics. We played Canada, Australia, the Japanese national team, and Korea. The Koreans were small, so they relied entirely on the three-point shot. They knew anything around the basket would be blocked. So a player would drive to the lane and as soon as the defense collapsed on him he would kick it out for a perimeter shot.

The Japanese team was unbelievably disciplined; when a player came out of the game he would stand at attention in front of the coach, who would say a few words to him, then he would walk down the bench and sit down. It made my coach's heart sing. Karl Malone was on our team. He wasn't "the Mailman" yet, but he was learning the route. He was about 6'9", 250-plus pounds, all of it muscle. During the game we had a three-on-one fast break with Karl in the middle. A Japanese guard, about 5'8", was blocking the middle of the lane: He wasn't moving and Karl wasn't slowing down. You could see this coming. Oh no, I thought, this is going to be a disaster. The Japanese guard probably had his eyes shut tight, knowing he was about to be run over by a train, but he stood his ground. Then it was just like the scene from *E.T.* in which the kids on their bikes reach the roadblock and suddenly take off into the air. Malone leaped up into the air, spread his legs, and went right over the top, right over him, then wham! he slammed it down. The basket was attached by wires to the ceiling of the building—and three minutes later that basket was still shaking.

Either the French team or the Spanish team had an American playing for them who was really a dirty player. He liked to throw his elbows, and in a couple of earlier games he had coldcocked a number of guys. When we were playing his team, he swung an elbow at one of our people, and one of our reserves, Kentucky's Winston Bennett, leaped off our bench and *wham!*—this was a different kind of wham!—he nailed the guy. That started a knockdown brawl. This was my first international coaching job, and as I watched players punching each other, I suspected it wasn't going exactly as I had planned. We got out on the court and got it stopped, and the Jones Cup committee reprimanded Winston Bennett. From a coaching standpoint we never should have let it happen, but this player just deserved it, and he needed to be stopped before he really hurt someone.

We won the tournament without a loss. Based on that success, two years later I was selected to coach our national team in the FIBA World Championship. That was quite an honor, although, honestly, until that point I didn't even know there was a world championship in basketball. But in Europe these championships were very important. Most countries entered the core of their Olympic teams. We had always put together a team of college players, so we hadn't won the gold medal in thirty-two years. The last American team to win it had been a touring semipro team.

I thought it would be fun. Of course, it was impossible to know how drastically these championships would impact our regular season.

My assistant coaches were Bobby Cremins of Georgia Tech, Jerry Pimm of Santa Barbara, and Scott Thompson. Initially, Bobby Knight and

Pete Newell invited about sixty kids to try out for the team in Colorado Springs. From that group I selected fifteen players to come to Tucson for the final selection of my twelve-man squad. Among the players I wanted were David Robinson, Tommy Amaker, Rony Seikaly, Derrick McKey, Armon Gilliam, Charles Smith, Reggie Williams, and Kenny Smith. With a twelve-man roster some of the players at the end of the bench wouldn't get a lot of minutes, and if all twelve players believed they deserved to be playing, that back end of the bench was going to be an unhappy place. It would destroy team chemistry. So I also invited Steve Kerr and Sean Elliott, Brian Shaw of Santa Barbara, and Tom Hammonds of Georgia Tech. I knew that these were the kind of kids who wouldn't complain about playing time. I also knew they would work hard in practice and the experience would be very good for them.

I also put 5'3" Muggsy Bogues from Wake Forest on my list. Before I invited Bogues to Colorado Springs I'd asked Dean Smith for his opinion. He told me, "The best thing I can tell you is that when we play Wake Forest I tell our guards, 'If you don't see Muggsy, pick the ball up. If he's not in front of you, he's coming to take the ball away from you.' "

At the tryouts in Colorado Springs he'd been our best point guard. But Pete Newell and Bobby Knight, both of whom had a lot of experience in international basketball, told me it wouldn't be wise to invite Muggsy to Tucson. If you invite him, they told me, he's probably going to play well enough to make the team—and you're not going to beat the Soviets with a 5'3" point guard.

I said, "I'm not concerned about whether or not we can beat the Soviets. I just want a chance to play the Soviets."

On a hot night in July the McKale Center was packed for our last scrimmage. We divided the squad into what we believed to be pretty even teams. At the half Muggsy's team had a twenty-point lead. We switched Muggsy to the trailing team; that was the only change we made. He brought that team from twenty points down to win the game. After that nobody ever wondered if he belonged on the squad.

Players just loved to be on the court with Muggsy. The instant someone got open, Muggsy was going to get the ball to him. We felt we needed a point guard who was going to be able to get the ball downcourt quickly, and nobody was quicker than Muggsy. Unless we had a fast break we insisted on our point guard passing the ball to the wings. By getting it to the wings we get good angles to feed the big man in the post. There was no one who could run the post like David Robinson, and Muggsy could move the ball ahead to make certain he got it in a scoring position.

To prepare for the tournament we played several games in France. We opened against the French national team in Paris. This was the seventh- or eighth-rated team in Europe; they hadn't even qualified for the World Championships—and they beat us by twenty-five points. They just destroyed us. The next day, on the train going to Lyon to play in a regional tournament, Rony Seikaly from Syracuse read the game story in the French paper. "One thing for sure," the story concluded, "the United States will not be playing in Madrid." Meaning we certainly weren't going to make the finals.

The world championships were held in Spain. We easily won our first three games, played in Malaga, but our next game, against Puerto Rico, was a battle that came down to the last minute. David Robinson hit a jump shot for the 73–72 win.

During the tournament we used an off day to visit the famed Rock of Gibraltar. Bobbi and Christi, who had come with me to Spain, had gone to England for a few days to watch tennis at Wimbledon. As we were getting off the bus in Gibraltar, one of the sportswriters with us, Greg Hansen, mentioned to Steve Kerr how unusual it was to see me relaxing in such an exotic place.

Kerr responded, "Oh, I don't think any rock is going to impress Lute. He has Bobbi."

The semifinals were played in Orvieto, in the Basque Country. We lost our first game there to Argentina, 74–70. Argentina was a good team, and I don't think our players gave them the respect they deserved. We just didn't play with a lot of intensity. I remember walking to the locker room after the game trying to think of something positive to say. The team was already down, and I didn't need to bring them down further. In the locker room I told them, "When we're in Madrid and they're putting the gold medals around our necks, we're all going to think back and remember that the key to winning the world championship was the loss to Argentina." I still tell people I had my fingers crossed behind my back when I said that.

That loss meant we had to win our next two games to remain eligible for a medal. I don't think anyone was too surprised that we'd been beaten; absolutely no one expected us to win the tournament. In our next game we beat Canada. That meant we had to beat heavily favored Yugoslavia to get into the medal round. Yugoslavia was a very good team, led by future Hall of Famer Drazen Petrovic. In the previous two decades Yugoslavia had won two world championships while the Soviet Union had won the other three. The past year they had beaten the Soviets to win the European championship.

To beat Yugoslavia we had to stop Petrovic. He was the heart of that team. Scott Thompson had been scouting Yugoslavia and he did a masterful job. He charted how often a player caught a pass and put the ball on the floor before shooting, how many times he went left or right, whether or not he had a midrange game, how often he went to the basket. From that scouting report we knew Petrovic had to put the ball on the floor before he did anything. The first thing he did when he got the ball was dribble, and everything that followed came off that dribble. The obvious strategy would have been to put Derrick McKey on Petrovic. Derrick was a really good defender, so it would have been a good matchup. But we didn't go that way.

Generally, on offense a player will have more trouble with a defender who's quicker than he is than he will against a player bigger than he. So we decided to assign 5'3" Muggsy Bogues to guard 6'5" Drazen Petrovic. I told Muggsy, "Petrovic has to dribble before he shoots. Use your quickness to force him outside. When he gets the ball, get right up on him. If he gets by you and goes to the bucket, he'll have to get by David." Muggsy just loved the idea. He's as great a competitor as I've ever known. When the teams came out to play and Muggsy lined up with Petrovic some spectators thought we were kidding, but Muggsy was just so quick that we decided it was worth the gamble. If it didn't work, we knew people would think we were crazy.

I told Muggsy, "Just don't let him catch the ball anywhere near shooting range. The second he catches it, you stick your nose right in his navel. Don't let him dribble." Our thinking was that Muggsy could disrupt Petrovic, take him out of his game. We knew that Petrovic would try to take advantage of the height difference by posting up. Our plan was that when Petrovic posted up, Muggsy would move in front of him to prevent him from getting the ball, and if they tried to lob it over his head David Robinson, McKey, or Charles Smith would play the pass as if Petrovic was their man.

As soon as Yugoslavia realized we were serious about this, they tried to attack inside. It was the obvious thing to do. Muggsy got great help from McKey and Charles Smith, and that strategy failed. Petrovic went scoreless for the first eight minutes and we opened up a 19–2 lead. Petrovic was the key, their offense started with him, so when he was neutralized there was very little they could do. Petrovic scored one basket in the first half, when a teammate stole the ball and threw it ahead to him for a layup. I think we were up twenty at the half.

Petrovic was so frustrated that when he got the ball on the first play of the second half he tried to dribble over Muggsy's head and then chase it down. It was very funny. Every time Petrovic got the ball, Muggsy was right there with his nose in Petrovic's navel. He just wasn't able to dribble and shoot. We took him out of his game and won relatively easily.

Muggsy became the most popular American player in the games. They called him "the Little Black Giant." Everyone assumed that David Robinson would be our featured player, and if not him, then Kenny Smith. But whenever we had a press conference, there would always be a big crowd around Muggsy and a few stragglers talking to David.

David Robinson had a big reputation, but, in fact, when he was playing at the Naval Academy he very seldom played against people his size having his skills. Against that competition his size and natural skills had enabled him to dominate the game, but against players at this level he struggled. Just about every time he got the ball he would get fouled, but he wasn't strong enough to fight through the foul and get to the basket for the two points and a foul shot. From day one we had started working with him on faking with his upper body. We wanted him using head fakes and shoulder fakes and ball fakes to get the man guarding him in the air. But he had to learn to separate his lower body from his upper body, to make sure he kept his legs bent so if his guy went into the air he would have the power in his legs to go through that hit and score and get the opportunity for a three-point play. We worked him in practice every day on separating his upper and lower body and staying flexed. Even on games days we worked with him. Every player on the team watched us working with him. They knew how much we needed David if we were to have any chance at a medal.

In one of our preliminary games David got the ball underneath, made a great fake, and the defender went up into the air. He came down as David was going up. David got the basket and the foul. And our bench just exploded. Everybody jumped to their feet and started cheering. They knew how hard he had worked to make it look easy. I think that was one of the key moments in bringing the team together.

We opened against Brazil in the medal round, which was held in Madrid. Brazil was led by Oscar Schmidt, a 6'8" guard who was probably as good a pure shooter as anyone in the world. You had to pick up Oscar—Brazilians are always known by one name—at half-court because he'd shoot from anywhere. In international competition teams generally play a half-court game—they weren't used to teams playing full-court defense against them, and with five minutes left in the first half we were up by twenty-six. Late in the game we were just running out the clock. Steve Kerr was in. He saw an opening and started to drive to the basket. The defender guarding Charles Smith picked him up at the free throw line. Kerr went up in the air to pass to Smith. He saw the pass was covered so he started turning in the air—he landed wrong and went down. It was obvious right away that he was badly hurt. Injuries on the court are always ugly, whether it's one of your players or the opposition, but this was devastating. Steve had worked so hard for three years to transform himself into a star. He was poised for a great senior season, and to get hurt in that situation, when the game was essentially over, was just awful.

He had suffered a torn anterior cruciate ligament and severely damaged other ligaments in his right knee. It was a very serious injury. In the locker room the team doctor told him right away that he would be out for at least the next season—and warned him that he might never be able to play at this level again.

We played the Soviet Union for the championship. This was a team that had played together for several years in the European championships and the Olympics, led by Arvydas Sabonis. In the semifinals they had been down to Yugoslavia, but made an incredible comeback to win in the final few seconds. I'd left the game with a few minutes to go because I figured it was over. When Bobby Cremins came back and told me the Soviets had won, I didn't believe him. It wasn't until he showed me the box score that I was convinced it was true.

Our strategy against the Soviets was to take away the three-point shot. We picked up their shooters at least three feet beyond the three-point line. I told our perimeter players, "If somebody drives, don't pay a lick of attention to him; leave it to the post guys to pick him up. Stay with your man. The whole purpose of driving is to get you to leave your man, and then they're going to kick it out to him for a three-point shot. So don't come off him. These guys can shoot." We played well and were in control most of the game. We were up eighteen with 7:45 left in the game. But then the Soviets made a furious comeback. Sabonis started knocking down threes from anywhere on the court. Part of the reason they were able to come back was that without Steve Kerr I had to play our guards more minutes than they should have played, and they got tired near the end. They cut our lead to two points with fifty seconds on the clock, but Kenny Smith went over Sabonis for a layup, and we held on for an 87–85 win. We were the world champions!

When we were marching toward the stand to receive our medals, Charles Smith stopped me and said, "You know, the key to winning the gold was the loss to Argentina." To me, that was the absolutely perfect thing to say. I didn't tell him about having my fingers crossed when I'd made that statement.

The thrill of the world championship was tempered by the injury to Steve Kerr. The entire Arizona basketball community was stunned. They had all been through the terrible days of his father's murder; they had seen him grow from a serviceable player into a preseason All-America; the Steeeeeeeve Kerrrrrrr cheer had become part of the fun at the games; and he was the leader on and off the floor of a team that people believed had top-ten potential. Now there was a pretty good chance his basketball career was done.

We struggled throughout the 1986–87 season. Kenny Lofton and freshman Jud Buechler took Kerr's place at the point, but neither one of them was a true point guard. We finished 18–12, and only a game behind champion UCLA in the Pac-10 with a 13–5 record, but we could have been so much better. We blew leads late in the game eight times, and we lost four games by one or two points; nine of our losses were by less than five points. We were close, we were competitive, but we lacked the leadership and decision making that we needed. Too many times the wrong player had the ball at the end of the game. In an early-season game at UNLV, for example, we were up thirteen points and still lost 92–87, and Vegas went to the Final Four that year. So we were good, just not good enough. It's impossible to even guess how much better we would have been with Kerr. That was the season the NCAA instituted the three-point basket and he was our best three-point shooter.

After a couple of months of rehab, Steve Kerr was able to start shooting again. He had only limited mobility, but he was the first guy at practice every day, and after practice was over he'd stay until we forced him to leave. Scott Thompson, who had probably been the best shooter in the Big Ten his senior year at Iowa, worked with him. Scott was a good athlete but lacked quickness, so he had had to learn how to get his shot off quickly. He had to learn how to catch the ball in shooting position, and that's what he began working on with Steve. Traditionally, most right-handed shooters catch the ball with their left foot forward, then step into the shot with their right foot. It's catch, one step, two step, shoot. What we determined was that you could get your shot off much more quickly, and with better rhythm, if you use a jump-stop. We teach our players that when the pass is in the air, they are in the air. As the pass is in the air the player is actually off the floor; he catches it and lands in a jump-stop with his right foot slightly ahead of his left foot. There are several advantages here. When the player catches the ball, his legs are already flexed and ready to go into the shot. The player is already moving forward into the shot when he lands; he has already established his rhythm. And the fact that both feet hit simultaneously is a huge advantage, because either foot can then become the pivot foot. He can move either way without any kind of crossover step. We started that with Steve, who needed that extra split second to get his shot off, but now we require all our players to do it. We knew Steve was going to miss the entire season, but we were hopeful that he would regain complete mobility.

It was a difficult year in other ways, too. Any coach who tells you he gets along with every one of his players is not being truthful. It's human nature. When you get a group of people together, you're going to be more comfortable with some of them than with others. What makes coaching difficult is that you can't play everybody. You have a lot of talented players who want to play and think they should be playing and only a limited number of minutes to distribute. Every player we recruited had been a star in his high school or junior college program. None of them was used to sitting on the bench. So those who didn't get as much playing time as they thought they deserved were going to be unhappy. I always tried to be honest with my players. Years later, for example, my grandson, Matt Brase, who was a star in junior college, wanted to come to Arizona. I told him he would be welcome, but that he would be a scout team player; he wasn't going to get any meaningful playing time. He still wanted the experience of being part of our program. He came to Arizona and understood his role, and had that great experience.

There were times I told people they weren't going to get playing time, and if they wanted to play they should consider a different program. Some players did that. We felt Bruce Wheatley would benefit from an additional year, for example, so we asked him to redshirt. He didn't agree; he felt he should be playing more, so he decided to transfer. That was his decision. I offered to help him find the right place, and he eventually played for my former assistant, Ken Burmeister, who had become head coach at Texas-San Antonio.

It isn't always easy. We had one player who just didn't want to fit into the program. He insisted on doing things his way rather than the way I demanded they be done. So we butted heads a lot. I insisted the team dress appropriately when traveling, for example, and he had his own laid-back California style. Finally, when he intentionally broke Craig McMillan's nose in practice one day, I'd had enough. I left it up to the team whether he should stay on the team or be asked to leave. After practice one day they held a secret vote. They put slips of paper reading "yes" or "no" in a hat. I counted the votes and the next day this player was released from the team. He transferred to a California school.

But that season my biggest battles were with junior college transfer Tom Tolbert. Tolbert was . . . unique. Years later, when he was playing pro ball for the Golden State Warriors, he dyed his spiked hair bright white; with us he often wore any kind of wild clothing. My job was to make him accept structure and get the most out of his ability. Tom just wouldn't practice hard. He was good enough to play at his own pace and get by with it, but I wanted him to work a lot harder than he wanted to work. We'd been warned about that by his junior college coach at Cerritos Junior College, a friend of mine, Jack Bogdanovich. "The kid has a lot of ability. If you can just get him to play hard, he definitely can play for you." But no matter what I tried, he just didn't hustle. So we battled often and sometimes loudly. Tolbert could take it. And sometimes he'd give it back. When I wasn't on him, assistant coach Kevin O'Neill took my place. But Tolbert took everything we could give him.

There's a story he tells now that I never knew about at the time, but is pretty representative of our conflict. One day at the end of practice I had the team running outside around a mall area. It was about a mile and a half. "I was just beat," Tom recalls, "and I didn't want to run. There was a fountain on the mall. It was maybe a foot and a half deep, so while I was running I looked back to see if the coaches were watching. When I saw they were just talking, I ducked in the fountain and got all the way underwater except for my head. Our trainer was walking around making sure everybody was running and he saw me. 'Don't tell anybody,' I said. I waited until everybody came around again, then joined the pack. I made sure I was in the middle so they wouldn't notice my shoes were sopping wet. I thought they were going to notice that I was wet and figure I was really working hard, really sweating. But they didn't even notice."

That was perfect Tolbert. I remember one night during his senior year, his second year at Arizona, I went home and sat down with Bobbi.

When she asked me about practice, I told her, "You know, something was different today and I'm not really sure what it was." And then it dawned on me. "Oh, I know what it is. I didn't yell at Tolbert today." He still claims that if he played four years for me instead of two I might not have any hair left—but I like to remind him that he's not the only player I've yelled at and my hair is still there.

Kenny Lofton was another player with whom I had my share of disagreements. Maybe I had Roz's share, too. And Thompson's. Kenny felt I didn't let him shoot enough. There was a reason for that. Our game has always been based on percentages. I explained it to him, "You're shooting percentage is in the mid-thirties. When you can hit more than 50 percent on a shot, then you can shoot it. But it doesn't make sense for you to be taking more shots than someone shooting 50 percent right now, does it?"

By the end of his sophomore year it seemed obvious to me that he wasn't going to be able to play in the NBA. I know he would dispute that, but I had enough experience to be able to judge it. He couldn't be a point guard in that league, and he wasn't a good enough shooter. But he was a tremendous competitor and as quick as any player I had ever seen.

At the beginning of each season we have a team softball game. Kenny's speed on the baseball diamond was unbelievable. No matter where he was playing in the outfield, it seemed like he covered the field from foul line to foul line. If the ball was hit to the outfield, he could catch up to it. At bat, all he had to do was make contact and he was going to beat the play. So at the end of Kenny's sophomore season I had a conversation with Arizona's baseball coach, former major leaguer Jerry Kindall. The baseball team had won three national championships, the last one a year earlier. I told Jerry, "You guys really need to take a look at Kenny."

He worked out with the team on a Saturday. "Obviously he's got a lot to learn," Kindall told me. "He doesn't get the bat around on curve balls . . ." But he recognized his potential. The baseball team played sixty games a year, so baseball players miss more classes in one year than our kids do in four years. That first season Kenny played with the junior varsity, so he didn't have to travel. The following year he made the varsity, but didn't start. He was mostly a defensive replacement or a pinch runner. There were major-league scouts at all of our games and a lot of our practices and the Houston Astros loved the things he could do with speed. At the end of his junior year they drafted him in the seventeenth round. The NCAA allowed athletes to play professionally in one sport and remain eligible in another sport, so he played basketball with us his senior year. After playing A-ball the summer of 1988 he returned to school to get his degree. Two years later he was playing Triple A in Tucson. A year later he was in the big leagues to stay.

It worked out for him. As it turned out, his contract was larger than Sean Elliott's NBA contract. It took awhile, but our relationship ended up just fine.

I do get after players in practice. I tell players that I get on them because I care, but sometimes they don't see it that way. You can't make everybody happy. There have been players who didn't like me at all, that's one of the downsides of being a coach. But you can't compromise your standards to fit the needs of each individual player. Some players changed their views after they graduated and matured, but whatever they thought about me, they loved Bobbi.

Bobbi's role was easy to define. She did everything that needed to be done that I couldn't do. She was as soft as I was hard. No matter what was happening on the court, she was the Rock of Gibraltar of our program. Bobbi always cared. And she had the gift of knowing the right thing to say at the proper time. In another one of those terrible incidents, Joe Turner's first cousin was killed by a police officer. There had been a robbery in the area a couple of days earlier and the police were conducting an investigation. Turner's cousin was not a suspect, but the police reported that he was shot running away. This was the second person close to Joe Turner to be killed. As soon as he got the phone call he wanted to go home, but his mother insisted he stay in Tucson.

Bobbi provided the support he needed. As soon as she heard the news she went over to his dorm and read scripture with him. Just to give him some peace and inner strength. Then she made sure that the whole Wildcat family was there through what was really a tough time for him. She just wanted to make sure he wasn't alone.

She knew a lot more about the kids' lives off the court than I did. She didn't pry. She had raised five children, so she had a pretty good sense of when the kids were down and might need a lift. She knew when to step in and when to keep out. So when our players had personal problems they confided in her, not me. They called her Mrs. O or Mom O. Much of the time she didn't share that information with me, although if she heard me complaining about someone she might tell me to go a little easy on him, that his girlfriend just broke up with him or he was having problems with a professor.

As in every other college basketball program a lot of our players came from the inner city, where their families didn't have a lot of time to teach them etiquette. Bobbi decided that would be her job. Sometimes at dinner she would sit with the freshmen at the training table and point out little things to them, which fork to use, where to put your napkin. On occasion she would take the whole team out to a very nice restaurant. With this first group it was sort of a disaster. One night she was trying to explain to them which fork to use and they were picking up their food with their hands. For several players this was the first time they'd ever had lobster—and they thought that was the greatest experience they'd ever had. They loved the melted butter, and from that night on they would ask for it with whatever they were eating. Chicken, steak, just dip it in that butter.

On another occasion Bobbi and Kim, Roz's wife, took the team to Tucson's Plaza Hotel for a buffet. They spent quite a bit of time explaining all the basics and finally the kids were allowed to stand up and get into the plate line. One of the players stood up and held his napkin in his hand, wondering what he was supposed to do with it. I could tell he was confused. Finally, he just shrugged, stuck it into his back pocket like a handkerchief and got in line. I pointed him out to Bobbi, with this big white napkin hanging out of his pocket, and said, "Sometimes you just can't cover everything."

Bobbi was also concerned about the way the team dressed. She didn't try to set any rules, and she was never critical, but she would make sure the kids were dressed in a way that properly represented the program. She was hands-on: If a collar was up, she'd put it down, if a tie needed straightening, she would do it. She was always easy with compliments. This was her extended family, and it extended three decades.

The 1986–87 season ended with an overtime loss to UTEP in the first round of the NCAA tournament. Earlier in the season we'd lost to Utah at home, 68–67, and as we were coming off the court, Tom Tolbert had predicted this team was going to be in the Final Four. I wasn't happy with that at all. I don't think any coach likes his players making statements like that, particularly after a loss. But even just three games into his career at Arizona, Tolbert recognized that we had the talent to be very good. It just took a little longer than he thought it would.

In the 1987–88 preseason Associated Press poll we were ranked seventeenth, the first time Arizona had ever been given any preseason recognition. A lot of coaches like to keep a damper on expectations, but I was still trying to build support for our program. "We have no obvious weaknesses," I admitted. "We have great competition in preseason practices." I'm a big believer in making everything you do in practice competitive. I like to see winners and losers, and I like losing to have some sort of consequence, from running laps to extra shooting. At our practices the winning group drinks water, the losers run sprints. In previous years, though, there had been a substantial drop-off in the talent level between the starters and the reserves. That makes obvious sense. But this team was extremely competitive; the second team pushed the starters very hard from the very beginning.

It was a well-balanced team. Sean Elliott, Tom Tolbert, Anthony Cook, Craig McMillan, and Steve Kerr were the starters, and each of them could score. Joe Turner and Kenny Lofton came off the bench. But the key to this season was the return of Steve Kerr. He'd spent a year rebuilding his knee. In practice he looked great, but you really never know how well a player has come back from serious injuries until he's tested. If he could regain his mobility, he would give us the floor leadership—as well as a deadly three-point shooter—that we'd lacked.

It didn't take us long to find out how good we were. We opened at the Great Alaska Shootout, traditionally one of the toughest tournament fields, by beating Duquesne 133–78. That was the most points any Arizona team had ever scored. In the semifinal we crushed Michigan, the ninth-ranked team in the country. I always talk about a "slanted floor," meaning when we've got the ball the floor goes forty-five degrees downhill but when our opponents have the ball it is forty-five degrees uphill. Making that happen is the result of conditioning and execution. We slanted the floor against Michigan; we just ran their legs out from under them. Then we played Syracuse, the top-ranked team in America, a team with future pros Rony Seikaly, Derrick Coleman, and Sherman Douglas. After trailing most of the game, we came back to beat them 80–69 to win the tournament. After that championship the AP ranked us ninth, the highest ranking in Arizona history.

In early December we traveled to Iowa City to play Iowa. We'd played them in Tucson the previous season, they'd beaten us 89–80 on their way to thirty wins under new coach Tom Davis, but this was different. This was sort of a homecoming for me. I honestly didn't really know how I would be greeted, and I was probably a little nervous about it. Many people still felt I had betrayed them by leaving. And they hadn't forgotten Bobbi's quote about my having created a monster. But we had a lot of ties to Iowa. Fans never give up their seats there, so when I looked up, I knew I would see many familiar faces. We still had the friends we'd made while living there. Also, three of my children had married Iowa grads. As I told reporters, "My grandkids' baby gifts usually include black and gold shirts or pajamas." Even without that added emotional burden it was going to be a great game. We were 6–0 going in and ranked fourth, and Coach Tom Davis's Iowa team was also 6–0 and ranked third.

From the moment we got off the plane we were the focus of attention. As somebody said, when we walked through the airport the moppers stopped mopping, the ticker takers stopped taking, and security stopped securing. That was the reaction we got wherever we went.

Tom Davis's teams always pressed full court, so the day before the game we held a closed practice at Carver-Hawkeye Arena. Our practices are usually open, with people wandering around, but this time I wanted all the doors closed. We shut it down. Our scout team, the reserves, did a great job running Iowa's press against our starters. The starting team looked terrible; they couldn't beat the press. It was a bad practice, and I wondered if I was allowing all the hoopla about this homecoming to get to the team. Particularly after a reporter asked Steve Kerr, "Is this a typical practice the day before a game?"

Steve shook his head, "No way. You can tell Coach really wants this one more than he's ever wanted a game. Usually the assistants do some things. Not today. Coach O ran the whole practice."

The night before the game Bobbi and I got together with most of our close Iowa friends. These people were living there, they were part of the community, and even they wondered what the reaction would be when I walked into the arena. I told them, "If I know Iowa fans, they're going to be receptive when we come in, but as soon as the game gets going, they're going to be screaming their heads off for the Hawks. I know that once the ball goes up, I won't have to worry about the reaction." I said it as confidently as possible. The truth was that's what I hoped was going to happen.

Bobbi and I tried to pretend that this was just another basketball game, another one of the thousands we lived through together, but it wasn't. It had a deep personal meaning—as well as being a national event. It was perfect for the media: The number-four team in the country was playing number three, the team he used to coach, in a game played in the arena he helped get built.

Admittedly, I was uptight in the locker room before we took the court. Finally, it was time. As I walked out onto the court the Iowa fans started cheering. They didn't just yell, they cheered, "Lute. Lute. Lute." It was a wonderful welcome home. Deep down I'd believed that would be the reaction, but you never know. I was thrilled. Absolutely thrilled.

The game definitely lived up to the anticipation. It was as intense as any game in which I've ever been involved. There were a lot of great players on the court that night. The only time the crowd got a little testy was at the end of the first half. Iowa's Jeff Moe was a superintense player; he was one of those players who pumped his fist to encourage the crowd after a great play. On the last possession of the first half Steve Kerr knocked down a three-pointer at the buzzer right in Jeff Moe's face. Steve was never a showboating type, he wasn't going to pump his fist, but as the two teams were leaving the court he went alongside Jeff and made the motion. Just what Jeff Moe would have done. He didn't touch him, he just made that pumping motion. When the crowd saw that, they got all over Steve. Throughout the entire second half every time he touched the ball they would start booing. It didn't seem to bother him at all; in fact, he was such a tough competitor it probably made him focus even more.

The game was close all the way. We had very little difficulty beating their press. Our reserves were really happy about that. They were telling each other that they had run Iowa's press in practice better than Iowa was running it. We were leading by a few points most of the second half, but with about four minutes to go, Sean Elliott fouled out. I didn't complain about the calls, but he certainly didn't get any breaks. That was a real problem for us because he was our leading scorer and essential to the way we attacked their press. But Jud Buechler came off the bench and played big for us. With time running out, Iowa had to start fouling, and obviously the smartest thing to do is foul the player coming off the bench cold. Jud knocked down four straight free throws and we held on to beat them 66–59. But when the game was over I think we all agreed we didn't want to do that again. It was just too emotionally draining.

Ten days later the polls named us the number-one team in the country. Number one! I told the kids that it was nice, that it was something we'd worked for and earned, but that it really didn't mean anything unless we were number one at the end of the season. I told them that, but it did mean something. It meant that in five years we had built a nationally recognized program. It feels good to be number one. Good? It's tremendous. This was a very big deal for a small city like Tucson. Nothing like this had ever happened before. The players were like rock stars. Everywhere they went people wanted their autographs. Tickets were already hard to get, now they became impossible. Having a ticket to the game became a status symbol. People were calling the athletic department and offering to pay just about any price for tickets, only to be told that there were no tickets at any price.

The entire city embraced the team. The rest of the country was looking forward to March Madness; in Tucson we were in the middle of December Madness. If people couldn't get into the game they watched on TV or listened on the radio. One couple postponed their wedding—twice—to avoid a conflict with one of our games. Charity dinners were moved to different dates. Supposedly babies were named after our players. Our home games had become civic events. Bobbi would get to McKale about a half hour before tip-off. The pep band would let everyone know she was there by shouting, "Hi, Bobbi." She'd smile at them and give them a little wave, then she would work her way up to her seat in section 16, stopping along the way to talk to everybody as if they were her best friend, even those few people she'd never met before.

A week after being named the number-one team in the country we played undefeated and ninth-ranked Duke in the Fiesta Bowl Classic in Tucson. This was a real test for us: the great Duke tradition against our suddenly successful program. It seemed like from the very beginning of the game Duke Coach Mike Krzyzewski was on the officials. In the Atlantic Coast Conference he's known for working the refs to his advantage, but in Tucson he was less successful. The game was another close one, but we held on to the lead. At one point their All-American, Danny Ferry, ended up standing at the sideline near our bench. He said something like "Nice hometown refs."

"Just play the game," I told him. Our trainer, Steve Condon, said pretty much the same thing.

Then from the other end of the court Coach Krzyzewski yelled to me, "Don't you yell at my players."

That's when it started. Krzyzewski and I started yelling at each other. I really got angry. The officials brought us together to try to settle this dispute, but instead I got even more upset. I'm the stoic coach, the one who doesn't get ruffled, who maintains his composure, but this time I lost my temper. For a team like Duke that does not get a lot of fouls called against them at home to complain about officiating was absolutely ridiculous. Now, I will tell you I don't curse. I'll say "Dang" or "Bull-loni!" or "Judas Priest." I'll yell at people, but I don't curse at them. But there are people who were there that night who will tell you I did curse. Danny Ferry and Steve Kerr later played professional ball together and became close friends—and Ferry apparently continues to insist that I cursed that night while Kerr defends me.

For the record, Danny, I don't curse.

Also for the record, we beat Duke 91–85.

Since then, I've gotten to know Coach K. We're both on the Nike Consulting Staff and we both work at Michael Jordan's Fantasy Camp most summers. Even when we're working, his cell phone is constantly ringing. He's always getting calls to do commercials or make an appearance somewhere. One day I just shook my head and told him, "You know, Mike, it's really getting a little ridiculous. Even here at fantasy camp you're getting all the calls."

As the number-one team in the country we were getting a tremendous amount of publicity, nationally as well as locally. It's fun and very satisfying to see your team on the cover of *Sports Illustrated,* but Tucson is larger than Iowa City, so Bobbi and I were able to maintain our privacy. My own public image had been pretty well shaped by this time; I was the guy with the white hair that never moved, who dressed impeccably and demanded perfection. Reporters wanted to know more about me; they wanted to know what I was really like behind the locker room door. So I think they were surprised when Steve Kerr told them, "Despite his heroin addiction, he's doing well for himself."

What made this team special was that it was a team in the purest sense of the word. Every player, whether he was playing regularly or not, was supportive of every other player. This was a team in which the reserves actually became known nationally. They were an unusual group known as the Gumbys.

The original Gumby was a green animated clay figure who had his own TV show in the 1950s. He looked sort of like a gingerbread man, but he could be bent in any direction and he never got any respect. The name had been given to the reserves who didn't play very much a couple years earlier by Bruce Fraser. The starting players and key reserves, particularly the stars, are always going to get a lot of publicity, but the scout team works as hard as anybody on the squad and we've always pushed the media to feature them. At Iowa, a local TV station did a special about our scout team, which we called the F Troop—after the bumbling cavalry in the TV show—and people who deserved recognition received it. But that was nothing compared to what happened with the Gumbies at Arizona, the group who caused the NCAA to institute new rules for behavior on the bench.

Fraser was our first Gumby. One afternoon Q, as Fraser was known, and Steve Kerr were shopping in a mall and Q had bought a little rubber Gumby. Q related Gumby to his own situation. Like just about everybody else on our squad, he had been a star in high school—our roster was a collection of all-city and all-state and Mr. Name-Your-State Basketball—but for some reason when he got to us he had problems shooting. That kept him on the bench. Rather than sulking about it, or complaining, he accepted his role on the team. He set an example for everyone else. He worked hard in practice, didn't complain, and rooted for his teammates. He didn't get a lot of meaningful minutes, but when he did get in a game he had the whole arena rooting for him.

Before each game Q would stick his rubber Gumby figure in his sock. For good luck. The only person who knew about it was his best friend, Kerr. One night we were playing Washington State in Pullman, Washington. It was about 30 degrees outside, and he'd been sitting on the bench for two hours. I put him in the last minute of the game. When you've been sitting that long it's tough to get loose, you kind of run up and down stiff-legged. Q tried to take a shot and got knocked down. As he fell, this little rubber Gumby came bouncing out. The ref looked at him with disbelief. "That's mine," Q said, sticking it back in his sock.

I didn't notice it. Even if I had, I wouldn't have known what it was. I missed the original Gumby era. After Fraser graduated in 1987 I'd hired him as a graduate assistant coach, and he started referring to the scout team as Gumbys. They began to take pride in the name. They took a situation that could have been a negative and turned it into a positive.

When local reporters wondered where this nickname had come from, Fraser explained, "We're the Gumbys because we do whatever Coach wants us to do. He bends us this way, he bends us that way. In practice we pretend we're Iowa, or USC. We're just disposable and totally manipulated. We're the Gumbys."

"We do get abused," Mark Georgeson said. "We get no calls in the practices. But it's a good experience. Everyone should be a Gumby at least once."

They were also good. The Gumbies consisted of Harvey Mason, Matt Muehlebach, Jud Buechler, Sean Rooks, Craig Bergman, Mark Georgeson, and Brian David. There were future pros sitting on the bench. In practice Q would often scrimmage with the scout team. Some of these players could have transferred and played elsewhere, but the team spirit was so strong that nobody did. These people could play. When they scrimmaged the starters, they won a reasonable share of the games. They took a lot of pride in that. In fact, after we had beaten USC, Coach

George Raveling said that our second team probably would have finished second in the Pac-10. Starters couldn't be Gumbys. There's a classic photograph taken minutes after Sean Elliott fouled out of the Iowa game: There he was with the Gumbys on the bench, waving a towel, looking like he belonged, like he wanted to be part of the Gumbys.

After games in which they hadn't played I always gave them some extra work in practice. I wanted them to get extra wind and keep up. If we needed them, I wanted to make certain they would be prepared to play. The players referred to these scrimmages as "Gumby Classics."

Their participation wasn't limited to our practices. During the game they were our loudest cheerleaders. They would be standing up and yelling encouragement and waving towels. They even developed several choreographed moves, if Kerr hit a three-pointer they would move one way; when Sean Elliott dunked they would do something else. They had a whole routine. A local sportswriter heard about the Gumby Classics and wrote a piece about the Gumbys. It really caught on in Tucson. People started rooting for them to get into the games. Somebody made Gumby T-shirts, we had fans coming to the games dressed in complete Gumby costumes. When we got to be number one, Dick Vitale mentioned them on TV, *Sports Illustrated* wrote about them, and it became a national phenomenon. Mattel, the toy company, began sending us boxes of merchandise; Gumby heads, Gumby underwear, Gumby shampoo bottles. It was fun, but I wanted to make sure we didn't lose focus on what really mattered, which was winning basketball games. Obviously in direct response to the Gumbys, after the season the NCAA passed several rules restricting conduct on the bench. Players could only stand up for a certain amount of time, they couldn't wave towels, they instituted a list of do's and don'ts to insure that the bench didn't detract from the play on the court.

A year earlier the Chicago Bears football team had recorded a video, so we had our own theme song. Harvey Mason's father was an established musician, and Harvey had inherited his love for music. And his talent. He'd been writing songs his whole life. A local radio DJ, Mike Elliott, asked him to collaborate on a song about the team. Harvey wrote the music and Elliott wrote most of the words for "Wild About the Cats," which Harvey produced. It was a soft rap song in which the players talked their lines between the chorus. Steve Kerr, for example, promised, "I'll drill it in from three-point land," while Craig McMillan sang, "I'd better find the open man and get the ball down low."

While a critic commented, "It's not exactly a masterpiece; or, for that matter, a minorpiece," the city loved it. It was played all the time on the most popular radio station. It was a big hit, number one in Tucson. Even our band started playing it at our games. For Harvey Mason it was the first hit in what was to eventually become a wonderful career in music—he has written and produced for many of the top performers in the music business—and for us it added to the wonderful spirit of the season.

For a coach it was a dream season. This was a team capable of executing the offense exactly the way it was supposed to be done, while still playing very good defense. When you're in the middle of something like that, you try to keep it going, make whatever adjustments are necessary on the court, and make sure you maintain control of everything that happens off the court. With success and the ensuing celebrity comes a lot of temptations, not all of them positive. I just made sure they stayed focused on their job.

But even a dream season like this one has its bumps. After beating Duke we lost our first game of the season to New Mexico by two points. Then we won eight more in a row and lost at Stanford. Those were our only two losses of the regular season. We finished 31-2, winning the Pac-10 conference title and the postseason tournament. In a season of great moments one of the rare unpleasant events came when we visited Arizona State at the end of the regular season. The rivalry between us and ASU was intense. Before I got to Tucson ASU had beaten the Wildcats regularly, but in the past few years we'd done very well against them. And the fact that we were a nationally ranked team made the rivalry even stronger. While we were warming up before the game a group of . . . Call them whatever you want, but these people began taunting Steve Kerr about the assassination of his father. They yelled despicable things at him, obviously trying to destroy his concentration. It was more than disgusting. Several of our players had to be restrained from going into the stands after the hecklers. Clearly these people affected the team: Steve Kerr hit his first seven shots, six of them three-pointers. We shot an incredible 75 percent in the first half, setting the school record, and we beat them 101-73.

We'd been eliminated in the first round of the NCAA tournament the three previous seasons. A few of the local sportswriters were starting to blame me for those losses in the early rounds. Sometimes they wrote that I couldn't coach, other times they wrote that I overcoached. Years later I would be criticized for losing early-round games to lower seeds, but here I was getting criticized for losing to higher seeds. Nobody enjoys being criticized, but I understood that it's part of every coach's job. What I didn't like was being criticized unfairly. This was our fourth consecutive appearance in the tournament. Our seniors had earned an invitation to the tournament every year, an amazing accomplishment. Believe me, I didn't like losing to anybody in any round. I didn't like losing a meaningless game against a team nobody ever heard of in Italy, so you can just imagine how I felt losing in the Big Dance. Those first few seasons I knew the reality was that we weren't good enough to win it all, but that never stopped me from believing we could win. Once you begin to accept the possibility of defeat, you're on your way to being defeated. But this season was different. We had won thirty-one games. We were 17–1 in the conference. We'd gone 5–0 against teams from the Big Ten. We knew we were capable of beating any team in the country.

Our first-round opponent was Cornell, a team we knew we knew we should beat easily, but we treated that game no differently than if we were playing UCLA, Duke, or Iowa. We got game films. The assistants broke down their offensive and defensive tendencies and scouted their players, and by the time our kids took the court they knew what to expect from their opponent. Right-handed, left-handed, likes to drive, good pull-up jumper, always goes to his left, puts the ball on the ground before shooting, poor three-pointer shooter—they knew how many points per game each player scored, how many rebounds he got and fouls he committed. Was he a good defender? Was his first step quick? What were each player's strengths and weaknesses?

We were the number-one seed in the West. In that opening-round game we beat Cornell by forty. So much for the first-round problems. Then we played Seton Hall, led by 6'9" 250-pound Mark Bryant. On TV broadcasters Billy Packer and Jim Nantz both were saying Seton Hall had a real good chance to upset Arizona. Bryant was big and strong, but we were so much quicker and better balanced. We beat them by twenty-nine points to move into the Sweet Sixteen in Seattle.

Ironically, we played Iowa in the West regional. They tried to press us again, but we were just too quick for them. This time we beat them by twenty points to move into the Elite Eight. That set up a confrontation with Dean Smith's 27–6 North Carolina Tar Heels for a spot in the Final Four. The Tar Heels were loaded; they had J. R. Reid, Scott Williams, Rick Fox. They were second seed, but they were still favored. Supposedly, their tough inside game would prevent us from running. People still believed the best West Coast teams weren't as good as the best East Coast teams.

I don't remember if I took the time to think about the fact that I was coaching against Dean Smith, a man I'd respected for so long and who had had such a profound influence on my own coaching philosophy. Dean Smith was never afraid to try something new, something different: He created the four corner-offense, and at the beginning of his career he actually substituted five players at a time. He was one of the true innovators in college basketball. It was from Dean Smith that I learned it was okay to try new methods of coaching, but before this game I probably didn't think about any of that. The thing about the tournament is that everything happens so fast there is no time for anything except work. I certainly didn't pause to savor our early-round victories; as soon as one game ended we got busy preparing for the next game. I didn't even have the time to think about Al McGuire's elevator advice, to take time to enjoy the moment.

The North Carolina game was a good old-fashioned heavyweight toe-to-toe brawl. We battled for every point. At halftime we trailed 28-26, only the second time in the whole season that we'd been behind at the half. One of the great things about our team was that any one of our starters could step up and make the difference. We took whatever was available. In our opening game against Cornell, Tom Tolbert had injured his back so badly that we weren't sure he'd be ready to play for the rest of the tournament. While he played, he obviously was hampered. In the first half against North Carolina he managed only one basket, one free throw, and one rebound. At the end of halftime I took him aside and asked him flatly, "Tom, do you really want to go to the Final Four?"

"Yes," he said. "Yes, sir."

"Then prove it."

In the second half the endless battles we'd fought in practice paid off. In the first fourteen minutes of the second half Tolbert personally outscored North Carolina 16-12. We won by 70-52, holding the Tar Heels to only twenty-four points in the half. We were going to Kansas City to play for the national championship.

When the buzzer sounded, the kids started celebrating at midcourt. But I stood in front of our bench, looking up to the stands, waiting for Bobbi to make her way down to the floor. This was our victory. I didn't know it at the time, but the network had focused its cameras on us. Bobbi finally made it through the cheering crowd to the court, and, for an instant, we just looked at each other. Both of us knew how much it had taken to get us to this moment. I was stunned to see her on the court; she never, ever, had done that before. I can close my eyes and still see her standing there, wearing a black and white outfit, with a cat face on the front of it. I took her in my arms, lifted her off her feet, and twirled her around, then kissed her. As millions of people watched, we danced round and round.

I think what surprised me most was how many people saw Bobbi and me dancing. For years afterward people would tell us they had seen it and how good it had made them feel. And when we went out recruiting, it was amazing how many mothers commented on it to me.

In the locker room after the game the team had one objective: to muss up my hair. The whole team, the starters and the Gumbys, came after me. It was, as everything had been that entire season, a team effort. If that's what they wanted to do, they had earned that right. The truth is, I have a full head of white hair, it's all natural, and when I comb it into place it stays there. I don't use stickum on it. The team did a fine job messing it up—and when they were done, I brushed it back into place and it looked like it hadn't been touched.

In the postgame press conference Dean Smith was asked how it felt to come so close to the Final Four and not get to go. Dean smiled, then said, "Well, look at this way. We came closer to Arizona than anybody else in the tournament. We only lost by eighteen."

That night I went right back to work with my assistant coaches. We were going to play the University of Oklahoma in the semifinals. Coach Billy Tubbs's Sooners had finished the season as the top-ranked team in the country, and we were right behind them. We were the only two teams in the nation with more than thirty wins. In the other semifinal game Duke was playing the University of Kansas.

You expect that dream seasons will have dream endings. Then you confront reality. There are so many things that can go wrong in any game; one unlucky bounce of the basketball and all the planning and practicing makes no difference. Some nights the ball goes in the basket, and other nights the same shot hits the rim and bounds away. This just wasn't our night. Oklahoma was able to dominate inside and led 39–27 at halftime. Our problem was that Steve Kerr was having a poor shooting night. He missed his first shot, a long jumper from the corner, and could never really get going. Steve was a great shooter. That season he had set the still unbeaten school record by hitting 57 percent of his three-point shots. For his entire career he hit 55 percent of all his attempts. But not that night. That night he hit only two of twelve three-point attempts, he was two of thirteen from the field. Steve always said it was like there was a lid on the basket. Shots that looked like they were in just rattled out. When you look at tapes of the game his mechanics seemed no different from any other game, but the ball just wouldn't fall. Even Sean Elliott's thirty-one points and eleven rebounds weren't enough, as we lost to Oklahoma 86–78.

I've spent most of my adult life in locker rooms, but I don't think I've ever been in a locker room that was as sad as our locker room after that game. I think we were absolutely shocked that we'd lost. There wasn't one person there who didn't believe that if we went out and played them again the next day we wouldn't have beaten them. It was a very emotional scene; a lot of people had tears in their eyes. I did something that I hadn't done before, and the whole team joined together for a great hug. Some of the players remember it as the first time since they'd been at Arizona that I completely let down all the barriers, one of the few times I'd expressed an emotion not directly related to basketball or school.

Maybe so.

All losses hurt, but some losses do hurt more than others. Every coach reacts differently to a loss in a big game—anger, frustration, depression—but we all hurt. Some people just hide it better than others. For some of us the feeling is a lot more than a personal disappointment; it's like you've let down people who were depending on you. The old saying is, it's only a game. For most people it is, and the next day they'll get back into their normal routine. They won't forget about it, but they'll put it aside. But when that game has been your life as long as basketball had been Bobbi's and my life and our job, then it's a lot more than that. A lot more.

The press conference after the game was difficult. Anytime you've got a real chance to win the national championship—and this team was capable of that—then losing just has to tear your heart out. That's the most difficult thing about this tournament, you're not allowed one slipup. This was a painful loss. The last thing I wanted to do was talk about it. These press conferences are not something I particularly enjoy, but they are a requirement of the job. So I went and I answered all the questions, but at the end the result was still the same: Oklahoma 86, Arizona 78.

This was one night that Bobbi didn't give me a time frame in which to get over the loss.

I spent a lot of time trying to figure out why Steve Kerr had such a rough shooting night, because he never even had a bad practice. He was that consistent as a shooter. But there was one thing that was different that night: His mother was at the game. The Kerr family had been good friends with King Hussein of Jordan, who had been educated at the American University in Beirut. After Malcolm Kerr had been assassinated Anne Kerr had been transferred to the American University in Egypt. When we reached the Final Four, King Hussein contacted her and graciously offered to fly her to the game on one of his planes. As an example of how crazy things can be with NCAA regulations, we were later investigated to see if Mrs. Kerr's acceptance of this trip was a violation of the rules. If King Hussein had been an Arizona booster, we probably would have been hit with a three-year penalty.

This was one of the very few games in Steve's entire career that she was able to attend. I coached Steve for five years and I never saw him have an off day shooting, so I have to believe that the fact that his mother was at the game affected his performance. I think he was trying so hard to have a perfect game for his mother. After he missed his first few shots the pressure just grew and grew. Shooting is as much mental as physical; sometimes it seems like a great player can almost will the ball into the basket, and I think Steve's desire was so strong that it took him out of his natural game.

It had been a memorable season. Sean Elliott was honored as our first consensus All-American, Steve Kerr had made the AP's All-American second team and was also named the U.S. Basketball Writer's Most Courageous Athlete, and I received several Coach of the Year honors. Also for the first time, pro scouts started talking to Sean Elliott and Steve Kerr. Today that sounds obvious—considering that more than thirty Wildcats who played for me have been drafted by the NBA. Since the draft was shortened to only two rounds in 1989 we lead the nation in draft picks—but not at that time. At that time players didn't come to Arizona to prepare to play pro basketball. It wasn't really part of their thinking. Our kids were really impressed that Sean might play pro ball. They used to sit in the back of the bus telling him that after he made the pros he'd have to come back to see the team play.

"I don't know if I'm going to make it to the NBA," he told them honestly. He really didn't know how good he was going to be. None of us did. For a short time after that season he considered coming out early, leaving school to play pro ball, but eventually decided against it.

In the past several Arizona players had been drafted; Pete Williams had gone in the fourth round, Eddie Smith was a seventh-round pick. But after the 1988 season both Tom Tolbert and Steve Kerr were second-round selections. The odd thing was that Steve Kerr's serious knee injury actually proved beneficial to him and to us. Without Steve Kerr that season there was no way in the world we would have gotten to the Final Four. And I don't believe that he would have gotten a chance to play in the NBA had we not gone to the Final Four. That gave people a chance to see how good he was—even if he did have a poor shooting night against Oklahoma. And I don't believe we would have gotten to the Final Four a year earlier, in what would have been his senior year, even if he had been able to play. We had a very young team, and they simply were not ready for prime time. It's strange to say that an injury proved to be so lucky, but in this one case it did.

At the end of that season we also lost assistant coach Ricky Byrdsong, who left to become head coach at Detroit Mercy College. Everyone who had come into contact with Ricky loved him, although there was that one time when I came into contact with him and we ended up arguing. In practice one afternoon I was demonstrating a high pick-and-roll. Ricky was defending the player I was using as a pick. I rolled off the pick, my shoulder just touching his shoulder, and Ricky stepped out to guard me. Ricky was moving as I hit him and we both went down. I fell right on top of him. I didn't think it was funny; I treated practice seriously. "That's a charge," Ricky called out, putting his palm to the back of his head, the official's signal for a charge.

"It's not a charge," I yelled at him. "You were moving. That's a foul." Ricky didn't back down. We had a real argument. That's a charge. No, it isn't, it's a block. You don't know . . . We were like two kids arguing on a playground, and the players stood silent, astonished at what was going on. And trying very hard not to laugh.

It was impossible to stay mad at Ricky, though. He was one of those people who was always smiling, and to whom things just kept happening. Ricky was forgetful. I don't know how many times he flew out of Tucson without his driver's license or credit cards. His wife, Sherialyn, who coached our woman's team, often had to put whatever he'd forgotten on the next plane so he could rent a car. When we play Oregon State, we stay outside Eugene at a place called the Valley River Inn. On the day of the game we take a bus into Corvallis, where the game is played. After the pregame shootaround we'd go to a nearby hotel, have our meal, and get dressed for the game. One afternoon I was in my room in the hotel when I got a panicked call from Ricky. "Coach, do you have an extra pair of dress shoes with you? I left mine back at the Inn." Ricky took great pride in his appearance. He was always well dressed. Of course, he also had huge feet, at least a size 13, maybe larger.

I explained that I'd brought only one pair with me. "Why don't you just wear your white tennis shoes?" He couldn't do that, he said; he was wearing a black pinstriped business suit to the game and tennis shoes would look ridiculous. I suggested he call George Kalil. George is a large man; he wears a size 16EEE shoe. "They're like boats," I said. "But don't worry about it, nobody's going to notice."

As it turned out George did have an extra pair of shoes. After trying them on, Ricky called me back. "I can't wear these things," he said. "They're like boats on my feet."

"Look," I said, "they're better than white tennis shoes. Wear a few extra pairs of socks and nobody'll notice." When he finally knocked on my door I couldn't help looking down. It was almost as if he was wearing oversized clown shoes. I kept a straight face and said, "Oh, they look great."

"You don't think anybody'll notice?" he asked again.

"Absolutely not," I reassured him.

It was a tradition at that time that the players would be waiting for the coaches in the lobby. As we walked through, they would get up and head for the bus. Ricky was walking with me, trying to stay far enough ahead of the team so that they couldn't see his shoes. It worked for a few seconds, then Kerr asked loudly, "Hey, Bigfoot, where you going?"

Ricky glared at me. I shrugged. "Don't worry. Nobody else'll notice."

Generally what happens before a game is that the assistant who has scouted our opponent stays in the locker room while we warm up and writes down the points we want to cover about our opponent on the chalkboard. Ricky hadn't scouted Oregon State, but he decided to stay in the locker room. Finally, just before the game he came out and took his seat on the bench. I'm sure Ricky thought he had gotten away with it. But as the starting players made their way out to center court, Booker Turner, one of the best referees in NCAA history, came over to our bench. The entire arena was watching him to see what was going on. He stopped in front of Ricky, I think he pointed at his feet, and told him, "Ricky, make sure you keep those boats out of my way!"

There was also a very serious side to Ricky. Tucson did not have a very large African-American population. Some of our kids, who had grown up in the inner city, felt left out. Ricky and Sherialyn would invite them to their home, throw little parties, to make sure they felt welcome. Ricky was always there for them. For some of our players Ricky and Sherialyn's friendship made a tremendous difference in their adjustment to the University of Arizona and the city of Tucson. Ricky made people welcome.

But Ricky was leaving, and so were Steve Kerr and Tom Tolbert. These were three people who had helped establish the program. They had done an amazing job. We were a national powerhouse, number two in the country. The only thing we hadn't accomplished during that period was win the national championship.

As the 1988–89 season began we believed we had a great shot at that championship.

7

I never set out to become a bobble-head doll. My dream growing up was to coach basketball. What I didn't anticipate was the celebrity that came with success. The media attention I got both at Iowa and Arizona has led to a tremendous amount of opportunities. I've turned down many more than I've accepted. Believe it or not, I'm not particularly comfortable making public appearances off the court, but I have done a great variety of things that seemed to make sense. I've done everything from bank commercials to bobble-head dolls.

I think many people would agree that there is too much commercialism in college athletics, but the reality is that with gender equality in scholarships and skyrocketing costs in every aspect of a major college basketball program, you're just not going to be able to continue to compete successfully without corporate support unless you're one of the heavily endowed universities or accept funding from the state, which we have not done. As in any business, and college sports is a big business, our costs rise every year. At most schools the revenue generated by the major sports, primarily basketball and football, has to pretty much support the entire university athletic program. At Arizona that's nineteen sports. The expenses and revenues of the basketball program are only part of the overall athletic budget, and our success helps support those sports programs that lose money. That's the way it works. Our basketball program has a yearly income of slightly more than $16 million, which, according to *The New York Times,* is the highest income of any team to make the 2006 NCAA tournament. Even then it takes a tremendous effort on the part of our athletic director, Jim Livengood, and his staff to keep the athletic program in the black.

The odd thing is that the more success you have as a basketball coach, the less time you actually have to coach basketball. Anyone in a position like mine knows that for every hour spent on the court I probably spend twenty hours doing other things for the good of the program, including public relations, charity work, and recruiting. That's in addition to the increased responsibility that coaches now have for their players twenty-four hours a day.

I've always done as much as made sense to help raise the profile of our program. If in addition it enabled me to earn some additional money, there's certainly nothing wrong with that. Unlike professional teams, the only relatively permanent person in a university sports program is the head coach. Players graduate, assistant coaches leave for other jobs, but the head coach stays for the longest time, and if the program is successful he becomes the best-known member of the team.

This is how I became a bobble-head doll. Alltel, a cell phone company that had been a great supporter of the program, asked my permission to put out the doll as a promotional item. The sample they showed me had my white hair and was wearing a navy blazer. I admit it, the first time you touch your own bobble-head, there is an urge to kind of bobble your head, but I didn't do it. I knew my grandchildren would love it, and I suspected at least a few of my former players wouldn't mind shaking that head. It actually turned out to be nice, for a bobble-head. Alltel gave away some of them while many others that I've autographed have been auctioned off at all kinds of fund-raisers. I checked eBay in early 2006, and at that time there were 532 bobble-head dolls being auctioned off. None of them were mine. However, Rick Pitino's bobble-head was going for $24.

I've also done several local TV commercials. When I first got to Tucson a luxury-car dealer asked me to do their ads. However, another dealer was loaning cars to the university, so I wouldn't do a commercial for his competition. I did, however, become the spokesperson for the automobile dealers association, so I was representing all of the car dealers in Tucson. I was the spokesperson for a paint company and for Sparkle Dry Cleaners, "The cleaners for particular people." I also did public service announcements for a beverage distributor to encourage responsible drinking, but the commercials that attracted the most attention were a series I did with then-Arizona State coach Bill Frieder for the Valley National Bank, which later became Bank One. Frieder is . . .

Frieder is . . . really difficult to describe. He can't sit still for a second. He's very bright, has a great business mind; he's a card counter, so he's not permitted to bet in the casinos in Las Vegas. And he was a fine basketball coach, too.

The bank approached me first. I reminded them that there is such a competitive relationship between us and ASU that the people in Tempe might not do business with the bank if I was in their commercials. They then suggested Frieder and I do the spots together. Most of them were pretty funny. I was the straight guy; it turns out that was a role I was born to play. I'm Norwegian. Frieder was not the straight guy, also a role he was born to play.

The commercials were so popular that when Frieder and I were recruiting the same kids during his home visits, he would show them the commercials. When I asked him why he was doing that, he admitted, "I have to have something I can sell."

We stopped doing the commercials when Frieder was fired in 1997, but people still ask both of us when we'll be doing more of them.

The corporate relationship that has proved beneficial to the university has been my relationship with Nike. I'm an original member of the Nike Consulting Staff, and the university is one of the few schools with a head-to-toe Nike program. Nike provides all the equipment for each of our nineteen intercollegiate sports teams, men's and women's, and they pay us for that exclusivity. That's a huge saving for our program. Huge. A pair of quality sneakers can cost as much as $120, and our players go through at least six pairs a season. I remember when I started coaching there were two types of sneakers: high-tops and low-tops. Now there is a sneaker built specifically, not just for every sport, but even for the different positions. They make shoes for guards that allow for a lot of cutting, or shoes for the bigger players that support more weight. Years ago there was a shoe designer, and the only options for the consumer were what size and color to buy. Now there are shoe engineers. All of the major sports equipment manufacturing companies, and not just Nike, use computers to design sneakers that provide the necessary support.

I know some people complain about the close relationship between corporations and university athletic programs, but it's a fact of collegiate sports life, and, properly supervised, these relationships are mutually beneficial. And for colleges, at least, extremely important.

I don't really enjoy doing commercials. I admit it, I'm not a natural actor. In fact, some people might describe my acting ability in those commercials as wooden. Of course, a few of my former players have described it as "cement." I'm always comfortable speaking in public about basketball because that's the subject on which I have expertise. Ask me about a zone defense and I can talk for hours. But for some reason I can never really explain—particularly to myself—I once accepted an invitation to make a motivational speech at the America West Arena in Phoenix. Among the other speakers were Zig Ziglar, certainly one of the most popular motivational speakers in America, and former British prime minister Margaret Thatcher. We sold out the arena, as well as the convention center next door, where it was broadcast on closed circuit.

I can't imagine what I was thinking when I accepted this invitation. Even in the privacy of the locker room I'm not a dynamic speaker. I don't want my team charging out the door screaming; I want them to be calm, determined, and confident. So standing in front of 20,000 people who were there to be motivated made me extremely nervous. In my speech I emphasized the same things I teach my players: Be well prepared, work hard, and work with other people, and if you do that, good things will happen. I probably quoted Teddy Roosevelt, who said, "It is not the critic that counts; not the man who points out how the strong man stumbles or where the doer of deeds could have done them better. The credit belongs to the man who is actually in the arena, whose face is marred by dust and sweat and blood . . . who at the worst, if he fails, at least fails while daring greatly." And "Far better it is to dare mighty things, to win glorious triumphs even though checkered by failure, than to rank with those poor spirits who neither enjoy nor suffer much, because they live in the gray twilight that knows not victory nor defeat."

At a basketball clinic I'm speaking to my peers; even if they don't speak English, they all speak basketball. In my career I've conducted at least three hundred clinics all over the world, all through Europe, Asia, Australia, and North and South America. I think the first clinics I gave were in Australia in 1986, right after we'd won the world championship. When I conduct a clinic, one of the first things I tell the coaches in the audience is that I don't want them to fill notebooks with the things I say. What I want to do is make them think about their own philosophy of coaching and maybe come away with one or two ideas that would be valuable to them. I always finish my presentation by telling the audience if they are ever in the states to please let me know, because they are welcome to come to Tucson. That's where I learned a very important lesson: If you invite an Australian he's going to come.

Within months after that first clinic the head coach of the Australian National Team and his family came to Arizona, as did the head coaches from the Melbourne area, the Sydney area, Canberra, and Brisbane. We had the head woman's coach come, the assistant woman's coach, the head coaches from the youth basketball programs in each of their states and territories; we had club team coaches. At least twenty coaches came, many of them with their spouses. That was twenty years ago, and Australian coaches are still coming to Tucson. I've lectured in Australia six times. I haven't spoken in Africa yet; I've been invited, but we haven't been able to work out the time.

Basketball coaches are an amazing fraternity, united by our love for the game and the never-ending quest to be just a little bit better next season. I remember giving a clinic in a small town in the Czech Republic, not far from the Polish border. The town was so small I don't even remember its name. We were in a small well-used gym. I wondered if anyone would show up, and when I walked in, there were probably a hundred coaches from around the world sitting there.

The farthest I've gone to coach basketball was China. I went there for the first time in the late 1980s to conduct a clinic with Villanova coach Rollie Massimino and Don Casey, then head coach at Temple. We were invited to Kunming, at the end of the Burma Road, by the Chinese Basketball Federation. On the flight our guides taught us how to use chopsticks by making us practice with them until we could pick up marbles. That was pretty much our entire instruction for the trip. So if anybody ever needed marbles picked up with chopsticks, we were ready.

The Chinese were determined to build an internationally competitive basketball program. They knew they had to start from the bottom and build up, so they brought in six hundred youth coaches from all over China. We worked with an all-star team of sixteen-year-old girls in the morning and an all-star team of sixteen-year-old boys in the afternoon. The youth coaches were the perfect audience for a coach. They paid attention to every single word and didn't make a sound, and then they listened as our interpreters translated for them. The entire clinic was run like a military operation. After we finished an entire day of instruction, all those coaches would have dinner—and then attend a night session at which they would study tapes made that day and be tested. That night session would go on until midnight, and they would be there ready to work early the next morning.

One afternoon in China while I was demonstrating the proper way to slide on defense, I pulled my hamstring. It was incredibly painful, but I managed to finish the session. After the clinic I asked for medical help. The medical director asked me, "Have you ever had acupuncture?"

I hadn't, I said, but if it would help I'd try anything.

Truthfully, I wasn't too sure about it. Acupuncture was just starting to gain acceptance in the West and all I knew about it was that it involved sticking you with several long needles. The acupuncturist was a woman. I laid on my stomach and she stuck several needles into my hamstring. These needles were hooked up to some sort of machine. Through an interpreter she told me to let her know when the current became too intense for me. And then she turned on the machine. Instantly, my hamstring started break-dancing. It felt like it was being turned inside out. I could feel my whole hamstring. "Okay, that's enough," I said quickly.

"But, sir, that is lowest current possible," she said.

Oh. Well, then, go slow. Very slow. I had never felt anything like that in my life, but it really helped. The next day I was still hobbled, but I was able to work the clinic.

Five years later Bobbi and I returned to Kunming for an Asian coaches clinic. We did a lot of sightseeing on these trips, and this time we went out into the countryside to visit a commune. We watched an elderly woman carrying buckets of water that she would dump onto plants. That was their irrigation system. This woman was wearing a wide-brimmed straw hat and Bobbi told our interpreter she wanted to buy that hat. The interpreter told her no, it wasn't necessary to buy an old used hat; we would stop and she could buy a new one. Bobbi was insistent. "I want that hat. I'll give her ten dollars for it."

The interpreter told her she could get a new one for fifty cents.

Bobbi was always polite. "I'd like to have that one," she said. "Would you check with her?"

The elderly woman thought Bobbi was crazy. Ten dollars for an old hat? Some of the other women were laughing about it; the indication was that Bobbi was a fool. She did buy that hat for ten dollars. I had no idea why she wanted that particular hat. When we came home, we hung it on the wall. Every time I walked by it, it reminded me of how incredibly fortunate I have been. Every time. It helped me keep my life in perspective. That ten-dollar hat turned out to be an awfully valuable lesson.

The success of our program at Arizona also made me very attractive to other programs. Arizona had changed the state policy limiting coaches to one-year contracts, and the head coaches of our major sports were given five-year deals. That didn't stop other universities from calling from time to time just to see if I might be interested in another job. It seemed like whenever a job in the Pac-10 opened up, the papers began speculating that it was going to be offered to me. To stop that, I signed a noncompete clause that prohibited me from moving to another Pac-10 school. Through the years I've also received several feelers from NBA teams. They weren't specific offers, just calls to ask me if I'd be interested in meeting to discuss the situation. I've never seriously considered accepting an NBA job. Chuck Daly, who had coached with great success in both college and the pros, once told me that on the pro level there are times you just have to look the other way. You have to pretend you don't hear what the players are saying. That's just not me. I've always believed that little problems turn into big problems if you don't deal with them. When the good of the team is concerned, I can be confrontational with an individual, and at the pro level you just don't have the leverage you need. I've also worked with enough pro players and agents to know I wouldn't be able to work with those egos.

All of these calls were flattering. It's nice to be wanted, but we were very happily settled in Tucson, and there was only one other job that intrigued me: In 1989 a scandal at the University of Kentucky in which a booster had given money to a player had caused Eddie Sutton to resign. The NCAA had placed the basketball program on probation. C. M. Newton had been named the new athletic director to try to clean up the mess. I had gotten to know and respect him when he was on the U.S. Olympic Basketball Committee. During the 1989 Final Four in Seattle he started talking to me about the job. He invited me to Lexington— this time with Bobbi—to see if we would be interested in the job.

Kentucky was going through tough times. The Wildcats had just had their first losing season in something like a half century and nobody knew how stiff the NCAA penalties would be. The program would have to be rebuilt. One of the reasons that Newton wanted me was because of my squeaky-clean reputation. And I have to admit the Kentucky job interested me. It was still one of the most prestigious jobs in basketball. And the great Kentucky tradition makes recruiting much easier. If you loved college basketball, you had to admire what had been accomplished there for so many years. That's why Bobbi and I even considered it.

Once again, the newspapers found out about it. It became a major news story in Tucson. Everybody started talking about it. We were supposed to fly to Kentucky on a Saturday morning. On Friday afternoon Bobbi picked up our grandchildren, Julie and Matt Brase, at their school. As she was driving them home, nine-year-old Julie started crying. "What's the matter?" her grandmother asked.

As the tears rolled down her face, she said, "Mama Bobbi, it's okay. We understand if you and Papa Lute want to go to Kentucky."

Bobbi was waiting for me when I got home from practice. "We have to talk," she told me. If you ever want to influence a grandmother, there is no stronger weapon than tears. We got out our yellow pads and talked for hours. Finally Bobbi told me, "I just don't think I could leave the family."

That night I called C. M. Newton and told him, "Don't send the plane." I don't know for certain that job was going to be offered to me. And I never found out. Eventually they hired Rick Pitino. And it was finally clear that Bobbi and I were in Tucson to stay. As I told the media, "We want to stay here as long as people want us here." And we assumed they would want us there—as long we kept winning basketball games.

In response to the Kentucky offer the university gave me a new five-year contract that paid a little more than Bill Frieder's new contract at ASU. I got some criticism for that; some sportswriters claimed that I had used the Kentucky offer to hold the university hostage. That wasn't true. If earning as much money as possible was my objective, there were several other, more lucrative deals waiting for me. Based on my record of accomplishment and the way we ran the program, I could have taken a job that would have made me one of the highest paid coaches in the country. Instead I signed a new contract that paid me slightly more than the new coach at ASU.

Great success also creates great expectations. We'd gotten to the Final Four in 1988, so even though Steve Kerr had graduated, the least our fans expected was a return trip the following season. The very least. In fact, the cover of our media guide even teased, *Final Four, and a Whole Lot More?* The only thing "a lot more" was the national championship, which was a pretty substantial expectation.

To win the national championship you need at least one great player, and we had that with Sean Elliott. And we had a very solid veteran group surrounding him. Preseason polls ranked us eleventh, but I believed we were a lot better than that. The only thing we lacked was a really experienced point guard.

We finished the 1989 season 29–4, ranked second in the country, and repeated our 17–1 record in winning the Pac-10 regular season title as well as the conference tournament. The four games we lost were all on the road, and we lost them by a combined total of fifteen points. So we were sixteen points from perfection, not a very big margin. We extended our winning streak at McKale to thirty-three games, the longest streak in the nation, and Sean Elliott became our first National Player of the Year. Anthony Cook, listed at 6'9" but that was a stretch, was an honorable-mention All-American. The first game we lost was to tenth-ranked North Carolina in the early-season Tournament of Champions played at Charlotte, practically a home game for the Tar Heels. Sean Elliott fouled out with more than five minutes to play—the first time in more than a season that he'd fouled out—and they beat us 79–72, the most points we lost by the entire season. When we beat UNLV at home by eleven points in early December, it was becoming clear we could be very good. By early February we had regained the number-one ranking, and all the attention that came with it. After Oklahoma beat us in Norman to drop us to number two, I admitted, "We have the potential to be a great basketball team. We're not there yet. We still don't do all the little things."

Mostly, by that, I meant protecting the ball. There were games in which our guards were great, but at other times they seemed to lose their focus. A great team is consistently great, and we played uneven. One of our biggest tests of our season came in late February, when we played ninth-ranked Duke in a nationally televised game at the Meadowlands in New Jersey. I always like playing on the East Coast because the program gets media attention we don't otherwise receive, and it gives kids from the big eastern cities a chance to see the kind of exciting ball we played. It definitely helps recruiting, and it's an exciting road trip for our players.

No matter how many thousands of games you've coached, whether it is a early-season game against a struggling team or a meeting with a national power in a packed arena, the feeling you get being on the sidelines, directing your team, is always exhilarating. You just never get tired of it. I loved it when I was coaching high school in Minnesota, and I never lost that passion for it. Everything else you have to do is the preparation, from monitoring the boys room at the high school level to recruiting and the countless hours of practice at the major college level. Coaching the game is the payoff. Putting the players you've taught out on the court to execute the strategy you've planned is what being a coach is all about. In any sport.

The truth is that during a game—even a late-season matchup between two top-ten teams on national television—once the game starts the surroundings never even enter your mind. You forget all about the cameras; the cheering becomes background noise you barely notice. The only thing you're aware of—and I think this is true of most coaches—is the five-on-five right in front of you. You're focused completely on making the necessary adjustments—how do we counter that defense? when do I make a substitution?—and they have to be made on the run. It's not like you have time to huddle up and call a play. I remember when I was coaching baseball in high school I kept thinking, there must be something I should be doing right now? There has to be something I can do to change the flow. In basketball everything happens right in front of you, and it happens so quickly that you have to stay focused on the moment.

There isn't even time to get nervous. I get nervous sitting the stands watching people I care about playing. My granddaughter, Julie, grew up to be one of the greatest players in Arizona high school history. My grandson Matt was a fine high school player who starred on his junior college team before walking on to the team and playing for me at Arizona. Bobbi and I went to as many of their games as possible. Sitting in the stands with nothing to do but cheer was very hard for me.

So the fact that we were playing a very high profile opponent like Duke really didn't make me nervous. If anything, it was a terrific opportunity to measure our ability going into the tournament. It was an intense game, so intense in fact that I got called for two technical fouls. For me, that's about a season's worth in one game. We jumped out to a nineteen-point lead, then we lost our intensity and Duke came all the way back to go up by eight. With under a minute left we were tied at seventy. That's when your star is supposed to step up—and Sean Elliott did. He hit a long three-pointer over Danny Ferry, then a few seconds later hit two foul shots to lead us to a 77–75 win. We regained the number-one ranking in the country, and for the first time in our history that's where we finished the regular season.

Once again we were the number-one seed in the West. After beating Robert Morris and Clemson, we went to Denver to play fourth-seeded UNLV in the Sweet Sixteen. I thought we were a better team than we had been when we'd beaten them by eleven at McKale early in the season. So while I knew it would be a tough game—every game against a Tarkanian-coached team is a tough game—I believed we were going to win and go back to the Final Four. We were good enough.

There are just so many factors that have an impact on a game. The only advantage UNLV had over us was a deeper bench. They played more people than we did. Denver was one of the few places where that made a significant difference. Our players were extremely well conditioned, but Denver is at a very high altitude. The air is thinner. Sean Elliott and Anthony Cook never wanted to come out of a game. Both of them just wanted to get every minute of playing time. But five minutes into the game they had their hands up telling me they needed a breather.

UNLV was playing at the same altitude we were, but they were much higher. They were playing the number-one team in the country, so emotionally, they were sky-high. And with their bench they were deeper, too. With about half a minute to go we were up two and Matt Muehlebach tried to go inside to Sean Elliott. Elliott was tightly guarded, so Matt ended up walking. UNLV came downcourt with ten seconds left in the game. Kenny Lofton was guarding Anderson Hunt. Hunt put his left shoulder into Kenny. Kenny went down, which he really didn't have to. It was a flop. That push wasn't enough to knock him down. It could have been called a charge or a foul, but at that point in the game no official is going to make that call. When Kenny went down Anderson Hunt had a clean look. He hit a three-pointer at the buzzer from twenty-six feet out and UNLV beat us 68–67.

It took me a few seconds after Hunt's shot went in to understand our season was over. It doesn't sink in right away, there's still a part of you that believes there must be something that can be done. It takes a little time to accept the finality of it. Then begins the inevitable second-guessing.

I think everybody was stunned when the buzzer went off. It wasn't just me. A three-point shot at the buzzer. Game over. Season over. Dream over. We were the number-one team in the country. It was as if we had gotten close enough to touch the top of the mountain, but had failed to make it to the summit.

For a lot of programs the season would have been a tremendous success. But when people expect you to win the national championship, anything less is a big disappointment. Only three years earlier our fans would have been overjoyed by what we had accomplished. A top ranking, twenty-nine wins, the Sweet Sixteen. Instead, it was a tremendous letdown. Even during the regular season our locker room after a loss is never a pleasant place to be. That's the way it's supposed to be. Every coach wants his players to feel the loss. People speak to each other in low voices or whispers. Every once in a while someone snaps angrily at somebody else or slams his equipment into the locker. When I walked into our locker room after this game I told them what I knew to be true, even if I didn't feel it completely at that moment. "Don't let a few seconds destroy what we've accomplished the entire season. Be proud of how hard you worked to get here."

Then I went back to the hotel and watched the game again—and probably again after that. When you're as involved every second of a game as I am, it never ends with the final buzzer. I can't turn it off because the buzzer sounded. That's the way I've always been, win or lose, from high school to the Final Four. After every game, I need to talk about it, to think about it, to relive it, and, when technology made it possible for me to get a video of the game as soon as it ended, to watch it. If we were on the road in a hotel, usually some friends or family members would come back to our room with us, and I'd sort of sneak into another room and put the tape on. If my family wasn't there, I'd grab anyone who was there to watch it with me. And as we watched I'd make comments and ask that person's opinion. It didn't matter who it was; if somebody was walking by in the hall I'd ask their opinion. I'd go forward and reverse, analyzing the game play by play. Look at that, he should have made that pass. How could that ref miss that call? What's wrong with that player's release on his free throw? What should I have done there? I didn't lose my temper at the video, although admittedly at times I got frustrated. It was more just a way of winding down.

A lot of people can't understand how I can bear watching a game we've lost again, particularly a heartbreaking loss like that one. Believe it or not, it makes me feel better. When you spend so much time preparing for a game, it takes time to get it out of your system. Looking at the game allows me to relax gradually. If I don't watch it, I'll just remember an unnecessary foul or a missed free throw or some minor violation that turned the game around, all the negative things. By watching it I can see all the things we did right. I get a much clearer picture of the game. During the season that'll help me prepare for the next game; at the end of the season it just makes me feel better. And having watched hundreds of games many times, I know one thing for certain: At the end the score is always the same.

For me, the loss to UNLV marked the end of the beginning at Arizona. That core first group we'd recruited was gone, after having done an amazing job building a strong foundation of excellence. Now young coaches were looking to me for the same things I once learned from Wooden and Dean Smith and Pete Newell. I'd often get letters from high school coaches asking me for advice. My philosophy has always been simple: There are a lot of very knowledgeable coaches in the game, but what makes the biggest difference between coaches is preparation and attention to detail. Actually, in many cases being prepared means paying attention to the details.

If your team has been properly prepared when it goes out on the court, then it's just a matter of playing the way they've been taught and executing the plan for that game. Preparation means paying attention to the smallest details. Learn how to do it correctly. Practice it until it becomes natural. Then practice it some more. Then do it in the game. A relatively basic play, for example receiving a pass and hitting a jump shot, is the end result of countless hours of work and practice. We break that play down into each of the smaller elements that make a difference between success and failure. Both the passer and the shooter have to execute correctly. The difference between getting the shot off and having it blocked is less than a split second, and if either one of them makes a small error—so minor that almost nobody in the arena is even going to notice it—an open shot suddenly becomes a pressured shot and the shooter's percentage goes way down. If the player receives it at his waist and has to bring it up, that might cost him the shot. If he has a habit like putting it on the floor—like Petrovic—that could cost him the shot. If the pass is too low or off to a side, that could cost him the shot. We want the passer to hit the shooter right in the shot pocket, so he can start his shot as he receives the pass, every time. And that takes preparation, repetition, and attention to detail.

There isn't any substitute for putting in the hours. There are no shortcuts. Next to my family and my faith, coaching basketball has always been the most important thing in my life. What made it easier was the fact that the whole family got completely involved in basketball. Our kids knew that every Tuesday and Friday night they were going to be at the game. And that they were going to be sitting with Bobbi. Our children grew up expecting to see people they had never seen before around the house. Usually tall people. No Thanksgiving or Christmas dinner at our house was ever the same; those players who couldn't go home for whatever reason would be with us. If we had a game over the holiday weekend, we might have the entire team for dinner. Often when I went to watch high school games or camps, I'd take our kids and later our grandchildren with me. Some of the kids were a little more helpful than others. My daughter Jodi, for example, would tell me which player had the best legs or looked the best in his uniform. The

NCAA tournament was sort of like our annual family reunion: Everybody who could get there went. I used to let my grandchildren choose one road trip a year to travel with us. Usually they wanted to go to California. When our kids or grandchildren weren't with us on the road, either Bobbi or I would call them after every game to talk about the results.

At times it got pretty tough. As much as I loved the game, it required spending too many nights to count away from my family. Without Bobbi's understanding and complete support it would have been absolutely impossible. There were times when it seemed like she had to raise our family by herself, and I know she got very frustrated. Our life wasn't as predictable as it had been in those years when I was teaching and coaching in high school. The pressure at Long Beach and Iowa and Arizona was much greater; doing the job correctly required many many more hours, but the rewards were far greater. Anybody who believes you can be successful at almost any job without the support of your family and friends or without sacrifice and dedication just isn't going to be successful.

Successful coaches know that the basketball season isn't a season, it's a year-round job. On the college level meaningful games in March are won by spending days recruiting in high school gyms in April, or in the summer tournaments in July and August, by making high school and home visits in September, and in practice sessions in October and November. While we still focused our recruiting efforts in California, our success enabled us to recruit nationally, and eventually all over the world. Until the early 1990s we hadn't had any success recruiting in New York, for example. Our feeling has always been that we can waste a lot of time and money recruiting in the East because, when the final decision has to be made, a kid usually wants to play close enough to home to allow his family and friends see some of his games. We've had several kids tell us that the distance was not a problem; usually, though, when it got time to make a commitment, distance had become a big problem. But one afternoon we got a call from coach Bobby Oliva at Christ the King High School in Queens, New York. That's a quality program. Kids there learn how to play basketball, but we felt it was just too far away for us. Coach Oliva told us that one of his players, Khalid Reeves, wanted to go to a school out west. The reason, Khalid told me later, was that he had decided he wanted to get away from snow. His first choice was any school where it was hot all year round. Well, we qualified for that. So we began recruiting him.

There are a lot of different ways we find out a player's decision. Often it's a phone call. When Jason Gardner, who was to become one of the best players in the country, called me from Indianapolis, he said, "Coach, I'm narrowing my schools down."

I asked him, "What schools are you considering?"

"Arizona and Lute Olson," he said. I took a silent, deep, grateful breath. At the level we recruit there are more failures than successes, so we really compete for every good player. The recruiting process can take years. Literally, there are kids we began tracking in seventh and eighth grade. Bobby Knight once got a commitment from an eighth-grader. Recruiting an eighth grader? The youngest player we've ever recruited was Nick Wise, who was already a 5'7" *ninth*-grader when we offered him a scholarship! Generally, when you recruit a player that young, size matters; usually he's already a tall kid and you know he's going to get bigger, but every team Nick played on won. Even as a thirteen-year-old he was a great passer, a great ballhandler, and could shoot it. His father was a high school coach, so Nick understood the game. He just wanted to get the recruiting process done; he wanted to enjoy high school, so his father let it be known he would make an early decision. Other major universities were also recruiting him, but he wanted to come to Arizona.

Generally, it takes a lot longer than that to recruit a player. When a kid you've been watching and talking to and visiting for years commits, there is that one split second when you just want to cheer.

The way I found out Khalid Reeves was coming to Arizona was probably the most unusual. I walked into a bathroom at an all-star tournament Khalid was in one of the stalls. "Hey, Coach," he greeted me.

"How you doing, Khalid?" I said. Then I asked him. I was mostly kidding because I certainly didn't expect an answer in the bathroom. "So are you going to sign with us?"

He didn't even hesitate. "Yeah," he said, "I'm coming to Arizona."

"Great," I told him. What else can you say in that situation? I think it is accurate to say that this was the only time I recruited a player in a bathroom.

Khalid's teammate in our backcourt, Damon Stoudamire, was someone we first started following when he was a ninth-grader. I saw him for the first time playing in a summer tournament at Long Beach State. He was really small at that time, maybe 5'5". When you see a young player at that point, you have to look at his skills and just assume he is going to grow. You look to see how quick he is, how much he understands the game, his ability to create openings for other players. It was obvious Damon had been well coached. Anytime he stepped on a court, he was immediately the leader. The name Stoudamire is big in basketball in Portland; his dad played, his uncle played. I doubt there was a day of his life he didn't pick up a basketball. I remember, the first time I saw him play, the other team tried to press. He was a human press breaker; even then he was clever handling the ball. Once he got a step on a defender, there was no way anybody was going to catch him. It was obvious he was going to be special. He had to grow a little bit, but he had the talent and the desire. So over the next few years we made the permitted contact and let him know we were interested in him. Even after he had decided to come to Arizona we had to wait until he got his SAT scores in. I told him, "I wouldn't want to take you and then if things don't work out with your test scores you'd have to explain to people why Arizona couldn't take you." Eventually he made his scores, and almost four years after I saw him play we signed him.

By the turn of the century we literally were recruiting all over the world. The days of sitting in a local gym and discovering an unrecruited gem like Steve Kerr were long gone. Whatever anyone feels about it, the reality is that college basketball has become a multibillion-dollar business. In 2002 CBS signed an eleven-year $6 billion deal for the TV rights to NCAA basketball. The same rights that CBS had paid less than $20 million for in 1985 were now valued at more than half a billion dollars a year. In addition, the major conferences make their own television deals. TV rights to Pac-10 games are held by Fox Sports Network which, unfortunately, is more of a regional network, meaning that a national channel like ESPN can broadcast only our nonconference games. In addition to television and radio rights, colleges also make money from merchandising branded equipment. There are a lot of kids out west wearing Arizona Wildcat jerseys and sweatshirts, and a successful major sports program has been proven to help attract students. So a lot of people make a lot of money in a lot of different ways from college ball. Obviously we can't afford to travel to different continents to scout young players, but the world of basketball has gotten much smaller. Playing in the NBA is now a realistic dream for players from every continent. And it's a lot easier to accomplish that if you've played college ball in the United States.

In the 1980s and early '90s our recruiting efforts were pretty much limited to a few hours from Tucson, but by 2001 our Final Four squad consisted of Loren Woods from St. Louis, Michael Wright from Chicago, Jason Gardner from Indianapolis, Gilbert Arenas from Van Nuys, and Richard Jefferson from Phoenix. As basketball became a truly international sport, we began hearing from people on just about every continent. Players almost everywhere in the world follow American college basketball. College teams now tour Europe, Asia, and Australia every few years; coaches on all levels attend clinics everywhere. Many games are televised and just about every game is taped. American players routinely play for professional teams on just about every continent. So the top programs have become known worldwide.

When Ndudi Ebi, a high school player who had committed to us in 2002, elected instead to enter the NBA draft, for example, we had an available scholarship, and we desperately needed a big forward to fill Ebi's spot. Assistant coach Josh Pastner started working the phones. Like every program we have a large network of friends, alumni, and coaches all over the world with whom we keep in contact, basketball people. A coach in Europe told Josh there was a 6'10" kid in Belgrade, Serbia-Montenegro, who could play for us, although he didn't know his amateur status. A few years earlier the prospect of a young man from Serbia who spoke little English being recruited to play basketball in Tucson, Arizona, would have been impossible, but that had ceased to be true. His name was Ivan Radenovic, and we set out to learn as much as possible about him. It turned out his father had carefully protected his amateur status. He was eligible to play college ball. We found out he had played on a junior national team against good competition and done well. We talked to some people who had seen him play and got good reports. We looked at a lot of tape and finally made contact with him. It wasn't just a matter of his ability. No matter how good he was, he had to be able to do the required schoolwork. So he began studying English. Fortunately, Ivan is very smart and his sister spoke fluent English. Eventually he passed the SATs and qualified for admission. That was probably the longest-distance recruiting we've done so far.

Also starting in the 1990s, promising young foreign players began attending American prep schools to prepare themselves both academically and athletically for our colleges—as well as to be seen and scouted by major college programs. Mohamed Tangara, for example, from Mali in West Africa, was playing at Mount Zion Christian Academy in Durham, North Carolina. He had been brought to America by a man named Linzy Davis, who had become his legal guardian and arranged for him to enroll at Mt. Zion. I first saw Mohamed play at the Nike All-American camp. I just loved the way he played with such great passion for the game, but I didn't think we had a chance to get him. Kids from North Carolina, with all those great programs in that area, tend to stay there. When Linzy told us Mohamed wasn't locked into staying on the East Coast we began recruiting him. It turned out that the weather in Tucson is similar to Mali's.

I remember when he came to Tucson for his official visit. We let him play in the annual softball game; what we didn't know was that this was the first time he'd ever played softball. It wasn't exactly like watching Kenny Lofton play. Somehow Mohamed got on base, and the next batter hit a long drive into the outfield gap. Mohamed started running. He rounded second, then he rounded third, and raced home—and then he rounded home and kept going back to first.

Once this annual softball game almost cost us an important recruit. When Mustafa Shakur, a great young player from Philadelphia, made his campus visit in 2002 he participated in the game. Mustafa was ranked the number-one high school point guard in the country, and with Jason Gardner graduating we needed him to play the point for us. He'd told us that we were his first choice, that he was 99.9 percent sure he wanted to play at Arizona, but he hadn't committed officially. In the softball game he was playing left field for the underclassmen. One of our graduating seniors, Ricky Anderson, hit a bomb way over the left-field fence. It was gone the moment it left the bat. But Mustafa took off after it. The ball went flying way over the wall—and a split second later Mustafa slammed into the fence. One of the players who was there later said it looked just like Wile E. Coyote hitting a wall and falling straight down flat on his back.

Oh jeez, I thought, that's not good. We just killed our top recruit. Meanwhile, all the other kids were laughing. My next thought was, okay, even if he isn't dead, the fact that nobody yelled to warn him about the fence and everybody laughed when he crashed into it was probably enough to convince him not to come to Arizona. Later that day I asked him how he felt when he was lying there and all the other guys were laughing. "I'll tell you the truth," he said. "If it was somebody else lying there I would have been laughing, too."

That's when I felt confident we had our new point guard.

For a simple game in which you just put the ball in the basket, basketball had changed in just about every possible way since I had begun coaching. It had become a truly international game; the players were bigger and stronger and faster; the addition of the three-point shot and the incredible ballhandling and shooting skills of the players had fundamentally changed strategy; the evolving relationship between the colleges and the NBA—in which colleges serve as a kind of minor league for the pros—had resulted in changes in recruiting and retaining players; the equipment, from headband to sneakers, had been redesigned and stylized; technology, ranging from videotape to training equipment, had become very sophisticated. Ironically, probably the thing that has changed least are the kids themselves—what has changed fundamentally are the pressures they have to deal with.

At Long Beach State my responsibility for my players had been pretty much limited to the period they were with me. That changed a long time ago. As their coach, I become responsible for them twenty-four hours a day throughout the entire school year. I had to fulfill the recruiting promises I had made to their parents about caring for them. I had at the same time to ensure that their behavior reflected well on the entire program, for it had great influence on our ability to continue to attract quality people and players. Just by coming to Arizona to play basketball they were guaranteed a great deal of attention in Tucson—basketball players are stars in town—and not all of it would come from people concerned about their welfare. It was part of our job to protect them from those people and those situations. We tell our players right away: You're vulnerable now. You're a celebrity, and people want your attention. They also want your money.

While our players may be talented and mature on the basketball court, sometimes it is easy for them—and us—to forget that off the court they are still teenagers, subject to the same peer pressure as every other teenager—and facing even greater temptation. At this point in their lives, though, because of their unique talent, they have a lot more to lose than most people their age. So at the beginning of every season we now have experts come in to talk to the team about drugs, gambling, the NCAA regulations, and the range of problems that can happen with women. We go through it all. If you are in this situation, this is what can happen and what can't happen. We remind them how much they have at stake—not just their responsibility to the program—but what they have at stake for themselves. Many of our players have the ability to play pro basketball, and that opportunity can disappear with one immature decision. Our players don't have the luxury of making teenage mistakes.

The way we let them play the game has changed, too. The game has evolved, and any coach who doesn't recognize it and adapt to it isn't going to be coaching very long. That "old school" closed a long time ago. When I got my first college coaching job, I was older than most coaches—and even that was more than three decades ago. My age has never been a factor in coaching—except to a few of the schools we recruit against. I have heard stories from our recruits that other schools pointed out to them that I was older than the coach at that college, and then the recruiter wondered aloud how much longer I'd be coaching. The point was quite simple: If you were going to Arizona to play for Lute Olson, he might not be there for the next four years. They would also suggest that I was stuck doing things the same way I had done them for many years.

All the kids had to do was watch one of our games to know the type of basketball we play at Arizona. It's more accurate to say that we've evolved with the game rather than simply changed. No question about it, I give the kids a little more freedom to be creative on the court than I did years ago, but still within some pretty strict limits. One example, there was a time I wouldn't let our kids make behind-the-back passes. The fans love a flashy behind-the-back pass, the players love making them, but generally it's a low percentage play—so we didn't let them do it. We weren't interested in flashy and fancy, just in getting the job done. The legendary Pistol Pete Maravich gets a lot of credit for adding flash to the game, but as unbelievable as he was handling the ball, his teams didn't win. I don't believe Pete's teams ever won a championship. So I didn't like behind-the-back passing, not because it was too flashy but just because it wasn't the highest percentage play. When that was no longer true, I changed. In certain situations it's become the most efficient pass. We allowed Mike Bibby to use a behind-the-back pass when it was the most intelligent way of getting the ball inside. I didn't want him using it just for flash or to get the crowd ooohhhing and ahhing, and he had a lot of that ooh and ahh ability.

We never used to allow bounce passes under the basket, either. It was a low-percentage pass in that situation. But now when a guard drives for the basket, a big man will move to meet him. The defender is going to have his hands up to try to block the shot, so we'll use a bounce pass there instead of a direct pass. I also allow guards to use a behind-the-back air-pass to a forward in that situation.

One of the many important things I learned as a high school coach is that you have to adapt your system to the players, rather than trying to fit players into a predetermined style. The best system is the system that allows you to take advantage of what your players do best. That's true in any field. So we do adapt to fit our personnel. Prior to the 1993–94 season our offense had been dominated by big men up front. But that season we had three very talented guards on the team, Khalid Reeves, Damon Stoudamire, and Reggie Geary. So we had to find a way of keeping our best players on the court for the most minutes. If we had used a traditional rotation, one of those three would have spent considerable time on the bench. Instead, we became arguably the first team to play a three-guard offense. It was a significant change. We emphasized our quickness. Almost every team we played was bigger than us. Reggie Geary was the key to making it work. Reggie was 6'2" and some games he had to guard a 6'9" forward, but he had very, very long arms and was a great leaper so he could do it. Because of his quickness he gave big players much more trouble than another big, tall forward would have. This was our Muggsy Bogues philosophy: Guard your opponent from the front and depend on backside help if they lob it over your head. Whatever we lost on defense we more than made up on offense, as few big forwards could guard someone as quick as Reggie. To counter his speed many teams that usually played man-to-man were forced to play a zone against us. And when a team has to change its basic defensive philosophy, we know we have a big advantage. Our three guards averaged more than fifty points a game and took us to the Final Four.

When I started coaching, players stayed in college for the full four years. When we recruited a player, we knew he was going to be there four seasons, so we had time to let him grow into our system. In those early years at Arizona playing in the NBA was not something the players focused on. For most of the kids it was more of the impossible dream. But as the younger players got better, the NBA began drafting them before they graduated. Players who believed or were told they would be drafted left school with eligibility remaining. And with the NBA offering multimillion-dollar contracts, who could blame them?

At the end of every season I meet individually with each player to talk about the season and his future. All our frontline players have the ability to play professional basketball on some level. Before meeting with our seniors I speak to people in the NBA to find out how teams are projecting them in the draft. They give me a realistic report, so I have a pretty good idea whether a player has a chance to be drafted and, if so, what round he will go in. Money-wise, that makes a big difference. The scouts and general managers, however, are not permitted to talk about underclassmen. Instead, the NBA's senior vice president of operations, Stu Jackson, acts as sort of a clearinghouse. If an underclassman wants an assessment of his chances to be drafted, we'll contact Jackson and he'll find out from the teams how much serious interest there is in a player. For example, Hassan Adams and his mother met with me after his junior year in 2005 and told me they were thinking about testing the NBA waters. Jackson reported that most teams believed Hassan would be taken late in the second round, although two teams said they would consider drafting him late in the first round. When we shared that information with Hassan and his mother, they decided he would not declare himself eligible for the draft and instead return for his senior year.

I know some people believe every coach will try to convince his best players to stay in school, because that is what's best for the program, but it's just not true. The more players a program puts into pro basketball the more desirable that program will be for the better young players. We want those kids to know that if they come to Arizona, we will prepare them to play pro basketball. I never, never tell a kid to stay or go. I simply lay out the facts as I know them. In many cases the better players come from impoverished inner-city backgrounds, and a pro contract allows them to move their entire family to a better environment. If I pushed a player to stay an additional year for my benefit and that player got hurt, I would never be able to forgive myself. I suspect that's true of most responsible coaches.

The kids generally have a pretty good sense of whether or not to leave. At the end of his junior year Sean Elliott had the opportunity to come out. He wasn't sure what to do until we went to Los Angeles for the Wooden Player of the Year awards. The night before the awards dinner we went to a Clippers game. We got tickets right down on the floor. I think Sean was surprised how big and physical the NBA players were. That game convinced him that he wasn't ready to succeed in the NBA; he just wasn't physical enough to deal with the pounding. He stayed in school for his senior season, was the Player of the Year, and signed a contract worth about $6 million more than he would have gotten a year earlier.

Mike Bibby started to consider coming out in 1998, right after his sophomore year. I was told by the NBA that Mike Bibby would be a lottery pick, meaning one of the first ten picks, if he decided to leave school. From a financial standpoint there was no question it was something he should do. I met with Mike and his mother, Virginia, right after the season. Mike's father, Henry Bibby, had played in the NBA nine season, so Virginia knew all the pitfalls. At our meeting I told him, "I don't think it's a case of whether you can play or not. You can play, you know that. You're going to have to pick up your defense a lot, but you can handle that.

"The main thing I wonder about is if you're ready to handle the stuff away from the court, all the time you're going to have on your hands, the fact that all the other guys are a lot older than you. It's a whole different situation. It's not like hanging out with your buddies. It's a business."

Virginia understood that and made plans for family members and trusted friends to move with him. Mike was the second pick of the 1998 draft.

For Gilbert Arenas it was not a question of his ability to play on the pro level, but rather his maturity. Gilbert had not been heavily recruited out of high school; somehow he'd managed to stay under the radar. He was from Van Nuys, California, and because his father made him stay in summer school, he played in only one of the major high school tournaments. Cal State Northridge was the only other school recruiting him, and DePaul came in at the end. Apparently UCLA and USC had both scouted him and didn't think he fit into their plans. It was my assistant coach, Rodney Tention, who scouted him and really believed he could play. I went to see him. He wasn't playing against top-level competition, but he was so quick it seemed obvious he had tremendous potential.

He was seventeen years old his freshman year, and very immature. I used to say he was seventeen going on thirteen. We roomed him with Jason Gardner, hoping some of Jason would rub off on him. They became best friends. I used to ask Jason how he dealt with Gilbert. "I love being his roommate," Jason told me. "He gives me something to laugh at all the time." In the middle of a lecture one afternoon, for example, as the professor wrote some notes on the screen, the lights suddenly went out—and when they went on, only one of a couple hundred students was missing. Gilbert. He was a bright kid, and funny, and very coachable. A very likable person.

Gilbert matured as a player very quickly. By the end of the 2001 season he was playing extremely well. We made it to the Final Four, and in the semifinals he got hurt, partially separating his clavicle. He couldn't lift his hand above his shoulder. We lost the championship game to Duke 82–72. Had Gilbert not been hurt, I think we probably would have won that game. That's how important he had become. Toward the end of that season we heard rumors that street scouts were telling him if he entered the draft he'd be a first-round pick, probably around twentieth. First-round picks get guaranteed contracts, which in Gilbert's case would have helped solve some family problems. We spoke to several NBA teams and found out that they really liked his game, but no one was certain he'd be a first-round pick. At our meeting I told him that he had the ability to play in the NBA, he could score on anybody, but neither I nor Coach Tention thought he was mature enough. He was still a teenager. We really thought he should stay for at least another season. He wasn't sure, he was hearing one thing from us, another thing from various agents who had a shot at making a lot of money representing him. I think he was leaning toward staying, but when Richard Jefferson and Michael Wright decided to come out, he just got caught up in the momentum. It turned out that the agents were wrong; rather than being a lottery pick he was the first pick of the second round, meaning he didn't get a guaranteed contract. He was absolutely furious.

Fortunately, it turned out very well for Gilbert. He has become one of the best players in the league, eventually signing a much larger contract than the number-one pick that season, Duke's Shane Battier.

When one of my players and his parents tell me they're thinking about entering the pro draft, I'll offer to put them in touch with several top agents who have proved to be honest and competent. Then I'll speak to those agents to find out what rumors they're hearing about this player. Finally, I'll put the agent and the family in touch with each other. I want them to hear the facts from a reliable source other than me. I have something to gain by the player staying; the agent may have something to gain by the player entering the draft. It is not illegal for a player and his parents to talk to an agent. As long as they don't make an agreement, they remain eligible.

We try to keep our kids away from those street agents. Street agents have always concerned me because many of them will tell a promising young player almost anything to get him to sign a contract. You're going to be a lottery choice; sign with me. You're going to be drafted in the first round; sign with me. I can get you four million; sign with me. Some of these agents will flat out lie. They create smoke. They do it because they know they can't compete with legitimate agents who provide a range of professional services—they don't just take a percentage of their contract—and believe their only real chance is to get to a kid before these experienced professionals get involved. The best high school players see Kobe Bryant and Kevin Garnett succeeding in the NBA directly out of high school and believe they can do it, too. Most of them can't. At one point I was told that through the years at least fifty-six kids, both high school players and college players, had been practically guaranteed by street agents that they would be first-round picks and, based on that, had given up their eligibility—and then were not drafted. That didn't affect the agents—the agents just went looking for the next sucker—but it destroyed the careers of many of these kids.

Ndudi Ebi is a perfect example of what can happen to a kid. He was heavily recruited out of Houston's Westbury Christian High School. Coincidentally, one afternoon Steve Kerr happened to be in Coach K's office at Duke when Ebi walked in with his student host. Steve did not know that Ebi was the focus of a torrid recruiting war. When Coach K introduced them, Steve, with his dry sense of humor, asked Ebi, "Do you have a chance to go to Arizona?" When Ebi said he did, Steve asked, "Well, then, what are you doing here? Why would you consider Duke when you can go to Arizona?"

Coach K did not get the joke. Maybe the only thing that Steve could have done that would have been worse was tell Ebi about all the snakes on the Duke campus. We won that particular recruiting battle. When Ebi committed to Arizona, he told us that he intended to stay in school for at least three years. We were thrilled. He was a potential All-American and certainly, with a lot of work, a future pro. We immediately stopped recruiting other players for that position, confident that we were set there for at least the next two years. Then some agent got hold of Ebi and convinced him he would be a lottery pick, or at worst he'd be taken somewhere in the teens. I was stunned when Ebi informed us he had decided to enter the draft. I believed it was a terrible mistake for him, but there wasn't anything I could do about it. A lot of these kids come from real poverty, and the chance to earn a substantial amount of money for their family can be overwhelming. It's hard to wait in that situation. "I'm not saying I'm ready for the NBA now," Ebi told reporters, "but I'm ready to get drafted now."

He ended up being selected by the Minnesota Timberwolves with the twenty-sixth pick. He just wasn't ready to play pro basketball. He had neither the experience nor the strength, both of which he would have gained in college. In two seasons with the Timberwolves he appeared in nineteen games and played a total of eighty-six minutes. Wolves coach Kevin McHale worked with him for hours and hours after practice, but as McHale explained when he cut Ebi in November 2005, "He didn't have the opportunity to work on his game and improve his game other than with me working after practice."

By 2006 he was playing in the NBA's Development League. This was a kid who easily could have been a lottery pick; instead, he listened to the wrong people and maybe destroyed his career.

At least the NBA has changed its rules. Now a player has to be at least nineteen years old to be drafted, which is old for a freshman, and he has to have been out of high school for at least one year. Maybe that'll deprive some future Kobe of an extra year in pro ball, but it'll probably save the careers of a lot of other kids.

So the draft has changed drastically, too, but one thing I haven't changed is my principles. Personal integrity, respect for other people, hard work—that hasn't changed at all. As a coach I still emphasize discipline and making my players responsible for their actions. I haven't made adjustments in those areas. But I have long been aware that kids want you to be aware of their culture, and whether you like it or not, at least respect it. I've always tried to show an interest in those things that are important in their lives. When you and your wife raise five kids, you get some pretty good experience at that. For example, the team notices right away if I'm wearing clothes that are in their style. Believe me, I'm not going to wear baggy pants lower than my waist, but I do try to pick up a shirt or something that is popular with their age group so they get the feeling that I'm at least partly cool. When Tommy Hilfiger was popular, I'd buy a couple of those shirts. They noticed when I wore them.

The job has also required me to keep up with technology. While I don't regularly play video games, I do as much text messaging and e-mailing from my Blackberry as the NCAA permits. Like most people my age I relied on my grandkids to teach me how to use the available technology, but I also had my assistant Josh Pastner, who's very good with computers. In our locker room we have a big-screen television and top-quality stereo equipment. There's always music playing. I tolerate hip-hop, that's what the team chooses to play, but, admittedly, it's not exactly what I listen to in my car. Basically, I listen to anything else.

One change that has remained constant throughout my career is the way my relationship changes with my players after they graduate. During their playing careers I'm not interested in being friends with them. Bobbi was their friend. That's not my job. I'm their coach, their teacher, and to accomplish that it's necessary to maintain enough distance to ensure respect. While they are at Arizona I want my players to learn how to play the game of basketball at the highest possible level, but, more important, to learn about life and enjoy the college atmosphere. I try hard not to get in their business—unless it becomes necessary.

That changes when they finish their careers. Then the barriers go down. Well, if not down completely, at least they're lowered. In 2005, for example, we had a reunion of the 1987–88 team. There was a charity fund-raising dinner—which included a comedy sketch in which I would appear with several players—scheduled for Saturday night at seven. The former players were supposed to be in the ballroom, completely dressed, at four thirty for a brief rehearsal. As I learned later, at four o'clock they were all sitting out by the pool, debating whether or not they should stay there and be late for the rehearsal. Almost twenty years later and they were still worried about me being angry at them.

I maintain relationships with many of my former players. My current relationships go all the way back to players I coached in high school. Pretty much whenever and wherever we're playing on the road a former player is going to be there for the game. I encourage them to spend time with our active players to reinforce the concept that they have become part of a long and very proud tradition. Whenever I get the opportunity I go see our players who are in the pros. I'll regularly get calls from former players who need some sort of recommendation; the one I'll never forget was Joe Turner, who came back to America after playing pro ball in New Zealand and applied for a job in social services as a planned parenthood counselor, basically a pregnancy prevention case manager. "But Joe," I said when he called, "you've got six kids."

"Well," he said, "I guess that makes me an expert on the subject."

Sometimes the players have a more difficult time making the transition than I do. Once, I remember, we were having another reunion and the players were at my house for a small party. They were shocked when I actually had a beer with them, but not nearly as surprised as they were later that night. Several of the players jumped in the pool or got pushed into the pool with their clothes on. As soon as I saw that, I knew what was going to happen. One way or another, I was going to end up in that pool. So very quietly I went inside and put on my bathing suit—and I will never forget the expressions on their faces when I jumped right in there with them.

A few of them who were there, however, swear that even underwater my hair never moved.

I've got too much to do in the present to spend a lot of time focusing on the past, but I try to maintain contact with many of my former players. I'm very proud that so many of them have become good friends. I've been to numerous weddings, I know their wives and their children, I know where they're living and what they're doing. It's a very large extended family. Bobbi and I were there when Steve and Margo Kerr got married in Tucson, when Reggie and Candy Geary got married in Newport Beach, and when Kevin and Alex Flanagan got married in Sonoita, Arizona. Kevin is 6'9" and Alex, a reporter for ESPN, is probably 6'2", so when their first child was born, instead of sending them a present I sent them a letter of intent. I didn't care if it was a boy or a girl, I just knew it was a future basketball star.

There are times I'll pick up the phone and call my former players just to say hello, particularly during the holiday season. I really try to be available to them if they decide they can use my support. And at those times in my life when I've needed them, they've always been there for me.

It's amazing how long and far that ball bounces.

8

The first few years in Tucson our fans had been satisfied with some meaningful victories as long as we played exciting, competitive basketball and continued to show improvement. As we got better, they were somewhat satisfied if we had a shot at the Pac-10 title and went to the NCAA tournament. Eventually, it was almost taken for granted that we would be ranked in the top ten and receive an NCAA tournament bid—we've gone to more consecutive NCAAs than any team in the country—and then the goal became reaching the Final Four. Winning twenty-five games, winning the Pac-10, that wasn't enough. Almost anything less than a national championship was considered a disappointment.

We had gotten to the point where almost nothing else mattered but winning the final game of the season. Obviously that was our goal, every minute, every day, but, truthfully, I got sick and tired of hearing people criticize our kids—and sometimes me, too—for not winning the championship. Lose at the buzzer in the Elite Eight and everyone starts wondering "What happened? You lost." Lost? We won more than twenty games every season and made it to the last eight teams still playing. That's a tough standard. People forget how many great teams and coaches never won a championship. Oregon State's Ralph Miller was as fine a basketball coach as I've ever competed against. He was Coach of the Year twice and elected to the Basketball Hall of Fame, yet he never even got to the Final Four. I've always felt it was unfortunate that people placed so much emphasis on winning that final game.

It is, however, the reality. I accept it. Living with those expectations is part of the job. I wasn't obsessed with winning the national championship, but any coach who claimed that he didn't have the desire to find out what it's like to win that last game, just one time, is lying.

We have one of the nation's best records in the NCAA tournament; we've made it to the Sweet Sixteen a dozen times, eight Elite Eights, and four Final Fours. But throughout my career I've been criticized as a coach who couldn't win the big games. Rather than focusing on our success, some people in the media preferred to point out our early tournament losses, when we were eliminated from the tournament in early rounds by teams ranked much lower than us. In 1992, for example, we lost our first-round game to fourteenth-ranked East Tennessee State. A year later we dropped our opener to fifteenth-ranked Santa Clara. After that loss one of the local car dealers even ran an ad asking, "What's the biggest upset of the year? Arizona losing to Santa Clara or the price of the new . . ."

If I said anything to defend myself, I was criticized for being thin-skinned. If I didn't respond, I was criticized for being cold and aloof.

The criticism didn't affect me. After you've been a high school boys' room monitor, you kind of learn to keep things in perspective. The losses certainly did bother me; they probably hurt me a lot more than even our biggest fans. I hated to lose in high school; imagine how it feels to have a team you believe is capable of playing for the national championship and you lose in an early-round game. Of course it hurt.

That first game is always difficult. It's not that we're playing the toughest opponent, but just about every coach of a highly-seeded team will tell you how relieved he is to get past that first game. We're usually coming right out of the Pac-10 tournament, where we've played teams we've played before, with referees who've worked our games, in a familiar atmosphere. Basically, whether we've won or lost that tournament, we're in a comfort zone. The NCAA tournament takes you out of that zone. The change is about as abrupt as being on a beach one day, then walking through a door into a snowdrift. And sometimes, depending on what region we were sent to by the committee, that's exactly what happened.

The tournament is unlike any other part of the season. During the season we try to maintain a daily routine. That's impossible during the tournament. During the tournament, for example, we only get an hour and a half on the court to practice, so we have to do all our stretching off the floor. The day before the game we get only forty minutes on the court; a lot of teams use that time just to shoot and then go somewhere else to practice. There are daily press conferences, and—except on game day when practices are closed—there are always people in the stands. It's a completely unique environment. For us there is usually a lot of pressure. As soon as the brackets are announced our fans are looking two or three games in, trying to figure out who we might have to beat in the Sweet Sixteen and Elite Eight to get to the Final Four.

It isn't that easy. Games are a lot easier to win on paper. Many talented teams are seeded low in the tournament. Maybe they play in a mid-major conference that doesn't get too much publicity, maybe they had some key players hurt and lost games they otherwise might have won, but there are always sleepers at the bottom of the brackets. Because most of the time they're just happy to be in the tournament, there's no pressure on them. They play as loose as can be. In some situations they've already played and won a game in the tournament so they're feeling confident and are not nervous. What we've done sometimes is pressure lower-seeded opponents at the beginning of the game, both to get our players moving and to get the butterflies out of our system. If you can prove right away you're a superior team, normally you'll be in pretty good shape, but the longer a low-seeded team stays with you, the more confidence they develop, and the more pressure builds on the favored team.

You can feel it happening. A underdog has the best night of its life: They hit some threes, they get a few early fouls on your key players, the ball bounces their way a couple of times. In really neutral arenas the crowd almost always gets behind the underdog, and suddenly we start feeling the pressure. It happens. It happens to a high seed every single year. An East Tennessee State or a Vermont or Bucknell seems to come out of nowhere to defeat a highly ranked opponent.

Except they haven't really come out of nowhere. They've been good enough to win their conference or win enough games to earn an at-large invitation. In 1992–93 we were a young, talented team. We had Chris Mills, who had transferred from Kentucky and become an All-American, Damon Stoudamire, and Khalid Reeves. At one point we won nineteen straight games and were ranked number three in the country. We won the Pac-10 with a 17–1 record. It was an amazing run, and when you're in the middle of a streak like that, sometimes it seems like you just can't be beaten. The NCAA made us the number-two seed in the West, scheduling us against fifteenth-seeded Santa Clara in Salt Lake City.

Santa Clara had finished third in the West Coast Conference, but had gotten red hot and won the conference tournament to earn a bid. They were a good shooting team, and they had a 6'2" kid nobody had heard of yet named Steve Nash. We just had one of those terrible nights. They got out to a big lead. We scored twenty-five straight points to get back into the game, but give Santa Clara credit, they came back to take the lead. Nash hit six consecutive free throws at the end of the game, and they beat us, 64–61.

A lot of people consider it one of the major upsets in NCAA tournament history, but Santa Clara turned out to be a very underrated team. While Nash was there they went to the Big Dance three out of four years. A season after beating us, they upset Jason Kidd's thirteenth-ranked California, and the following season they beat defending NCAA champion UCLA.

After the devastating loss to Santa Clara, everybody pretty much considered our season a disaster. It wasn't. It was a great season. We finished 24–4. But it's that last game that sticks in everybody's mind. For months afterward the local paper wrote about it. And it just added to the growing criticism that I couldn't win the big game.

The only possible response was to win the big game. The following summer we took the team to Australia for twenty-seven days to play ten exhibition games. The tour had been planned a year earlier, but it came at the perfect time. After two consecutive first-round losses it was a welcome opportunity to regroup. It was a terrific experience. I remember one afternoon we were scheduled to go diving on the Great Barrier Reef. Khalid Reeves loved fish. He used to talk about fishing and aquariums, but being from New York City he had never learned how to swim. The day before the trip several of our kids had Khalid out in the hotel swimming pool trying to teach him how to swim. But as soon as they let go of him—boom—his big butt would carry him straight to the bottom of the pool. He was about as bouyant as lead. When we got out to the Barrier Reef the next day, Khalid had decided he wasn't going in the water. No way, no how. Steve Condon, our trainer, was determined to change his mind. Finally, Steve and I persuaded Khalid to put on a life jacket and a snorkel; we each took him under one arm and paddled just a few feet away from the boat. We did that, and I could feel him relaxing, so we went a little farther from the boat. He was beginning to feel comfortable, so we went even a few more feet. He felt confident enough to put his head down into the water. After a few seconds his head popped up and he said excitedly, "There's fishes down there!"

Khalid was thrilled. We couldn't get him out of the water. He couldn't believe all the different types of fish swimming just below him. Meanwhile, we were drifting away from the boat. Finally, I said to Steve, "Let's get his face out of the water and wave to the people back on the boat."

We got his attention. When he lifted his head out of the water, Steve told him to go ahead and wave. He had a big smile on his face—until he realized how far we were from the boat. He panicked, grabbed Condon in a headlock and held him tight. Khalid was fine, but Steve's face was turning brighter colors than the fish. I thought we were all going to drown. I could just imagine the headline: COACH OLSON DROWNS AFTER BIGGEST LOSS OF CAREER!

The trip enabled the team to bond in ways even I didn't know about for a long time afterward. One night, for example, several players went into a club with the team managers and apparently some of the locals made a couple of racial remarks. Then one of them walked over to Dylan Rigdon and said to him, "Do you remember me? Do you remember me?" Before Dylan could respond, this guy coldcocked one of our managers, Lou Baltus, who went sliding across the dance floor. The fight ended up in the middle of the street. The players were scared the press was going to find out about it. They knew how the Tucson papers would report it: UNIVERSITY OF ARIZONA BASKETBALL TEAM JAILED AFTER 3 A.M. BAR BRAWL, but they were even more afraid I was going to find out about it.

The next day they did the only thing possible: They went to Bobbi for advice. "Did you hear about the fight?" She hadn't. They told her the whole story, then asked, "Do you think Coach is going to get mad?"

"Did you guys start it?"

"No."

"Then I wouldn't worry about it."

With All-American forward Chris Mills and seven-foot center Ed Stokes graduating, we were left with three very good guards, Stoudamire, Khalid Reeves, and Reggie Geary. This was the season I had decided to install the three-guard offense, and we used this trip to experiment with it. We weren't big, but we were very quick, we handled the ball well, and we had great team chemistry. We won nine of the ten games, and by the time we got home we'd pretty much put the loss to Santa Clara way behind us and were playing well.

At the beginning of the '93–94 season we were just barely ranked in the top twenty. We won twelve of our first thirteen games. We beat Oklahoma State with "Big Country" Reeves. We blew out Michigan with Jalen Rose and Juwan Howard as Reeves put on a show. Our only loss in that span was to Kentucky; Khalid made two free throws with three seconds left to put us up by a point, but they got a fluke tip-in at the buzzer to beat us 93–92. Once again we won the Pac-10, this time with a 14–4 record.

We were rewarded with the number two seed in the West. This time we easily beat the number-fifteen seed, Loyola of Maryland, then beat the number-seven seed, Virginia. We played great team defense to beat Louisville in the Sweet Sixteen. Damon Stoudamire scored twenty-seven points and added eleven rebounds as we beat number-one seed Missouri to get back to the Final Four. The season that had started in Auckland, New Zealand, was going to end in Charlotte, North Carolina.

For the time being, at least, the media had stopped focusing on our early-round tournament losses. Instead, a few of them pointed out that this was my fourth trip to the Final Four—and that I was sixty years old—and wondering if I would ever win a title, or would I be known forever as a good coach who got close but could never win the biggest game?

We played Arkansas—and President Clinton, the former governor of Arkansas, showed up to root for Nolan Richardson's Razorbacks. A reporter told Joseph Blair that the president of the United States was going to be at the game and asked him if he was a Democrat or Republican.

"Neither," Joseph told him, then gave the absolutely politically perfect answer, "I'm a basketball player." Later he added, "One thing that I knew for sure, he wasn't there to help me."

Stoudamire hit a three-point shot at the end of the first half to tie the score, but they beat us 91–82. Stoudamire just had an off night, hitting only 5 of 24 shots, including 2 of 13 from the field. We were in foul trouble a lot of the game; all three of our guards played with four fouls. So we got killed on the free throw line. They hit only 20 of 32, but we only took a total of 16 free throws. It was still a great run for us. In the finals, Arkansas beat Duke to win the national championship.

The one thing every coach can expect is the unexpected. With most of the team coming back the following season we were ranked in the top five preseason; some magazines were picking us to win the national championship. That was our intention, too. Our motto that season was "Play on Monday," meaning that we had played in the national semifinals on Saturday and this season intended to make it to the national championship game played on Monday night.

In 1994–95, it was one of those up-and-down seasons where we just couldn't seem to get momentum going. We played some great games—

at the end of the season we were trailing Washington State by thirteen, I believe, with slightly more than a minute left. We came all the way back to tie it at the buzzer, then won in double overtime 114-111. But then we lost to Arizona State—also in double overtime, 103-98, finishing the regular season 24-6.

As I've written, to win a national championship a team needs to be great and needs to be lucky. We were good, but we weren't lucky. During the season, for example, Damon Stoudamire was suspended for several games by the NCAA for a technical violation involving a plane ticket his father had accepted from an agent. It was a mistake rather than an intentional violation. Damon had done nothing wrong, he wasn't even aware where his father had gotten the ticket, but it was against the rules. Many things have happened during my career that have made me excited or angry or proud. As a coach you really never know the impact you have on your players. You work at it, you hope, but you never really know. Some of the players on the team felt I hadn't adequately defended Damon, but during his suspension he stood up in front of the whole team and told them flatly, "I don't care what you guys say about Coach, but he's got your back all the time."

That was one of the times that made me proud.

The committee seeded us fifth in the Midwest region. We opened against Miami, Ohio in Dayton, Ohio. The last week of the season our center, Joseph Blair, had suffered a badly sprained ankle. Stoudamire was suspended for the first game of the tournament, and forward Ben Davis couldn't play because of an NCAA violation that had taken place when he was at Kansas. Blair tried to gut it out, but he couldn't make it. He hobbled around ineffectively. Without three of our starters we lost our opening game to twelfth-seeded Miami. Naturally that started the whole early exit story again.

For Bobbi and me the seasons had taken on a comfortable rhythm. We had come so far together since we'd struggled through those cold North Dakota days and nights. We'd raised five children and were now grandparents; we'd traveled the world, always to the sound of a bouncing basketball. Like every other couple we had our disagreements. She could get very frustrated with me, but there wasn't a day we weren't in love with each other. Money never played a big role in our life, whether we had it or not. Our life just wasn't focused on possessions. For years we'd had our little joke; Bobbi would tell me, "I'm going to get you a Rolex watch."

I would respond, "No, you're not. I won't wear it. It's just out of character for me." Spending that much money on a watch, whether or not we could afford it, was not something I was comfortable doing. One thing I didn't need was another watch. I have a lot of watches, I have drawers full of watches. Everybody in my family has a watch. You get a watch just for making the NCAA tournament. If you make it to the Final Four, you get a Final Four watch. If you win, you get a gold watch. Most tournaments award watches, the league gives watches, special events hand out watches. Believe me, there would never be an instant when I didn't know what time it was.

There was one time when a watch was very helpful. Bobbi and I and Paul and Betty Weitman had been invited to a special wine tasting at the Joseph Phelps winery in Napa. Those are wonderful wines and we were enjoying ourselves. The young man showing us around was an Arizona graduate and a big basketball fan. I noticed he kept looking at my watch. Finally he asked, "Coach, is that a Final Four watch?" When I told him it was, he asked to try it on. It looked very good on him, and he got up the courage to ask me if I would consider trading the watch for a case of Joseph Phelps Insignia, a very expensive, wonderful wine.

"Well," I said, sighing, "you know that watch has a lot of meaning to me." It did, too, just like the dozen or so exactly like it I had thrown into a drawer at home.

"It would really be special for me," he said.

How could I turn him down? I was thrilled. I don't make deals like that all the time; in fact, I'd never made a deal like this in my life, and I loved the wine. A couple of weeks later the case arrived at my house. Every bottle had been signed by the winemaker, so each one of them was worth several hundred dollars. I put the bottles into the wine closet. I was feeling great about my deal. The next weekend Bobbi and I went away somewhere, and when we came back Sunday night I happened to look into the garbage can—which was full of empty Insignia bottles.

One of my sons, Greg or Steve, had invited some friends over. I never did discover which one of them was the guilty party. All I knew is that I had a garbage can filled with empty bottles and a young man in Napa was wearing a Final Four watch.

So Bobbi knew I really didn't want a Rolex. She knew I was adamant about it. I wasn't going to wear it. Period. But on my sixtieth birthday she handed me a gift-wrapped box. "This is from the whole family," she said. So now it wasn't just Bobbi. It was Bobbi and all the kids and their husbands and wives and our grandchildren who wanted me to have a Rolex. She had me outnumbered.

I got even. We were in a shop in Mexico and she found a beautiful necklace, but she thought it was just too expensive. Later I snuck back to the store and bought it for her, but I didn't give it to her right away. I waited a few weeks—until *her* sixtieth birthday. We were playing in Los Angeles and our good friends from Iowa, Jim and Bobbie Stehbens, had flown out to surprise her. After the game we went to dinner—and I surprised her with the necklace.

She did have one extravagance. Bobbi liked shoes. The shoes she loved best were any shoes on sale. Bobbi and our granddaughter Julie were best friends. Every year Bobbi would take Julie and our other grandkids shopping for school clothes. Once, Bobbi and Julie were in San Diego, Julie told me many years later, and walked right into a big shoe sale. Bobbi bought Julie two pairs—and bought thirteen pairs for herself. "Oh, Papa Lute'll be fine about it," Bobbi confided to her. "But let's just not tell him what we bought today." So she snuck them into her closet. Generally I didn't notice when Bobbi wore a pair of new shoes, but for the next few months it seemed like every few days she was wearing a pair I'd never seen before.

I'd ask her, "Are those new?"

"Oh, no, honey," she would tell me. "I've had these for a while." After all those years, she knew how to get around me pretty well.

We opened the 1996 season by beating Long Beach State, Arkansas, Michigan, and Georgetown to win the preseason NIT. We were a veteran team, with five senior cocaptains, and early in the season were ranked as high as third. But we were erratic. We lost several conference games. By early February, when we played Coach Bob Huggins's number-five Cincinnati in the 7-Up Shootout in Phoenix, we had dropped to sixteenth in the AP poll. We were down nine points with six minutes left and fought back to tie it, but the Bearcats were taking the ball out of bounds under our basket with a few seconds left. They inbounded it to Danny Fortson, who turned and went up for a jump shot, but Michael Dickerson stripped him cleanly. Miles Simon grabbed it at the top of the key, took a quick glance at the clock, and then heaved it about sixty-five feet. Miles has always claimed he knew his "shot" had a chance as soon as he released the ball. Maybe he did, on the films he's running with his hands up victoriously. Incredibly, the ball went right through the basket for a buzzer-beating upset.

That was a pretty special and perfect ending to my five hundredth career victory.

One of the lowest moments of the season came days before the beginning of the spring semester when Joseph Blair was declared academically ineligible by the university's board of regents, not by the NCAA, ending his season and his career. "Academically ineligible." Those are tough words. With the billions of dollars paid by television for rights to college basketball games, with the intense recruiting battles and the constant media pressure focused on a major program like ours, it's possible to forget that our players are college students. I emphasize, from their first day at Arizona, we're here to prepare you for the day the air ball goes out of the basketball. Don't let basketball use you; use basketball. I say it over and over. And then again. And I make it clear to them that if they don't do their work in the classroom they are not going to play. We back that up, too.

Many people believe college basketball players don't have the same responsibilities as other students. That's true. They have more. They have to do the same work as other students and they have much less time to do it. I have always taken our academic responsibilities seriously. For some of these kids school has never been stressed. We stress it. Our university requirements are actually tougher than the NCAA's. The NCAA requires athletes to take twenty-four academic units a year; we require fifteen units per semester, plus an additional three-unit course from the middle of May to mid-June. We do help freshman pick a reasonable schedule that allows them to get acclimated to college. Every freshman has to spend a mandatory number of hours each week at the Academic Center—usually fifteen—and as they prove their ability to handle college courses we reduce that number. The hours can be during the day, on weekends or nights, that's up to them. We have required study times on the road. We have an academic advisor, Lisa Napoleon, who travels with us. Only players with a grade point average over 3.0 are excused from the Academic Center, and they still have to check in weekly with Lisa. Several times a week assistant coaches spot-check classes to make sure our players are where they're supposed to be. And there are penalties for missing study halls or classes. If one player misses one class, for example, we bring the whole team out at six o'clock the next morning for a run. That puts a lot of pressure on each player to do what he needs to do.

We've suspended players for missing classes, and we've had players suspended by the university or NCAA for their grades. Key players, starters. The day we opened the 1996–97 season against North Carolina in the Hall of Fame Tip-off Classic starting guard Miles Simon was declared academically ineligible. Miles was our leading returning scorer. In the locker room before the game my assistant, Phil Johnson, asked me how I thought we would do. I told him the truth, "Phil, I don't have the slightest idea what's going to happen. We could get beat by forty or make a game out of it." Miles was out, and our freshman point guard, Mike Bibby, was playing his first college game. He was the first freshman to start for us in ten years, so we had no idea how he would respond. We won by eleven.

I told Miles, "There isn't anything we can do about it. It's up to you to get your academics in order so you can play next semester."

Nobody made it easy for him to regain his eligibility. At one point all he needed was a B in a class, and the professor gave him a C. He had to take an extra course to finally regain his eligibility. The situation got so tough for him that he considered transferring. I sat down with him the day before he had to make his decision and told him, "The team wants you back. I want you to play, but you've got the responsibility to get it done. Nobody can help you do it."

We had a different problem with Gilbert Arenas. One day, as I was getting ready to go to practice, I got a call from our academic counselor—at the time it was Jennifer Mewes—telling me that Gilbert was two written assignments behind in a class. Gilbert was already on the court shooting when I got there. I told him I wanted him to take a shower and go see Jennifer.

"After practice, you mean?"

"No, I mean right now." When he started complaining, I told him, "Gilbert, being able to practice is a privilege. You have to earn that right. But you're not allowed to practice until you get all your assignments turned in."

He couldn't believe I was serious. Gilbert had the potential to be a great player, and maybe in the past that had enabled him avoid some of his responsibilities. But I'd run my program one way throughout my entire career, and I wasn't going to change for any player.

The following morning Gilbert's roommate, Jason Gardner, came by the office and told me, "Coach, Gilbert didn't sleep all night long. Every time I woke up his light was on, and he was working."

He turned in his assignment and we never had another problem with him. It's something we deal with seemingly every season. In 2005, for example, forward Jawann McClellan missed the first half of the season because he didn't keep up with his work. We've lost very good players for academic reasons. In 1996, for example, we signed 6'7" high school All-American Stephen Jackson, who eventually became an NBA star, but he didn't qualify and briefly attended junior college before dropping out and eventually going into the NBA.

The graduation rates of college basketball players that are often cited to condemn college programs are greatly misleading. These statistics make no allowances for players who leave early for pro ball or those who spend more than four years earning their degree. Nowadays the average college student takes about five and a half years to get a degree, yet if an athlete doesn't complete his degree in four years the program is penalized for that. Several of our players have returned to campus while playing pro ball to complete their education, among them great players like Miles Simon, Damon Stoudamire, A. J. Bramlett, and Richard Jefferson.

This is an issue that makes me furious, because every program gets thrown into the same pot. I would guess that more than 90 percent of Division I coaches work really hard to make sure their kids get an education and graduate, but most of the publicity centers around those programs that don't graduate their kids. The heart of the problem is the way graduation statistics are compiled: When we played Duke in 2001 for the national championship, Loren Woods was a fifth-year senior because he had had to sit out a year after transferring from Wake Forest. He graduated—but not statistically. Because he entered Wake Forest and left that program without graduating, he counted against them, but because he didn't matriculate first at Arizona, we get no credit for him. On the NCAA books he's a negative for Wake Forest, too. That year we only had one senior starter. Jason Gardner and Gilbert Arenas were sophomores, and Richard Jefferson and Michael Wright were juniors. Of those five, only Jason returned the next year. Loren graduated but didn't count, and the other three left school to play pro basketball.

Kids who leave or transfer count against us. Ruben Douglas started for us his freshman year. The next season, when it became obvious in pickup games that Gilbert was going to take his position, Ruben decided to transfer to New Mexico. He played there, and graduated and got his degree. But he counts against us as another player who didn't graduate; he doesn't count as a graduate for New Mexico. In 2003 a terrific kid named Beau Muhlbach made the team as a walk-on. When we had a scholarship available we gave it to him. When it became apparent the next season he was never going to get any significant playing time with us, he decided to transfer to Texas A&M. Beau was about a 3.6 student and very competitive, so he wanted to play. He probably had fifty credits when he transferred. So with a high average and a lot of credits, it was obvious we had done our job academically, but as soon as he transferred he counted against us.

There are people who believe that coaches will try to get rid of kids who can't help the team in order to get his scholarship back. The NCAA has written its rules so as to prevent that from happening. I have never run a kid off in my career, never, and I think there are only a few coaches who have. Kids transfer for all types of reasons. I've suggested to the NCAA that when a player decides to transfer that the university president should put together a faculty panel to determine the reasons for this decision. If it is a life reason, rather than being pushed by the coach, he shouldn't count against the program.

Some of the NCAA rules made it very difficult for players to complete their education. One rule, for example, states that to stay eligible a player has to have completed a specific percentage of units toward a degree each year. That sounds fine, but, for example, if he's a junior and decides to change his major, he can't do it and stay eligible, because he will not have completed a sufficient percentage of requirements toward a degree. Channing Frye was an education major, and he was completely up-to-date in the classroom. At the beginning of his junior year he decided he wanted to change his major. That created a problem. If he changed his major, he wouldn't have enough credits toward graduation in that major to remain eligible. So he had to continue to take education courses that did not apply to his new major.

He completed his course requirements for an education major. But at Arizona an ed major can't do the student teaching until he has completed the course work, so that meant Channing would have to be there for the first semester of his fifth year in order to earn his degree in education. When the year ended, he was drafted by the New York Knicks. His choices were to play pro basketball for millions of dollars or student-teach to get his degree. We hope he's going to play pro ball for the next fifteen years, but until he completes his student teaching, he can't get his degree. So he will count against us.

Like other players who came from impoverished backgrounds, Joseph Blair was just trying to do too much. He was using his scholarship money to help support his family at home as well as his own two-year-old child. He was trying to go to school, play basketball, and raise a child. It just was too much for him. It wasn't a matter of Joseph not being able to do the work, he just couldn't keep up with everything.

We finished the 1995–96 season ranked eleventh, and finished second in the Pac-10. In the NCAA tournament we beat Valparaiso, then Iowa, to move into the Sweet Sixteen. We were playing Kansas in Denver. We were playing really well by that time—even without Joseph Blair, who had been averaging almost nine rebounds per game—and I was pretty confident. That's where the luck came in again.

The night before the game we went out to a steakhouse. Usually, when the team eats at a restaurant we preorder so we don't have to wait. Our dinners are ready when we get there. We ordered salad for everyone and all the kids had the house dressing except for forward Joe McLean. Joe wanted Thousand Islands dressing. He spent the whole night in the hospital with food poisoning, getting fluids. He was released from the hospital only two hours before the game.

Joe was able to play a few minutes, but he was very, very weak. Still, we were winning with less than a minute left. Then Jacque Vaughn hit a jump shot to put Kansas ahead, and they beat us, 83–80. Joe McLean was our best defensive player. If he had been healthy we could have won that game.

Our only returning starters for the 1996–7 season were Miles Simon and Michael Dickerson, and Miles was academically ineligible and had to sit out the first half of the season. I knew we had a lot of talent, but we were a young, inexperienced team. With five seniors gone, we were starting three juniors, a sophomore, and a freshman, Mike Bibby. I thought we were a season away from really competing for the national championship. Sometimes, though, you get good—and lucky.

We played erratically the first half of the season, going 10–4. When we were good, we were as good as any team in the country. We played undefeated fourth-ranked Michigan in Auburn Hills, Michigan, early in the season and lost in overtime by a basket, after leading scorer Mike Bibby had fouled out with nineteen points. And sometimes we didn't play very well. We went to Los Angeles just after Miles Simon regained his eligibility and lost on the road to both USC and UCLA for the first time in six years.

When Miles returned, I had him coming in off the bench, and he was struggling. He wasn't accustomed to that role. We needed him to provide leadership; Jason Terry, who had filled in for him, was doing a good job, but Miles Simon was that special kind of leader who gave everyone a boost of confidence. We were a better team with him in the starting lineup, but I didn't know who to replace.

Jason Terry made that decision for me. After the two losses in Southern California he came into my office and told me, "Coach, we have to get Miles back in the starting lineup."

"I know that, J. T.," I said. "What I don't know is who we're going to take out."

"Well, Mike Bibby couldn't handle it. He's a freshman. That would ruin his confidence. You can't take out Michael Dickerson, because it would be a killer for him, and we need his scoring. So it's obvious the only guy who can handle it is me. And that's fine. I like coming off the bench. I know I'm going to get my minutes, so it's not going to be a problem."

We made that change, although we never found the consistency we needed. We lost our last two games to Stanford and Cal to finish 19–9, but only 11–7 in the conference. Our fifth-place finish in the Pac-10 was the worst we'd done since our first season in Tucson. It was also the first time in years that we were considered a "bubble" team, meaning there was some question whether we'd get an invitation to the tournament.

The committee made us a fourth seed in the Southeast Region, sending us to Memphis, Tennessee, to open against thirteenth-seeded University of South Alabama. That was a tough draw for us because on offense they played a slow, deliberate style and were an excellent defensive team. Their coach was Bill Musselman, who had been at Minnesota when I was at Iowa. He knew what he was doing. As we watched tapes of their games, it was obvious they were a fundamentally sound, well-coached basketball team.

The game was exactly what we had anticipated. They played slow and deliberate offense, a tenacious, relentless defense. They'd run twenty-five seconds, thirty seconds off the clock every possession. We were trailing most of the game. We were down ten with seven minutes left. I know that Miles Simon, for sure, and maybe some of the other kids, were thinking, oh, no, not again, not another first-round loss.

There wasn't too much I could do in that situation except make sure the team kept its composure. I just reminded them to keep playing our game, follow the game plan, and keep plugging. Maybe I tried to get them to raise their intensity. The half-court pressure we'd been applying the whole game finally began paying off as South Alabama turned the ball over fourteen times in those last seven minutes. Jason Terry and

Miles Simon led us on a 22–4 rally, including seventeen straight points, for the victory.

Two nights later we played twelfth-seeded College of Charleston, a physical run-and-gun team with a twenty-three-game winning streak. There were people picking them to be the Cinderella team, the low seed that breaks into the Sweet Sixteen. With three minutes to go, we were tied, then Bibby hit a three-point shot. With twenty-nine seconds left he hit a free throw to put us up four, and we won 73–69. Bibby, the Pac-10 Freshman of the Year, scored thirteen of his eighteen points in the last seven minutes to get us back to the Sweet Sixteen.

That set up a rematch with Coach Roy Williams's Kansas Jayhawks, who'd beaten us by three a year earlier. On paper, this didn't figure to be much of a game. Kansas had exactly the same players who had beaten us, led by Jacque Vaughn, Paul Pierce, and All-American Raef LaFrentz, while we'd lost five players from that game. The Jayhawks had been ranked number one in the country just about the whole season; they were 34–1 and a heavy favorite to win the national championship. We'd barely gotten by South Alabama and the College of Charleston.

The oddsmakers made Kansas a ten-point favorite. But we honestly believed we could beat them. It wasn't just talk, either. I mean, our kids really believed they were better than Kansas. At a press conference before the game a reporter asked Michael Dickerson how it felt to be the underdog. Michael Dickerson was a quiet, confident player, but he was never cocky. He was actually surprised by the question. He couldn't believe we weren't favored.

That was the attitude we brought onto the court. Nobody was intimidated by Kansas's record or ranking. We felt we would have beaten them a year earlier if Joe McLean had been well. We knew we were quicker than they were, and we had a big advantage in knowing how they played while we, with a different team on the court, had changed. Our game plan was simple; they were big, we were fast. We were going to pressure them the whole game. This was when all those laps we'd run were going to pay off. They weren't going to get a single uncontested shot.

I didn't give any kind of motivational speech in the locker room before the game. I treated it just like every other game that season. We went over our game plan, and I told them that if we executed as we were capable of doing we would win.

We played close to a perfect game. With 3:28 to go, we were up thirteen points, but Kansas didn't quit. They played just the way you'd expect the number-one team in the country to play down the stretch. They went on an 11–0 run. With 21.1 seconds left, we held a one-point lead, 83–82. Bibby calmly hit two free throws; Kansas missed three three-point attempts, and we won 83–80.

You savor games like this one forever. The memory of that night and that team always makes me smile. We were confident before the game, but that was based more on what we believed we were capable of doing than on what we'd accomplished during the season. After that game we knew we were good enough to beat any team in the country.

At the press conference a day later one reporter just couldn't resist reminding me about those first-round losses. "What about the year you lost to the Richmond Spiders?"

"We didn't play them," I told him. But I wasn't about to let that question ruin a great time, so I added, "But we might have lost if we did."

I don't remember if I spent any time thinking about winning the national championship. I doubt it. I rarely waste time thinking about any game except the next one. There were still several very good teams between us and winning it all, but we'd peaked at exactly the right time. The question was whether we could sustain it. But I certainly was aware that I might be running out of chances to win it. As I'd said after we'd lost to Kansas the previous year, "The closer you get to the end of the line in your career, the more important every tournament becomes. Twenty years ago I figured there was plenty of time . . . I'm running out of birthdays to get it done."

We were going to play tenth-seeded Providence in the regional finals. The real danger after a big win is that you're going to be a little flat the next game because all the kids are going to be hearing from their friends and fans is how great they were the last game. They get overconfident. Providence was a big, physical team from the Big East, good enough to have knocked Duke out of the tournament in the second round. After the selections had been announced, I was asked to pick the sleepers, the underrated teams that could go a long way in the tournament. The first team I'd named was Providence. They had a great guard, God Shammgod, a big front line led by Austin Croshere, and a fine coach, Pete Gillen. As big as our upset over Kansas had been, I brought the team back to reality by asking them, "How many people remember what teams made it to the Elite Eight?"

I told the team we needed to play forty minutes of Arizona basketball, but I was wrong. It took more than that. We were up twelve with six minutes left, up seven with a minute left, but Providence just kept coming. In the last minute we turned it over twice; they hit two three-pointers and tied the game. They even had a shot at the buzzer to win it, but missed a long jumper. In the overtime we regained our composure and beat them, finally, 96–92. That was one of those games that an hour after it's ended you're still thinking they might come back. I did my best to maintain my calm demeanor, but I did admit to some writers after we'd beaten Kansas and Providence that I might have to pinch myself to make sure this was really happening.

This was my fourth trip to the Final Four, the third time with Arizona. In our locker zoom after the Providence game I told our guys, "We've had this opportunity in the past. We can bury all that talk about the '88 team and the '94 team if we step up and get the job done."

I have to admit I hadn't expected to be in this situation. I believed this team was a year away from reaching its potential. Which shows you how wrong the coach can be. The morning after the Providence game Bobbi and I woke up in our hotel and started laughing. The first thing we had to do was cancel a vacation trip to Acapulco, which we had planned to take after we were eliminated. Even that was a problem. Every year after the season ended Bobbi and I would take a vacation, but we had no way of knowing when our season would end. There is no way of knowing how many rounds you'll survive in the NCAAs. So each year after we received our invitation to the tournament, Bobbi would make a flight reservation for the time period after the first round, another after the regionals, and another after the Final Four to ensure we'd be able to get a flight we wanted. We'd cancel the flights we couldn't use. If we won a game, Bobbi would often joke with those reporters we knew well, "Cancel the reservation!" This time, though, when Bobbi said that, one reporter thought it was necessary to ask some of our players how they felt when they found out before the game that their coach had already made a reservation to go on vacation after the game. The meaning was obvious: I had so little confidence we would win that I made plans to go on vacation after the game. That wasn't true. I explained the situation to the kids—which they understood—and didn't bother dealing with the media.

So after Bobbi canceled the next round of reservations, we went out for our morning walk, held hands, and talked about this team. As a group, it was as close a group as we'd had, a bunch of really nice kids. We hadn't planned on going to Indianapolis—but we were extremely thrilled to have to change those plans.

None of the experts on television or in the newspapers gave us any chance to win at all. We joined three number-one seeds, North Carolina, Kentucky, and Minnesota, in Indianapolis. The whole week before the Final Four all the talk was about those three teams. It was as if we were there to fill out the dance card. It was sort of, Who's the fourth team in this thing? Most people just dismissed our win over Kansas as a fluke. We were going to play North Carolina, our second game against a number-one seed, in the semifinals.

North Carolina was a heavy favorite. People ignored the fact that we'd opened the season by playing and beating the Tar Heels—without Miles Simon and in Bibby's first college game. Thirty-two games later we were a much more experienced team, with a deeper bench.

The Final Four was being held in the RCA Dome in Indianapolis, the site of my first Final Four with Iowa in 1980. That year the team had stayed at the same hotel as our fans, one of the biggest mistakes I'd ever made. The players were besieged by well-meaning—and partying—fans. I never made that mistake again. This time we stayed in a hotel downtown. We took the whole second floor, and security kept everyone except the players off that floor. Even families weren't allowed. This was a place for the players to get some rest and for us to do our work; it was not a place to hold a celebration.

We had a pretty loose schedule. The team had breakfast together, we watched tapes, we went to the dome and practiced, and we had a curfew. Other than that the kids were on their own; my feeling was that the worst thing we could do was sequester them in a hotel. The more time they spent there the more they would feel the pressure. I wanted the kids to get outside and enjoy the activities. That was one of the reasons we stayed right in the middle of town. I remember Dick Vitale said that wasn't a good thing to do. He said, You go outside and you run into Arizona players right in the middle of everything. They're too distracted, they aren't going to be ready to play.

I disagreed. We did our work first, and then we let them be kids.

Several members of my family were there. Our grandkids, Matt and Julie, had been traveling with us for the last few games. Matt usually sat next to Bobbi. For the Kansas game he wore a red, button-down shirt. After that game she told him, "We have to wear the same outfit for the next game." When we beat Providence, she said, "Matt, you're my good luck charm. You have to sit right next to me. And wear the same shirt." So he was next to her for the rest of the tournament. Wearing the same shirt. Cleaned, I hope.

North Carolina, led by Vince Carter, was on a sixteen-game winning streak, the longest in the nation. In the first few minutes of the game they proved how good they were, jumping out to 15–4 lead—and making us look badly overmatched. They were running on us, something few teams had been able to do all season. We were supposed to be the team with speed. We called time-outs to try to regain our composure. I didn't want the game to get out of reach. As I said later, "I thought our guys did a real good job of getting Carolina overconfident that first ten minutes."

When you've coached long enough, you neither panic when you fall behind nor relax when you get ahead. Good teams may have bad spurts, but almost always they'll make it up and play a good game. The key to us getting back into this game was playing defense and taking away all their fast breaks and alley-oop baskets. We began mixing up our defenses. We'd been playing a straight man-to-man and we started throwing in a little zone; we applied some full-court pressure. We stopped their running game cold and forced them into their set offense. By putting more pressure on their guards we prevented them from getting the ball down into their normal operational zone. Instead of the first pass being made twenty feet from the basket, it had to be twenty-eight, and that totally disrupted what they had been doing. They didn't get many good looks; they started missing shots and turning the ball over. Our speed totally neutralized their height advantage.

On offense we hit a couple of three-pointers, then Miles Simon drove into the lane and did an up-and-under. All of a sudden our people had their confidence back, and you could just see North Carolina wondering, Wow, what's happening here?

In the locker room at halftime I asked the team how they thought we'd played. Lousy, they said. They were right. We had been awful, but we were leading by three points. Going into the second half we were very confident. Mike Bibby, who'd hit only one shot in the first half, got hot, hitting five three-pointers in the second half. Miles Simon had twenty-four points. Defensively, we did a good job pressuring Vince Carter into poor shot selection. He missed shots that probably under normal circumstances he would have made. Their other guard, Shammond Williams, hit only one of thirteen shots. We won 66–58. We were going to play the defending national champions, Rick Pitino's Kentucky Wildcats, for the championship.

What we did not realize that night was that we had given Dean Smith, the man I had learned so much from and greatly respected, the final defeat of his career. Several months later he announced his retirement.

I'd spent a lot of time in my career with the media, but I'd never experienced anything like this. Reporters were everywhere. It seemed like someone was analyzing everything we did. Obviously, a lot of the attention was on the fact that this was my fourth trip to the Final Four and we'd never won. In various ways, I was asked several times if I would feel my career was a success if I never won a national championship. My response to that question has always been that winning a championship would be wonderful, but to me that's not what it's all about. I've spent my life as a coach, working with kids, having an impact on their lives. The success of a coach shouldn't be measured only by how many games he or she had won or how many kids ended up playing in the NBA or WNBA. The real test should be whether or not you made a difference in the lives of the young people who played for you and whether they were going to make a difference in a lot of other people's lives. There was a coach who once said to determine how successful he had been you need to see what his former players are doing five or ten years down the line. I believed that. That's why we insisted on our players doing community service while they were with us. So I didn't feel that I needed to win the national championship for my career to have been a success. I understood other people felt differently—that's the world of sports—but it wasn't the scale I used to measure my career.

I wanted to win; believe me, I wanted to win. I've never stopped being competitive. I've been coaching for fifty years, and I still want to win every scrimmage. And reaching this game had been a goal since I started coaching at Long Beach. For the first time in my career, it was one and done. Win or lose, this was the last game of the season. I tried to keep things as normal as possible, but it was hard. I couldn't take two steps without someone wishing me luck or putting a microphone in front of me or asking if I had any extra tickets. And, of course, for the media the story became, Can Lute Olson finally get the monkey off his back?

We'd beaten North Carolina Saturday afternoon, the championship game was going to played Monday night. We practiced Sunday. We went through some tapes with the team, and we outlined our strategy for the championship game. Then we went on the floor and practiced. I've probably run five thousand practice sessions. That one I remember.

I remember it because it was so normal, just like a thousand others. We spent a minimum amount of time on the floor. We did some shooting, spent some time working on the defenses, and then spent the rest of time preparing to deal with Kentucky's press. Kentucky had played a swarming full-court pressure defense the whole season, but they hadn't played it against a team that could handle the ball like we could. In fact, at his press conference Rick Pitino said he didn't think his team could press Arizona. He didn't have the manpower, he said.

Who knows, maybe he did feel that way at least a little bit. "Right," I said when reporters asked me about that. "And he's going to play a zone and slow the ball down, too." I didn't pay any attention to that. We prepared, as we would always prepare, against what the team has done all season.

Defensively we made several adjustments. Forward Ron Mercer was a great player for them. They set all kinds of screens for him. Our plan was to play him differently than anyone else. As soon as he came off a screen, even before he got the ball, we were going to double. Every single time he came off a screen, we were going to double him aggressively. Bennett Davison, Jason Terry, or Michael Dickerson was going to be in his face every time he came off a screen. That would force him to catch the ball a little bit farther out than he was used to. If he didn't get the ball, we'd just drop back. When one defender popped out on Mercer, the other one would have to drop back to protect the post. And if Mercer didn't get the ball, but another player tried to exploit our defense by driving to the basket, the first defender had to drop back into the post area. That required our post players to really work well together, like defensive backs in football, but they were capable of doing it. That was our plan. Make it difficult for their primary scorer to get his shots, forcing them to depend on their secondary scorers to beat us. All we had to do was execute.

Pitino had been telling the truth. At the beginning of the game, they didn't try to press us. That was a surprise, and a huge confidence boost. Later in the first half, when they did try to pressure us, we handled their press well. The reason we were so effective against their press was because everybody on our team could handle the ball. Our center, A. J. Bramlett, was very much the key to that because we had him flashing to the middle of the court to receive a pass and distribute to a wing man. We also had worked against a pretty good copy of their press in our practices. The people who played the most minutes of the game get the attention and the stardom, but our scout team, the reserves that only the biggest fans ever heard about, contributed tremendously. We were well prepared for Kentucky's press.

It was a classic basketball game. Two great teams slugging it out basket for basket. We pretty much shut down Mercer, holding him to thirteen tough points, five under his average. The most amazing statistic was that he only got nine shots the whole game. But forward Scott Padgett hit the boards for them and scored seventeen points. The game was tied sixteen times and there were eighteen lead changes. I think it might have been tougher for my family and our fans watching the game in the stands and on TV than it was for me. As usual, I was so completely focused on each possession that I didn't have time to be nervous. With nineteen seconds left in the game Bibby found Bennett Davison under the basket for an easy layup, putting us up by three. Seven seconds later Kentucky's Anthony Epps hit a clutch three-point shot to send the game into overtime.

After all those years of maintaining a businesslike atmosphere, during the break before starting the overtime I really got fired up. If there was one time I got in everybody's face, this was that time. I knew how tired everybody was, how much emotion and energy each one of them had exhausted. How depressing it was to be up three with twelve seconds to the national championship and have your opponent hit a really tough shot. I crouched down in front of my team, I put my hands on them. I was shouting at them, "Did you guys come this far to lose it now? Are you going to finish the job? The toughest team is going to win this game. Are they tougher than we are? The toughest team is going to be national champions!"

We were the tougher team. Just after the overtime period began, I looked out on the court. Almost without exception every Kentucky player was leaning over and holding onto his shorts. That's a sign of exhaustion. They just looked drained, while our guys looked fresh, ready to play all night. For the first time I felt we had them.

They couldn't keep up with us in the overtime period, so they were forced to foul. We scored 10 points in the overtime—every point from the free throw line. On defense we held Kentucky to a single basket until six seconds were left and the game was essentially over. We won 84–79.

We'd completed an incredible run. We were the first team in NCAA history to beat three number-one seeds to win the national championship. Miles Simon, who'd missed the whole first half of the season, had completed an amazing comeback. He scored fifty-four points in the final two games and was named the tournament Most Valuable Player.

When the game ended, I kept my Norwegian cool. I think every coach remembers Jimmy Valvano running around in complete joy after North Carolina State won the championship. I think every coach wonders what that moment actually feels like. I found out: The reality was that I don't think I was capable of feeling anything at that point. I was beyond that. It was pure happiness.

As I went to shake Rick Pitino's hand, Bennett Davison, with permission from Bobbi, snuck up behind me and mussed up my hair. That was as close to being doused with Gatorade as a basketball coach was ever going to get.

When I turned around, Bobbi was standing there, just beaming. She wasn't screaming or jumping. That wasn't Bobbi. She was standing there, a beautiful, satisfied, proud smile on her face. The first thing she did was reach up and straighten my hair. Around us, all over the court piles of players were growing.

Bobbi and I were ushered over to Billy Packer and Jim Nantz for the traditional interview. I can't remember what I said; I don't think she said anything. I think she was just overwhelmed. Then we cut down the nets and posed for team pictures and finally headed for the locker room. That's when the rest of our family joined us on the court. My whole family had played a role in my coaching career, from the recruits our kids and grandkids entertained to going with me to high school games to being supportive, so we all shared in this moment. We'd gotten there together.

Very few coaches have gone through this more than once, so everything is new. There are people all over the place to direct you to the proper place, to tell you what happens next. The whole postgame is well planned; the winning coach and team just gets plugged into it. Finally I went into the locker room. The locker room was closed for about ten minutes. There was a lot of hugging and laughter; I told the kids how much this team meant to me and how proud of them I was. Then, finally, I went to meet the media with several players. I was pretty certain what the first question was going to be. "Coach, do you think this will finally take the monkey off your back?"

There have been times in my life when I probably would have gotten angry about that question. But this wasn't one of those times. Instead, I said, "I know I'll go to my grave with some people still talking about some of those losses, and I feel bad for them." A reporter asked if I considered the criticism unfair. That's one of those questions to which there is no real good answer, which is how I answered. "If I say yes, that makes it sound like I'm whining. All I've ever asked is for people to consider the facts, to look at our record. Make your own decision, but please look at the facts."

The record was pretty good. Over the past decade we had compiled the best winning percentage in the country. During that period the only teams who had been to more Final Fours than us were Duke and North Carolina. In NCAA games, after beating North Carolina, we were 5-0 against ACC teams.

The press conference seemed to go on forever. As I answered question after question after question, Bobbi stood patiently on the side, occasionally leaning against the wall. If I close my eyes, I can still see her standing there. It was after one in the morning when I finally started to stand up, but a reporter asked one last question. I looked at Bobbi and asked her, "Will you wait one more second, dear?"

She smiled. "I've waited forty-five years for you," she said. "I'm surely not going to stop now."

Bobbi and I had been blessed to have found each other.

After the press conference we went back to the hotel for the presentation of the National Association of Basketball Coaches trophy. Finally, Bobbi and I got back to our suite. It was a garden area and a party was well in progress. The team was there; our family and friends were there. Everyone was so excited. We put the tape of the game on the TV and watched it; this time I had no problem finding people to watch it with me. It was just a whirlwind. By the time I got to bed it was 5:00 A.M.

An hour later I was up and appearing on *CBS This Morning*.

Our chartered flight back to Tucson took off right after breakfast. When we landed, we all climbed into convertibles for the drive back to campus. All the way to the university the road was lined with cheering people. There were so many people there I thought there wasn't going to be anybody left at the stadium, but as our caravan pulled into the football stadium I saw right away that I was wrong. The stadium was packed. A stage had been set up and just about every member of the team spoke. I don't remember precisely what I said; I know I thanked the fans for the support they had given us for so long, and how proud we were of the team and how well they had represented themselves, the university, and the state. A night later I was a guest on Jay Leno's show. On the show Jay Leno handed me a can of "Lute Spray"—to prevent my hair from getting mussed up.

This was the biggest sports event in Tucson history. Everybody had a story they wanted to share with us. We even heard from a young man who told Bobbi that his wife gave birth during the game. As a precaution, they had called ahead to the hospital to make sure there was a TV in the labor room. Between contractions they had cheered us on.

When the rally broke up, so many people tried to get close to the team, it got scary. Security broke down completely, and people just rushed the stage. It felt as if we were going to get trampled. Michael Dickerson started hyperventilating, and there wasn't too much we could do. We managed to get over to McKale, which is very close to the stadium, and got the team safely sequestered in our locker room. That was pretty much the first chance we had to settle down. We'd been celebrating since the final buzzer sounded.

I went up to my office and the president of the United States called. As we spoke, it became clear to me why President Clinton was such a successful politician. It was such a relaxed conversation it felt like I was speaking to an old friend. He told me he had a knee injury which limited his mobility, and that had allowed him to watch the whole tournament. The conversation ended with an invitation for the entire team to visit the White House.

After that we still had to battle to get out of McKale. The arena was entirely surrounded by fans. Nobody wanted the celebration to end. Finally, though, we got home—and the whole family was waiting there for us. But that was the first chance I had to just sit and talk and go through all the good thoughts that came from the Final Four. And then I enjoyed the greatest feeling I've ever experienced in my career. The season was over and we were the last team standing. There was no one left to play. When I was in high school, we had won the North Dakota state championship. In 1986 we'd won the world championship. Both of those times the feelings had been beyond description. Unbelievable. But nothing like I was feeling at that moment. Who else was there to play? The Chicago Bulls?

I was completely relaxed. I sat there thinking about all the difficulties the team had overcome during the year to win the championship—and knowing, too, that we would be in the record books forever as the first team to beat three number-one seeds, three of the most storied college basketball programs, Kentucky, North Carolina, and Kansas.

The feeling was extraordinary. It lasted for almost three days. Then I was back out on the road recruiting again.

9

We were the big target as the 1997–98 season began: We were the defending national champions. We were ranked number one. We pretty much had the whole team coming back. Three players, Miles Simon, Mike Bibby, and Michael Dickerson, were named to preseason All-American teams. So every loss would be considered an upset, and anything less than a second national championship would make the entire season a disappointment. There was a lot of pressure on us to be perfect.

After opening with three wins, we lost the championship game of the Maui Invitational to third-ranked Duke. We lost again two games later in Chicago's Great Eight tournament to number-two Kansas. We were very good, but not perfect. Not yet. Usually at the beginning of the season you have to fit your new players into the system. You have to find out those things the team does well and where you need to do some work. You have to live with freshmen mistakes. We didn't have any of those problems. What we needed to do most was establish consistency. We had three very good shooting guards, and chances of all three shooting poorly the same night were pretty slim. We won twenty-three of our last twenty-four games, losing only to USC by a point in overtime in that run. We averaged almost ninety-two points a game. We won the Pac-10 again with a 17–1 record.

Nobody was surprised that the NCAA made us the number-one seed in the West region. There were a lot of people picking us to repeat as champions. Truthfully, I thought we had a real good chance of doing it. We were playing very well. This time we had no problems in the first round, beating Nicholls State 99–60. Then we beat Illinois State, 82–49, to move into the Sweet Sixteen. After beating number-four seed Maryland, we only needed to beat Utah to return to the Final Four. We'd played them a year earlier and had beaten them by eight, they just couldn't handle our press. Utah came out of the Western Athletic Conference, and it had been more than three decades since a team from the WAC had gone to the Final Four. But they were coached by Rick Majerus, and were led by All-American guard Andre Miller and 6'11" Michael Doleac. They'd made it to the Elite Eight the previous season. They could play the game of basketball.

And that night they played it a lot better than we did in every department. They played a triangle and two against us; that's a kind of "junk defense" in which they guarded Bibby and Simon man-to-man and their other three men played a zone. They took us apart, beating us 76–51, our worst tournament defeat ever.

We couldn't do anything right. On offense we shot a miserable 28 percent, which included four-for-twenty-four three-point attempts. Mike Bibby was three for fifteen from the field with only one assist, Miles Simon one for nine, Michael Dickerson two for twelve. Bramlett and Davison managed to take only twelve shots the whole game. We weren't much better on defense; Andre Miller had no problem breaking our press, and had the first triple-double anyone had ever gotten against us, and the only one in the entire tournament. They destroyed us inside; fourteen of their seventeen field goals were dunks and layups.

When you lose a game like that, you spend a long time trying to figure out what went wrong. I remember coming home the day after the game. I know I should have felt good about the year, we'd finished 30–5, but I was heartsick. I found out that winning a national championship once doesn't diminish your desire to win it again. Instead, it makes you appreciate how hard it is to win it all, and you just want to experience it one more time. I couldn't sleep that night. So I went out on our deck, threw some blankets over me, and just sat there, looking out at the city lights.

Eventually, from sheer exhaustion, I drifted to sleep.

This time we used our plane reservations. Bobbi and I went down to Mazatlán, Mexico with the Stehbenses and had our usual wonderful time. I love being on a beach, and Bobbi and I got to take our early morning walks. A few weeks later we went to Europe, where I was conducting a series of coaching clinics. I did several clinics in France, then we went to Prague, the capital of the Czech Republic, with Paul and Betty Weitman for several more clinics. Eventually Bobbi and the Weitmans took a train to Vienna while I conducted a clinic in a small town in the Czech Republic, near the Polish border. It was maybe the oddest of all the clinics I'd done. Usually, after completing the instruction, I respond to questions. For the first time in the hundreds of clinics I'd conducted, I could really sense quite a bit of resentment. One questioner implied that American coaches seem to believe they know more about basketball than anyone in the world. None of the other coaches in the audience disagreed. I responded that if that was what they thought, I was sorry, but that certainly wasn't my intention. I explained that all I was trying to do was explain how we teach elements of the game, whether it is offense or defense. When I went to clinics as a young coach, I said, I wasn't looking to pick up twenty ideas, rather I was hoping to pick up one or two things that would help me in my teaching. "Look," I finished, "I don't want you to feel like American coaches have all the answers, because, believe me, we don't."

After finishing that clinic, I met Bobbi and the Weitmans in Vienna. It was a wonderful time. Bobbi and I were with close friends in a beautiful city. I hadn't forgotten that Utah game—I never forget the losses—but I'd gotten past the pain. I was already starting to get excited about the coming season.

I did another clinic Sunday afternoon. That night we were getting ready to meet the Weitmans for dinner when Bobbi told me she wasn't feeling well and was going to stay in the hotel. That was very unusual, very unusual. Bobbi never complained. Even when she wasn't feeling well, she did whatever she had planned without complaint. She would never show the kind of pain or discomfort she was in because she didn't want to bother anybody else. Years earlier, for example, Bobbi and George Kalil were walking into Pauley Pavilion before a game with UCLA when a kid locking up his bike on the level above them dropped the metal lock. It hit Bobbi in the head and knocked her down. They rushed her to the arena medical office. Bobbi and George spent more than half the game in there. Bobbi was hurt, even years later every once in a while it would bother her, but she never missed a game, one of our children's events, or even a night out because of it. Bobbi was a social person; she loved being with our friends, so when she told me in Vienna that she didn't feel well enough to go out, I was concerned.

At her insistence, I had a very quick dinner with the Weitmans. I suspected her discomfort might have been caused by something she'd eaten. I was concerned, but I thought she probably would feel better after a good rest.

When she got up the next morning she still felt lousy. We had planned to take a boat ride down the river from Vienna to Budapest, but because Bobbi wasn't feeling well, we took a car. We called the hotel doctor that night. After examining her he prescribed some pills. She took them, but they didn't help at all. I was getting very concerned. I got a specialist to come to the hotel to examine her.

Our nightmare was beginning. This doctor took me outside the room. This is an emergency, he said. She has a major problem and you need to try to get her back to the United States as quickly as possible.

I sat with Bobbi and told her the truth. The doctor said we had to get back to the States to get the best possible care.

She looked at me. "I want to see my grandkids," she said forcefully. She understood this was serious, and whatever happened, she wanted to be with her family.

Paul Weitman went to the American consulate and told them that the wife of a famous American basketball coach needed help to get back to America. But by the time he got back to the hotel she was feeling even worse. She was in terrible pain. Whatever was happening was happening very quickly. There was nothing we could do but react. And the most important thing was to deal with the pain.

We called an ambulance and raced to the hospital. This was supposedly the best hospital in Budapest. I was expecting an American-style hospital, something similar to the clean, well-lit hospitals that provide some sense of reassurance. This was more like a dirty warehouse. It was dark and gloomy; it didn't even have air-conditioning. It felt like a construction site. They wheeled Bobbi into the elevator and that elevator didn't work. Every bump was agony for her. Finally they managed to get her upstairs where the doctor could see her.

After examining her, the doctor told me in broken English that she had an intestinal blockage and if he didn't operate immediately her intestines would burst and she would die.

Two days earlier Bobbi and I were enjoying a working vacation; we were in the middle of a comfortable life. Now we were in a dark, dirty hospital being told she might die. I had no choice. We didn't have time to get a second opinion. Even if we had the time, we had no place to go.

They operated at one o'clock in the morning. I sat in the waiting room with the Weitmans. Waiting and not knowing and being in a strange place was torture. All I kept thinking about was that we had to get back to Tucson where she would get the finest care in the world.

The operation did not take long. When the surgeon came out, I could see by the way he was walking that it was bad. He didn't speak English, but we had an interpreter. As I sat in the surgeon's office with the Weitmans he told us that the blockage was being caused by a large tumor. He had cut out enough of the tumor to relieve the immediate problem. A tumor. Bobbi had ovarian cancer, he said.

I heard him say it, I heard it translated, but it didn't really sink in. In that situation I didn't even begin to think about long-term treatment. What mattered was the next day, the next hour, and then we'd worry about the days after that.

Bobbi was in the recovery room. It was incredibly hot in there, and the nurses were sitting at a table just outside the room smoking. There were no private rooms in this hospital. At first they put her in a multi-patient room where the loudest sound was people moaning. We finally managed to get her into a double room. There wasn't even a fan in the room. At night we couldn't keep the window open and the lights on because of the mosquitoes. The hospital was on a busy road, so there was a constant roar of traffic outside. The best hospital in Budapest, supposedly, but it was the most deplorable situation imaginable. There wasn't even any toilet tissue in the bathrooms, so you'd see people walking in the hallways carrying their own tissues.

I was so used to being in control. I ran my team. At home our lives basically ran around my schedule. I had assistants to take care of most of the minor things in my life. Here I was practically helpless. We were in a place where I didn't speak the language, in a hospital with seemingly antiquated medical facilities.

And then Bobbi's temperature started rising. She had a raging fever. We needed to get her fever down. Paul Weitman raced back and forth to the hotel to bring back trash bags filled with ice. Paul and I went out and bought a fan and a foam cooler so we could prevent the ice from melting. Bobbi, naturally, insisted that we share that ice with the woman in the next bed. Gradually, her fever started falling.

It was obvious things were not getting better. Bobbi was in a tremendous amount of pain, but they wouldn't give her any pain medication. One of the doctors spoke just enough English for us to understand him. We understood him to be telling us that they had decided they were going to have to do more surgery. That was our greatest fear. I was certain that she could not survive a second surgery. So it wasn't going to happen.

In the past Bobbi and I had done a lot of charitable work for the university arthritis center and cancer center. Bobbi had served as the cochairman of the local American Cancer Center Society and among other things had chaired two benefit concerts. I have never been too comfortable using my fame to get special treatment. But this time I didn't hesitate. Bobbi had earned everything special we could give her. I called the director of the medical center, Dr. Dean Dahlen, for advice. Don't move her, he told me. Don't do anything yet. He immediately sent our family doctor, Dr. Michael Maricic, and an emergency surgeon, Dr. Daniel Spaite, to Budapest to take control of her care.

We were thinking of any way possible to get Bobbi home. I called Robert Sarver, who now owns the Phoenix Suns but at that point was a banker. He was a close family friend; he'd dated Christi for a long time and he and Bobbi had become close. He had a plane that could fly that distance. As soon as he heard what was going on he offered any help he could give.

I called home. Our granddaughter, Julie, answered the phone. For some reason I don't remember, several of our kids and grandchildren were at our house. As soon as Julie heard my voice she asked, "What's wrong?"

"I need to talk to your mom," I said.

As soon as I told Jodi she began making plans to fly to Hungary. She intended to fly out the next day. The grandkids got poster board and began making GET WELL MAMA BOBBI signs for her to bring with her. Jodi didn't have a valid passport, so our congressman, Jim Kolbe, got in touch with someone at the passport center in Houston. Jody flew to Houston the next day and was issued an emergency passport. So it took her an extra day to get to Budapest.

The two doctors from the University Medical Center arrived in Budapest the next day. Dr. Spaite was the head of emergency transportation at the university. After examining Bobbi he told me she couldn't be moved. "She's bloated," he explained. "She can't fly. She won't be able to withstand the pressure. There'll be a small window when she would be able to make it home." We had to be ready to move immediately during that time period.

Dr. Spaite and Dr. Maricic told me that the Hungarian doctors wanted to take Bobbi back into surgery. They were both adamant that they would not allow that to happen. She's too weak, they said. She couldn't survive another surgery. They promised me, "No one is going to take her anywhere. We're not leaving this room." And they didn't.

One of them sat there while the other one slept. They just wouldn't leave her. If they hadn't come over, I don't believe Bobbi would have made it home.

Dr. Dahlen had put us in contact with Dr. David Alberts, an oncologist who was the director of the Arizona Cancer Center—and one of the leading ovarian cancer experts in the world. We were unbelievably fortunate to have the best doctor for her condition at the university. Dr. Alberts was so calm, so reassuring; he was the first person to give us any hope. "It's treatable," he told me. "We just have to get her back here."

Her temperature stabilized, but it wouldn't go down. We couldn't fly home until it did. Dr. Alberts knew an excellent Hungarian doctor who had recently spent a year working at the University of Arizona. He got in contact with this doctor, who happened to be on a skiing vacation in the Alps, but he agreed to cut short his trip and meet us in Vienna. To make the situation just a little worse, the hospital in Budapest wouldn't release her until the entire bill was paid. In cash. They didn't know anything about health insurance. They wouldn't take a credit card. They wouldn't even take a check. Cash. The situation was getting worse and worse. The loss to Utah seemed about a thousand years ago. Paul Weitman and I ran around to ATM machines all over the city getting enough money to pay the bill. Finally we got an ambulance. They called it an ambulance, but it was little more than a delivery van with a bed in the back, and we moved Bobbi to Vienna.

The University of Vienna Hospital was comparable to any American hospital. Doctors there finally gave her the pain medication she needed and gradually her fever came down. We flew back to Tucson on Robert Sarver's Gulfstream, which had been outfitted as a flying hospital. Someone had set up a bed, with the necessary IVs, we had two nurses, and the two doctors flew with us. Our son Steve met the plane. As soon as Bobbi was out of sight he broke into tears because she looked so bad. Then Dave Alberts took charge of her treatment.

Bobbi was diagnosed with advanced ovarian cancer. Dr. Alberts put her in a wing called 3 Northwest, which is where the seriously ill cancer patients are treated. When he examined her for the first time, he discovered she had what is called a frozen pelvis. That meant the tumor was so large there wasn't even enough room for him to put his hand into the pelvis. It's apparently a very tough point at which to begin treatment. Bobbi was diagnosed with stage 3 cancer in her pelvis and upper abdomen. There was, however, some promising news; the cancer hadn't spread to any of her other major organs. Dave Alberts was always optimistic. It's treatable, he insisted.

What had happened to Bobbi and me wasn't unusual. We knew it happened to other people every day. We just never even considered the possibility something this terrible could happen to us. Without any warning we suddenly found ourselves in the middle of a new world, a world with a different and strange vocabulary, with new people, with really scary possibilities. All the plans we'd made were gone. Our old life was gone. The schedule we'd lived by for decades—this time for recruiting, this for the preseason, this for the season—that was all done. It was a really steep learning curve for us.

Throughout it all Bobbi's spirit was phenomenal. She was the one trying to make everybody else feel better. She immediately established a close bond with Dr. Alberts. At the very beginning of their relationship she made him promise that he would never come into her room without a smile on his face.

The treatment philosophy at the University Medical Center, and as I learned at most of the top cancer centers, is that you begin by using chemotherapy to shrink the tumor to the smallest size possible—in Bobbi's case, to about the size of a quarter—and then you do surgery. So Dr. Alberts and his oncology nurse, an amazing woman named Ardie Delforge, who became a close friend, immediately began chemo.

It was impossible to keep Bobbi's illness secret in a small town like Tucson. Rumors were already spreading that the situation was much worse than it was, and we wanted to stop them. So we issued a press release: "During the past several weeks there has been much speculation about Bobbi's health. We want to end any rumors and confirm that Bobbi is being treated for ovarian cancer . . . Her diagnosis was confirmed shortly after we returned from a trip to Europe. Because of our desire for privacy, we hesitated making her condition public until we as a family understood the implications of this disease and what we are facing.

"Bobbi and I want to assure everyone that she is doing great and we have every reason to believe her prognosis is excellent . . .

"We are very grateful for the thoughtfulness and concern that everyone has expressed . . . We also appreciate the respect for our privacy and hope this will continue as we move forward . . ."

Bobbi didn't want sympathy, and she didn't want people spending their time—or hers—talking about her cancer. But she never tried to hide it, or shied away from talking about it. "I just feel I've had a wonderful life," she told a reporter for the *Arizona Daily Star*. "God has a plan for all of us, and if that's his plan, that will be it."

Tucson was amazingly supportive, mostly by not making a really big deal about her illness. And when we attended Reggie Geary's wedding in early August, which was sort a reunion of recent players, everything seemed normal.

We learned more than we ever wanted to know about ovarian cancer. Like most people, until we were in the middle of this we didn't know anything about it. Risk factors include an early first period, as early as age eleven or twelve, and a late menopause, in the midfifties. Typically, a woman who contracts ovarian cancer has had two pregnancies at most; Bobbi was unique, having had five children. Most of the women who get it haven't used oral contraceptives, meaning that they have had their period month after month after month. Other risk factors include a Western diet and a lack of physical activity, so women who get ovarian cancer tend to be somewhat overweight.

It's a disease that often strikes well-educated professional women who may never have gotten pregnant. Birth control pills are very protective. Taking an oral contraceptive for two or more years reduces risk of ovarian cancer by as much as 75 percent. Physical activity reduces the risk of ovarian cancer by 30 percent. Knowing all this didn't do us any good; all we were concerned about was getting rid of it and getting our old lives back.

Bobbi spent the summer getting chemo to shrink the tumor. Normally I spent a lot of time during the summer going to the camps and getting to know the high school prospects. The NCAA permits the head coach and two assistants to recruit during that period, but we got permission for Coach Roz to go out in my place. So for the first time . . . for the first time in our lives, Bobbi and I spent a quiet summer at the beach.

We owned a small house we loved in Coronado, an island community in San Diego Bay. Dr. Alberts had arranged for Bobbi to have most of her chemo treatments at UC San Diego's cancer center. Bobbi and I started every day she felt strong enough with our early morning walk along the beach. On our walks we talked about the kids, the basketball program, the lives of our friends, just about anything—except cancer. We didn't avoid it—making plans for her next treatment was part of every day—but we tried not to let it become the only thing in our lives.

One of the first things we did that summer was shop for wigs. We knew the chemo would cause Bobbi's hair to fall out and we wanted to be prepared for it. Bobbi had always loved to shop, and on occasion she'd drag me along, but this time we went together to a store that specialized in wigs for cancer patients. It was as if we were shopping for dresses. She modeled several wigs for me, asking for my approval. How does this one look? What do you think about this one? Eventually we got two wigs, one a little more sporty and one dressier. She put them away for several weeks. When her hair finally started falling out, without saying anything about it she took the wigs out of her closet and started wearing them.

The one thing doctors couldn't control with chemo was fatigue. So Bobbi was often very tired. Most afternoons after lunch she would put an old movie on TV, usually something with a happy ending, and take a nap. In the early fall Dr. Alberts operated and removed the remnants of the tumor. Things looked good. Dr. Alberts wanted her to continue chemo to kill any remaining cancer cells, but things looked good. Bobbi knew all the statistics, she knew about survival rates—she knew that the life expectancy of a woman with stage 3 ovarian cancer is sixty-three months—and how tough it was to really beat this disease, but we never discussed it. Bobbi had brought some materials home from the hospital but we didn't look at them. She said, "I don't want to find out any more about this than what I know right now." And I had decided to listen to Dr. Alberts rather than reading statistics. As he said, "In our large database in the study, many women are seven to ten years after diagnosis and still disease free." We knew she was being treated by the best ovarian cancer doctor in the world. He was optimistic. Things looked good.

When Bobbi's cancer had been revealed, some people speculated I might have to take a leave of absence from the program, or even retire. At first, even I didn't know what was going to happen. I had taken the summer off to be with her, but as Bobbi's health improved, there was no reason not to go back to work. We were a very young team in 1998–99, starting three freshmen, among them Richard Jefferson and Michael Wright.

Freshmen are like spring, they come with hope. You look at their raw ability and anticipate working with them and watching them grow. We were very lucky to get Richard Jefferson. His mother, Meekness, was a minister and motivational speaker who travels throughout the country and owns a small bookstore near Phoenix, about thirty-five minutes from the Arizona State campus. Bill Frieder had recruited him; he probably even showed him those bank commercials. Fortunately for us,

Meekness would not allow him to go to ASU because their nickname was the Sun Devils. She said she would never allow her son to go to a school that had the devil as a mascot. Frieder was no longer there anyway, having been fired during Richard's senior year, which left Arizona State's coaching situation unsettled. We became an easy choice for him.

Bobbi's health was good enough for her to come to our games. It was almost as if nothing had happened. The band was still greeting us, Hi, Lute, Hi, Bobbi, and she was still sitting in her usual seat across the court from me. But there were always little reminders that things were different. Often, for example, when I looked across the court I'd see our new close friends, Dr. Alberts and his wife, Heather, sitting near Bobbi. Dave had been attending Arizona basketball games before I got there. The first time he and Heather went with Bobbi, Dave sat between them. When the game started, he opened up a red folder and started going through a pile of papers. Bobbi asked Heather, "What's he doing?"

"Dave's working," Heather explained. "This is what life with Dave is like. He works all the time, everywhere he goes."

Instead of complaining, Bobbi leaned back in her seat, satisfied. "That's good," she decided. "I like the fact that my oncologist is working all the time." She looked directly at Dave. "Just keep working."

Bobbi didn't miss any home games. It was pretty amazing. Generally we played home games on Thursday and Saturday, then went on the road the following week. If she had to have any type of procedure done, she'd schedule it for Sunday, after a home game, so by the time we got home she'd be well enough to go to the games. That's how we got through the season.

In November, we celebrated our forty-fifth anniversary. The fact that she was doing so well made it an extra special occasion, we had the whole family there. And she surprised me. When we were married in 1953, Bobbi had a wedding dress and a going-away outfit. Her going-away outfit, the clothes she changed into at the reception before we left for our one-night snowed-in honeymoon, was a beautiful green velvet fitted suit.

At our anniversary party she disappeared into our bedroom for a little while, and when she returned I looked at her, and I was stunned. She was dressed in her going-away outfit. She'd kept it. She still fit into it. And she still looked beautiful.

There are moments that mean so much they couldn't possibly be planned. I didn't think about how to respond. I'd had long-stemmed roses delivered to her earlier in the day. I took one of the roses and I got down on my knee in front of her and I told her that I loved her and asked her to marry me all over again.

When you can make your children cry with joy, you must be doing the right thing. Bobbi and I had been through a lifetime together. After you've raised five children you've pretty much dealt with the complete range of good times and troubled times. We'd gotten to this moment, and we still had each other. I think that's what we saw in each other's face that night.

Dave Alberts became a constant presence in our lives. He was always looking for the next treatment, always upbeat. There was a company in Switzerland working on a promising new drug, for example, and he tried everything to get it. We didn't want to get too excited because it was still experimental, but Dave told us the initial results had been very promising. The problem was that the company had only a limited amount of the drug and needed all they could produce for clinical trials. Dave tried hard to get it, he spoke to everyone, but in essence it came down to the fact that the company couldn't afford to give it to anyone with only a slight chance of long-term survival; it might not help her, and if it didn't, it would skew their test results. They wanted to show survival data. All of us kind of dismissed it as just another step. Dave told us there would be other methods we would use, but it was difficult news to hear. You invest yourself in hope, and any little piece of bad news is very painful.

Dr. Alberts remembers that every time he had to give her some bad news she would respond by ordering him, "No frowns, just big smiles."

1998–99 was an erratic basketball season, but that had nothing to do with Bobbi's illness. From the moment I got to the office until I left at night I was focused on basketball. I was as passionate about the game—and about winning—as I'd ever been. There might have been nights when I got home a little earlier than usual, but I worked just as hard, and just as long, that season as I'd always done.

We finished a credible 22–7, second in the Pac-10. That earned us a number-four seed in the Midwest region. We played thirteenth-seeded Oklahoma in the first game, and we lost 61–60 on a tip-in. It was one of those games. Michael Wright, who'd had a fine season, averaging almost fourteen points a game, was inbounding the ball with forty-eight seconds left. We were up a point. Oklahoma wasn't pressing. But somehow Michael stepped over the end line before making the pass. We lost the ball. It's the kind of play that doesn't happen once a season, but it happened. It was a simple mistake, a mistake that any player could make, magnified by the moment. Oklahoma missed a three-point shot. The ball bounced away from our rebounders. They got a follow-up; they missed that, too. Then they managed to get a tip-in to put them ahead. Literally, that's the way the basketball bounces. We still had a chance to win. Jason Terry, the leading scorer in the Pac-10 and the conference Player of the Year, missed a short jumper. Richard Jefferson got the rebound and missed another jump shot. We were eliminated.

The previous three seasons we'd been 11–2 in the tournament, but the next day the media was writing about our first-round losses again. There wasn't much I could do about it. We'd won twenty-two games starting three freshmen. I remember that when Bobbi and I left the arena after that game, the one thing we weren't thinking about was cancer. Both of us were devastated by the loss.

Bobbi went through four rounds of chemo and three surgeries, and at the sports awards banquet in the spring we were able to announce that, according to all the tests, she was cancer free. Bobbi got a long standing ovation. We didn't tell anyone at that time, but "cancer free" was the medical term. It didn't mean completely cancer free. Dr. Alberts told us that there was still one little spot, but it was small enough for her to be considered medically cancer free. The fact that spot was there made me feel she wasn't out of the woods.

We were living with cancer. Dealing with it had simply become part of our lives, and with a little luck it would be a part of our lives for a long, long time. On July 3, 1999, we were reminded how lucky we were. Ricky Byrdsong, who had been my assistant coach when I first came to Arizona and had quickly become a close friend, was shot and killed by a white supremacist while he was jogging outside his Skokie, Illinois, home with his two children. He was killed by a racist because of his skin color. It was the most senseless crime imaginable; Ricky never had an unkind word or thought for anyone. I don't think there was any person who met Ricky who did not like and respect him. He was a man you couldn't help but admire. A man who didn't hate anybody in the world was the victim of a hate crime.

Like everybody who knew Ricky and Sherialyn, our whole family was devastated. Ricky was one of those people who always had a smile on his face, who made other people smile. At the press conference after he had been fired as head coach by Northwestern, for example, he held up a sign reading WILL WORK FOR FOOD.

Sherialyn asked me to speak at his funeral. She wanted the service to be a celebration of a wonderful life rather than a solemn service. The church was more than filled; they had to set up speakers outside so everyone who wanted to be there could participate. Among the mourners were several of our ex-players; Steve Kerr served as a pallbearer. I was the first speaker; and I talked about Ricky and his big feet and Ricky forgetting his shoes and forgetting his driver's license. I also told them about the night we were out recruiting and Ricky, looking for anything positive to say about me, told the parents of this young man, "Coach has never been arrested."

There were more than a thousand of us there that day to honor him, and we all laughed with love for him. We all cried a little, too. Maybe a lot.

Ricky was not a particularly successful basketball coach—if you measure success by wins and losses, but if you measure it by the relationships you make in your career, by the impact you make on young lives, or by the footprint you make in the earth, Ricky had very big feet.

After everything that had happened, the predictability of the basketball season was very welcome. We were depending on three freshmen again—Gilbert Arenas, Jason Gardner, and Luke Walton—so I knew we'd have to go through the whole learning process. We stayed in the top ten all season, although we had some key injuries, particularly Richard Jefferson, who missed almost eight weeks with a stress fracture, as well as all the normal problems.

Our biggest game took place in early January. We were ranked fifth—and we were playing number-one-ranked and undefeated Stanford on their court. We were good, but we were inexperienced and very thin. We only had eight scholarship players. Before the season three players decided to transfer, among them Luke Recker, who left when his girlfriend was injured in a car crash. A Lithuanian player decided to return home. To fill out the bench we recruited a player from the football team, Peter Hansen, a kick-blocking specialist. When he got into a game the crowd would cheer, "Block that kick! Block that kick!"

Two freshmen, Gardner and Arenas, were starting in the backcourt. So when Richard Jefferson broke his right foot three minutes into the game, we knew we were going to have to gut it out. This was when all those extra laps paid off. At the beginning of the second half we took the lead with an 18–4 run. Stanford came from ten down to get within a point with thirty seconds left, but Jason Gardner hit two free throws to seal the upset win—and the six hundredth victory of my coaching career.

"The five hundredth is easy to remember," I told reporters. "Miles Simon's sixty-five-footer beat Cincinnati. The six hundredth win, against number-one Stanford, is not one I'll forget, no matter how many senior moments I may have."

Bobbi described my reaction perfectly, saying, "He doesn't say anything, but I think he's excited."

Four hundred and seven of those wins took place in Arizona. In honor of our success athletic director Jim Livengood decided to name the court at McKale the Lute Olson Court. It wasn't something I expected, but I certainly appreciated it. The ceremony was held the Thursday following the win at Stanford, after a tough game with Washington State—we won by five—they set up chairs right on the court. While I was sitting there I wondered whether, if we'd lost, they would have taken my name off the court.

I remember standing there that night with my arm around Bobbi's waist, as the fans cheered and the university unveiled the court with my name on it, feeling so proud. The Lute Olson Court. My name had appeared on a lot of awards and trophies and plaques, I was quoted in the newspapers almost every day, but this was special. This was from my family, my very large extended family. And while it was my name that appeared in the middle of the court, this was really a tribute to the entire program we had built—all the kids who provided so many thrills for so many people for so many seasons, and all the assistant coaches and the managers and the support staff. Everybody who had contributed to creating an era of excellence at the University of Arizona.

That night I was also feeling that Bobbi and I had made it through the roughest period of our marriage. I would never have dared use the word "cured." I could barely say the word "remission." We both knew there was always the chance that her cancer would return, but that night I felt we'd gotten through the worst of that terrible period.

We finished the season 27–7, and the NCAA made us the number-one seed in the West. When we were healthy we were that good, but we weren't healthy. Just before the tournament we lost 7'1" Loren Woods, our top scorer and second leading rebounder, when he fell during a game against Washington State and compressed several discs in his back. He was lost for the rest of the season. Eventually he required two operations, and doctors had to put four screws and a plate in his back. Richard Jefferson was back, but far from full strength. We were able to beat Jackson State in our first game, but we were just too thin and lost to Wisconsin 66–59 in the second game. In that game Jefferson got into foul trouble and played only twenty-four minutes, getting only five shots, and we just didn't have the experience or the depth to overcome those problems.

Obviously it was a disappointing end to the season, but with the whole team coming back next season, it was easy to get excited about the possibilities. But even before we could get started, we got some more bad news. In mid-May Coach Scott Thompson, who had played for me at Iowa and then spent six seasons as my assistant at both Iowa and Arizona before becoming a head coach at Cornell, was diagnosed with colon cancer. During the time we'd worked together, Scott and his wife, Rebecca, had become our close friends. So Bobbi and Scott spent a lot of time on the phone that summer, trading cancer stories. It was the perfect relationship: Both of them were more interested in providing support to the other one than spending time feeling sorry for themselves.

Throughout that summer Bobbi continued seeing Dave Alberts for treatment. The two of them had developed a special, wonderful relationship. Dave Alberts has the doctor's gift of making every patient feel that they are his most important patient, but he's a very serious guy. Bobbi had broken through that serious barrier right away. When I was working, our daughter, Jodi, would drive her to the hospital. Jodi claims that Bobbi would flirt with Dave right in front of her. "Jodi, you'll have to leave," Bobbi would tell her. "Dave's here. Let me close the curtain, Dave, so we can be alone." Or she'd sigh and tell him, "Dave, sometimes I wish you weren't my doctor because we could have so much fun together." Dave would often call to check on his patients while he was working out on his exercise bike. One afternoon he called Bobbi, huffing and puffing and she told him, "If this is an obscene phone call, Dave, well, you just go right ahead."

Of course, as Jodi points out, Bobbi charmed every man she met. She had a way of flirting so that everybody knew it was meant in fun, but it was her way of letting them know how much she liked them. She was always telling men, "No wonder your wife loves you. You're so this and that. You can come over to our house anytime and I'll cook you dinner." Or, "It's a good thing you and I aren't single."

For me, it was as close to a normal summer of scouting and preparing for the season as possible. We were anticipating a great year. Including Luke Walton, we would have six men capable of starting. We were starting five future pros, every one of them a legitimate candidate for the Wooden Award, given annually to the Pac-10 Player of the Year, which was unprecedented. So when Richard Jefferson told reporters, "If you had to draw up a college basketball team, how could you draw up a better team? At our best we can beat any team in the country," nobody disagreed. The AP ranked us preseason number-one.

It started as a dream season, but one night in early November it became my worst nightmare. As every family who has been through this knows, you wake every morning hoping it's going to be just another day, but you're always fearful it isn't. Somewhere in the back of your mind you're always wondering if this is going to be the day you've been dreading. Bobbi and I were home one night in early November, a normal night at home, when she told me she had a terrible pain in her stomach. "I have to go to the hospital," she said. That was so unlike her. Usually when she was in pain she'd take some pills and lie down, but not this time; this time she admitted the pain was unbearable. "Please take me to the hospital."

Ardie was there to meet us. We checked her into 3 Northwest under an assumed name. As soon as she got there, they began giving her pain medication. For the next eight weeks, the hospital was our home. We were still hopeful that her cancer was treatable, if not beatable. Dr. Alberts never told us it wasn't.

I was with her every possible minute. I would get there early in the morning to wake her up. I'd bring as much work as I could with me, and when she dozed off, I sat at a little table there and got it done. Sometimes I'd stay until lunch, then leave for practice. I'd come back when that was done, and we'd spend the night talking or watching TV. Then, when she was getting tired, the nurse would come in and give her medication to allow her to relax and sleep. I'd sit on the bed and we would hold hands and say the Lord's Prayer together. Then usually I'd go home, although there were some nights that I slept on a rollaway bed in her room. Whether I had stayed there or gone home, when she woke up in the morning I would be there. That was our routine. If we had a home game, I would stop and visit with her on my way to McKale. Unfortunately, the TV sets in the hospital did not get our games, so Dave Alberts would go to the hospital right from McKale to describe to her what had happened. I would come by after every game, although by the time I got there she was usually asleep.

It was Bobbi's wish that we keep the fact that she was in the hospital private, but that was almost impossible. She was registered under a different name, but in Tucson we were both instantly recognizable. We were often in the newspapers or on TV. At first Bobbi and I would take our morning walks around the area, and when she could no longer walk, I would take her out onto the patio in her wheelchair. So many people recognized us or knew that Bobbi was there, but, amazingly, nobody, absolutely nobody, talked about it to the media. If the media knew, it was not reported. This was a secret shared by an entire city.

There were things I had to do that couldn't be avoided. Before the season started, the conference has a media day to generate publicity for the upcoming season. It was being held in Los Angeles, and if I wasn't there, people would wonder why. The doctors told me she would be fine. My plan was to fly there in the morning and return in the afternoon. I did my interviews with TV and radio in the morning, then spoke to the print media. As I was going in to the media luncheon my daughters Jody and Vicki called and told me to come home on the next plane. Bobbi had gotten a lot worse. Dr. Alberts had put her on a respirator. When I spoke to him, he acknowledged it was very serious.

The next flight to Tucson didn't take off for more than two hours. I stayed at the luncheon and answered questions about the team. That was one of those many days I could never forget. Sitting there talking basketball, responding to questions, when my heart was breaking. At that moment there was only one thing on my mind, and that was the one thing I couldn't talk about.

I was trying to live two lives simultaneously. Late one night, I remember, Bobbi had had a bad day and they done some surgery to make her more comfortable, so I was with her in the intensive care unit. The hospital was very quiet and Dr. Alberts was sitting with me, telling me what he was doing to try to control her pain. I got a call from the mother of an important recruit. She was so excited, she said. Her son had decided to come to the University of Arizona to play basketball for me. It was the intersection of my profession and my life. I really was pleased to hear that, and I had to show my enthusiasm. It was a moment Bobbi and I had shared so many times in our life: Guess who just called and committed? For the first time, I had no one to share it with.

We opened up the season at the Maui Invitational in Hawaii on November 20. Bobbi was going through a particularly difficult time. The surgeons had to operate several times, trying to fight off different attacks. One operation lasted almost nineteen hours, and she spent the next nine days in intensive care. Bobbi was a fighter. I had considered taking a leave of absence to stay with her. Obviously, everybody would have known something was desperately wrong if I wasn't in Hawaii, but Bobbi insisted that I go. "You get over there with your team," she said. "I'm here and I'm okay." I didn't know whether to go or stay home.

I didn't know what to do. I spoke with Bobbie Stehbens, and she offered to come out and stay with her while I was gone. Offered? She insisted.

When Bobbie Stehbens came into Bobbi's room for the first time, she had the hardest time keeping from breaking down. At that time Bobbi had just come out of another surgery and couldn't speak. To communicate with us she wrote notes on a clipboard. Typically, she wrote funny things, trying to make light of the situation.

I went to Maui, knowing that Bobbie Stehbens and close friends like Betty Weitman and Norma Slone and her sister and our girls, people we loved, would be with her all the time. Dr. Alberts promised me that if there was a significant change, they would call me immediately. We had a private plane standing by to fly me home.

The players may have suspected that her condition had gotten worse, but if they did, they didn't show it. We were loaded, and we opened the season ranked number one. In Hawaii we beat eighth-ranked Illinois to win the tournament.

I raced back to Tucson. Bobbi had actually gotten a little better. Through all the ups and downs her spirit never wavered an inch. We never talked about mortality; it was always about the future, always, "When I get out of here . . ." One time, I remember, in early December Dave Alberts came to see her directly after run-walking the Tucson Half Marathon, still dressed in his running clothes. At first Bobbi thought it was Robert Sarver, but gradually realized it was her doctor. "Where have you been dressed like that?" she asked. "What are you doing?"

"I just did the Tucson Half Marathon," he told her. Then described it to her.

She said firmly, "Next year I want to do that."

But Bobbie Stehbens told me later that they had spoken about the situation and Bobbi faced reality and accepted it. They talked about her disease and the different surgeries and treatments. Bobbie Stehbens told me that my Bobbi said some of the things she went through were for the family, not for herself. The closest she came to being angry was shaking her head and wondering, "How did I ever catch this?"

Bobbi's faith was very important to her. She never made a fuss about it, but she was a good Christian. I remember she once asked Dave Alberts, "Are you a believer?" Absolutely, he told her. "Good," she said, satisfied. "That's important." Later she told him, "I'm not afraid of death. I know where I'm going." Bobbi's mother had died earlier that year, and sometimes she would talk with Bobbie Stehbens about seeing her again. I know that her faith provided a lot of comfort. Throughout this whole horrible process Bobbi seemed more concerned about the effect it was having on the people she loved than about her own illness. She didn't want her illness to change the lives of the people around her.

In early December we were playing fifteenth-ranked UConn in Storrs, Connecticut. Bobbi's condition had deteriorated and Dave wanted to operate again. I didn't make the trip, instead giving the team to Jim Rosborough. The day before the game, we issued a statement explaining I had stayed in Tucson "because Bobbi was having a procedure related to her ongoing treatment for ovarian cancer."

That was the first time, I think, that people began to understand that Bobbi's cancer had returned. I had missed only one previous game in my career. Years earlier, I'd had the flu. That was tough for me. This decision was easy to make. The team played very well, but a disputed goal-tending call at the end cost us the game, 71–69. Two years later an official in that game apologized to Roz for that call, telling him, "I want you to know that I wasn't intentionally trying to do anything. It was a call from the heart."

I wasn't living my life day-to-day, it was more like hour-to-hour. We wouldn't give up hope. There was no question that the team was affected by everything that was going on. We didn't tell them very much, just that Bobbi was very sick. We tried to keep things as normal as possible, not too high, not too low, but that was impossible. Things weren't normal. I was able to return for our next three games, but obviously I was distracted. In practice I probably was even a little tougher than usual on the team, and usually I was pretty tough.

Our whole family, all our children and grandchildren, came to Tucson for Christmas. Everybody wanted to be with her, and Jody had to take charge when I wasn't there. A couple of days before Christmas all of us—I think there were twenty-four people—squeezed into her room for a little ceremony. Our pastor, Mark Roessler, was there with his wife and two girls. Dr. Dan Spaite, the doctor who'd flown to Budapest two years earlier and from then on was with Bobbi all the time, came to Bobbi's room that night with his wife and their son and daughter and led us all in Christmas carols. It would be accurate to say that no one in that room had ever felt the love for our family and the meaning of Christmas more than that night in Bobbi's hospital room. We knew we were saying good-bye to her.

A few days after Christmas I coached the team in the first game of our annual Fiesta Bowl Tournament. We beat Butler by a dozen points. The next night Dave and Ardie came over to the house. I knew why they were there. "There's nothing more we can do," Dave told us. "It's just a matter of time."

We talked about time, about keeping her comfortable, and about bringing her home.

We had scheduled a shootaround, a shooting practice session, for the following morning. December 30, a Saturday. We were playing Mississippi State in the tournament championship game that night. I went to the arena and asked the coaches to come in to my office. I'm taking a leave of absence, I told them. Roz'll be coaching the team. I don't know when I'll be back. It depends.

There were some tears. Somehow I managed to maintain my composure.

Then we called the team into the locker room to tell them I was taking an indefinite leave of absence. "I have to take some time off to be with my family," I began. "I don't know when I'm going to be able to come back. As soon as possible, I promise you. I want all of you to know that I'm proud of you, of what you've accomplished so far . . ." Then I just couldn't say anything else. I'd held it together for so many weeks, I just couldn't do it anymore. I wiped away the first few tears, but it . . . I just couldn't do it anymore. I couldn't finish. The kids knew. They knew.

I left the locker and walked down the hallway with one of our senior managers, Jack Murphy. Murph's father had died a year earlier, and we'd spent some time together talking about it, getting through it. Jack reminded me of my own words. We'd talked about love and life and focusing on the wonderful memories. Jack told me how sorry the whole team was, how much the team loved Bobbi. It was a tough day, a tough day. Then I went home.

The kids were shaken by the news. "We're all upset," Loren Woods told a reporter. "Mrs. Olson is like a second mother to a lot of us."

Richard Jefferson added, "This is devastating. Mrs. Olson was very instrumental in recruiting every player who has ever come here." For the game that night several players paid tribute to Bobbi on their uniform. Richard Jefferson wrote MRS. O on his elbow pad. Gilbert Arenas wrote her name on the ankle tape. Guard Lamont Frazier wrote it on protective padding covering his forearm.

The burden on the coaches and players was enormous. It was a game they all wanted to win so badly that they had a difficult time focusing. We lost the tournament final to Mississippi State, 75–74.

We planned to bring Bobbi home right after New Year's. We'd hired nurses. Jody and her husband, Jon, had purchased a hospital bed large enough that I could sleep in it with her. We'd gotten all the medical supplies we needed, including the pain medication. Everything was in place.

For many years Bobbi and I had spent New Year's Eve with Paul and Betty Weitman. Most of the time it was just the four of us. From the moment I'd taken my leave of absence, I'd basically been living at the hospital. Paul suggested I come to his house New Year's Eve and we'd have something to eat. Bobbi was receiving a lot of morphine at that time, and Dr. Alberts assured me he'd call if . . . That's all we had left, if . . . And finally, when . . .

Our daughters had taken turns staying with her when I couldn't be there. After I'd left, Bobbi's pain had increased. "I'm going to call Daddy," Jody told her. Bobbi asked her not to, but Jody insisted. "No, no, you want him here."

"No, I'm fine with you girls. I'm just happy you can be here."

Paul has a workout room, and I was down there, finding a release for some of the frustration I was feeling, when Dave Alberts called. "We need you to get up here as quickly as you can," he said. Some of our kids were in her room by the time I got there. Her sister arrived soon after. Our grandkids came. Dave had given her drugs to control the pain, so she was not conscious. There wasn't anything we could do but wait. The arrival of the New Year passed pretty much without notice. I was at peace, too; Bobbi had been through so much, so very much, that I just couldn't stand to see her suffer anymore. When her breathing finally became labored, I climbed into the bed and held her tight in my arms until it was over.

"Bobbi faced her illness with great courage," I said in the statement to the media. "Her love of family remained her priority, and even in her last moments she continued taking care of and comforting all of us."

Our grandson, Matt Brase, added, "She died today, 01/01/01—No. 1 wife, No. 1 mother, No. 1 grandmother. Always No. 1."

I spent the next few weeks in shock. It was like I was living in a nightmare, like it hadn't really happened. It couldn't be real. I was numb. That feeling, or lack of feeling, just wouldn't go away. No matter what I was doing, where I was, who I was talking to, my mind just kept coming back to Bobbi. The only escape I had was watching the team play on television, and even that escape lasted only a few minutes at a time.

The first few days the house was constantly filled with people. Bobbi had touched so many people. Truckloads of food arrived—Chinese,

Mexican, Italian. I think every restaurant in the city sent something. It seemed like everyone in Tucson had a story about Bobbi they wanted to share. In *Sports Illustrated* Curry Kirkpatrick wrote, "No coach's wife was closer to her husband, his players, their university, an entire state; none was cherished more. When she unveiled her smile, a booster opened his pockets. When she prepared her apple pancakes, a recruit was sold. When she said what really mattered, her husband of forty-seven years melted." That seemed right.

There were some other things that needed to be done. Bobbi had not been afraid of death. But she wanted to be prepared for it. When she got really sick, she met with our pastor, Mark Ressler, to make certain that everyone in her life had been forgiven for whatever kinds of problems she might have had; she didn't want to leave this world until she was fine with everybody. Then she dealt with me. There have not been that many people in my life with whom I didn't get along, but one of them was *Arizona Daily Star* columnist Greg Hanson. About six years earlier Khalid Reeves had been accused of something that later proved to be completely false. It was nothing, but Greg wrote a column claiming that while Khalid was going through this problem, I was on a vacation and, basically, all I'd done in the two months since the season ended was vacation. I was furious. I called the editor of the paper and the sports editor and said I needed to speak to them. Maybe they were still concerned about the possibility that I might sue over the false accusations made in the uniform story, but for whatever reasons they came to my office. I showed them my calendar. I went through five straight weeks in which I had not taken one day off—including Sundays. Bobbi had kept track. I had worked 283 straight days. I told them, "I want you to know I will never talk to Greg Hanson again in my life." And I didn't. What happened is that the beat writer would come to our press conferences or call me to ask a few questions, and my answers would wind up in Hanson's column. It was an unpleasant situation for everybody.

Bobbi had told Pastor Ressler that she wanted to make sure she was okay even with Greg Hanson. And then she said to me, "Honey, I hope when I'm gone you can get together with Greg."

When she died, Greg wrote an unbelievable article about Bobbi. It was just beautiful. I called him and asked him to come to my office. "Okay," I said, "we're starting from day one right now. I can't tell you how much I appreciated your column." Ever since that day we've had a good relationship. Thanks to Bobbi.

Five days after her death we held a private memorial service. The following Sunday a larger memorial was held at McKale. Several thousand people attended the service, among them dozens and dozens of former players. No matter how old they were, they were her kids forever. Among the speakers at the family service were Bobbie Stehbens, Sherialyn Byrd-song, and Dave Alberts, who pointed out that, if Bobbi were there, "she'd tell us now that we have all these wonderful people gathered together, we ought to have a wonderful party, not a funeral service."

Justin Wessel spoke for the current team, promising "our team is go-ing to play harder than any team has ever played" in her memory. Steve Kerr spoke for the many players who had been part of the program. "You can't talk about Bobbi without mentioning her utter beauty," he said. "She was a stunning woman. When she would walk into a room the place would light up with her grace and her style . . . Boy, I get a kick of people who say, 'That Lute Olson, he walks into a room, heads turn, people stare.' Hey, Coach, they weren't looking at you. But I have to give you some credit. When you turn on the TV, the announcer says, 'Boy, that Lute Olson, he sure can evaluate talent.' They weren't kid-ding. You had her pegged at an early age . . ."

The following Sunday more than 3,500 people attended the memo-rial service at McKale. The service was televised in Tucson on all of the major networks. After all the years we'd spent walking into McKale, when I walked in that day I felt like I was home. Right after Bobbi died I'd had an idea about a tribute that I felt would be appropriate. I spoke to Jim Livengood about it, and he immediately agreed it was a very good idea. He got permission from the board of regents. So by the time I walked out onto the Lute Olson Court, its name had been changed for-ever. The new name, the Lute and Bobbi Olson Court, had already been painted there. And her name will be on that court as long as we play basketball there.

At the service they read an open letter to her that had been written by Bruce Fraser, "Thanks for coming on every road trip," he wrote, adding, "Coach would've been impossible to deal with without you."

Among the many former players who were there was Sean Rooks, who was then playing for the LA Clippers. The truth is that when Sean was playing for me at Arizona, we didn't have a good relationship. I felt he didn't work as hard as he was capable of working. The kids called him Wookie, and I used to shake my head in frustration, "I gotta hold a two-by-four over Wookie's head all the time." So I was on him a lot. Sometimes a coach has to be tough on a player. You can't worry about being every player's friend. I know Sean didn't like it at all, so we butted heads. That made Sean exactly the type of person Bobbi would care most about; he needed positive reinforcement and she'd given it to him. As hard as I was on him, she was the opposite. The Clippers had a game the night of the funeral, so Sean went to the morning shootaround in LA, then flew to Tucson. After paying his respects, he flew back to Los Angeles for the game that night. When he had been at Arizona, Sean had done everything possible to resist running around the track, but nobody, absolutely nobody, made more of an effort to get back for the memorial than he did. One thing I know for sure; he didn't make that trip for me.

That is the kind of effort that I could never forget. Since then Sean and I have become good friends.

After the service many of our current and former players got together. In the program we'd always emphasized the fact that the team was a family, and I think that day every one of our players felt that relationship. Players from different eras told me later that they felt like they had known each other for years. There was an extraordinary sense of camaraderie. Well, they'd all eaten Bobbi's pancakes.

During the service Justin Wessel remembered that his mother had been nervous about him coming all the way across the country to play at Arizona, but Bobbie had assured her she would take care of him. Sometime later his mother had explained to him, "That's why you're her favorite."

"Mom," he'd responded, "that's the way she treats everybody."

"I know," she'd apparently agreed, "but you're still her favorite."

When Steve Kerr spoke, he talked about that, how just about every player believed he was Bobbi's favorite. And then he added, "They were wrong, of course. I was her favorite."

Tom Tolbert laughed at that. "Are you kidding me? It was me. Bobbi and I were a lot alike. We loved to have fun, loved to laugh. I loved her to death."

Reggie Geary wasn't surprised to hear all that, but still said, "I felt like I was her favorite player. When I was talking to her, she made it seem like whatever I was saying was the most important thing in the world to her. She was very much a motherly figure." That became the one thing we all laughed about, the fact that so many people were convinced Bobbi had liked them best.

"For two years she prepared us for her exit," George Kalil said. "She wanted to go out twinkling."

We played Cal at McKale the night before the funeral. Everybody was feeling enormous pressure. The kids wanted to win that game for Bobbi. Before the game there was a moment of silence. And then two fans each placed a closed rose on her seat. "They were closed red roses," one of those people explained. "They typify that there is still growth. Fans, the team, and the city of Tucson can look forward to the beauty that was exemplified in Bobbi Olson's life."

I watched the game in my bedroom with Jody and a few friends. I'd coached more than a thousand basketball games, but sitting there in my bedroom that night was harder than any one of them. I felt very comfortable with Coach Roz in charge, but I really was concerned how the kids would react. We won the game, 78–75, when Michael Wright hit two free throws with fifteen seconds left to put us ahead. It had been a struggle; our big center Loren Woods, who normally maintained control, just lost it after an official made a questionable call. The official called a technical on Loren and when Loren moved toward him, he called a second technical and threw him out of the game. At that point his teammates had to hold him away from the official. Loren's reaction was more out of frustration than anger, and I understood it. I don't remember him having another technical called on him in his career. But he just wanted to win so very, very much.

Two nights later we lost at home to number-two Stanford, then went up to Washington and beat both Washington and Washington State. The team was 3–2 under Roz and playing well.

I was sixty-seven years old and alone for the first time in my adult life. I spent the next week with my family, trying to decide what to do. In this situation there was no right or wrong, no path to follow. There was a lot of speculation in the media that this might be the time I walked away. I had each of my children come over to the house, and we took a walk and talked about it. Each one individually. Vicky felt that this would be a good time for me to leave: I'd accomplished every goal and it was time to walk away from the long days and nights, the pressure to succeed, the inevitable criticism, and just enjoy the rest of my own life. I think Jody felt the same way, but she told me, "Dad, you have to do what you have to do. You'll know it when it's right."

Eventually you just have to follow your emotions and rely on the fact that your intentions are good. One morning I woke up and knew what I had to do. I'm a coach, that's who I am. I had to coach.

10

For a time, I was lost. Without Bobbi, without basketball, I didn't seem to have any direction. For almost a half century Bobbi and I had done everything together. We were best friends. Learning to live without her was a tremendous adjustment for me. I was living with an empty feeling that wouldn't go away. My daughter Christi and her four children had moved into the house so I wouldn't be alone. Basically, I spent my time looking for something to clean: the garage, the house, the backyard. Steve told me, "Dad, this isn't healthy."

Finally I realized that the best therapy for me was to go back to work. I thought back to the time Steve Kerr's father was assassinated in Beirut. I told Steve to take as much time off as he needed, but only a day later he told me he needed to come back and practice. "The only time I can forget about things is on the court," he said. Now I understood exactly what he meant. Maybe I wasn't ready emotionally, but I felt I owed it to the kids to get back. A lot of them were suffering, too. Bobbi had been a big part of their recruitment and their life on campus. They had lost a good friend.

We had a team meeting to talk about the situation. Toward the end I asked, "You guys have any questions?"

Loren Woods wasn't a guy who said a whole lot, he kept his feelings inside, but I remember he asked, in these words, "When are you coming back so we can get on our way toward getting that ring?"

If I had any doubt about being ready to come back, it ended with that question. I had to get back, more maybe for them than for me. These kids had come to Arizona to play basketball in our program. They had made a commitment to me, and I felt a responsibility to them. The fact that we were playing USC and UCLA the following weekend, games we had to win to stay in the race for the Pac-10 title, was a major factor in my decision.

I also was hoping that maybe by immersing myself in work I could escape the pain for at least a little while every day.

We didn't make any official announcement. I spoke to Roz, then just showed up for practice Monday morning. I began by apologizing to a team for the first time in my career. "Guys, I'm very sorry for being as hard on you as I've been this year." They understood. "Now I need you guys more than ever. I have to be honest with you. I'm going to be back out there, but I don't know how I'm going to feel."

Later that day Eugene Edgerson told a reporter, "It took Coach about five minutes before he started getting on us."

We played USC the following Thursday night. The team had publicly dedicated the remainder of the season to Bobbi. Judy Kessler, who was in charge of booster and ticket sales, had asked my permission to place a red rose on Bobbi's seat. I thought that was a very nice gesture, but I knew that seeing that empty seat, looking at the new name on the court, that was going to be very, very hard. The pep band wanted to do something, too. Before the game they wanted to say their usual "Hi, Bobbi"—and then point to heaven. But our family thought that would just be too hard to deal with before every game.

There were times during the day on Thursday I wasn't sure I was ready for it. When I walked onto the court that night, January 15, I received a standing ovation. The crowd chanted my name. That reception didn't surprise me; the support from the community had been tremendous, and it made the night just a little easier.

We beat USC 71–58. Once the game started, I was fine. I was where I needed to be. I was a coach and I was coaching. And after the game I walked across the floor to the pep band, to thank them personally for attending the memorial service. At the press conference that night I said I really appreciated the support from our fans, but that I hoped from that point on we could just come out our normal way and play basketball.

I hoped so, but for me I knew that wasn't going to be true. We'd opened the season ranked number one, but with all the turmoil we had dropped to twenty-first. Once we were able to regain our focus, we finally started playing to our talent level. When I was working I was okay,

I was distracted, but the rest of the time I just couldn't avoid thinking about Bobbi. We had always driven to home games together, for example. Now Christi made sure my grandson, Jimmy, went with me. The normal route took me right past the hospital. When Bobbi was sick, I'd always stopped there on my way to the game. Now, every time I drove by I just got that awful feeling. I kept thinking that I needed to go back up to 3 Northwest to thank everyone, but I just couldn't do it. It was months before I could even go back to the hospital.

The worst part of my day was coming home at night and not having her there. My daughters knew that, so they continually invited me to their homes for dinner, or the whole family came over to the house on Sunday. They tried, but I was alone. At the end of the day I would get into bed and watch television or put on a CD and hopefully drift to sleep.

We won eighteen of our last twenty-one games, including the last six straight. We finished the season in Palo Alto against first-ranked Stanford. It was a classic basketball game, two heavyweights slugging it out. With five seconds left we were trailing by a point. Jason Gardner inbounded the ball to Loren Woods, who bounced a pass inside to Michael Wright. Michael powered his way to the basket for a two-foot layup and a 76–75 victory.

We were the huge sentimental favorite going into the NCAA tournament. The committee made us the number-two seed in the Midwest region. The Hollywood aspects of the story were unavoidable: The coach's beloved wife dies; the team dedicates the season to her and wins the national championship. The tournament hadn't even started and some people were wondering who would play me in the movie.

That was a tremendous amount of pressure to put on the team, but by this point they were used to it. We easily beat Eastern Illinois and Butler to advance to the Sweet Sixteen. We beat Mississippi, setting up a meeting with the number-one seed in the Midwest, Illinois, in San Antonio. After the game I described it as "a battle and a war." This was a game to show to anyone who doubts basketball is a contact sport. We took the lead early in the game, so Illinois had to foul to stay in the game. And foul. And foul. Six Illini fouled out. We shot fifty-six free throws, including twenty-four in the last five minutes, making forty-three of them, en route to an 87–81 win. Arizona was going to the Final Four for the fourth time. Ironically, the finals were being played in Minneapolis. At the end of the most difficult year of my life, I was going home.

As we drove into Minneapolis I was very surprised to see billboards bearing the message: FOUR BOBBI. Meaning it would have been her fourth trip to the Final Four—and we were playing for her. All over the city thousands of fans, not just Arizona fans, were wearing FOUR BOBBI pins. Every reporter wanted to talk to me about Bobbi. I heard the same questions over and over and over. Fortunately, all five of our kids had come with me, as well as six of our fourteen grandchildren. So the Olson family was present in force. Bobbi was, too. "She's here," our grandson Matt said. "Her spirit is here."

Once again, we just weren't lucky. During practice two days before we were leaving, Luke Walton caught the thumb of his right hand, his shooting hand, in Gilbert Arenas's jersey, fracturing it. He could play, but it was difficult for him to shoot. It was one of those bizarre injuries that just happen.

We played Michigan State in the semifinals. We were up two at halftime, but opened the second half with a 16–1 run. We played classic Arizona basketball: be tough on defense, force turnovers, convert. Defend and run. After that run the game was pretty much over. They didn't get closer than nine points and we won, 80–61. The Spartans were the fifth consecutive number-one seed we'd beaten.

We had one more left. We were playing Duke with Shane Battier for the national championship. I've been around basketball long enough to understand the realities of the game, but there were a lot of people who believed we were fated to win this game. There was a good chance for the kind of storybook ending the media just loves.

The bad news was that during the Michigan State game Gilbert had tried to force his way through a screen and took a shot to his upper chest. He suffered a partial separation of his clavicle. He couldn't even lift his arm above his shoulder. He didn't practice on Sunday and wasn't close to full strength for the game against Duke.

We weren't able to write the fantasy ending everybody anticipated. Loren Woods really stepped up, scoring twenty-two points and grabbing eleven rebounds, but Duke beat us 82–72. The game was a lot closer than the final score, we got within three points four different times, the last time with only 2:31 left, but Battier kept responding. If Gilbert Arenas had been even close to healthy, he would have been the leading scorer and we probably would have won. But he hit only four of seventeen shots. We shot only 38 percent for the game. "It's really tough," I said after the game. "All the emotions the team had to go through, and they withstood them and did a great job to get to the final game. Someone's got to lose. Duke is deserving. We gave them a good run and couldn't get it done."

The officials weren't kind to us. Even Billy Packer, broadcasting the game, criticized the officials for a series of pro-Duke calls. There was one call in particular that I think turned the game around. Duke's great guard, Jason Williams, got in early foul trouble. Then late in the first half he was guarding Jason Gardner. When Gardner drove crosscourt Williams lost his balance and fell over him. If Jason Gardner had gone down or lost possession of the ball, the officials would have had to call a third foul on Williams, no question about it. I feel certain that would have made a tremendous difference in the outcome of the game. Jason Gardner was so strong that he took the collison and didn't even turn over the ball. The crowd started booing at the no call, but, no harm, no foul. Duke 82, Arizona 72.

After the game I felt the sense of disappointment you feel at the end of a long roller coaster ride. In a few weeks I'd experienced unbeliev-able lows and tremendous highs. Now it was all over. When the media asked me how I was going to get through the next few months, I told them, "I've heard from so many people who have lost their life partners and they said it's those memories that will be there all your life and the pain will start diminishing eventually. Never totally. So it's a fact of life, so it's there. Like I've said, thank goodness for family and great friends."

I was telling the truth, I had received numerous letters from people who had lost a loved one later in life. The message in so many of them was the same: You never forget, the memories stay warm, but you do go on with your life. Live life, they all wrote.

We'd lost a basketball game, but as a coach I don't know that I'd ever been more proud of a team. The team had been on an unexpected and difficult ride, too. After the game Loren Woods said, "Coach Olson has taught us so much since we've been in the program, and we all have learned as much as we could learn from him. He's taught us courage, patience, dignity for the program, and dignity for yourselves and your families.

"That's not about Coach Olson. It's just about growing up. All of us seniors came to college as boys and we're leaving as men."

Richard Jefferson added, "This year I learned so much about life and so much about how I need to be for the rest of my life."

As I've said, I had my whole family around me.

Loren Woods had been our only senior starter. I expected at least one underclassman would declare for the NBA draft, maybe two. I don't think I was prepared for what happened. A week after the season ended, juniors Richard Jefferson and Michael Wright announced they were leaving school, and so did sophomore Gilbert Arenas. This was a very close team, these kids loved playing together, and I think that when Gilbert saw the team breaking up, he kind of got caught up in it. We were very proud of the fact that we had four players drafted, Richard Jefferson was the thirteenth pick, Gilbert Arenas thirty-first, Michael Wright thirty-ninth, and Loren was the forty-sixth pick. I was happy for each of them, but we had a tremendous rebuilding job to do. We'd lost four starters. I had to find a way to put a competitive team on the floor the next season. That's what our fans expected. We had some terrific recruits coming in, among them Channing Frye and Salim Stoudamire, Damon Stoudamire's cousin. It was a time of renewal.

As my family had always done when the season ended, we went to the beach at Coronado, where we tried to make things as normal as possible. My kids and my grandchildren never let me be alone, which was very important. Doing the things alone that Bobbi and I had done together for so many years was indescribably painful, but the second time I did them it got just a little easier, and the third time . . . My daughters did as much as possible to fill the emptiness. When we had recruits come up, for example, Christi was always there, and Jodi and Vicki would come over. They knew without my saying a word that if we were going to create a family atmosphere for the recruits I needed their help.

When Christi was ready to move out, Jodi and her husband, Jon, moved in. Sundays were the hardest days for me. When Bobbi was alive we'd usually have the family for dinner on Sunday nights. "We're grilling tonight," we'd tell them. "Come over." The kids made sure that for a long time we didn't miss many Sundays together. If possible, we actually did more things together, as a family, than we'd done in the past, as we all tried to deal with the emptiness.

The end of the basketball season is the beginning of the awards season. For the second consecutive year I was named a finalist for induction into the Basketball Hall of Fame. Among the other nominees were Mike Krzyzewski and Temple's John Chaney. I didn't get in—Coach K, John Chaney, and Moses Malone were elected—but as I had explained to Bobbi a year earlier, just being nominated was a tremendous honor. That was still true, but this time I was very disappointed. It seemed to me that if I was ever going to make it, this would have been such a natural time, with the run we'd had that year and everything surrounding it. And this time, being elected would have meant so much more to me than ever before, because it would have been seen as a celebration of Bobbi's life as well as my career. From a professional standpoint I believed this was an honor I'd earned. My career record was equal to many of the coaches who had already been inducted. Comparing my record to some of those coaches, a North Carolina columnist wrote, "If Lute Olson isn't deserving of being in the Hall of Fame, then you shouldn't have a Hall of Fame." Looking at it, I did believe this was a result of the bias against West Coast basketball. Maybe because our games start later and aren't seen regularly on TV in the East we don't seem to get the respect that we deserve. This has been a complaint of mine for a long time; it didn't start this year. I see it in tournament seedings, I see it in All-American selections, and I hear it when supposedly knowledgeable people talk about college basketball. There isn't too much we can do about it, except continue to beat eastern teams. There was no question in my mind that if I had been coaching in the East I would have been elected. If I didn't get in that year, after everything we'd been through, I had to question whether it would ever happen.

I did receive one honor that was extremely meaningful to me. I was named the recipient of the John Wooden Legends of Coaching Award. More than anyone else, John Wooden had been the coach I'd tried to emulate. There was great satisfaction to know that—at least according to the committee that made the selection—I'd succeeded.

Some people were still wondering if I was going to retire. Retire? I needed basketball more than ever. As I told the media, "If I had ever said anything to Bobbi about getting out to spend more time with her, that would not have gone over. She didn't believe in retirement."

I had always replied to that question by explaining that I would keep coaching as long as I had my health, as long as I had the energy the job takes, and as long as I felt I was doing justice to the program. Now I had another reason. My goal when I started coaching was that I would be a better coach this year than I had been the year before. I still felt that way.

For the first time in more than a decade, when the 2001–02 season began we weren't ranked in the top twenty-five. Nobody knew how good we might be. Including me. We had nine scholarship players, six of them freshmen. We had one returning starter, Jason Gardner, and one returning reserve, Luke Walton. At the beginning of the season I admitted to Roz, "I flat-out don't have the slightest idea how we're going to do this season."

I changed. Or maybe I just adapted to my new circumstances. I probably spent more time with this team than I had with any other team, mostly because I had the time to spend. I had a lot of one-on-one conversations with them, I even joined them at the training table. I was still a disciplinarian; somebody has to be the head coach, you have to be demanding and not very flexible on important matters where the team is concerned, but maybe I had become a little more understanding. I also began spending more time than I had ever before at the charity and promotional events I had always attended. In the past I'd go to these events and get out of there as soon as Bobbi felt it was appropriate. That changed. At our annual Fiesta Bowl tournament, for example, I spent three nights at the dinners.

When we'd gone on the road the previous season I'd always taken one of my kids or grandkids with me. This season good friends like Paul Weitman, Bucky Dennis, a close friend since my year at Long Beach State, Bob Felix, a retired orthodonist who had become close with Bobbi and me when his wife died, and, always, George Kalil, traveled with me. It was very important for me to have someone I could talk to about things other than basketball. It was also time for my family to go back to their own lives.

Apparently Bobbi and I had passed down our love of the game to our grandchildren Julie and Matt Brase. While Bobbi was fighting her illness, Julie had broken the Arizona high school scoring record while leading Catalina Foothills to the state championship as a junior and to the semifinals her senior year, and had been recruited by a lot of the major programs. She finished her career as the second all-time scorer in Arizona high school history—five points behind Mike Bibby. "Papa Lute, why didn't you let me know," she complained when she found out about that. "I could have beaten that easily."

She narrowed her college choices to New Mexico, Arizona State, and Arizona. I told her through the whole recruiting process that I wasn't going to interfere, but if she had any questions to call me. It was very strange being on the other side of the recruiting process. She'd called a number of times to talk about it. I tried very hard to be neutral. This was her life; this was a decision I wanted her to make. I reminded her that she was going to be playing with whatever team she picked for four years, the team was going to become her family, so she should feel very comfortable. I told her to be sure she was comfortable with the coaching staff's philosophy, that they played the kind of ball that she liked. Finally, make sure the school has a strong academic program in your major.

When the time came for Julie to make her decision, she was leaning toward Arizona State. They had a new coach, Charli Turner Thorne, whose style she liked; she'd had a great time on her campus visit, and it was far enough from home—but not too far. Truthfully, the relationship between Arizona and Arizona State has not been a good one, going all the way to the incident with Steve Kerr, although Frieder and I tried to change it. If Julie really wanted to go to Arizona State, I . . . I . . . When she called me to discuss it, I told her honestly, "Julie, I don't care where you go as long as you're happy—and I can watch you practice every single day."

She hung up the phone and told Jody, "You know what, Mom, I don't think Poppa is being very neutral anymore." She played four years at Arizona. She was the captain three years. After graduating in 2003 she became an assistant coach at Loyola Marymount, and in 2005 was hired as an assistant by the WNBA's Phoenix Mercury. So at least part of me ended up in the pros.

Every season begins with a mixture of confidence, curiosity, and a little anxiety. Maybe at the start of the 2001–02 season there was a little more curiosity than normal. We had a lot of talent and little experience. From the first day of practice almost to the very end it was a memorable season. What this team lacked in experience—only two players had gotten meaningful minutes the year before—it made up for with desire and teamwork. We started unranked, but a week after beating number-two Maryland and fifth-ranked Florida to win the Coaches versus Cancer tournament in Madison Square Garden, we moved into the top ten. A month later we beat then sixth-ranked Illinois at the Southwest Showdown. In late December we won our own Fiesta Bowl Classic honoring Bobbi Olson. I learned not to focus on her name on the court. When I saw it, right there, it just brought back too many memories.

At the end of the regular season we beat number-twenty-five Cal and number-twenty USC—opening the second half with a 19–4 run to take control of the game—to win the Pac-10 tournament, which was being held for the first time in twelve years. I had not been in favor of reviving the conference tournament. I felt pretty strongly that if we spent more time thinking about the student-athlete and not the money it wouldn't have been revived. We just ended up beating up on each other before starting the NCAA. I thought that was too much, but as long as we had to play it, I was very pleased to win it.

In the opening round of the NCAA tournament in Albuquerque we barely got by fourteenth-seeded Santa Barbara, 86–81. They hit 16 of 27 three-point attempts and were within a basket with under two minutes left. About all I could say after that game was "We survived one."

Luke Walton had twenty-one points and Channing Frye had eighteen and eleven rebounds as we beat Wyoming 68–60 to advance to the Sweet Sixteen for the ninth time in fifteen years. It was a great run, but that's where it ended. We lost to a veteran Oklahoma team in San Jose, 88–67. We were up 37–32 at the half, but they dominated the rest of the game on their way to the Final Four.

In addition to the great basketball, a lot of college basketball's business gets done at the Final Four. It's the one time and place that coaches, athletic directors, corporations, everybody involved with playing and merchandising the game get together. So win or lose I'd usually be there. That year it was being held in Atlanta.

I'd spent most of the day before the semifinal games over at CNN. During the season we'd played three of the final four teams, so a lot of reporters wanted to ask me about them. As I walked into my hotel room that night the phone was ringing. Cedric Dempsey, the man who'd hired me at Arizona and had become NCAA president, explained that he and his wife, June, were going to a meeting of the board of the NCAA Foundation out at Coca-Cola headquarters and wondered if I'd come along with them. Cedric and June are wonderful friends, and the chance to spend an evening with them—as well as get a free dinner—appealed to me. "Give me ten minutes to change," I told him.

Of course, Cedric didn't mention that he wanted me to speak to the group.

During the reception before the dinner June Dempsey took me aside. "I know you don't like to be put in a position where you're sitting with a woman," she said, "but there's a single lady here who's on the advisory board and everybody else is here as a couple. Would you mind if I sat you next to this lady?"

"That's not a problem," I told her.

"Her name is Christine Toretti," June said. What I did not know is that June had told this woman that she was going to sit her next to a "cute, single" coach named Lute Olson.

And Christine had responded, "Who's Lute Olson?"

The fact was, I hadn't had any kind of social life since Bobbi's death. I was sixty-seven years old, and I certainly didn't see myself getting married again. Through the years Bobbi and I had occasionally talked about what we wanted the survivor to do after one of us died. When we traveled we would see widows on our trips, and it seemed sort of lonely for them not to have someone to share their life with. Bobbi had wanted me to promise her that if she died first I would remarry. I told her there was no way in the world I was going to do that. Then I'd tell her the same thing and she'd say, Nope, if you go first the family will be there, and I'm not going to remarry. I feel confident that if I had died, as personable and attractive as she was, men would have been standing in line. After Bobbi's death I got a letter from Norma Slone, a good friend, who told me that Bobbi had always said that if she died she didn't want me to be alone.

I wasn't alone. I had my family. I had my team and my former players and all my friends. So I definitely wasn't alone. Besides, Bobbi was a beloved person in Tucson. I knew it would be difficult, if not impossible, for anyone to move into that situation.

As I later discovered, I was very naïve. My kids told me that within weeks of Bobbi's death people were asking them what I was going to do about the rest of my life? Did I plan to remarry? Jody in particular couldn't believe that other people could be so cold about it.

Our whole family has always been actively involved in local charities. I've also required our players to do some volunteer work, things like speaking at schools or using their local fame to draw people to events. Rather than changing, we became more involved. A respectful period of time after Bobbi's death I began getting phone calls from the chairpersons of different organizations asking if they could auction off a dinner with Lute. I assumed that meant I would go out to dinner with several other people. So I agreed—provided I could bring one of my daughters with me. Truthfully it never occurred to me that they were auctioning me off for a date. But that's exactly what they were doing. There was generally some pretty spirited bidding, so a good amount of money was raised by the charities, but I always took Jody or Vicky or Christi with me. They were my protection.

After one of these events, Jody was appalled that single women were trying to get her father's attention. She complained that they had been flirting with me. Until she told me that, I hadn't known it.

I didn't date. I had no real desire to date and even if I had, I didn't think I'd be good at it. I'd been happily married my whole adult life. I started getting phone calls from friends telling me in the nicest possible way that they wanted to introduce me to this person or that person. I did go out on one date. One time. She was a lovely woman living in

Phoenix. I took her to a dark outdoor restaurant, hoping no one would recognize me. The fact that I was so concerned about being recognized was all the evidence I needed that I wasn't ready to start dating.

The first person who said something to me that at least made me think about dating was Bobbi's sister, Yvonne. We were in Coronado, sitting out on the deck having a glass of wine before dinner, when Yvonne suddenly asked me, "When are you going to get on with your life?"

"Excuse me?" Coming from Bobbi's sister, that just caught my attention.

"You've been grieving for a long time." Then she talked about Bobbi and the way she lived her life with such joy. "She wouldn't want you to be this way."

I told her I didn't know. When I was ready I would know it, but honestly, I didn't think that time would come.

So that's where I was fixed when I sat down next to Christine Toretti. I couldn't help but notice how attractive she was; she had wide-open, expressive eyes and a warm smile. She laughed in all the right places, and, most important, she was so easy to talk with. I was attracted to her immediately, not only because of her appearance but because she made everything feel so natural. We talked so much that neither one of us really ate our dinner. We talked and talked and talked and the next thing we knew dessert was being served. As I found out, she was the divorced mother of three boys and lived in Indiana, Pennsylvania, a small town fifty-five miles outside Pittsburgh. She was the chief executive officer of a big land-based gas and oil drilling company, she was a Republican National Committeewoman, and she knew slightly less than nothing about college basketball. Her own athletic participation was pretty much limited to learning how to ice skate so she could play hockey with her sons.

Very early in our conversation, for some reason, I mentioned that my son, Steve, was getting married that summer in Positano, Italy. Her whole face brightened. Two of her friends had just been appointed ambassador to Italy and ambassador to the Holy See, the Vatican, and she offered to arrange pretty much anything we wanted to do through those people. That was very nice and, as I was to learn, typical. Christine loves to connect people to make nice things happen.

While we were talking about the beautiful gardens at the American embassy in Rome she suddenly looked at me and said, "Oh my God. I know you. You're the guy who coached Arizona last year in the Final Four. We rooted for you. You're Afro man's coach!"

As I discovered, Christine had taken her ten-year-old son, Matt, to the Final Four a year earlier, when we'd lost to Duke. When they got to the game, she asked him who they should root for. "Well, Mom," he'd told her, "there's this really cool guy. He's got a big Afro and he wears white kneesocks and white knee pads and he plays for Arizona." That was Eugene Edgerson. "We rooted for you," she told me.

I was really enjoying our conversation, so much so that I'd pretty much ignored the man sitting on my other side, the CEO of a major insurance corporation. Apparently Christine had been speaking with him before I got there. So in the middle of dessert she took my arm and whispered, "The man to your left will absolutely kill himself tonight if you go through this dinner and don't talk basketball with him, because he played in high school and is really excited that you're sitting here. So, as much as I'm enjoying this, you really need to talk to him."

A few minutes later Cedric Dempsey stood up and announced that I was going to say a few words about what people were going to see this weekend. That was as big a surprise to me as it was to everyone in that room, but I did as asked. When I finished, several people came up and started asking questions and when I glanced at our table, Christine was gone.

It had been a long time since I'd been as comfortable with an attractive woman as I was that night, and I was disappointed she'd left. I had to walk through the lobby of the hotel where the NCAA officials were staying to get to my room, so I sauntered around the lobby for a few minutes hoping she might still be in the lobby. I intended to ask her to have a drink. When I didn't find her, I went back to my room.

It didn't occur to me that she might be interested in me, but later I found out that she had gone back to her room and Googled my name. The first thing she discovered was that I was sixty-seven years old, twenty-three years older than she. That bothered her, she admitted to me; she never thought I would be interested in someone her age.

We hadn't even exchanged contact information. The semifinal games were played the next day. I was going to be sitting with the Dempseys. Apparently, while I was doing some pregame interviews with Jim Nantz for CBS, Christine had come by and told June, "I'm looking for Lute. Is he here?"

Knowing how much I protected my privacy, June suggested, "Oh, honey, if you just write to him at McKale, he'll get the message."

"Who's McKale?" Christine wondered.

When I sat down, June told me about this conversation. I was pleased. I found out where Christine and her son were sitting—unfortunately, it was right in the center of a long row—and wrote my phone number on the back of a business card someone had handed me. The excuse I made for myself was that she was going to introduce me to our ambassador to Italy. Then I went up into the stands and I started climbing over people, excuse me, I'm sorry, squeezing my way down the row, sorry, until I got to her. Handing her the card, I said, "June said you stopped by. This is how you get in touch with me."

She asked if I would take a picture with Matt. We got that done and I went back upstairs. So that was how we met.

We found ways to keep in touch. She sent me the photograph and asked me to sign it for Matt. I would call from time to time just to chat. There weren't a lot of silences in our conversations. We were becoming phone friends. Whatever I felt at that time, we were living thousands of miles apart and both of us had very hectic schedules. It didn't seem likely our relationship would ever become more than a nice friendship.

Then, in early June, something quite wonderful happened. I was elected to the Basketball Hall of Fame. This is something you don't campaign for and you can't win, but it's certainly the biggest honor you can earn in basketball. When the phone rang at home and I was told, "You've been elected," I didn't really know how to act or what to say. Having been disappointed twice, I'd done my best to put it out of my mind. I had just come back from a long three-week Australian tour with the team, so I was exhausted, and I'd pretty much even forgotten that they were voting. So that call came as a sort of shock to me. I was asked to keep it secret for a day. Well, that was difficult. The first person I told was my son, Steve, in Italy. I figured no one there would be asking him about Hall of Fame results.

I was elected with Magic Johnson; Larry Brown; Kay Yow, North Carolina State women's coach; the Harlem Globetrotters; and, coincidentally, the late Drazen Petrovic, whom Muggsy Bogues had guarded in the 1986 World Championship, when he was a young Yugoslavian star. Petrovic had died tragically in a car accident.

I was proud. I was incredibly proud. I was also aware that many other people had played a role in my success. I was getting the attention and the acclaim, but I hoped that all those other people felt proud of their contributions. Even with the joy that came with it, there was still that hollow feeling that came with the realization that Bobbi wasn't there to share it. This was her honor just as much as it was mine. A lot of people had offered me a lot of good advice about dealing with the loss of a life partner. You learn to live with it, they said. Eventually the pain diminishes, they said. At a great moment like this one, I felt her absence.

My problem was that the induction ceremony was scheduled for the following September 27, the same weekend my son Steve was getting married in Positano, Italy. Obviously there was no way I was going to miss his wedding, so we had to figure out some sort of arrangement. The Hall of Fame agreed to let me videotape my acceptance speech, which would be played at the ceremony, and then allow me to show up the following year when the class of 2003 was inducted. I asked Jim Livengood and Roz to represent me at the ceremony, but in addition I had to choose someone to present me for induction. That was like choosing a best man. It was actually a difficult decision because there have been so many best people in my life, so many people who deserved that recognition and I didn't want to anyone to feel overlooked.

Finally I asked former California coach Pete Newell, who had been one of my heroes just about my entire career. He'd also been a close friend for three decades. When I was just getting started I'd hired one of his former assistants as my assistant because I wanted to learn how Pete Newell did things, and I'd based a lot of my defensive philosophy on his work.

The Hall of Fame sent a production van to my house to tape my speech. I really worked on that speech. I wrote and rewrote and rewrote it. I read it over and over to my family. I used the kids as my sounding board. I knew the hardest part to get through would be my tribute to Bobbi. I was concerned about becoming too emotional, so I rehearsed the speech many times. I was steeling myself for it.

We thought it would be nice if it looked like I was speaking from Italy, so I stood in front of our dining room furniture. It was actually French, but it looked Italian enough. Part of my personality is being prompt. Our practices are scheduled to the minute. I like to be where I'm scheduled to be when I'm scheduled to be there. So I was ready to go right on time, I had reached an emotional peak—and then they called to tell me the truck had some kind of mechanical problem and wouldn't be there on time. I had to do it again. I couldn't relax, or sit down or even catch my breath. Finally, they showed, and we got it going.

Basically, this was a thank-you speech to all of my players from high school through the years at Arizona, the athletic directors who hired me, from Del Walker who risked his own job at Long Beach City College to my current boss Jim Livengood, who inherited me and became such a good friend. I acknowledged the support staff, especially my secretary through most of the years at Arizona, Lydia Burch, and all my assistant coaches. I made a point of singling out my associate head coach Jim Rosborough, who had been with me for twenty-three years and was one of the main reasons the Iowa and Arizona programs had been successful. I thanked my family, my five children, and thirteen grandchildren, who had always been there for me, for the "big wins and the disheartening losses."

Then, finally, it was time to talk about Bobbi. I was okay when I started, but it got a lot tougher for me. "The most difficult thank-you is to Bobbi," I said. "She is truly the Hall of Famer in our family. I married Bobbi when she was eighteen years old, before she was old enough to know what she was getting into. Like she loved saying, I chased her until she couldn't run anymore. She worked to put me through school . . .

"Bobbi was the real head coach, the number-one recruiter and the team mom. Every player who has ever played for me knows these things to be true. Bobbi was my inspiration, my number-one supporter, my true love and my very best friend . . ."

It was getting very hard for me to hold it together. "She was truly the wind beneath my wings. I know she's looking down on this special occasion, and I also know she's loving every minute of it." Roz told me later that when it was played at the ceremony, and when the lights were turned on, there wasn't a dry eye in the room.

While the ceremony was taking place I was with my family in Italy. I did glance at my watch and imagine what was going on back home. I can't say honestly that I didn't feel a little bit wistful about not being there to accept the greatest honor of my career, but this was not a situation in which there was a choice. My family always came first.

While I was in Italy I also found myself wondering about Christine. We had continued speaking, but still at a safe distance, and very much on a friendly basis. Our conversations grew longer and longer. I found myself doing things I had always thought I didn't like very much. Talking on cell phones, for example. I thought they were intrusive. I didn't understand how people couldn't get through an hour or two away from the phone, but once we started talking, I found myself using a cell phone more and more. Sometimes our conversations went on for hours. Once, I remember, several months later, she was driving from Tallahassee, where she'd had dinner with Florida Governor Jeb Bush, to Hilton Head, where she was to meet her close friends. It was late at night in the East, and it was a long drive; we spent more than an hour on the phone. That just wasn't like me.

I was interested in her. I wouldn't admit to anything more than that. We still hadn't been out on an actual date. We hadn't even seen each other since meeting at the NCAA tournament. Finally, we were both going to be in California the third week of August. A couple of weeks before then, I suggested, casually, that if she was available we might have dinner. In my mind it wasn't exactly a date, just two friends getting together. I made a reservation, but we didn't speak for a couple of weeks. She didn't know if I'd even remembered. Finally I called the day before and told her I'd pick her up about four in the afternoon.

When I picked her up at her hotel the clerk went to get her. Christine asked the clerk, "What do you think?"

The clerk shook her head, "He's not your type." Apparently Christine thought, Well, how do you know what my type is?

We went up to Dana Point, one of my favorite spots, and walked for a while. It's a beautiful area, like being in Europe. It took a long time for me to get comfortable, this was all so new to me. Talking on the phone was a lot easier. A friend of mine named Bucky Dennis owns a restaurant, Cannons, which overlooks Dana Point Harbor and San Clemente. I don't think there's a restaurant with a prettier view in the world. I told Bucky about Christine and how we'd met, and I asked him if he and his wife would like to join us for dinner. I guess I felt edgy that I was on a dinner date, and Bucky was a little bit of a security blanket. He decided, or maybe they decided, that we should have dinner alone.

We were sitting out on the deck. A wedding was going on inside, behind us. Christine and I had a bottle of Duckhorn wine, Bucky's favorite, and gradually I began to feel more comfortable. It was hard for me to accept the fact that I was on a date. I hadn't been on a date in almost half a century. So I didn't think about it. I just had a good time. It had been a long time since I'd felt so good.

We sat there for at least four hours, talking about our lives. Christine was divorced. Her father had built the drilling company, but after being squeezed by a bank he had committed suicide. She'd taken control of the company and made it very successful. She was also involved in a lot of positive programs to help people, among them women's empowerment programs, and seemingly she was quite independent. She'd started a retreat for women who were in the Young Presidents' Organization. She called it the Golden Door Group, and it was a place where women could safely unburden their souls about the difficulties they were facing as female CEOs. People who hadn't experienced those pressures just couldn't understand how hard it is for a woman in that position, but these women would understand each other's concerns.

Coincidentally, she had lived in Arizona twice. When Christine was a child her mother had moved to Carefree, Arizona, and she'd gone to sixth grade there. Years later she'd dropped out of college and moved to Phoenix. She enjoyed the desert, she told me. What I really liked, though, was the way her face just lit up when she talked about her kids. I knew that feeling. She told me that she had learned how to play ice hockey so she could coach her kids and play with them in pickup games. "You can play psychological games with little kids," she explained. "If you trash-talk them you can get them to take their eyes off the puck."

Well, I liked the thought of a woman who learned how to ice skate so she could trash-talk her kids.

I told her the story of my life. The short version. Much later she told me that when I was telling her about the day my father died, how he had just trimmed my hair and brushed off the loose hairs, that all of a sudden she didn't see me as successful coach, to her I was a vulnerable little boy. "My heart just melted," she said. "And I was like flat on my face in love."

I didn't notice that. I had no idea how this dating thing worked.

The next day she called me from the airport. Her Golden Door group was leaving and she'd gone to the airport very early to say good-bye to her friends. Her own flight to Pittsburgh didn't leave for several hours, so I suggested I show her around San Diego and Coronado. I picked her up, but as we approached my house in Coronado I saw that Matt and Julie were there. I'd thought they were going to the beach. "Let me show you some more of Coronado," I told Christine. What I was really thinking was, I can't stop because then I'd have to introduce Christine to Matt and Julie. It turned out that the hardest thing wasn't telling my kids about Christine, but telling my grandchildren. I wasn't ready to introduce her to my family.

We drove around for a little while, until I saw that their car was gone. Then I pulled into the driveway. Unfortunately, just as we walked into the house Matt and Julie returned. They'd forgotten something. I was busted. I introduced Christine as a member of the NCAA committee. I think they believed me. Eventually they left, and after they were gone I asked Christine to stay for a few more days. I hadn't planned anything like that. As usual, I didn't have a plan, but I was enjoying being with her. She couldn't stay, she said. She had to get home to her kids. Obviously, though, there was some kind of connection between us.

A few days later I was in Las Vegas working at Michael Jordan's Fantasy Camp. An overnight package arrived at the hotel from her. Inside was a small tape player with a cassette in it. When I played it there was only one song on it, sung by Grant Hill's wife, Tamia, "You put a move on my heart. . . ." I thought there was probably more than that on it, but that was it, one song. I tried fast-forwarding it, reversing it, everything, just that one song. I couldn't figure it out. When I called Christine, I said, "I got this tape from you, but something must have happened because there's only one song on it."

She said, "That's the only song I wanted you to hear."

Well. This really wasn't something I was used to, and it made me very uncomfortable. This relationship was about to get serious, and I didn't know that I was ready for something serious.

She was in Chicago, she continued, then suggested, "I can catch a flight and come down."

I didn't feel comfortable dating anyone. I told her that I just had too much to do. I explained that I was planning to meet some friends, Bill Frieder and his wife and Nike representative Eric Lautenbach, and I couldn't change those plans. Both of us knew it was an excuse, and both of us pretended it wasn't an excuse. I knew she was upset, but there wasn't too much I was capable of doing about it.

Another time Christine called from Dallas and asked if I could meet her there. "I'm sorry," I said. "I have another commitment." That was true. I did have something I had to do.

Christine's reaction was pretty straightforward. She told me, "Okay. Well, good-bye, Lute Olson." She said it in a way that made clear it was final. I thought, that's that. Truthfully, though, I suppose I was at least a little relieved. At least I didn't have to make any decisions. No matter how much I enjoyed being with Christine, I knew there wasn't a place in my life for another person. In addition to my family and friends, as *Sports Illustrated* reported, Bobbi had been loved by the entire city of Tucson, by the whole state of Arizona. I thought it would be just about impossible for another woman, any other woman, to fill that place. If I was going to be with someone else, I believed, I couldn't do it in Tucson. That wouldn't work. I wouldn't put a person I cared about in that situation. I wouldn't do that to someone as nice as Christine.

So if I ever was going to be with another woman, I would have to retire and leave Tucson. So, as far as I was concerned, I would have to choose between coaching and being with someone. I also still loved coaching.

It seemed like our relationship was over almost before it started, but as a little time passed, I realized how much I liked having her in my life. I missed our conversations. I missed knowing she was there. An odd thing happened next: Neither Christine nor I remember exactly how or when we started talking again, but we did. As friends. Just as friends. We were very careful about calling it anything more than a friendship. We didn't tell anybody about it.

In September I went to Italy. I was traveling with the Stehbens and my in-laws, the Gragsons. Christine had arranged a guide for us, as well as dinner with the American ambassador to the Holy See. It was a wonderful day and I wanted to thank her. I left several messages for her, and she never called me back. Uh-oh, I figured, she's mad at me again. I began wondering what I'd done this time. I was beginning to get frustrated.

Christine really was mad at me. For some reason she wasn't getting any of my messages. As far as she knew, she'd gone to considerable trouble to make arrangements for me and I hadn't called to thank her or tell her about it. This was getting to be like one of those romantic comedies where events and mistakes keep the couple apart. Christine had to be in Florence to work on a project for the Young Presidents' Organization. And as she was getting on the plane to Italy her assistant asked her, "Are you mad at Lute Olson?"

"Why?"

"Because he just called and asked why you weren't calling him back."

Coincidentally, we were going to be in Florence while she was there. When we finally spoke, I invited her to join us for dinner. We had dinner alone the first night, but the second night we were going to join the Stehbenses and the Gragsons. This was the first time we were going to meet members of my family together. When I went to pick her up, she was probably more nervous than I'd ever seen her. "I don't know if I can do this," she said.

"Of course you can," I told her.

"What if she doesn't like me?"

Knowing Christine, knowing Yvonne, I assured her that wouldn't be a problem. And it wasn't. I hadn't prepared Yvonne; I hadn't told her that I was attracted to this woman. That didn't matter, Yvonne went out of her way to make her feel comfortable.

Christine and I went out for dinner the next night. At the end of that night I couldn't pretend even to myself I wasn't interested in being with her. I invited her to go to Lake Como with me and the Gragsons for the weekend. I know that she was surprised when I asked. Admittedly, I was still probably a little surprised I was asking.

No matter how old you are, some things never change. Christine excused herself and went to the ladies' room—and called her mother. "Lute wants me to go with him to Lake Como for the weekend. What do you think I should do?"

"Come home tomorrow," her mother said.

Christine told me, "I called my Mom and she said, 'You tell Lute Olson thank you, but I have to go home.'"

Christine then called her friend and political assistant, a woman named Bernie Comfort, who was close to Christine's sons. "Do you think the boys would mind if I didn't come home until Monday?" Go ahead, Bernie told her.

Christine had a big smile on her face when she came out of the ladies' room. "I can go," she said. She told me she was very happy that Bernie had approved, because otherwise she would have had to keep calling people until she found someone who said it was fine.

There was no one moment when we acknowledged that we were a couple, and there were still some very high hurdles ahead of us, but this was certainly the beginning.

At that time Christine didn't know too much about sports. Her ex-husband was a golfer and former football player, and his father had been an assistant football coach at Penn State, so she had a little bit of knowledge about football. She didn't know a thing about basketball. At business she was brilliant; she knew how to calculate the cubic feet of gas in a certain volume but didn't know a free throw from a personal foul. But being Christine, she immediately set out to learn as much as she could. She started by reading every book she could buy, beginning with *Basketball for Dummies.* She watched each of the instructional videos I'd made several times. She called the cable company and subscribed to Fox Sports Arizona so she could get every one of our games. Her friend Bernie had played basketball in high school, and Christine asked her to become her teacher. "Okay," Bernie said, "how many seconds can you stay in the key?"

Christine just looked at her. "What's the key?"

"Oh, boy," Bernie said. "We are in big trouble."

The two of them watched game after game on TV. They would get together late at night to watch our games. Christine started reading the sports pages and figuring out the meaning of a box score. And she learned.

Christine and I spoke on the phone every day, often several times a day. Once again, I'd gotten very busy preparing for the season. With our entire starting five returning, we were ranked number one in the country. I knew we were going to be very good. Those five—seniors Luke Walton, Rick Anderson, and Jason Gardner, and sophomores Salim Stoudamire and Channing Frye—had averaged sixty-seven points a game the previous season in winning twenty-four games. Walton and Gardner were preseason All-Americans. Unfortunately, very few teams, except Coach Wooden's legendary UCLA teams, had been able to maintain their top ranking throughout an entire season, but that was the kind of problem you want to have to deal with.

Christine and I kept trying to figure out how we could get together. Finally, we met in Las Vegas the first weekend in November. We had such a wonderful time, again, that I knew we had to deal with the reality that this relationship wasn't going anywhere. I told her that weekend that she could never come to Tucson. I tried to explain to her how difficult it would be for any woman to try to occupy Bobbi's place. We were caught in an ironic situation; I cared about her too much to be with her. I knew what was going to happen and I didn't want to put her through that.

Christine wasn't scared by my warnings. "Let's just see where this goes," she said realistically, "You know, Lute, I think you'd be really surprised how strong I can be."

We really did come from two completely different worlds. She had done so many different and difficult things in her life, but I still didn't believe she understood how difficult it would be for any woman coming into my life to live in Tucson. Christine, meanwhile, heard my words, but took another meaning from them: She realized I had strong feelings about her.

Falling in love when you're young is easy because you don't know very much. Falling in love after a lifetime is much more difficult. It wasn't just me Christine would have to deal with, it was my family and my extended family, it was the city of Tucson, it was my career and all the responsibilities that came with it.

I told her all that, but she made it clear she wanted to try. Okay. During that weekend in Las Vegas we went from you can never come to Tucson to would you like to come to Tucson for the Thanksgiving weekend. There was going to be a ceremony that weekend and I was going to receive my Hall of Fame ring. I wanted Christine to see what she would have to deal with if this relationship went any further. She told me she'd love to be there.

A couple of days later I sent her a copy of the video I'd made for my Hall of Fame induction. When she watched it, when she saw me expressing my love for Bobbi, she was devastated. She started crying hysterically. "That's it," she told Bernie. "I can't compete with this. It's over."

When she told me she wasn't coming to Arizona it was my turn to be upset. That wasn't the reaction I expected at all. "I never should have sent that to you," I told her. "We should have watched it together." As we spoke, she calmed down. And agreed to come for the Thanksgiving weekend. Not Thanksgiving dinner, though. We had the whole family as well as Julie's college basketball team for dinner. I don't think either one of us was ready for her to meet the whole Olson family.

Until I'd met Christine I'd been sure I was never going to get married again. I'd had a long and wonderful marriage to a wonderful woman. Now, to my surprise, I was no longer so sure. Christine had been through a very difficult divorce, and she was also sure she was never going to get married again. Here we were, to our surprise, moving in small steps in that direction.

Christine's mother lived in Carefree, Arizona, so Christine arrived early and spent Thanksgiving with her. She drove to Tucson on Friday. I was as nervous as a teenager. On Saturday I brought her to my house for the first time. She'd spoken on the phone to Jody, but I hadn't actually told Jody we were dating. We had mutual friends, I said. She was a friend. I think Jody began to understand it was more than that when I brought Christine to the house.

There were memories of Bobbi all over the house. Christine looked at all the pictures and asked me a few questions. I pointed out a few things to her and we got through it. Christine told me later she had decided, if it's worth it, we'll figure out how to make it work.

I'd told Christine I was going to take her over to McKale on Sunday, but doing that was more difficult than I had expected. We managed to stay busy all day, avoiding the subject. Finally, about four o'clock, I suggested, "Are you sure you want to go over there?"

"Yes," she said. "I'd really like to go."

Maybe it was me who really didn't want to go. I wasn't sure that Christine fully appreciated how deeply Bobbi was revered, not only in the community, but in the state, and how difficult it would be for anyone to deal with her legacy. The Lute and Bobbi Olson Court was evidence of that love. I didn't know how she would deal with it. McKale was locked, so there was no one there. I had the keys. I took her into our Hall of Champions and showed her the numerous trophies we'd won. Then we walked out into the arena, to see the Lute and Bobbi Olson Court. We just stood there for a few seconds, looking at it. I glanced at her, trying to figure out what she was thinking. And finally she said, "That is really cool."

"What's that?" Both of us were looking at the court rather than each other.

"It's just so neat that not only you, but your wife and your family, can make such an impact on the school and the community that they honor you like that."

I guess that was the moment when I accepted the fact that I wanted to marry this woman.

This was new territory for me. As strong as Christine seemed to be, though, I still didn't think it could work. It was becoming obvious to me I was going to have to choose between a career I loved and the woman I had fallen in love with.

We began talking about it. This should have been one of the most difficult decisions I've ever had to make. We began talking about the future, and suddenly the answer seemed obvious. "Maybe the best thing would be for me to retire," I said. I felt I had a commitment to the kids I'd recruited, but in two years, three years, when they had graduated, I would have fulfilled that.

She was stunned that I would make that offer. It wasn't something I wanted to do, I wasn't ready to retire, but if that's what it took for us to be together, then that's what I would do. I'd made my decision. I wanted to marry her. Christine understood that this was the greatest gift I could give her. But she had no intention of accepting it. "Oh no, you won't," she said. "You're not quitting coaching because of me."

"Christine, I just don't think you know how hard it would be for anyone to come in here . . ."

She was insistent. "You don't marry someone to change them," she told me. "You marry them because of who they are and what they do, and if you really love them, you find a way to make it work. If we love each other, we'll get through it."

We'll get through it. I listened, and I hoped she was right.

A month later Christine returned to Tucson with her three boys for the Fiesta Bowl tournament. It was time for me to tell my family about Christine. About us. There were all the reactions you would expect, including a lot of tears. It was very hard for the kids. None of them tried to talk me out of it, but their feelings were very mixed. At best. I understood their feelings. Julie, particularly, was very upset. So we sat down and talked about it. I told her, "Christine isn't replacing Mama Bobbi. No one's going to replace her. But she's a wonderful person, and being with her makes me very happy."

I think she just needed to hear that. She looked at me and brushed away her tears, and said, "Okay, you can date her."

It was also very hard for Christine's three boys. Her oldest son, Joe, was going to London for film school, so it was not an immediate issue for him, but her two youngest sons, Matt and Max, would have to move to Tucson. They were not at all pleased about leaving their life in Pennsylvania to come to Arizona.

Love isn't always easy, but Christine was right. If you want it enough, you figure out how to make difficult things possible.

Christine and I would spend hours on the phone every night. I would sit outside, under the stars, as we spoke. One night, I remember, it got so late that my son-in-law, who didn't know I was still out there, locked all the doors. Christine had gotten me locked out of my own house.

The team improved steadily throughout the season. Although we'd been as low as fourth in the rankings, we were back to number one when we traveled to Lawrence, Kansas, to play Roy Williams's sixth-ranked Jayhawks. I invited Christine to meet me there. My plan was that we would have a quiet dinner after the game and I would ask her to marry me. Christine had figured it out. I'd been asking her pretty obvious questions, like what kind of engagement ring she'd like, and I'd told her that after the game rather than joining my friends we were going to a very special restaurant by ourselves.

At the hotel she was in the room right next to mine, on the same floor with the team. The only people I'd told about my relationship with Christine were Paul and Betty Weitman. At the game I sat her next to George Kalil, another friend named Jim Slone, as well as Paul and Betty. George and Jim wondered why she was in my seats. She told them that she was on the NCAA Leadership Advisory Board. "But why are you here?" George asked politely.

"Because of Lute," she said. Nothing else. Whatever George was thinking, he didn't ask any more questions.

We played terribly that first half. Christine wasn't quite sure what was going on, but she knew it wasn't good. Betty knew Christine and I were going to dinner after the game. We were down thirteen at halftime and she leaned over to Christine and said, "I don't think dinner's going to be very good tonight."

Christine turned and said, "Betty, you don't know the half of it." She was sure we were not going to get engaged that night.

In the first few minutes of the second half Salim Stoudamire caught fire, scoring eleven quick points to get us back in the game. I don't think anyone ever cheered as loudly as Christine. We came all the way back to win, 91–74.

Christine and I went to the nicest restaurant in Kansas City. It was snowing and it was very cold, but I was as happy as I could be. We'd just beaten one of the best teams in the nation on their home court, and I was about to ask the woman I loved to marry me.

We sat in a banquette. I just kept waiting for the right moment, and waiting. It had been almost fifty years since I'd asked a woman to marry me, so it didn't come easily. Finally Christine had to ask me, "You're going to ask me something, aren't you?"

"Yes, I am," I told her. "Christine, will you marry me?"

She had the biggest smile on her face as she told me, "You're going to have to get down on your knee to ask me that question."

The restaurant was crowded with Kansas fans who'd been watching the game on television. Several of them had recognized me. "You've got to be kidding me?"

She wasn't. She pushed back the table. This was a moment of decision.

I got down on my knee and again asked her to marry me. Then as quickly as I could, I sat back down.

Christine was so thrilled with my proposal that she asked me to do it again.

We were officially engaged.

11

It did not take long for Christine to find out exactly what she was getting into. We'd decided to keep our engagement a secret as long as possible, because we didn't want to take any attention from the team. The team was playing very well. We were 15–1 when I asked her to marry me, then we lost to Stanford before reeling off another ten wins. As Christine told me, "This year's about fourteen young men. It's not about a man and woman getting married."

We'd decided to get married after the season, in early April. Christine had called the headmaster of her boys' school to make arrangements for them to attend our wedding. She confided to him that she was getting married, but asked him not to tell anyone. Things didn't quite work out that way.

Maybe a half hour after Christine had spoken with the school a society page reporter from a Pittsburgh paper called her. Christine is well known in Pittsburgh, where she serves on numerous corporate, political, and charity boards. "You've been holding out on me," this woman said. "I hear you're getting married."

Christine is a very strong person. It takes a lot to get to her; this got to her. She was afraid I would see it as some sort of betrayal. She worried that people close to her whom she hadn't told would be hurt if they read about it in the paper. The columnist agreed to wait several days before printing the story.

The first thing she did was call me. I could hear the apprehension in her voice as she told me, "They're going to run the story next Monday, but the good news is it's going to be in the society column, so I don't think anybody'll pay attention to it."

During practice on Tuesday my secretary, Lydia, came down to the court. We've worked together since I've been at Arizona and she rarely speaks with me during practice. "Coach, I'm getting a lot of calls about you getting married. They're going to run the story if you don't deny it."

Well, so much for secrecy. We decided to hold a press conference the next day. It was very much a last-minute event, so only sixty-seven reporters showed up. Sixty-seven! We didn't get that many when we were in the NCAA tournament. The press conference was televised by all our local channels as well as several stations in Phoenix. Who could have imagined people would be so interested in my personal life? Actually, they weren't. The first question asked was "Does this mean this is your last year of coaching?"

"No. Christine is looking forward to being part of Arizona basketball, and she shares my excitement about our prospects for next year."

I'd never discussed politics in my professional life. Nobody knows my political beliefs; I always believed if I spoke about them I'd be upsetting 50 percent of the people listening, no matter what I said. Christine is active in politics, so when I was asked where I was registered I assumed they were talking about voting. "In Arizona," I said.

It turned out they meant, Where were Christine and I registered for wedding gifts? I had no idea. When one of the reporters said I'd broken a lot of hearts, I told them how I felt about Christine, "Well, I know my own heart, and I'm very happy. This year has been unbelievable. I've really been blessed.

"It has been a difficult two years and four months for me. Those who matter most, my family, said, 'Dad, we want you to be happy. Life goes on.' "

My happiness was showing. According to the *Tucson Citizen*, "The coach, a widower the past two years, was happier than anybody had seen him since UA's overtime victory over Kentucky for the NCAA championship in 1997."

Christine came to Tucson for our final home game of the season, against Oregon. By that time the media was reporting almost daily on our engagement. I was off the sports pages again, but this time I was in the social column. Obviously, I was pretty anxious to see how Christine responded to the media crush. This was very different than anything she'd done. Christine was an extremely successful, accomplished woman, all of the publicity she had received had been due to her own work, but in Tucson she was "Lute Olson's fiancée," and there were a lot of people wondering about her. She arrived on Wednesday evening. On Thursday we had a meet-the-coach luncheon. Two hundred supporters were there, most of them very curious about Christine. She arrived with Bobbie Stehbens. As she was checking in at the door a great supporter of our program, Bob Strauss, was in front of her. Bob said to the woman checking names at the door, "Okay, where is she?"

Hearing that, Christine tapped him on the shoulder. "I'm here," she said, smiling, "right behind you." When I heard that story I felt confident she'd be able to hold her own in Tucson.

It was during that weekend that I think she began to really understand what she was getting into. She went to the game with Jody and Jon and as soon as she walked in it seemed like every photographer in Arizona descended on her.

As Bob Strauss told her, everybody here wants Lute to be happy, but they want that happiness to fit their own fantasies. At halftime a reporter approached her and asked, "What's it like to be engaged to Lute Olson?"

Among the many things I love about Christine is that she is her own person. "I have no idea," she said. "What do you think it's like to be engaged to Christine Toretti?" Almost as soon as those words were out of her mouth she regretted them. She had intended it to be a joke; instead it came out as a flippant remark. She didn't mind people thinking she was a smart aleck, but she was very worried that it would reflect poorly on me. By the next day she was so upset she was crying.

Bobbie Stehbens, who had come in for the weekend, sat down to talk seriously with her. "Christine," she asked, "do you realize what you're getting into?" This was the kind of frank conversation she needed. "This is going to be very difficult for you," Bobbie said. "You have to think long and hard about this." Bobbi wanted us to be happy, but she knew how difficult Tucson might be for Christine. She offered to help as much as she was needed.

Christine listened to her, but she was determined that if she was going to make our relationship work she had to face things head-on. So that's what she did, and that first weekend turned out to be great. She met the players and their families. It was a delicate situation, sort of coming into the program in the middle for most of the kids, and she handled it extremely well. She was determined, we both were, that nothing we did in our personal lives would have any impact on the team's effort to win the national championship.

We were good enough to do it. Once again we were ranked first. But as every coach knows, no matter how good you are, no matter how high you're ranked, once they toss up the ball, none of that matters. We had a ten-game winning streak when we played UCLA in the Pac-10 tournament. UCLA was ending its worst season in sixty years with a 10–18 record. We'd beaten them twice, by thirty-five and thirty-six points. And then we suffered what ESPN called, "The biggest upset in college basketball the whole season," losing in overtime, 96–89.

There isn't any explanation for why we played so poorly. That's basketball. That's why a coach can never take any game for granted. Jason Gardner, who would be named the Naismith Player of the Year at the end of the season, made only two of twenty shots. We lost the game on the foul line, hitting two of eleven in the overtime while they made ten of their twelve shots. As a coach you always try to find something positive in a loss, and the only thing I could say about this game was that if we had been overconfident going into the tournament, that stopped right there.

We were still the number-one seed in the West. We opened up the tournament in Salt Lake City with an easy win over Vermont, then we played ninth-seeded Gonzaga. Ninth-seeded? When the brackets were announced I thought Mark Few's Gonzaga Bulldogs were a lot better than that. The day before we played them I told reporters they were every bit as good as any of the number one or two seeds. I believed that, too. Gonzaga just didn't have a history of success at that level, which was probably why they were seeded much lower than their ability had earned them.

It was a great basketball game. With twelve seconds left we were up two—and missed a foul shot. With three seconds left they went for the win, taking a three-point shot. It missed, but they got a tip-in at the buzzer. Overtime. With fifteen seconds left in the first overtime they went ahead 89–87 on a layup, but Jason Gardner hit Luke Walton inside and Luke powered his way to the basket and banked in a turnaround to tie it. There's a very special feeling that only coaches get to experience when you watch kids you've worked with for years execute perfectly what you've taught them. You just know how many hours of practice and doing the same drills over and over went into making it look natural. In a sense, it's like knowing your kids have grown up.

In the second overtime Salim Stoudamire scored our last five points to put us ahead by a point. But they had the ball for the last shot. A basket wins the game. With six seconds left they missed a three, but got the rebound. Our whole season came down to one shot with one second left. They missed an eight-footer. We won, 96–95. You just have to be lucky.

Near the end of the long postgame press conference a reporter asked, "Before the start of the second overtime I looked up to where your family was sitting and Christine wasn't there. Do you know where she was?"

I've sat through literally hundreds and hundreds of press conferences, I've answered at least ten thousand questions, and this was probably the dumbest question I had ever been asked. At the start of the second overtime in the NCAA tournament did I know where my fiancée was? I couldn't resist. I said, "You know, usually during a game my first concern is to look over at the media and make sure they seem happy about the way things are going. After that I always look at big boosters because I know how important it is that they feel like I'm doing a good job. Third, every once in a while I like to look out on the court and call a couple of time-outs to make people think I know what's going on." Meanwhile, this reporter was writing down every word. "Then finally I'll check my family. But I don't know where she was, either." With one exception, every reporter in that room was laughing.

In the Sweet Sixteen we beat Notre Dame, 88–71, setting up a game with number-two Kansas for a trip back to the Final Four. For Christine this was a new experience. In the past her rooting interest at the Big Dance had been decided by an Afro and kneesocks; now she had a serious rooting interest. She was more than a fan now, she was becoming part of the program, and she brought the same intensity to basketball as she did to every other aspect of her life. After the Gonzaga game, for example, she described herself as "a total wreck."

On the night Christine and I had gotten engaged six weeks earlier we'd come back from a twenty-point deficit to beat Roy Williams's Jayhawks. In this game we were only down sixteen, but that was still in the first half. We were down fourteen with fourteen minutes to play when we went on an eighteen-point run to go ahead with 10:30 to go. Every game is different, unique, but they do take on patterns. This pattern began to seem similar, but Roy Williams is just too good a coach to let his team stop fighting. Our problem was we turned over the ball nineteen times, which Kansas turned into twenty-nine points; that's not our game and we can't win when we play that sloppy. With seven seconds left we were down three. We played great defense to force a shot-clock violation and got the ball back. There are a lot of decisions to be made in the last two minutes of a close game, do you foul, when do you foul, how long do you hold the ball, take a two or a three, but down three with seven seconds, you've got to go for three. Jason Gardner's shot was partially blocked, but Luke Walton got the loose ball and passed it back out to Gardner. He got a decent look but his shot bounced off the back of the rim. We lost 78–75. You just have to be lucky.

I had the experience to be a little philosophic about it; I had almost half a century to put a loss into context, but Christine was distraught. She was upset that she was so upset about the game that she couldn't comfort me.

In the past, after the Final Four, Bobbi and I took our little vacation. The end of this season was very different; at the end of this season Christine and I got married.

We were married on April 12, in a suite at the Bellagio Hotel in Las Vegas. We'd invited about thirty people, just our grown kids and their adult children and a very few friends. Bobbi's sister Yvonne was there with her husband, Ken. My son Greg was my best man, and Christine's goddaughter Suzy Jack was her maid of honor. We couldn't even invite my grandchildren. I know there were some hurt feelings, but we were in a small suite, and if we had started inviting more people we would have ended up hurting many other friends. It was an elegant, quiet ceremony; we had both the ceremony and the reception in the suite. I suspect two of the most surprised people there were Christine and me. Neither one of us had ever expected to be married again, but there we were, almost like kids, so happy to have found each other and be together.

Afterward our children each made a little speech. Christine's son Joe is a very accomplished speaker and made some appropriate remarks. Max is more of a quiet guy, but it was obvious he was speaking with real feeling. Matt is her youngest, and she'd warned me beforehand that he was so shy that he might not say very much. Well, Matt stood up on a chair so that everyone could see him, and his whole personality just burst out. He stole the show. If he kept going, we probably could have put his name on the sign in front of the hotel and sold tickets.

Getting married was the easy part. Now we had to figure out how to put our lives together. Both of us already had very full schedules; we had to find ways to combine them so we could be together. We lived almost a continent apart, we each had time-demanding professions, we had children and families and responsibilities, we had homes, and Christine's kids had their schools. So from the very beginning of our

marriage we spent a lot of time meeting each other and saying good-
bye to each other at airports. It seemed that one of us was always about
to leave for something, a game, a recruiting trip, a business meeting, a
family function; we accumulated a substantial amount of frequent flier
miles.

That was hard. As I'd known was going to happen, Arizona fans
were worried that I would be retiring or leaving Tucson. That I'd be
moving to Pennsylvania to be with Christine. The reality was that we
were going to try to live in both places. I don't think the people of Tucson completely accepted that until I signed a new five-year contract a
year later.

Not everyone in both our families immediately accepted our marriage. In that, Christine and I were no different than so many other people who put two families together. I know it's hard for children,
whatever age they are, to see a parent move into a new relationship.
There's a feeling that it's somehow disloyal to the other parent to em-
brace a new person. As a parent, about all you can do is hope that those
feelings change with time. So we did have the same problems in this
situation that almost everybody else does.

We didn't forget about Bobbi. It wasn't necessary for my family to do
that in order to allow Christine into their lives. I remember that first
summer the whole family came in for the Fourth of July weekend.
There were about thirty-five people there of all ages. One afternoon
Christine went to the mall to shop with Bobbie Stehbens and Yvonne.
Apparently they were talking about our marriage, how it was going, and
Christine was being very irreverent. Suddenly Yvonne started crying.
"What's wrong?" Christine asked.

"Oh," she said, "my sister would really like you."

Christine was really touched by that, but she dismissed it. "Well, we
would never meet," she said, but later she told me that was the nicest
thing anyone had said to her in relation to Bobbi.

It wasn't just a few of my kids who had trouble with all the changes.

Christine's son Matt had a difficult time adjusting to living in Tucson, too. She would drive him to school every morning, and as he got
out of the car, he'd tell her, "This is not my home." Then he'd slam the
door and walk into the school. His teachers described him as very
surly and morose. The situation got so bad that by the end of October
Christine had decided that if he wanted to, he could go back to Pennsylvania and live there. The whole situation was making both of us very unhappy. But when she flew to Indiana, Pennsylvania, in mid-December,

Matt was at the airport to meet her. "You know, Mom," he said, "I don't like it there."

"Believe me, I know you feel that way," she told him. "You've told me that a million times."

"But here's what I've decided. I'd rather be there with you than stay here and you not be here." Christine has always said that this was one of the best days of her life. Little by little, we were making progress.

The bad was only a small portion of it, of course. The Olson family has always been close. And it was those bonds that proved to be most important. Matt Brase, my grandson, had grown to be 6'6" and a good basketball player. My daughter put a basketball in his hands when he was about two years old; there was always a hoop up on the garage. Matt was good, but not really quick enough to compete on our level. After graduating from Catalina Foothills High he decided to go to junior college and played two years at Central Arizona College. He was a very good player for them, the captain of their team. When he finished his second year, he wasn't certain what he wanted to do. He had some offers from lower Division I and Division II schools, which was the right level for him. Indiana State was particularly interested in him. He could have played at that level. Matt had literally grown up inside McKale. He'd known all our players, been to all our games. One night he was working at a camp with some of our players and when they were done, Hassan Adams asked him what he was doing. When Matt told Hassan he was talking to a couple of schools, Hassan frowned, "Hey man," he said, "why don't you ask your grandpa to come be on the team? Why don't you walk on?"

Hassan had put Matt's dream into words. Matt had been afraid that if he didn't deserve to be on the team, people would believe he was only there because he was the coach's grandson. Later that night both Damon and Salim Stoudamire told him, "Yeah, do it."

Hassan gave him the confidence to speak to me about walking on to the team. Matt knew the reality was that he wasn't good enough to get a lot of playing time; he'd play on the scout team in practice and sit on the bench during competitive games, and he knew I couldn't get him a scholarship. That's the life of a walk-on, but it would be his dream come true.

So one night he called me, supposedly for some other reason. Finally he asked me, "Pop, I've been thinking about it. I'd really like to walk on at the U of A. What do you think, would you let me walk on?"

I told him the truth. "You know, Matt, you've been playing, not sitting. If you come to Arizona, you're only going to get a few minutes now and then. I know that sounds exciting to a lot of guys, but then they get here and the reality is that they practice hard but don't get a chance to play."

We talked about it some more. Matt said he understood all that. "I just want to learn the game," he said. "And who better to learn it from than you?" It was a much harder decision for me than it might seem. Matt and I had a very strong relationship; I didn't want to do anything to damage it. I did the only thing I could think of given the circumstances: I called his mother. It was the most unusual recruiting call I'd ever made. "He's not going to play," I told Jody. "He'll be on the scout team and he'll travel with us, but I just don't think he's of our caliber. Do you think he could handle it when I yell at him? The last thing I want to do is ruin our relationship."

Jody's answer was a good, strong maybe. "I'm staying out of it," she said. "I'm just your daughter and Matt's mother. If you guys want it to work, you have to work it out. Only take him if you think it'll be a positive thing."

Finally I agreed to let him walk on. In a different situation I might have been concerned that the players on the team resented the fact I was letting my grandson join the squad. But most of the team knew Matt. They'd played with him and they liked him. When Matt told Channing Frye about it, for example, Channing told him, "It's about time. You should have been here before." So Matt became the only grandson playing for his grandfather in college basketball.

Although we had only two returning starters and no seniors, we still were ranked fourth preseason. Certainly one of the keys to our season was my ability to get Salim Stoudamire to play consistently to the level of his talent. That wasn't easy. Salim and I had our confrontations. The basis of the problem came from the fact that he was an absolute perfectionist. He didn't think he should ever miss a shot, so when he wasn't shooting well, it affected his entire game. I reminded him over and over that basketball is a game of percentages. If you're a 60 percent shooter, which anybody would love to be, you're still going to miss four of ten shots. Instead of dropping your head, you should be thinking, great, I missed it, now the percentages are going to play into this, and I'm going to make six of my next nine.

Salim is a good person, with a big heart, but too often he was sad and moody. It seemed like something was always bothering him. I told him once, "You make me depressed just looking at you. I'm sure your teammates feel the same way. They don't know if you're upset at them or me or what."

We never knew what we were going to get from him. In the championship game of the Fiesta Bowl Classic, we played the Louisiana–Lafayette Ragin' Cajuns coached by my former assistant Jessie Evans. It was a game we should have won comfortably. Instead, in twenty-four minutes Salim took only six shots and didn't score a point. It took a three-point shot by Andre Iguodala with nine seconds left in the game for us to finally put it away, 72–69. But in our next game, against Arizona State at Tempe, Salim hit ten of fourteen shots, ending up the high scorer with twenty-six points as we won 93–74.

For Christine, this was her first real season as a member of the team. She had a lot to learn, too. Christine is an activist; she likes to roll up her sleeves and get involved. She likes to help things get done. At first, I think, she was very tentative. This was another area in which she was aware she was walking a thin line. She did not want anyone to think she was trying to replace Bobbi, but she wanted to make her own contribution. It wasn't easy. She wasn't comfortable, and she was worried about doing the right thing. She knew how Bobbi had created the family atmosphere that was so much a part of our program, so she began inviting the kids up to the house for dinner to make them feel welcome. Once she stopped worrying about doing it right, it became natural for her.

She's learned. When I was going through all those difficulties with Salim, she could see it was affecting me. So she began calling Salim every morning, trying to pump him up, but it didn't seem like it was working. One afternoon, on the way up to a booster club event, she got into an elevator with him. I wasn't with them, but apparently Salim was not happy to be at this event and said something about signing only four autographs. Four, that's it. Christine grabbed his shirt and told him straight up. "You will sign every autograph that's asked of you. You are not going to disappoint anyone."

Salim looked at her with amazement, one of those "who the heck do you think you are" looks—but he did sign the autographs.

There were some things she tried that just didn't work. We had some problems with the overall team chemistry that season, and she offered to put together a program that would teach personal development. It was the kind of program she'd built so successfully for her own company. She recruited a couple of experienced people to work with the players, but some people who had played important roles in the program for a long time didn't understand what she was doing. With so much to get done and a limited time to do it, they felt the time could have been spent better. Christine began to accept the fact that change takes time. Her enthusiasm and good intentions weren't enough. So one day she told Ryan Hansen, our director of basketball operations, that she was going to drop the personal development program. "I don't want to take over," she said. "All I'm trying to do is help. But I'm backing out now." And she did.

My grandson walked the same line. There were some students—not teammates—who assumed I'd let him walk on because of our relationship, but Matt paid no attention to those people. He proved to be a real asset to the team, working hard in practice, doing all the things we asked of him, and never once complaining about sitting down at the end of the bench. For my part, I tried to treat him exactly the same way I treated every other player, although he was the only player permitted to hug the coach.

Matt's attitude won the respect of our fans. A couple of sections used to hold up signs, PUT IN YOUR GRANDSON! suggestions like that. When he did play, always at the end of a blowout, they would really cheer for him. I remember once we were way ahead, the game was just about over, Matt drove for the basket, and the official called a charge on him. McKale just erupted in boos. The official was stunned. He'd made a meaningless call at the end of a blowout, and the crowd was screaming at him? He looked at Roz and asked, "What's that all about?"

Roz was laughing; we all were. "You just called a charge on Lute's grandson," he explained.

On another occasion Matt played and scored six points. At the press conference after the game one of the columnists, whom I've known a long time, said to me, "Well, after that, I guess Jody is gonna want to know why he's not playing more."

I nodded. "I know, and truthfully I'm worried about it because, you know, she has my home number."

We finished the regular season 19-8, including two losses to number-two Stanford and two losses to unranked Washington. By midseason we'd dropped out of the top ten, and we finished ranked twenty-second in the nation. Winning starts with good defense and we just weren't very good defensively, giving up 78.4 points a game, the worst in the last twenty-one seasons. We could score points, we led the nation in scoring at 87.1 points per game, but we couldn't stop good teams. For a coach, nothing could be more frustrating. You continue to look for answers, you try to find a way to plug the holes, but every time we plugged one we opened up another. By winning our first game in the Pac-10 tournament we'd won twenty or more games for the seventeenth consecutive season, the longest twenty-win streak in the country. But we just never established the consistency we needed; from game to game it was impossible to predict how we would play. In our second game in the tournament Hassan Adams tied his career high with thirty points, and nine rebounds, and we made twenty-four of twenty-five free throws—but we lost to Washington for the third time that season, 90–85. That was the first time in twenty-four years, the first time in my career, that Arizona had lost to the same opponent three times in a single season.

We had earned our twentieth consecutive invitation to the NCAA tournament, also the best in the country, but only as a ninth seed, the lowest we'd been seeded in eighteen seasons. We opened against eighth-seeded Seton Hall from the Big East—and we closed against them, too.

The game was typical of our whole season. With about fifteen minutes left we were up fourteen, but we just couldn't stand prosperity. We gave up too many easy baskets. Seton Hall had people going coast-to-coast for layups, and we lost 80–76. As good as it feels watching the kids you've coached for years use the skills they learned in pressure situations, that's how bad it feels to watch a team just fall apart, just forget everything you've been practicing day after day, hour after hour, and revert to playground skills. There's very little a coach can do in that situation. Call time-out, substitute, scream at them, but sometimes nothing works, and you just have to sit there and watch it.

That last loss again. It hangs over everything you do for a while, then other events take place and the frustration and what-ifs begin to fade and you begin to look forward to the next season with optimism and hope. Our entire starting five was eligible to return, but sophomore Andre Iguodala, who had been an extremely valuable player for us, decided to declare himself eligible for the NBA draft. He was only the sixth player I've had leave early, but it made sense. Scouts told us he would be a first-round pick. Andre had been the Illinois High School Player of the Year, and when he first got to Arizona he told me, "Coach, I want to play like Luke Walton. I want to be able to pass and rebound." Eventually he became the first player to lead the team in rebounds, assists, and steals the same season. When you recruit at our level, you're getting the top scorers from their areas, so generally you don't hear them talk too much about passing.

When he was drafted by the Philadelphia 76ers I told him, "You know Andre, it's a real good thing you're not that interested in scoring, because with Allen Iverson on the team you're going to have the opportunity to get a lot of assists, rebounds, and steals."

We still had the nucleus returning. By the end of the season Christine, like my grandson, had become a lot more comfortable with her role. But certainly her decision to become actively involved in one particular local charity has made a big difference in the community. One night we were sitting out on the patio and she asked me, "What do you want your legacy to be? How do you want people to remember you? Do you want it to be the Hall of Fame coach, the winner of a national championship?"

That actually turned out to be an easy question to answer. "I want it to be for helping to find the cure for women's cancer." There was nothing more important to me, having lived through the horrors of it with Bobbi and worrying about my daughters and my granddaughters every day. The thought of another person going through what we went through— and we were fortunate enough to have the best people and the best facilities available to us—is just terrible for us. It was ugly.

"Okay," Christine said, moving immediately into her business mode. "Then let's do it."

Shortly after Bobbi's death the whole family had begun looking for a permanent, meaningful way of honoring her memory. There were a lot of people who wanted to contribute something. We had a family meeting and invited Dave and Heather Alberts. There were a lot of individual tributes. For example, our son Steve, a chef, wrote a cookbook in her honor. Nike representative Eric Lautenbach wrote a song about her entitled "Reflections." We decided we didn't want to do a lot of different things, but rather focus on a few larger events that would enable us to make a real impact.

The first thing we could do was emphasize to women the difference that exercise could make in reducing the incidence of ovarian cancer. There had been a time when Dave Albert's wife, Heather, didn't even own a pair of running shoes. The first time her husband forced her to jog, she literally couldn't jog to the top of her driveway. Maybe a hundred yards. But after she talked with cancer doctors she realized the importance of exercise. Here is an amazing fact: The number-one thing people can do to reduce their risk of getting cancer is to exercise. Number one. It doesn't just cut the risk of ovarian cancer by 30 percent; large studies have shown that physically active people cut their risk of colon cancer by 50 percent. Dave likes to say Heather now thinks she invented running. In 2000 she'd founded Better Than Ever, a fitness and fund-raising program designed to get couch potatoes up and active. In 2000 BTE held their first half marathon, a 13.1-mile run–mostly walk in which participants were sponsored, in conjunction with the Tucson Marathon. She raised $24,000.

We remembered the afternoon Dave Alberts had gone to visit Bobbi in the hospital right after running the Tucson marathon. I want to do that next year, Bobbi had told him. Well, we decided this was exactly the type of event she would have loved, so the Bobbi Olson Half Marathon was born, with proceeds going to the Bobbi Olson ovarian cancer fund. Our goal was to raise money to support research for the prevention and cure of ovarian cancer.

We had a game scheduled against Mississippi State in Anaheim on Saturday afternoon. The next day the first Bobbi Olson Half Marathon was scheduled to be run. I flew home right after the game. I was the official starter. Before the race it was about twenty-six degrees and people were wearing running shorts and jogging around, mostly to keep from freezing to death, I thought. I ran and walked the 13.1 miles with ten members of the family and about five hundred other participants. I started walking with my family, but they were slowing me down. Thank goodness Stacy got a blister, so they stayed with her. Who says I'm not competitive? I finally caught up to my granddaughters, Vicki's daughters Katie and Kellie, and I ran with them. We left the rest of the family in the dust.

Not everybody finished the race that day, but that wasn't the goal. We raised more than $270,000 for the fund that afternoon. Since that first race, Better Than Ever has raised more than $1.25 million for cancer research and prevention at the Arizona Cancer Center.

In addition to Heather Albert's BTE, we also support the annual CATwalk, an event in which campus fraternities and sororities walk to raise money for the Bobbi Olson Fund—and in five years have raised more than $40,000, and the annual Quilt for a Cause, a wonderful event in which quilters in Tucson donate handmade quilts to be auctioned. In three years 208 quilts have been sold and $53,000 was raised.

We knew we could raise a lot of money in Bobbi's memory. The question was how to use it most effectively? Eventually we decided to endow the Bobbi Olson Chair in Ovarian Cancer Research. The first person to occupy that position was Dr. Setsuko Chambers, who came to the Arizona Cancer Center from Yale in 2004. Dr. Chambers, one of the very few gynecologic oncologist physician-scientists, was brought in to head the Arizona Cancer Clinic's new Division of Women's Cancers. This new setup brought all the breast and gynecological clinical and research programs together for the first time. Basically, it allowed them to put together a team to go after these cancers.

We had already been working on raising money for these programs when Christine got involved. Christine had much bigger ideas. In September of 2004 Christine threw a surprise birthday party for my seventieth birthday. She invited about sixty people for a dinner. After dinner she made a toast. She began by talking about the family she had married into and the wonderful lady who had created and nurtured this family. Then she explained that the family had a dream, and that dream was to make sure that the legacy of Bobbi and Lute Olson would live through the contributions we were making to the health of women. It was a lovely evening, an evening of hope.

We were making progress. A couple of weeks earlier, Scott Thompson, who is recovering from colon cancer, had accepted the job as senior director of development for the center. Dave Alberts had been appointed the new director of the Arizona Cancer Center, although he had not yet assumed the role. The Bobbi Olson chair had still not been fully funded, but we were close.

Then, in early January, the *Arizona Star* decided to do a profile on the basketball coach's wife, similar to a story they'd done on the football coach's wife. During the interview with Christine the reporter asked her which Tucson charities she was involved with. Christine had done a great deal of charitable work. She was chairman of the board of the Warhol Museum in Pittsburgh. She'd helped found a domestic violence shelter. She'd run several fund-raising dinners that raised more than a million dollars for various charities. She'd worked with numerous foundations. She'd raised a lot of money in politics; she definitely knew how to raise money. So she took this question as a challenge: What would she do for Tucson? "You know what," she responded. "We're going to create the definitive center for women's cancer treatment and research in America."

The reporter asked, "How much is that going to cost?"

"Oh," Christine said, "fifty million dollars."

Fifty million dollars? Fifty million dollars! The reporter was very surprised. "How are you going to do that?"

Christine didn't have an answer for that one. "Oh," she said confidently, "you'll see."

When the reporter was gone Christine called Dave Alberts and told him, "Dave, you're not going to believe what I just did."

Fifty million dollars!

The story announcing the new cancer center was published two weeks later. Dr. Chambers was thrilled; she'd accepted the job primarily because her husband had been hired as dean of the medical school and she wondered how much support she was really going to get. Now she knew she was going to get $50 million worth of support.

This really was a project that Bobbi would have wanted us to pursue. One of the few things that upset her when she had to go for chemo on a regular basis was that the treatment rooms were cold and sterile rather than being warm and inviting. Having to have the treatment was hard enough; doing it in a place that felt so foreign made it even harder. The people working there were welcoming, but the building was so cold. It was a big room, without real privacy, where people could see others getting sick. She really wanted the men and women who were coming in for their treatments to have a more homey place.

She tried to help while she was getting her treatment. She was constantly asking the medical staff if they needed anything more for their patients. Inevitably it wasn't medical equipment they needed, it was things to help with patient comfort. That was Bobbi: How can I help?

Initially we had envisioned building an outpatient treatment center, a comfortable place where people could come to get their treatment, maybe even in a private room, and feel as good as possible. But almost immediately the concept grew much bigger; it became a treatment center and a research facility devoted entirely to women's cancers.

To emphasize the fact that we were serious about this, two days later I announced that my family was making a $1 million gift to the Arizona Cancer Center to benefit the Bobbi Olson Endowment for Ovarian Cancer Research. It wasn't something we'd come up with overnight; it was something we'd been thinking and talking about, and this seemed like the best time to do it.

Dave Alberts was stunned when I told him about it. I thought about it in a very different way. When Bobbi and I were married, our entire savings consisted of what I had in my pocket. We spent our honeymoon night in a local motel. We'd lived for a decade, raising our kids, on a high school teacher's salary. And now I was able to make a million-dollar-gifts—and know that it wouldn't appreciably affect my family.

And the fact that Christine had been so supportive of it made it even more special.

Christine and Scott Thompson began working together. Within a month they had completed fully funding the endowment for the chair. To celebrate, we held a small ceremony. We invited about forty people. The whole thing was lit with candles, very understated and warm, just like Bobbi. As Christine said, "You could feel the angels in the room."

Throughout the night our friends stood up to talk about Bobbi. It had been a long time since I'd cried, but that night, among those people who had been so close to her, it was hard not to. I think some people probably felt a little uncomfortable, remembering Bobbi with Christine sitting right there. Then Pete Likens, the president of the university, said a few words. "We all loved Bobbi," he said. "We all loved her very much, and we will never forget her. What I've come to realize is that there is enough love in our hearts to love Bobbi and also love Christine."

No one had ever put that thought into words before. It was okay to love both of them. That was such an important night for Christine. In some ways it was her real welcome to Tucson.

Later that evening Christine and I were sitting out on the terrace with Dave and Heather. They were talking about the fund-raising program for the cancer center. Christine told Dave that we had to act as if we were at war with cancer. She quoted the *Tao of War*; if our goal is to build this center, she told him, then we have to be aggressive about raising the money to do it.

As she was speaking about it so passionately, my daughter Vicki came up from behind her. The two of them really had not been getting along at all. They hadn't spoken in about a year. Vicki had tears in her eyes. She said, "Christine, I just want to thank you for doing this for my mother."

They hugged.

That was a special night in so many ways.

I don't believe our work has made a significant impact so far, but I know we're on the right path. In early 2006 the National Cancer Institute issued a paper encouraging women with advanced ovarian cancer to be treated with the method developed by Dave Alberts, which calls for the direct administration of chemotherapy. According to *The New England Journal of Medicine,* women who received this treatment lived an additional eighteen months, raising the median survival period to sixty-seven months.

It's a very good start.

By the time the 2004–05 season started Christine was finding those places where she could make the greatest contribution. She was learning how to be the "team mom" while working with Scott Thompson and Dave Alberts on fund-raising efforts.

This was a veteran team with great talent. I knew how good we could be if we played to our potential. To reach that potential I thought they needed a challenge, so I gave them one: Win the national championship. Before the season began I admitted what everybody knew, we were good enough to win it again. In the past I'd said similar things, but with reservations: If we play to our potential we have an *opportunity* to win it. This time I admitted we were focusing on winning the last game. We opened the season ranked tenth in the polls. The experts decided that Salim was too inconsistent and that Channing Frye was "too soft" in the middle for us to be a championship team. Obviously, I thought that was baloney. Too soft, meaning that Channing wasn't a physical player. He wasn't tough enough. Channing used to joke about it, even calling himself a "ham sandwich," but it just wasn't true. Sometimes players get labeled early in their career and it sticks to them no matter how they improve. Channing had worked as hard to improve as any player I'd ever had; he had played in every game since his freshman year, he'd been beaten up, bruised and bloodied, and he still showed up. But because his game was finesse, people didn't appreciate his ability. I didn't understand how a guy could be soft who never backed off anybody, never missed a practice in four years, never missed a game, and played sick. It was ridiculous.

We played erratically at the beginning of the season. What was particularly irritating to me was that Salim's attitude didn't improve. As I've said, I have a master's degree in psychology and I'd had to put my education to use with him—without great results. During his junior season I'd had to suspend him for a game against Washington. It had made a slight difference. He returned against Washington State; I challenged him to guard Marcus Moore, who'd scored thirty-six and twenty-nine in his last two games against us, and he responded by holding him to five points.

Salim continued to frustrate me. He had enormous talent. I believed he was the best shooter in the country. I used to say, in Salim's case, any shot that's open is a good shot. "I don't care how many people are guarding him," I once told a reporter. "When you talk about the great shooters in our game today, you're kidding yourself if you think somebody is better than Stoudamire." When he was happy, when he felt good about himself, we would see that talent, but when he missed a few shots or got down on himself, it was as if he disappeared. When that happened, because he was such an integral part of our offense, he brought the whole team down with him.

For me, the final straw came in a game against Utah in early December. He played thirty minutes, took one shot the entire game, and didn't score as we barely managed to beat Utah and Andrew Bogut 67–62. They played a box and one against us—four defensive players in a zone while Salim was guarded man-to-man—but he still should have gotten some shots. I needed him to be a team leader and he just didn't seem interested. It was the thousandth win of my career, but I wasn't in a mood to celebrate. Instead, I suspended him. "Look," I told him, "ninety-nine-point-nine percent of the people are never going to meet you, and all they know about you is what they see on the court. I know you're a good person, but, believe me, you're not projecting that."

On the court he just looked like he didn't care. I wasn't the only one who noticed it. I often hear from my former players. I had received numerous phone calls from people who wanted to know what was up with him? What's his problem? These were people who had represented our program in a positive way. Few of them had ever met Salim, but they knew what the program expected of the kids—and that he wasn't fulfilling those expectations. I told Salim that he was letting down a lot of people, but most of all himself.

I also told him that the pro scouts knew he could play, but when they called, they all wanted to talk about his attitude.

Suspending him wasn't an easy decision. Four days later we were going to play undefeated twenty-second-ranked Marquette on national television. I wondered if it was fair to the rest of the team, but I just couldn't take his attitude anymore. I think a lot of people were surprised that I'd suspend our top scorer before an important game, but since my first day as a coach I'd taught that the team is more important than the individual. I'd suspended players for all kinds of reasons; academic problems obviously, but also missing a curfew, missing a meeting or a practice, fighting with a teammate, elbowing an opponent, and the general catchall, a lack of maturity. Often they were suspended for being teenagers, for doing the type of things that a lot of teenagers do, but things that basketball players can't do because they are in the spotlight.

I'd suspended both stars and reserves, including Sean Rooks, Gene Edgerson, Gilbert Arenas, Richard Jefferson, Ben Davis, even Jason Gardner, Loren Woods, Miles Simon, Joseph Blair. Twenty years earlier, when we played UCLA for our first Pac-10 title, Pete Williams and Morgan Taylor were sitting on the bench, and that might well have cost us the game. I've changed in a lot of ways, but my principles haven't changed.

With Stoudamire sitting on the end of the bench in civilian clothes we beat Marquette, 48–43. That was the least points we'd scored since 1985, but we won by playing great defense, they shot only 30.6 percent. Most important, Salim got the message.

He didn't start our next game, against Manhattan, but he came off the bench to match his career high with seven three-pointers, scoring twenty-three points. When he didn't start the game after that, he asked Roz, "Is Coach trying to test me?"

Roz nodded, "Yes."

He responded. In the four games following his suspension he hit 75 percent of his field goals, 79 percent of his three-point shots and fifteen of sixteen free throws. His whole attitude changed. One day he asked Roz why I was so easy on players like Jason Gardner, Jason Terry, and his cousin, Damon Stoudamire, when I was so tough on him. I didn't think I was so easy on those players, but comparatively, maybe. We gave him some tapes of those three players to take home. After watching them, he figured it out. Those guys were smiling when they were playing. "It looked like those guys were having fun," he told Roz.

The next problem I had with him was that he was overpassing. He was trying to get all his teammates involved. Finally I had him come into the office. I told him, "Salim, I love the fact that you're looking to get your teammates the ball, but you're hurting us by not taking the open shot. You have to look for your shot first." That's when he became the complete player we knew he could be.

Our relationship changed substantially after that. It was similar to what happened with Tom Tolbert years earlier. He drove me crazy for a year and a half, and then, the last half year, the lights came on.

We finished the regular season 27–6, and first in the Pac-10 at 15–3. I became Salim's most vocal booster. I just got so tired of hearing broadcaster Dick Vitale constantly telling viewers that Duke's J. J. Redick was the best shooter in college basketball that I began complaining. I told the media that I thought this was another example of East Coast bias at work. I had our sports information director, Rich Paige, put together a statistical comparison of Salim and Redick. To my surprise—I think to everyone's surprise—we discovered that at that point Redick would have had to hit seventy consecutive three-point shots to match Salim's shooting percentage. Seventy in a row to tie! It wasn't even close. Redick is a great shooter, but in his junior year he wasn't even in the same arena as Stoudamire. I gave those stats to our local newspapers and eventually it was picked up by other papers. I also sent it to Vitale, along with tapes of Salim and Redick. When I finally spoke to Vitale he told me, "You know what surprised me? I didn't realize that Stoudamire was that good a defender."

"Most people don't," I told him. "But since I've been here I think he's been our best defender four years in a row." I also said that Salim was the most underrated player in the country and just maybe the best guard I'd ever coached.

He wasn't the only player I defended loudly that season. It was frustrating to the whole coaching staff that people underrated Channing Frye, who had done everything we had asked of him—and maybe even more—during his career at Arizona. When we went up to Washington for two games he averaged twenty-eight points, shooting 85.7 percent. At the end of the week, however, the Pac-10 named the Huskies' Tre Simmons Player of the Week. Simmons is a great player and that week he averaged 26.5 points in victories over Arizona State and us. But when I heard that I was furious. I immediately wrote to Pac-10 commissioner Tom Hansen:

> *I am appalled at what has transpired recently within our conference ... Channing Frye just concluded one of the most impressive road trips, in terms of individual performance, in the history of this conference ... It is completely beyond my comprehension how you and your staff cannot have the instincts or common sense to do what is right ... Just in case you missed the games and/or did not see the box scores, Channing was 24 of 28 from the field and 8 of 8 from the free throw line last weekend.*
>
> *... It must take the box score hitting you square between the eyes before you finally see it. Therefore, in addition to the aforementioned shooting exploits, Channing also had 13 rebounds, 5 blocks and 3 steals, while playing 81 minutes! I ask you, what does it take? Would you like Channing to take tickets at the door and also sell concessions? I may advise him to do so at the upcoming Pac-10 tournament. If I seem incensed and furious,*

your senses are correct. To put it loud and clear ... I felt it was
totally disgusting not to have Channing Frye recognized. [He]
stands for everything that is right with college athletics ...

He deserves better. He deserves to be recognized for his hard
work and dedication, and whether it is through this letter or the
national media, I will see that it gets done.

And I did.

My praise for Stoudamire and Frye was well earned. In the Pac-10 championship game Salim scored thirty-seven points and was named the Most Outstanding Player—even though we lost to Washington 81–72. In our opening game of the NCAA tournament Channing Frye had thirteen points and seven rebounds—in the second half—to lead us to a 66–53 victory over Utah State.

We were playing very well. The last few games of the season Hassan Adams had stepped up his game another notch. Sometimes you can see a player mature over the span over a few games, and that's what happened to Hassan. He was getting assists, he was becoming much more of a factor on the glass, and he was scoring. Kirk Walters had made a great improvement as Channing Frye's backup. Just like you hope to do, we were peaking as we went into the tournament.

In our second game of the tournament Salim had twenty-eight points as we beat Alabama-Birmingham to reach the Sweet Sixteen. UAB loves to press, but teams generally can't press us for too long. When UAB tried, we ran right through it, forcing them to pull out of it and go to a half-court press. They wanted to wear us down with their quickness and aggressiveness, but that's our game. We ended up wearing them down.

That set up a meeting with Eddie Sutton's Oklahoma State Cowboys in the regional semifinals. Both Eddie Sutton and I were coaching in our twenty-sixth NCAA tournament. As I said after the game, "If no one cared who won, I don't think it could get any better than that."

I cared a lot. With twelve seconds left Oklahoma State was up a point, but we had the ball. As we came out of a time-out, there wasn't anybody watching that game who didn't know that Salim was going to take the last shot for us. During the time-out I had calmed everybody down and in a very businesslike fashion we talked about how we were going to score and defend. We were going to run a side pick-and-roll, I told them. Channing was going to set a screen for Salim. Oklahoma State had been changing up their defense throughout the game; sometimes they would attack the screen, other times they would come under it. I told Salim, "You're just going to have to read how they play you and make your appropriate move." This is the kind of moment we'd been preparing him for since the day he put on an Arizona jersey. He knew how to play the game.

We inbounded. Salim cleared the floor with a wave of his hand, then drove left. He was well defended. As a coach, that's about the time you just stop breathing. With 2.8 seconds left, he pulled up fifteen feet from the basket; he was off balance and the defender was up on him. Falling backward he took his shot—and hit it. One shot, a shot Salim had been preparing to take his whole life, and in the time it took a roundball to fly about fifteen feet, my anxiety turned to elation and Eddie Sutton's excitement became absolute dejection. I was elated, thrilled, excited, I was about as in-the-moment as it is possible to be. I was every bit as excited as I had been so many years earlier when we'd won meaningful games at Long Beach Community College. Every game is the most important game. The Cowboys' last-second shot bounced off the rim, 79–78 Arizona.

After the game, as I listened to Salim in the press conference, I kept thinking how far he had come in a few months, what a different kid he had become on the court. For the first time in his entire career, he looked like he was having fun. He told the media, confidently, "I knew crunch time would be my time."

Once more, we were a win away from going back to the Final Four. The only team we had to beat was the University of Illinois. The only team? Illinois had been ranked number one most of the season and was led by a great player, Dee Brown. A lot of people were picking them to win it all. Just to make the task a little harder, the game was being played in Chicago.

Chicago, Illinois.

It's an amazing game, basketball. It's incredible how quickly you can go from an incredible high to the deepest low. Not just from game to game, but from minute to minute within a single game. We've always been a team that plays for the streaks, we've won countless games by making a big run. Sometimes, though, they go the other way.

After the Oklahoma State game I'd told reporters it couldn't get any better than that game. Well, that lasted exactly one game. This was a home game for Illinois. A team playing in an arena packed with its fans has a huge advantage. It certainly doesn't create a level playing field. Or court. Rosemont Arena was just a sea of people wearing Illini orange, and tucked in a corner was a little section of Arizona fans. There was a time the NCAA wanted teams playing close to home because it would sell tickets, but now, with every seat sold out before the tournament begins, that's no longer necessary. It happens; there have been years we've played in our part of the country, but I've never been in favor of teams playing a series of postseason games a bus ride away.

Even though Illinois was the top-ranked team in the country I felt good about the game. We were playing well, and I knew our guys wouldn't be intimidated by them. We'd beaten several teams that played their style: They shot a lot of threes, and they were tough underneath. But we never doubted we could win that game.

We knew it was going to be a game of momentum switches; we'd have our time, then they'd have their time. For the first thirty-six minutes, though, it was mostly our time. We were just playing so well. The guys did an unbelievable job of moving the ball and being patient until we got the shot we wanted. We made some mistakes; we didn't take care of the ball and get out to meet the ball. I called a time-out because Channing had gotten the ball in the middle of their press a few times and kicked it back out to our guards. That's a no-no with us. You get the ball in the middle, you move the ball ahead and make them pay for pressing. I felt we were playing not to lose. The lead kept growing, we were up by seven, then nine, twelve, fourteen . . . Maybe the guys thought we could sit on it. I wanted us to be more aggressive. With four minutes left in the game, we were up fifteen points. I believe completely that if we had not been playing in an Illinois environment, the game would have been over. You could see on their faces of the Illinois players that they were down and out. But then they got a steal and hit a three, and the crowd got into it. They cut the margin to eight or nine, and the crowd just came alive. We always tell our players, if you're playing on the road and you hear the noise level go up, don't come down and take a quick shot. Bring it down, move the ball, make them defend. Because if you come down and shoot, even if you hit the shot, you don't change the momentum.

The other team is still in its rhythm. They're going to take it down and probably score. So what we try to do is get them to play defense for twenty-five or thirty seconds. The crowd gets a little tired of yelling. And then if you hit the bucket it'll deflate them. And even if you don't score, the fact that you've held it so long will have a bearing.

You could feel the momentum shift. You could see the look on Illinois faces that maybe, just maybe . . . They began picking up their intensity. Very seldom do you see the home team get tired, because when the crowd starts yelling, the adrenaline starts kicking in. When you don't have the crowd, you feel the fatigue. Luther Head hit a pair of three-pointers. Dee Brown scored on a floater in the lane. They stole the ball and Head scored again. They hit one big shot after another. When they missed, they got the rebound. They forced turnovers, then took advantage of every one of them. They played like a team that was 34-1. Believe me, in that situation you can feel the game start to slip away. You do everything you can to stop it, short of going out on the court and tackling somebody. We needed to make one play. We needed one stop, we needed one missed shot, we needed to score, we needed one rebound to bounce a little higher, a little farther out. One play and we were going to the Final Four. One play, that was all we needed.

Up in the stands Christine was sitting with her friend Bernie. "Tell me we can't lose, Bernie. Right, we can't?" She could barely watch.

Bernie told her, "There's no way you can be up fifteen points and lose. You hold the ball, make them foul. Don't worry, we're going to the Final Four."

The last couple of minutes the officials put their whistles away. A lot of people say you can't make a call at that point in a game; let the kids decide the game. I've always believed that's garbage. The kids should decide the outcome, but they still play by the rules. If it's a foul in the first minute of the game, then it should be a foul in the last minute of the game.

Illinois committed some obvious fouls those last few minutes of regulation, but I think the officials simply got caught up in the momentum of the game—and the cheering of 18,000 Illinois fans. Also, I think that the officials probably thought the game was over: Illinois was down fourteen, so maybe they let some things go that at another point they would have called. If I complain about the officials, however, it's just considered sour grapes. The truth is that Illinois played unbelievably great basketball those last few minutes. They did everything they had to do. They made pressure shots; they played with great determination and confidence. They deserve as much credit as they earned, but the officials still missed at least two obvious fouls: Once, Channing just got hammered on an inbounds pass. Seconds later, Mustafa Shakur got mugged. Illinois just ran right through him and took the ball without a call being made. Illinois scored on both plays. At that point we were in a double bonus situation. If the officials had called either foul, we would have had two free throws. Figure we make at least one, and they don't get the score. So it was at least a three-point turnaround caused by an official not making the call.

Now, admittedly, at some time during my career, maybe once or twice, there probably were games in which we were the beneficiary of a no call or a bad call, but I don't remember them. I suspect no coach remembers them. The only questionable calls, or no calls, you remember are the ones that cost you a game.

With thirty-eight seconds to go, Deron Williams hit a three-point field goal to complete a remarkable 20–5 Illini run in four minutes to tie the score at 80. We had a couple of decent looks the last few seconds, but Salim's shot at the end of regulation was blocked. So we were going to overtime.

During the time-out we regrouped. Our kids were down, and the momentum was going against us. We talked about that and I told them, "It's going to come down to who the tougher team is. Both teams have exerted a lot of energy. We just have to be tougher than they are."

In the overtime they kept rolling. They were up six with 1:57 left. That's when we showed our character. Hassan Adams hit five straight points to bring us back to within a point. We had the ball at the end of the overtime period, down 90–89, with one shot to win it. I called a time-out to set up a play. We didn't want to have to make a shot from the perimeter. Hassan Adams had been killing his man the whole game, so he was our first option. We wanted him to drive to the basket to put pressure on Illinois to make the stop without fouling him. Channing Frye was the second option. He was going to set up at the free throw line and slide down and get in position. Salim had been struggling the whole game, and he was really fatigued at that point. Knowing what a clutch player he was, remembering the shot he'd hit to beat Oklahoma State, where they had to play him tight, they had to assume he'd be our go-to guy. So he was going to be the decoy.

This is where luck plays a role. Their best defender was Deron Williams, and he had done a tremendous job holding Salim to nine points. During the time-out before the last play, Coach Weber was setting up his defense. He guessed that we would try to get the ball to Stoudamire, our best shooter. Williams told the coaching staff that he was exhausted; he didn't feel he could guard Salim. So they switched him over to guard Hassan Adams. That was luck: They had their best defender on the player we wanted to take the last shot.

We got the ball into the hands of the guy we wanted to take it to the hole; they had their best defender, who wasn't going to let him do that. We probably let too many seconds tick off before we started our offense, but Hassan never got a good look. He managed to get off a weak shot. It missed, and Illinois had completed a remarkable comeback to win the game. "It was a miracle," their All-American guard Dee Brown said after the game. Maybe.

Being on the losing side of a miracle is unbelievably painful. This game ranked close to the 2001 loss to Duke in the championship game as the toughest of my career. As hard as it was for me, I'd been through more than a thousand games, for the team this was just devastating. I felt awful for our seniors. This was our first group of seniors since 1987 that didn't go to at least one Final Four. We all knew that if we had gotten there, we were good enough to win it.

Our locker room was absolutely silent. The kids were sitting in front of their lockers with their heads down. "Listen up," I told them. "I'm so proud of you guys. I don't want you to let four minutes determine how you feel about this season. We had a great season. I couldn't be more proud of any other team. I want you to pick your heads up and be proud of yourselves. You guys are all winners. You're only the third Arizona team to win thirty games, you got a Pac-10 championship ring, you took the number-one team in the country to the last second in overtime. You guys fought as hard as you could. I am so proud of every one of you."

Then there were some hugs.

I had to go to the press conference with Channing Frye and Salim Stoudamire. I tried to make it as easy as possible for them. I spoke first, telling the media that if you didn't care who won and you watched that game, you saw a great college basketball game. Two teams that left everything they had on the floor. I never talk about the officiating and I didn't make an exception. This is about Illinois, I continued. They made the plays they needed to make down the stretch and we didn't. There was a reason they were thirty-five and one.

Channing and Salim handled the questions very well. Mostly they expressed their disappointment in the outcome but their pride in our effort. As I watched them, I thought about how far they had come in their four years at Arizona. About how much they had accomplished, both on the court and in their own lives. As bad as I felt, it was impossible not to feel very proud of them.

I had too many things that had to be done to spend time feeling bad. Christine was devastated. She was very good at dealing with losses when there were things she could do, but in this situation she was helpless. She did as much as she could to make me feel better, but this kind of loss was so new to her there wasn't too much she could do.

It was a long, quiet flight home. Everybody on the plane was sitting quietly. Nobody wanted to talk about it. About halfway home I started walking down the aisle trying to find out who had the tape of the game. My daughter Jody was on the plane. She couldn't believe that I would want to watch the game again. It was hard enough watching it the first time, but for almost fifty years I'd been doing things one way. It had worked out pretty well. So I wasn't going to change. She was right: That was a very hard game to look at again. No matter how many times I watched that game, we were always just one play away.

A few days later I went to St. Louis for the Final Four weekend. The NCAA had scheduled several important meetings and I wanted to be there for them. Among the subjects under discussion was a plan to revamp the academic requirements, and I wanted to get involved with that. I went to all the coaches' meetings. On the Thursday night before the Final Four weekend I always host a dinner for my former players who are now coaching. It's a great night. On Saturday I went to the semi-finals. That was tough. It was very hard watching that game from the stands when we had been so close to playing in it. People didn't really know how to approach me. A lot of the people there were head coaches, and they knew exactly what I was feeling. So many of them told me that they had been rooting for us to go all the way. There was a lot of "Sorry, Lute," and, "That was a great game," and, "Boy, that was close." I heard it all.

I flew home on Sunday because we had a team barbecue scheduled for Monday. The whole team watched the championship game together Monday night so it would be less painful. Kids recover from disappointment quicker than coaches. Illinois was playing Roy Williams's North Carolina Tar Heels for the national championship. Generally, in a tournament you want the team that beat you to win, but Roy Williams is a good friend of mine, and he was the winningest coach who hadn't won the championship. I wanted him to get that large monkey off his back. I think what made everybody feel a little better was that early in the championship game North Carolina had Illinois buried, and then Illinois made a great run at them to get back into the game. North Carolina held on to win.

After the season I met with each member of the team. When Hassan Adams came into my office, we talked about how painful it was to come so close to be playing for the national championship. You never know until you're in the game, but on paper we matched up better with North Carolina than Illinois did. While we were talking, the phone rang. Since my secretary, Lydia, put it through, I knew it had to be important. It was Steve Kerr. This was more than twenty-five years since Steeeeeeeve Kerrrrrrr! and his teammates had helped establish the Arizona tradition. That team put us in the polls for the first time, got us to the NCAA tournament, put us on the national map. But Steve and Hassan were members of a very large, very loyal, extended family. We knew it, and we felt it.

I said, "It's interesting that you called, because Hassan and I are sitting here, and Hassan was just wondering how long this pain will last."

"You know what," he said, "the unfortunate thing is that when anyone asks me about the semifinal game we lost to Oklahoma, my first thought was that I shot so poorly I cost us the game. I remember how terrible I felt after the game, like I'd let everybody down. Just tell Hassan that the pain will subside, but you'll never forget the game."

Steve Kerr was right. A few days later I was sitting in the bleachers of another high school gym, watching the future. The loss to Illinois wasn't forgotten. I'm still a bad loser, and I don't easily forget the last loss of the season, but I was already thinking about the next season. Salim would be picked by the Atlanta Hawks, the thirty-first pick in the NBA draft; Channing Frye would be the eighth pick, by the Knicks. They would be gone, but we had a strong nucleus coming back.

It didn't take too long for the anticipation of the next season to replace the sadness of the last loss in my mind. That's what being a coach is all about. That's the thing about true love: It may change, it goes through many seasons, but it never disappears.

12

Oklahoma City University coach Abe Lemons had a unique approach to the game of basketball. I remember hearing him lecture about strategy at a clinic in Chicago. "We have this two O, three X offense," he explained. "The Os are the only guys allowed to shoot the ball. The Xs don't shoot, they aren't allowed to shoot. If an X passes the ball to an X, he comes out of the game, but if an O passes to an X, he comes out of the game, too." Then he paused and smiled. "But the amazing thing is that the other team always guards the Xs!"

When he was coaching Texas, his team traveled to Lubbock for a game against Texas Tech. He felt his team was too tight and he wanted his players to relax. "I got together with my team and I told them, 'You know, every big-time basketball team has a curfew,' he said. 'So tonight, we're going to have a curfew. You can't come *in* before ten o'clock.' I didn't think that would be a problem. In Lubbock there isn't much to do after eight o'clock. Around nine I looked out my window and the guys were sitting on the curb looking at their watch. It got worse, I caught two guys trying to sneak *in!*"

I wish it was as easy as Abe always made it sound. It rarely is, though. Every season offers its challenges and rewards, although to get to the rewards you need to survive the challenges. The first challenge for us beginning the 2005–06 season was replacing Channing Frye and Salim Stoudamire, but I felt we had the people ready to do that. I thought we'd be a little rough at the beginning of the season and by the middle of the year we'd be as good or better than the team that had lost to Illinois.

People sometimes wonder how difficult it is to lose seniors like Channing and Salim, but after four years, and sometimes less, the seniors are ready to play pro basketball and in some cases four years has been enough for us, too. And if you didn't say good-bye to the seniors, you couldn't say hello to the freshmen.

For us the recruiting season began in late August, when high school senior Chase Budinger, who we'd been pursuing for three years, finally committed to Arizona. My assistant Rodney Tention discovered him long before anybody else. As a freshman he was a complete unknown, but a coach in a summer league called and told Rodney about him. Even as a sophomore he was barely rated in the top two hundred high school kids in the country, but we liked him a lot and started recruiting him. I went to see him play as often as was legal under the rules. I saw him play in late 2004, then planned to see him again after our afternoon home game against Washington State in January 2005. That was a game I expected to win, but Washington State ended our thirty-eight-game McKale winning streak, 70–63. It was just an awful loss. But as soon as that game ended I drove to Phoenix then flew to Orange County to watch Chase score fifty-one points against perennial power Mater Dei. Steve Kerr and Jud Buechler, who lived nearby and had been helping us recruit Chase, met me there with their families. It was a very good thing I was there, because after that game he was rated a top-ten prospect. I've been fortunate in my assistants, but kids want to play for the head coach. It turned out that my visit that day, after a rough loss, showed him how much I wanted him at Arizona, and it probably made the difference in his decision.

If you love coaching basketball, working with freshmen is especially rewarding. These are young people with raw talent, depending upon the coaching staff to take that talent and develop it. The NCAA allows us to bring freshmen in for one summer session. That allows them to take six units of core courses as well as play against our guys. In those games they get bounced around like a rubber ball. They know what hit them—experienced upperclassmen. To begin the 2005–06 season we were bringing in three true freshmen, J. P. Prince, Fendi Onobun, and Marcus Williams, as well as Mohamed Tangara, who had been hurt early in the previous season and been given a medical waiver.

Our problems began long before the season started. One of the people we were depending on to step up was Jawann McClellan. As a freshman the previous year he'd played in every game. He was an outstanding shooter and we expected him to become our second leading scorer and one our top rebounders. Jawann was enrolled in the summer program when his father suddenly died of an aneurysm. It was just awful, and Jawann was devastated. He had to drop out to go home. He came back for the second summer session and was there pretty much by himself. The coaches were away recruiting or on vacation; most of the other players had gone home. That's when the magnitude of his loss hit him.

I couldn't help but remember when the same thing had happened to me. It affects you forever, but the real impact takes some time before it hits you. After meeting Jawann, a university psychologist told me he was in no shape to handle this. He needed to go home and be with his family.

In the spring semester before his father's death Jawann had screwed up. He needed to complete this extra semester to remain eligible. When he dropped out, we appealed to the NCAA, telling the committee that he would have regained his eligibility if this horrible thing hadn't happened. The NCAA turned us down. Jawann was academically ineligible for the first semester.

That made us just a little thinner. We tried to be optimistic. Any coach will tell you that sometimes optimism is the only option. This might be okay, we decided, because it'll give Marcus Williams and some of our other kids more playing time. When Jawann came back at midseason we would be that much stronger.

We opened the season at the Maui Classic by beating Kansas. We lost our second game to Connecticut, then ranked second in the country, and our third game to fifth-ranked Michigan State in overtime. After beating Virginia we traveled to Texas to play Tom Penders's Houston Cougars. Two starters, Hassan Adams and Chris Rodgers, were late for our pregame meeting, so I sat them out for the first ten minutes. By the time I put them in, we were down 20–4. We actually came back and took the lead, but we missed some free throws and lost. We were playing well, but still had a losing record and were ranked mostly around twentieth.

We won our next four games, including a thirty-point victory over Utah in Salt Lake City to break their thirty-one game home winning streak. And then, for the first time in eighteen years, the first time since 1987–88, we dropped out of the top twenty-five. We had been ranked for 312 consecutive polls. It bothered me, I have to admit that. If we'd deserved to be dropped, okay, I accept that. We didn't. We'd won our previous four games; we'd won our last game by thirty, two of our four losses were to top-ten teams, and we had the fourth best RPI—that's the NCAA scale of success and takes into consideration scores and strength of schedule—in the nation. After 312 weeks in the polls, I thought we'd earned more respect than that. It wasn't something to make a big fuss about, and the only place it might really affect you if you drop out for a while is in recruiting, but I didn't like it. We didn't like it.

As the season progressed we got better and better. Ivan Radenovic really improved his game. He's an outstanding shooter from seventeen feet but not from twenty, so we took the twenty-foot shot out of his game. Instead of taking that shot, he faked the three, took one dribble to the basket and shot the seventeen-footer—and was hitting 50 percent. Marcus Williams took advantage of his playing time and came along faster than we anticipated. Kirk Walters progressed, too, but what prevented us from being a very good team was the lack of a consistent perimeter shooter. We were optimistic Jawann would fill that need when he came back. He became eligible in early January. We looked like we were going to be a very good team, and in his second game back he tore the ligament in his left wrist. They operated a couple of days later. He was out for the rest of the season.

We never found that three-point shooter we needed.

Every coach has to be a disciplinarian. It's as much a part of the job at Arizona as it was in high school. That part of it doesn't change. There isn't any magic secret to it. Recruit good kids, treat them with respect, be tough when you have to, and then try to be lucky. Things happen. Certainly one of the toughest disciplinarians I've ever known was Eugene Edgerson's high school coach. He had what he needed: A paddle and permission from his players' parents to use it. Make a one-handed pass? Smack. Not paying attention? Smack. In Gene's freshman year we were having some minor problems keeping everybody in order. One day Gene shook his head in disbelief and suggested to me, "You know, Coach, maybe you'd better get a paddle."

That became a joke, but there were times I wished I had something that worked as well. For example, I might have used that paddle when Andre Iguodala was at Arizona. Andre was a little bit on the stubborn side. He was a gamer, meaning that he wasn't our hardest worker in a practice situation. He just wanted to play, so if we were scrimmaging, he was full speed ahead, but when we were doing drills—and in our practices that's much of the time—we had to keep on him. When he decided to go pro, that might have hurt him a little. Scouts come to our practices, and they saw us butting heads. They also tracked his shooting in practice, and his percentage wasn't nearly as good as it was during games. He got a reputation that he wasn't the most coachable player. When I was asked about him by the pros, I explained that he was never a real problem; he was a good person and a good team member, but that at times he had to be pushed. Having the paddle might've helped me push him.

It might have also helped me during the 2005–6 season with Chris Rodgers. In midseason I had to suspend him. It was a case in which he had difficulty learning to play with four other people. He wasn't alone. That's the toughest transition for a lot of kids to make. He overdribbled the ball. Our other people didn't like playing with him. When he started becoming a problem in the practice situation, I had no choice. I dropped him from the team. This is not something any coach ever enjoys, but when a player begins taking too much of your time in practice without being productive you just have no choice. Sometimes the best way to get a player's attention is to suspend it. And when you do, you never know the outcome. I told Chris several specific things he had to do to be reinstated. To his credit, he immediately began working on them. It took him a month to fulfill his responsibilities. When he came to me and said he had done what I'd required, I spoke with his teammates to find out how they felt about him coming back. They were unanimously in favor of him coming back, so he was reinstated. By the end of the season he was voted our best defensive player.

With all the difficulties, we played erratically all season. We finished the regular season at a bumpy 18–11. We had been invited to the Big Dance twenty-one consecutive years, the longest active streak in the nation and second in history only to North Carolina's twenty-seven in a row, and there were some people speculating that we were on the bubble, that our streak might be ending. I didn't think that was true, because we played a difficult schedule, including several quality opponents on the road, we had a strong RPI and I knew the committee always looks at that. But still, twenty wins is usually the key. You get your twenty wins, you get an invitation. It was very possible we'd get those two additional wins in the Pac-10 tournament.

Difficult seasons tend to stay difficult. This was a difficult season. I had to suspend Hassan Adams, our leading scorer, for the tournament, when he was arrested and charged with driving under the influence of alcohol.

His arrest made headlines around the country. Immediately most people believed he was guilty. Unfortunately, part of the price for being a high-profile athlete is that when something like this happens, you're guilty until proven innocent. Even if you are proven innocent, many people will always believe you got away with something because you are an athlete. That does happen; absolutely, athletes are treated differently, but in Hassan's case there was more to the story than the headlines.

After Senior Day, our last home game, Christine and I invited all the players and their families, as well as some friends from Tucson, back to our home for dinner. According to NCAA rules, we're not permitted to have parents for dinner. I don't understand that rule; I just follow it. Parents have to cover the cost of their meals. To adhere to that rule we leave a basket out in front for the parents to put in money; we do have an honor system. Hassan had about twenty friends and relatives in town to see his last game at McKale, and it was at least an hour and a half before they got to the house. Hassan had finished his postgame interviews and then stood outside McKale signing autographs for every kid who asked him.

That didn't surprise me. Hassan is that type of person. It was later that night that I found out he had been stopped for speeding and arrested for DUI. When I spoke with him, he told me he had gone back to his apartment with his uncle and some friends and there he had a cocktail. One of our senior managers was having a party, and Hassan was driving there with several people in the car. The policeman who stopped him said he had tracked him on radar going forty in a thirty-mile-an-hour zone. Apparently he was tested with a Breathalyzer. "Probably six times," he told me, and he passed all the field tests.

I'm proud to have been Hassan Adams coach. He's a very good person. He pleaded not guilty and got an attorney. I had no choice but to suspend him, although, contrary to the reports, he was not suspended for DUI. He's innocent of that charge until the day he's proven guilty. Instead, I suspended him because we have a basic team rule: Don't do anything to embarrass the program. That rule applies equally to our leading scorer and our twelfth man. The publicity was an embarrassment to the program, so I felt I had no choice but to suspend him for the Pac-10 tournament.

Hassan accepted it without complaining. His mother, Connie, called me and told me she was also fine with our decision. In the opening game of the Pac-10 tournament, playing without our leading scorer and really the heart of our team, we beat Stanford, for our nineteenth win. We then lost to UCLA.

With only nineteen wins—only—there remained some speculation that we wouldn't get an invitation to the NCAA tournament. When I looked at the records of teams who had won more games than us, a lot of them, in fact almost all of them, had played a majority of their non-conference games at home. We had traveled. When the brackets were announced we were an eighth seed. That's a tough seed, because it sets up a second-round game with the number one-seed in the region. It made me wonder if we were really doing our team an injustice by playing our schedule. If, instead of playing only five of our eleven nonconference games at home, we had played ten of them there, I have absolutely no doubt we would have won several more games. Through the years we've won more than 90 percent of our games at McKale. If we'd won four more games we would have finished 23–6, and probably earned a number-five seed. So we are taking a serious look at the way we set up our schedule. It doesn't make sense to put ourselves in this kind of situation.

We played our first-round game against the ninth seed, Wisconsin. They had not been playing well at the end of the season, and we beat them easily. Hassan was reinstated. Playing only twenty-three minutes he hit ten of fourteen shots to lead us to a 94–75 win. We hit fourteen of our first twenty shots and got off to a 35–11 lead. Wisconsin never got within single digits. That was our twentieth win. Twenty wins: The media called it "a subpar season." And I suppose by the standards we've established, it was.

When Hassan was suspended, we got several letters from fans supporting that decision, but when he was reinstated, we got some letters complaining that this was a serious offense and by letting him play we were sending a very bad message. I respond personally to as many letters as I can, and I wrote back explaining that Hassan was innocent until he was proven guilty, which had not happened. If we had suspended Hassan for being charged with DUI and later he was deemed innocent, the school would face the possibility of a lawsuit because we had limited his opportunity to be seen by professionals in a playoff situation—and, more important, our actions would be a reflection on his character. In Hassan's case the penalty fit the crime—which was causing embarrassment to the university and the basketball program. Nothing else.

Our second game was against number-one-seeded Villanova. I thought we matched up well with them, but they had a huge advantage: The game was played in Philadelphia. We were fifteen miles from their campus; essentially it was a home game for them. This was pretty much the same situation that we faced the year before when we played Illinois in Chicago. I thought it might be a little better in Philadelphia because Kentucky played Connecticut in the first game of our double-header, and both teams had a lot of very loyal supporters. Their fans travel. We hoped they would stay for the second game and root for the underdog, and we were the underdog.

Well, I was wrong about that one. Really wrong. I don't know how it happened—maybe as soon as the first game ended, Kentucky and Connecticut fans handed their tickets to Villanova fans—but when we took the court, the arena was just full of Villanova fans.

Villanova was a very good team, basically playing at home. Early in the second half they were up twelve and we could have folded, but didn't. What this team lacked in perimeter shooting and depth we came close to making up in character. That's an intangible that no scale can measure. We made a great run, closing to within a point. With a minute and a half to go we were only down two. That's when the crowd really got into it. As Villanova's fine guard Randy Foye said afterward, "It was like a home game for us. When we needed a stop, we heard the crowd. It was important for us down the stretch."

We had to start fouling, and they knocked down their free throws. The final score was 82–78. We had fought ourselves into a position where we could have won it with a break or two. But we didn't get them.

At the end of every game both teams line up and shake hands. Usually nobody says very much beyond "nice game." It's generally perfunctory. If one of the kids on the other team is someone we had tried to recruit, I might say a few more words to him. As I was walking down the line after the Villanova game Kyle Lowry, a guard from Philly and a friend of Mustafa Shakur's, and someone we had not been involved with in recruiting, said to me, "Coach, it was a real honor playing against you and your team." That wasn't something I hadn't expected from a kid, and something very much out of the ordinary—but I thought it was typical of Coach Wright's program. I remember that almost as much as I remember how close we came to winning.

Almost. I couldn't help looking at what might have been if we'd won that game. It seems now that I have such pleasant memories from so many places. If we'd won, we would have gone to Minneapolis for the regional finals, where I had started my career and where we'd been in the Final Four in 2001, so we would have had great support there. The next stop would have been Indianapolis, where we'd won the championship in 1997, and where Iowa had made the Final Four in 1980, so we had supporters there too.

If.

The coach's lament.

I said a few words in the locker room after our game and on Monday met individually with each player. By then a lot of the emotion has dissipated; by then the seniors are looking forward to the draft and our returning players already have begun thinking about the next season—what role the new kids will play, where we'll be traveling, what they have to do to reach the next level.

When I walked out of the locker room after losing to Villanova, Christine was waiting for me. She had learned so much through the season. Early in our relationship she would be as down after a loss as I was. And once she got to know the kids, she even helped recruit some of them; she had a real emotional investment in the team. So when we lost, she hurt. We talked about it a number of times. I told her, "Despite how you feel inside, you need to put that aside. You need to be smiling outside the locker room. You need to tell them what a great job they did and how proud you are of them." I also told her, "You need to be supportive not only of the team, but of me at that point. You need to try to get me out of the depths."

That was a hard thing to do, to put on a happier face—and she did it. When we boarded the bus to the arena for the Villanova game, for example, she stood by the door, and every one of the kids gave her a hug before they went in. And after we'd lost the game she was standing right there providing support. No matter how badly a loss might tear her up inside, she now understands that this is part of the job of the coach's wife, and she does it.

Christine has made herself an important part of the program. I knew that had happened when I heard Mohamed Tangara tell a reporter, "Christine is great. I love her. She's a great person. I look at her like a mom." Among her many abilities is the fact that she's great about remembering meaningful dates, for example, and she loves giving gifts. I remember that she got really upset when I tried to explain to her that she could send a birthday card to a player but not a gift. She smiled incredulously, "I can't send them a birthday present?"

"No, you can't. That's not my rule, it's the NCAA's."

"That's the dumbest thing I've ever heard," she said. And then immediately began looking for the loophole. "How about the manager? Can I send the managers gifts?"

"All right, you can send a present to a manager." And the assistant coaches and the office staff—but she was still very upset that the NCAA wouldn't let her do what she does so naturally.

Christine became involved in almost every aspect of the program that didn't take place on the court, beginning with recruiting. Our initial contact with underclassmen is usually by phone. I've been making those calls for decades, but it's new to her. Fortunately, because her own boys are teenagers, she knows how to speak their language. I'll put her on the phone with a potential recruit, and somehow she knows what to say and when to say it. That's where her political background kicks in. She's a tremendous communicator. Now that some of the kids she first spoke with on the phone have joined the program, she has a real relationship with them and their parents.

She goes with me to their games, too. Once, I remember, I promised her a big night out. Well, it was, sort of. We played UCLA in the afternoon and, unfortunately, we lost. We went from the UCLA campus to the Convention Center where a Nike extravaganza was taking place. We met Bucky and Georgianne Dennis there. We missed the first half of the first game, but got there in time for the second half—and then stayed for three more games. That was four and a half games in one day for a woman who until she met me probably hadn't watched four and a half games in her whole life. Believe me, by then she knew what the key was. Fortunately, Nike had a hospitality room set up, and we were able to get in there for our big night out: hot dogs, potato chips, and salad. I don't know how happy she really was, but I tried to make her feel a little better. "As bad as this is," I told her, "just imagine. It's Georgianne's birthday!"

That was our big night out.

Christine has also begun teaching. We know how to prepare our kids to play basketball, but in addition to academics we also try to cover every aspect of their lives. At the beginning of each season we have a series of specialists come in to work with the team. We have our media people work with each player about the proper way of doing an interview, and we work with them about fulfilling their responsibilities to the public. We have representatives of the Tucson police department and our campus security talk to them about the potential problems with which they might be confronted. We have someone from the rape crisis center on campus talk to them about the potential difficulties of being a celebrity with the potential to earn a substantial amount of money. The FBI talks to them about gambling, pointing out the subtle ways that people might try to get information about the team, and emphasizing the fact that no one is going to do anything for them for nothing. We really talk to them about drugs, and Christine gives them a good introduction to etiquette. She has all these little devices she uses to teach. For example, which is the butter plate and where does the water glass go? Her technique is the basic BMW: from left to right, butter plate, meal plate, water glass. BMW. Simple. Believe me, if there's one thing our kids won't forget, it's BMW.

I've had to do some adapting to do, too, but I know it's been considerably easier for me. I had a lot less to learn. Often my role in Christine's life has been to accompany her to her events. Any time I can go with her, I do, because she comes to so many of mine. There have been times when I was one of a very few men present. Once, I remember, at one of her meetings there were about 150 successful women—and me. We were in Washington, and she had invited Pennsylvania's two U.S. senators and several representatives from Philadelphia to talk to the group about getting involved in politics in their communities. One after another these men would come in and start talking to the group, and gradually they would begin to make eye contact with everyone in the room—and then suddenly stop when they spotted sitting out there among this sea of women one white-haired man.

Our marriage has been a learning experience for both of us—a wonderful, sometimes challenging experience. I think pretty much like most marriages. When we met, I was a widower, she was a divorcee, and both of us had accepted the fact that we were never going to be married again. Both of us had an established lifestyle, and after meeting we had to learn how to change. I've learned, Christine has learned, our kids have learned, and slowly we're becoming a big family.

Christine is a very strong woman. In addition to being a single mother, she took her father's company from a very low phase to the largest privately held land-based gas and oil drilling company in America. She's been tremendously successful in politics. Although she's spent most of her political career supporting and managing other candidates, there are many people in Tucson who would like her to run for Congress. That's quite a compliment, and a request which she has turned down. She's the chairperson of the Andy Warhol Museum in Pittsburgh. She's founded organizations and run charities. And all of those things she has accomplished, every one of them, she did by herself. She is a natural leader. So it's been a huge adjustment for her to come into the basketball program, my program, and have to take a backseat. But she's done it, and she's done it extraordinarily well.

It's an unexpected life for both of us—and it's been very nice. In basketball, by the time one season ends the next season has already begun. The end turns out to be a beginning.

It has been half a century since I coached my first team. During that time there have been more than a thousand wins and too many losses. The numbers are easy to look up. In the record books that's how success is measured, but as any coach who cares will tell you, those numbers have little to do with real success. In the long term what really matters is how much players learn about life. I was so proudly reminded of that in January 2005 when my 1980 Iowa team held its twenty-fifth reunion in Iowa City.

That was a great group of overachieving kids; we didn't have the most talent but we were very close and played with incredible heart. We made it to the Final Four, and I will always believe that if Ronnie Lester hadn't been hurt we would have won the national championship. At that reunion we were all stunned to see Kenny Arnold. During his career at Iowa he was a burly 6'2", 200 pounds, but when he showed up at my house he was an emaciated 120 pounds. In 1985 he'd survived extensive treatment for a malignant brain tumor and seemed to be doing well, but, as we discovered, his condition had deteriorated the last few years. So much so that he wasn't going to come to the reunion—until Ronnie Lester flew to Chicago from Los Angeles and drove there with him.

"When we saw him," Mike Henry said, "we looked at each other and wondered why none of us knew about this. Kenny said he didn't want to burden us. We told him, 'We're family,' and everybody jumped on board."

The team raised a considerable amount of money to pay for his medical costs and help his mother, who was taking care of him. Then we hired an attorney to make sure he got all the disability benefits he was entitled to. Finally they found doctors to evaluate his condition and assist in his rehabilitation. The following March Mike Henry literally carried Kenny into my office. It was heartbreaking, but I was so proud of my team. Dave Alberts took charge. We were all very worried that his cancer had returned, but it turned out his problems were being caused by outdated medication. Once that medication was changed his condition began improving. "We were close then," Kenny told a reporter, but we're closer now. I've been blessed."

If anybody is looking for the definition of a team, check out the 1980 University of Iowa basketball team.

The following December we held another reunion, this time at my home in Tucson. Kenny was there, smiling this time. Afterward I received a letter from forward Mark Gannon. "Dear Coach O, I am writing this letter after a wonderful day of fellowship with a group of people who helped shape my life . . .

"I spend very little time today thinking of the ways you made me a better player, however, I use your lessons in life quite often. When you think of your family you must be overwhelmed due to the size it has grown to be . . ." It was signed, "Teammates for life, Mark Gannon."

None of this story appears in any record book, but for me, it has more meaning than any of the awards, any of the trophies.

It's amazing what a difference a roundball can make in so many lives. For me, it was love at first sight, and that love has lasted my lifetime.

Index